Lecture Notes in Computer Science 10866

Commenced Publication in 1973
Founding and Former Series Editors:
Gerhard Goos, Juris Hartmanis, and Jan van Leeuwen

More information about this series at http://www.springer.com/series/7411

Kaushik Roy Chowdhury · Marco Di Felice
Ibrahim Matta · Bo Sheng (Eds.)

Wired/Wireless Internet Communications

16th IFIP WG 6.2 International Conference, WWIC 2018
Boston, MA, USA, June 18–20, 2018
Proceedings

 Springer

Editors
Kaushik Roy Chowdhury
Northeastern University
Boston, MA, USA

Marco Di Felice
University of Bologna
Bologna, Italy

Ibrahim Matta
Boston University
Boston, MA, USA

Bo Sheng
University of Massachusetts Boston
Boston, MA, USA

ISSN 0302-9743   ISSN 1611-3349   (electronic)
Lecture Notes in Computer Science
ISBN 978-3-030-02930-2   ISBN 978-3-030-02931-9   (eBook)
https://doi.org/10.1007/978-3-030-02931-9

Library of Congress Control Number: 2018958765

LNCS Sublibrary: SL5 – Computer Communication Networks and Telecommunications

This Springer imprint is published by the registered company Springer Nature Switzerland AG
The registered company address is: Gewerbestrasse 11, 6330 Cham, Switzerland

Preface

We welcome you to the joint proceedings of the 16th International Conference on Wired/Wireless Internet Communications (IFIP WWIC). The conference constitutes a forum for the presentation and discussion of the latest results in the field of wired/wireless networks and aims at providing research directions and fostering collaborations among the participants. In this context, the Program Committee accepts a limited number of papers that meet the criteria of originality, presentation quality, and topic relevance. IFIP WWIC is a single-track conference that has reached, over the past 16 years, a high-quality level, which is reflected by the paper acceptance rate as well as the level of attendance. Following the conference tradition, there is a best paper award.

The 16th IFIP WWIC technical program addressed various aspects of next-generation data networks, such as the design and evaluation of protocols, the dynamics of the integration, the performance trade-offs, the need for new performance metrics, and cross-layer interactions. Moreover, we further solicited submissions on bio-inspired, machine-learning based, and data-driven approaches for network architecture and protocol design, and for wired/wireless system planning and optimization. WWIC 2018 received 42 submissions from 19 countries and five different continents, as a clear evidence of the international scope of the WWIC conferences. A highly selective review process allowed us to include 26 accepted papers, and to realize a high-quality technical program. The 50+ members of the Technical Program Committee rigorously checked the scientific quality and technical soundness of all the papers, as well as their degree of innovation and the adequacy of the presentation, and produced at least three single-blind reviews for each submission. From all research papers submitted, and based on the quality of the presentation, and of the indications of the reviewers, the program chairs elected the following best paper:

– "Ranged Name Retrieval: Design and Evaluation of a Flexible Data Retrieval Approach for ICN." Authors: Konstantinos Trichias, Lucia D'Acunto, Floris Drijver and Bastiaan Wissingh (TNO, The Netherlands)

The current edition of the conference was organized in cooperation with Boston University and Northeastern University: We thank these organizations for their great support. Finally, we would like to express our gratitude to all our colleagues for submitting papers to the WWIC scientific sessions, as well as to the members of the WWIC Technical Program Committee and the reviewers, for their excellent work and dedication.

July 2018

Kaushik Roy Chowdhury
Marco Di Felice
Ibrahim Matta
Bo Sheng

Organization

General Chairs

Kaushik Roy Chowdhury   Northeastern University, USA

Ibrahim Matta   Boston University, USA

Program Chairs

Marco Di Felice   University of Bologna, Italy

Bo Sheng   University of Massachusetts, USA

Publication Chair

Flavio Esposito   Saint Louis University, USA

Web and Publicity Chairs

Angelo Trotta   University of Bologna, Italy

Yuefeng Wang   Akamai Technologies, USA

Steering Committee

Torsten Braun   University of Bern, Switzerland

Georg Carle   Technical University of Munich, Germany

Geert Heijenk   University of Twente, The Netherlands

Peter Langendorfer   IHP Microelectronics, Germany

Ibrahim Matta   Boston University, USA

Vassilis Tsaoussidis   Democritus University of Thrace, Greece

Technical Program Committee

Sami Akin   Leibniz Universität Hannover, Germany

Paolo Bellavista   University of Bologna, Italy

Fernando Boavida   University of Coimbra, Portugal

Zdravko Bozakov   EMC Research Europe, Ireland

Torsten Braun   University of Bern, Switzerland

Marcos Caetano   University of Brasilia, Brazil

Maria Calderon   Universidad Carlos III de Madrid, Spain

Mehmet Can Vuran   University of Nebraska-Lincoln, USA

Domenico Capriglione	University of Salerno, Italy
Georg Carle	Technical University of Munich, Germany
Dave Cavalcanti	Intel Corporation, USA
Eduardo Cerqueira	Federal University of Para, Brazil
Stuart Clayman	UCL, UK
Marilia Curado	University of Coimbra, Brazil
Robson De Grande	University of Ottawa, Canada
Panagiotis Demestichas	University of Piraeus, Greece
Yue Gao	Queen Mary University of London, UK
Paul Gendron	University of Massachusetts Dartmouth, USA
Hao Han	Intelligent Automation, USA
Sonia Heemstra de Groot	Eindhoven Technical University, The Netherlands
Geert Heijenk	University of Twente, The Netherlands
Josep Jornet	University at Buffalo, USA
Andreas J. Kassler	Karlstad University, Sweden
Salil Kanhere	UNSW Sydney, Australia
Hana Khamfroush	University of Kentucky, USA
Ibrahim Korpeoglu	Bilkent University, Turkey
Yevgeni Koucheryavy	Tampere University of Technology, Finland
Peter Langendoerfer	IHP Microelectronics, Germany
Pascal Lorenz	University of Haute Alsace, France
Yao Liu	State University of New York, USA
Lefteris Mamatas	University of Macedonia, Greece
Xavier Masip-Bruin	Universitat Politecnica de Catalunya, Spain
Paulo Mendes	COPELABS/University of Lusofona, Portugal
Gianfranco Miele	University of Cassino and Southern Lazio, Italy
Enzo Mingozzi	University of Pisa, Italy
Edmundo Monteiro	University of Coimbra, Portugal
Liam Murphy	University College Dublin, Ireland
Ioanis Nikolaidis	University of Alberta, Canada
Panagiotis Papadimitriou	University of Macedonia, Greece
Paul Patras	University of Edinburgh, UK
Ioannis Psaras	University College London, UK
Danda Rawat	Howard University, USA
Amr Rizk	Technische Universität Darmstadt, Germany
Dimitrios Serpanos	University of Patras, Greece
Vasilios Siris Athens	University of Economics and Business, Greece
Burkhard Stiller	University of Zurich, Switzerland
Zhi Sun	University at Buffalo, USA
Violet Syriotuk	University of Arizona, USA
Chiu Tan	Temple University, USA
Alicia Trivino	University of Malaga, Spain

Ageliki Tsioliaridou   University of Crete, Greece
Honggang Wang   University of Massachusetts, USA
Fan Wu   Shanghai Jiao Tong University, China
Fengyuan Xu   Nanjing University, China

Contents

Vehicular and Content Delivery Networks

IoT and Sensor Networks

RTT-Based Congestion Control for the Internet of Things

Emilio Ancillotti, Simone Bolettieri, and Raffaele Bruno^(✉)

IIT-CNR, Via G. Moruzzi 1, 56124 Pisa, Italy
{e.ancillotti,s.bolettieri,r.bruno}@iit.cnr.it

Abstract. The design of scalable and reliable transport protocols for IoT environments is still an unsolved issue. A simple stop-and-wait congestion control method and a lightweight reliability mechanism are only implemented in CoAP, an application protocol that provides standardised RESTful services for IoT devices. Inspired by delay-based congestion control algorithms that have been proposed for the TCP, in this work we propose a rate control technique that leverages measurements of round-trip times (RTTs) to infer network state and to determine the flow rate that would prevent network congestion. Our key idea is that the growth of RTT variance, coupled with thresholds on CoAP message losses, is an effective way to detect the onset of network congestion. To validate our approach, we conduct a comparative performance analysis with the two loss-based congestion control methods of standard CoAP under different application scenarios. Results show that our solution outperforms the alternative methods, with a significant improvement of fairness and robustness against unacknowledged traffic.

Keywords: Internet of Things · CoAP
Delay-based congestion control · Flow pacing · Contiki OS

1 Introduction

The TCP/IP architecture has significantly evolved over the years to provide new functionalities and efficient support for mobility, content delivery, multimedia applications, etc. Nowadays, there is a large consensus on assuming that one of the most important drivers for the future Internet evolution is the design of solutions to enable access to services and information provided by billions of *smart things*, i.e. resource-constrained devices with sensing and actuation capabilities [1]. This network of physical objects embedded with IP-based networking capabilities is commonly known as the Internet of Things (IoT).

IoT networks differ from traditional wired computer networks in several ways. IoT devices are typically battery-powered and have limited computing power.

This work was supported by the SIGS project, funded by the region of Tuscany under the FAR-FAS 2014 framework.

K. R. Chowdhury et al. (Eds.): WWIC 2018, LNCS 10866, pp. 3–15, 2018.
https://doi.org/10.1007/978-3-030-02931-9_1

Furthermore, IoT systems often employ low-energy communication technologies, (e.g., IEEE 802.15.4, Bluetooth LE, etc.), which operate with smaller MTUs and lower transmission rates compared to traditional wired links. Finally, IoT networks have to rely on mesh communications to cope with limited communication ranges. For these reasons, many IETF working groups (e.g., 6LoWPAN [2], ROLL [3], CoRE [4]) have been established to modify the standard TCP/IP stack to fullfill IoT requirements, as well as to develop new protocols [5]. While important achievements have been obtained, the design of a scalable and reliable transport protocol for IoT deployments is still an unsolved issue.

TCP is the dominant transport layer on the Internet, which provides congestion control and reliable delivery. TCP has been primarily designed to efficiently deliver a large bulk of data over a long-lived connections without strict latency requirements. On the contrary, IoT applications are characterised by different communication patterns as IoT devices typically send small amounts of data either periodically or when sporadic events occur. In addition, IoT applications that implement actuation tasks may request low network delays. Lastly, most TCP congestion control algorithms perform poorly with lossy links, and when MAC transmission delays are similar to or longer than the retransmission timeouts. For these reasons, the Internet architecture for IoT networks only envision the use of an unreliable transport protocol (i.e. UDP). A stop-and-wait congestion control method and a lightweight reliability mechanism are only implemented in CoAP, an HTTP-like web transfer protocol for constrained environments.

CoAP uses the received ACKs to decide when transmitting a new packet. In addition, packet loss is implicitly assumed as a network congestion indicator and an exponential back-off is introduced between retransmissions to reduce sending rates. Recently, CoAP extensions are proposed to provide dynamic retransmission timeout adaptation [6]. However, recent studies have investigated the pitfalls of these techniques, such as unfairness and spurious retransmissions when offered loads are close to congestion [7,8]. In this work, we investigate an alternative approach for congestion control that employs measurements of round trip times to infer network state and to determine the flow rate that would prevent network congestion. We are inspired by some of the delay-based congestion control algorithms that have been proposed for the TCP under specialised conditions (e.g. data centres [9] or high-speed networks [10]). One of our aims is to show that reliable RTT measurements can be obtained in constrained environments with limited additional overheads. Differently from other similar schemes, we do not use fixed RTT thresholds to predict the onset of congestion. Instead, we leverage RTT variability to define a rate control scheme that aims at maintaining a low probability of data transaction losses. Our insight is that in 6LoWPAN networks RTT measurements are not a deterministic function of queue delays and propagation times, while the growth of RTT variance is a more efficient indication of network load increases. To prove our claims we implement the proposed rate control algorithm in CoAP, and we conduct a comparative performance analysis with the two loss-based congestion control methods of standard CoAP under different application scenarios. Results show that our solution outperforms the alternative methods, with a significant improvement of fairness and an increase of packet delivery ratios in presence of unacknowledged traffic.

The rest of this paper is organised as follows. Related works are discussed in Sect. 2. The proposed RTT-based congestion control method for CoAP is presented in Sect. 3. In Sect. 4 we introduce the simulation setup and we present the performance evaluation results. Finally, concluding remarks are discussed in Sect. 5.

2 Background and Related Works

The design of congestion control algorithms for reliable transport protocols in wired and wireless networks is a deeply investigated topic. In the following, we discuss the key design principles of congestion control solutions for TCP [11]. Then, we present a brief overview of CoAP and its congestion control mechanisms.

2.1 TCP Congestion Control

The majority of existing end-to-end congestion control proposals for TCP are based on the *congestion window* concept. Specifically, the congestion window is an estimate of the maximum number of unacknowledged data packets that a TCP flow can transmit without congesting the network. Thus, the TCP transmission rate can be indirectly controlled by adjusting the congestion window size. Typically, TCP senders update their congestion windows based on feedback signals they receive from the network. The most popular TCP congestion algorithms, such as TCP NewReno and its many variants, use packet losses as a binary congestion control signal[1]. However, loss-based congestion control algorithms are *reactive* schemes because they reduce sending rates only when network congestion causes a packet loss. The seminal work of TCP Vegas [12] introduces a *proactive* congestion avoidance method that tries to quantify the congestion state of the network before a congestion event occurs using round-trip delays. Specifically, the minimal RTT value is considered a baseline indicating a congestion-free network state. Then, the congestion window is decreased if the delay increases. Other modern TCP variants, such as FAST TCP and Compound TCP, use delay-based congestion control algorithms trying to maintain buffer occupancy at the bottleneck queue around some predefined thresholds. The advantage of such schemes is that they can stabilise the network around the full utilisation. The inherent weakness of delay-based algorithms is that their performance degrades if the delay measurements are noisy (e.g., due to delayed ACKs and route changes). Furthermore, minimum RTT can be a bias estimate of queuing delays in a non congested network. For these reasons, delay is typically used in hybrid congestion control schemes as a secondary congestion signal in addition to packet loss information [10].

---

[1] Typically, TCP packet losses are detected through the receipt of duplicate and/or selective ACKs, or the timeout of a retransmission timer.

2.2 CoAP

The Constrained Application Protocol (CoAP) is a web transfer protocol based on a REST architecture with a Request/Response interaction model. Requests and responses can be carried in *non-confirmable* (NON) or *confirmable* (CON) messages. The latter are required to be acknowledged once received by the destination endpoint. Reliability is then implemented by detecting message losses and retransmitting the packet (until a maximum number of attempts). Packet losses are detected by using retransmission timeouts (RTOs): RTO is set by the sender when a CON transaction starts; If the RTO expires before the ACK reception, the packet is retransmitted.

In CoAP, the congestion control regulates CON transmission: packet losses are interpreted as a congestion signal; therefore, retransmissions are spaced out using a binary exponential back-off (BEB) policy (RTO doubled at each retransmission). By default, the initial value for the RTO is randomly chosen from a fixed interval. Furthermore, the number of parallel outstanding transmissions towards the same destination is limited to NSTART, which is set to one in standard CoAP (i.e., no more that one notification per RTT to a client on average).

A more advanced congestion control scheme is proposed in CoCoA+ [6], which introduces an algorithm to dynamically adjust the RTO using measured RTTs. The key idea is to overcome the drawbacks of having a fixed RTO that could underestimate node's RTTs leading to unnecessary retransmissions or that could overestimate them leading to increased transaction delays. Specifically, CoCoA+ maintains two RTO estimators for each destination: a strong RTO estimator (RTO_s) uses RTT samples that come from transactions which did not require a retransmission, and weak RTO estimator ($RTOw$) that uses RTT samples of transactions that required less than three retransmissions. Individual $RTOx$, where $x \in \{s, w\}$, are computed using the following formula:

$$RTO_x = SRTT_x + K_x * RTTVAR_x, \tag{1}$$

where $SRTT_x$ and $RTTVAR_x$ denote the smoothed RTT and RTT variation respectively, as defined in RFC 6298 [13]; K_s is set to 4, while K_w is set to 1. Upon ACK reception, the computed RTO sample (weak or strong depending on the nature of the last sampled RTT) is used as input for a classical exponential moving average filter to calculate the RTO for the next CON transaction (RTO_{init}). A smaller K_w and a smaller weight for weak RTO estimates are used to avoid large increments in RTO_{init} due to large $RTTVAR_w$, which is affected by the high variability of RTT measurements of retransmitted messages.

Furthermore, CoCoA+ introduces a new back-off policy where the multiplicative factor, used to update the RTO, is variable and depends on the RTO_{init} value. Ideally, this should avoid that with short RTOs all retransmissions are occurring in a short interval, and that, on the contrary, with large RTOs unnecessary delays are introduced. Finally, CoCoA+ proposes an ageing scheme for the RTO estimate. Specifically, if no RTT samples are collected for a sufficiently long period of time, the RTO values should converge toward their initial value.

3   RTT-CoAP Design

RTT-CoAP is an extended version of the standard CoAP web transfer protocol that implements our RTT-based congestion control scheme for 6LoWPAN networks. Unlike classical TCP that employs a window-based congestion avoidance method, RTT-CoAP uses a rate-based algorithm that directly controls the pacing rate of packet transmissions to reduce traffic burstiness and data losses. As discussed in Sect. 1, we are inspired by recent delay-based congestion control protocols that rely on delay measurements for inferring network congestion [9,14]. The typical pitfalls of most delay-based congestion control schemes is that it is difficult to obtain a reliable estimate of RTT trends, especially in wireless networks. Furthermore, in constrained environments with small buffers and low transmission rates, RTT can not be considered a deterministic function of the queuing and propagation delays. Thus, it is not easy to define a RTT baseline that is indicative of network congestion. Most solutions simply assume that the minimum of all measured RTTs is the RTT value of a non-congested connection. However, the random channel access method employed in the 802.15.4 MAC standard, which cause huge variability of channel access delays, and bursty packet arrival processes leads to sudden fluctuations in RTT measurements. Furthermore, changing network conditions or network paths generate varying RTT measurements. Thus, single RTT values or the difference between RTT values may not be indicative of the network state. In the following, we explain our RTT measurement framework and how we leverage RTT variations to classify the different network states. Depending on the current network state coupled with thresholds on data transaction losses, RTT-CoAP updates the sending rate of each CoAP source to stabilise network delays and prevent packet losses.

3.1   Monitoring RTT Variations

We assume that a CoAP sender can use ACKs to obtain RTT samples. Specifically, an RTT measurement is obtained as the difference between the transmission time of a CON CoAP message and the time in which the ACK is received. According to Karn's algorithm [13], RTT samples should not be taken from packets that were retransmitted, as it is ambiguous to assign the ACK message to the first transmission of that packet or to later retransmissions. To remove this ambiguity we introduce the CoAP timestamp option: the CoAP sender places a timestamp in each CON message, and the CoAP receiver echos these timestamps back in the ACKs. Timing each CoAP message leads to a better RTT estimator without generating excessive protocol overheads, as discussed in Sect. 3.3.

Inspired by the TCP rules for computing retransmission timers [13], we exploit RTT samples to compute three state variables $SRTT_L$, $SRTT_S$, and $RTTVAR_L$. The first two state variables are obtained by applying exponential smoothing to RTT samples. The third state variable is the well-known smoothed estimate of RTT variations as computed in TCP. Unlike CoAP, we do not distinguish between weak and strong estimators but we use all CON messages to update the RTT state variables. More formally, let r be the latest RTT sample that is obtained by a CoAP sender. It holds that

$$SRTT_S = \alpha_S r + (1 - \alpha_S) \times SRTT_S \tag{2}$$

$$SRTT_L = \alpha_L r + (1 - \alpha_L) \times SRTT_S \tag{3}$$

$$RTTVAR_L = \beta_L|SRTT_L - r| + (1 - \beta_L) \times RTTVAR_L, \tag{4}$$

with $\alpha_S >> \alpha_L$. Using a small smoothing factor α_L is useful to remove the impact of noise on RTT measurements (e.g., due to random backoffs, or bursty packet arrival processes), and to obtain a more accurate estimate of the *long-term* RTT trends. On the other hand, using a large smoothing factor α_S is needed to monitor *short-term* RTT differences that occur due to sudden changes of network conditions. As better explained in the following, this improves the responsiveness of the rate control technique, especially when RTT samples are infrequent due to long network delays or low traffic intensity. It is important to point out that constrained devices have very limited memory, which makes impractical to implement more sophisticated averaging filters that require a long measurement history.

Our key idea is that the growth of RTT variance is a good indication of network state as a contention increase leads to longer backoff intervals, and higher variability of channel access delays. Thus, we leverage $RTTVAR_L$ variable to define *characteristic regions* of the network state, which will be used to determine the direction of sending rate changes (i.e., whether sending rates of CoAP sources should be increased or decreased). Let **S** denote the network state at the reception of an ACK. Furthermore, let us define the decision boundary $T(\gamma)$ as follows:

$$T(\gamma) = SRTT_L + \gamma \times RTTVAR_L. \tag{5}$$

To some extent, $T(\gamma)$ is analogous to a confidence level of the mean RTT, as it is a measure of RTT variability and it can be used to assess the distance of RTT samples from the mean. Now, we can identify four characteristic regions using the following decision boundaries:

- (**LC**): $SRTT_S < T(-1)$ (low congestion). In this state we can assume that there is no congestion in the network, as the short-term RTT estimate is well below the long-term averages. Thus, the sending rate can be aggressively increased.
- (**NO**): $T(-1) \leq SRTT_S < T(+1)$ (normal operating point). In this state, the short-term RTT estimate is comparable to typical RTT measurements. This corresponds to a normal operating point and the sending rate should left unchanged. Depending on the experienced packet losses a moderate increase of sending rates is also possible to check if more bandwidth is available.
- (**MV**): $T(+1) \leq SRTT_S < T(2)$ (medium variability). In this state, short-term RTT variability grows and this can be a signal of ramping network congestion. Thus, a controlled decrease of sending rate can be necessary to avoid congestion.

– (**HV**): $SRTT_S \geq T(+2)$ (high variability). In this state, the short-term RTT estimate is significantly higher that the long-term RTT estimate. Thus, the CoAP source needs to aggressively reduce the sending rate so as to return to the normal operating state as soon as possible.

3.2   Rate Control Algorithm

Algorithm 1 shows the pseudo-code for our rate adaptation scheme. RTT-CoAP maintains a single sending rate R for each connection and updates it on every ACK reception using the above-described state variables, coupled with a measure of the probability of data transaction loss. Specifically, each CoAP sender maintains also an exponential moving average, say μ, of the probability that a confirmable CoAP message is retransmitted. Since RTT-CoAP aims at keeping this probability very low, it employs two thresholds to respond to extreme cases of high packet losses or possible underutilisation of available bandwidth. We are inspired by the idea of control dead zones in TCP Vegas, which defines a range of network delays that correspond to a steady state during which no changes are applied to the sending rate. This approach is known to mitigate the impact of network condition fluctuations and to facilitate the convergence to a stable behaviour. More formally, we define L_{high} as an upper bound of the tolerable CoAP message loss ratio. It provides a way to infere that there is no more available bandwidth for the CoAP sender. Moreover, we define a low threshold L_{low} to filter out RTT spikes: RTT fluctuations above the *normal operating region* are not taken into consideration when the loss ratio is lower than L_{low}. The rate adjustments in the various states are described in detail in the following. At the reception of a ACK the CoAP sender updates the RTT state variables and the CoAP message loss ratio, and it determines the new sending rate. Basically, there are four possible conditions:

1. **S** $\in$ **LC** and there is a *fast increase* of sending rate (see line 3).
2. **S** $\in$ **NO** and there is a *slow increase* of sending rate (see line 5).
3. **S** $\in$ **MV** and there is a *slow decrease* of sending rate (see line 7).
4. **S** $\in$ **HV** and there is a *fast increase* of sending rate (see line 9).

However, if $\mu < L_{low}$ we can safely assume that no congestion is experienced. As a consequence, the decreases of sending rates are disabled (see lines 6 and 8). On the other hand, if $\mu > L_{high}$ the network is very likely operating under congestion state, and the increase of sending rates in the *normal operating* region should be disabled (see line 4). Concerning the rate adaptation, RTT-CoAP probes for more bandwidth by performing an additive increment step. However, the bandwidth additive increment is not constant. Specifically, RTT-CoAP differentiates between two regimes: a sending rate that is smaller than one CoAP message per RTT (called *base rate*, see line 18), and a sending rate that is higher than this value. In the first case, the rate increase will be proportional to the difference between the base rate and the current rate. In the latter case, the rate increment is a fraction of the base rate. The rationale of this design choice is to avoid that CoAP sources that already transmit faster than the base rate get a disproportionate advantage in comparison with slower flows. As in TCP Vegas, we follow an additive increase/additive decrease (AIAD) policy. Thus, when network congestion is detected and the sending rate has to be decremented, a linear decrement factor δ is selected following the aforementioned rules.

Algorithm 1. RTT-CoAP CONGESTION CONTROL

1: **function** UPDATERATE(**S**, $SRTT_L$, $SRTT_S$, $RTTVAR_L$,μ)

2:    **if** (**S** $\in$ **LC**) **then**
3:        $R = R + $ COMPRATE($R, SRTT_L, fast$);
4:    **else if** (**S** $\in$ **NO**)   **AND**   ($\mu < L_{high}$) **then**
5:        $R = R + $ COMPRATE($R, SRTT_L, slow$);
6:    **else if** (**S** $\in$ **MV**)   **AND**   ($\mu \geq L_{low}$) **then**
7:        $R = R - $ COMPRATE($R, SRTT_L, slow$);
8:    **else if** (**S** $\in$ **HV**)   **AND**   ($\mu \geq L_{low}$) **then**
9:        $R = R - $ COMPRATE($R, SRTT_L, fast$);
10:    **end if**
11: **end function**

12: **function** COMPRATE(R, $SRTT_L$, $speed$)

13:    **if** ($speed = fast$) **then**
14:        $\omega = 0.2$
15:    **else if** ($speed = slow$) **then**
16:        $\omega = 0.05$
17:    **end if**

18:    $R_b = \frac{1}{SRTT_L}$
19:    **if** ($R < R_b$) **then**
20:        $\delta = \omega \times (R_b - R)$
21:    **else**
22:        $\delta = \omega \times R_b$
23:    **end if**
        return δ
24: **end function**

3.3 RTT-CoAP Implementation

In this section we describe the key points of our implementation of RTT-CoAP leveraging Contiki, an open source operating system for the IoT. In particular, we use CoAP Erbium, a C implementation of CoAP for Contiki, that is compliant with RFC 7252 [4] and supports blockwise transfers and observing.

CoAP specification defines a number of options that can be included in a message. Specifically, CoAP uses a short fixed-length binary header (4 bytes) that may be followed by compact binary options and a payload. Each option instance in a message specifies the option number of the defined CoAP option, the length of the option value, and the option value itself. Since a length of a timestamp is typically four bytes, we follow an alternative approach for timing the CoAP messages. Specifically, the CoAP senders stores within a local table the timestamp of each transmissions of the same CoAP message, and use the retransmission counter as a one-byte timestamp option. The transmission counter is echoed in the corresponding ACK and it is used in the CoAP sender to retrieve the correct transmission time, and to estimate the RTT without ambiguity. Finally, we mark the CoAP timestamp option as: (i) a critical option, i.e., it must be understood by the receiving endpoint in order to properly process the message; and (ii) a safe-to-forward option, i.e., it can be safely forwarded by a proxy even if it can't process the option. The default value of this option is 0.

4   Performance Evaluation

In this section, we give the details on the simulation setup used to compare standard CoAP-CC, CoCoA+ and RTT-CoAP. Then, we presents results for a variety of different scenarios.

4.1   Simulation Setup

For our performance comparison we conduct simulations in Cooja, a simulation platform included in Contiki toolset, that allows to emulate off-the-shelf wireless sensor node hardware. At the physical (PHY) and MAC layers, the nodes implement IEEE 802.15.4, using a transmission rate of 250 kbps in the 2.4 GHz radio band. We do not use radio duty cycling (RDC) at the MAC layer to mitigate RTT fluctuations. To model realistic radio propagation and interference we use the Multipath Ray-tracer Medium (MRM), configuring MRM parameters to achieve a 100% success rate at 10 m and an interference range of 20 m.

RPL is used as routing protocol [3]. We consider two large network scenarios with 57 and 112 sensor devices, respectively. The nodes are deployed along concentric circles, and the distance between consecutive circles is 10 m. Nodes are CoAP servers that send observing notifications toward a common data collector node placed at the center of the network. We will assume that each server can generate two kinds of data flows: (i) a data flow made of NON-messages (*background traffic*); and (ii) a data flow made of CON-messages (*reliable traffic*). The main performance metric is the *aggregated goodput* measured as the number of successfully received acknowledgments (i.e. successfully completed transactions), and expressed in Kbit per seconds (Kbps). We also computed the flow fairness with the well-known Jain's Index applied to goodput measurements.

4.2   Mixed Traffic

The first set of experiments assumes that both background traffic and reliable traffic are active on the same CoAP source. The goal of this scenario is to assess the impact of an increasing congestion-unaware traffic on the reliable flow, which is instead regulated by the congestion control mechanism. More in detail, the reliable traffic has a packet generation rate of approximately 1 Kbps per CoAP source and it is maintained constant for the whole simulation. Such rate ensures that there is always a packet ready to be sent, thus, reliable traffic follows an asymptotic behaviour. Instead, the sending rate of the background traffic evolves as follows; it starts with an aggregate value of approximately 2 Kbps, and it is incremented every 400 s until reaching a maximum of about 44 Kbps, and finally it is reverted to 2 Kbps.

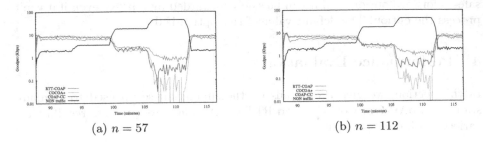

(a) $n = 57$ (b) $n = 112$

Fig. 1. Goodput under mixed traffic scenario for two network deployments.

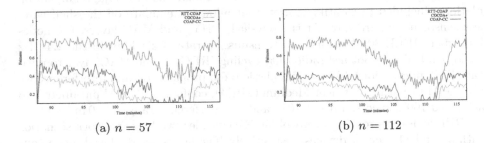

(a) $n = 57$ (b) $n = 112$

Fig. 2. Fairness under mixed traffic scenario for two network deployments.

In Fig. 1a and b we show the instantaneous goodput carried by the different protocols for $n = 57$ and $n = 112$, respectively. For convenience, we report the rate of the background traffic with a solid black line.

The results reported in Fig. 1a show that when the network is not congested, RTT-CoAP achieve a slightly lower aggregate goodput compared to both CoAP and CoCoA+ (the difference in goodput is compensated by a sensible increase of the fairness index as showed in Fig. 2a). However, as the background traffic increase RTT-CoAP tends to outperform both CoAP and CoCoA+, achieving about the same aggregate goodput in the presence of medium congestion (simulation time between 100 min and 105 min), and obtaining a sensible goodput improvement in the presence of high congestion. We can observe that when the background traffic reaches its maximum value the CoCoA+ flows almost completely stall. The main reason is that CoCoA+ (as CoAP) indirectly regulates the sending rate using RTO, which under consecutive losses can grow up to very large values [7,8], thus leading to nodes not sending data at all. Interestingly, CoAP is more resilient against non-confirmable traffic than CoCoA+ as RTO values are chosen in a fixed interval. On the other hand, RTT-CoAP can detect the onset of congestion earlier than CoCoA+, and it adjusts the pacing rate before overwhelming the network. Similar conclusions can be drawn from Fig. 1b. However, we can see that the gap between the algorithm is reduced when the number of sources increases. This can be explained by observing that CON traffic is asymptotic. Thus, it is enough that a few CoAP sources are able to get access to the channel to be able to saturate the available bandwidth. As better explained in the following, the downside of this asymptotic behaviour is an unfair share of the network bandwidth among the existing flows.

In Fig. 2a and b we show the fairness that is measured in the same settings of the above figures. The results clearly show that our proposed congestion control solution is able to significantly outperform both standard CoAP and CoCoA+ in terms of fairness, even when the network is deeply congested.

4.3 Homogenous Traffic

This second set of experiments assumes that each CoAP source generates only reliable traffic. The rate at which the application send the data to the CoAP layer is incremented every 300 s. The goal of this scenario is to assess the efficiency of our rate-based congestion control mechanism to fully utilise the available bandwidth while maintaining a fair share of network resources between the CoAP sources. To this end, Fig. 3a and b show the instantaneous goodput carried by the different protocols for $n = 57$ and $n = 112$, respectively, while Fig. 4a and b show the fairness index in the same scenarios. The results confirm that although the

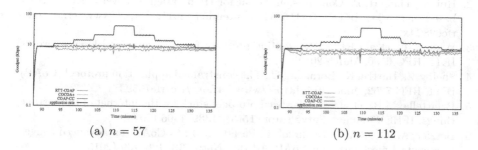

(a) $n = 57$ (b) $n = 112$

Fig. 3. Goodput under mixed traffic scenario for two network deployments.

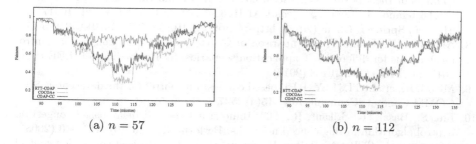

(a) $n = 57$ (b) $n = 112$

Fig. 4. Fairness under homogenous traffic scenario for two network deployments.

aggregate goodput achieved by RTT-CoAP is slightly lower than that achieved by CoAP and CoCoA+, RTT-CoAP guarantees a significantly higher fairness among different traffic sources. In particular, we observe an increment of the fairness index of about 250% when the offered load is set to the maximum value (simulation time between 110 min and 115 min Fig. 4b), while the goodput decrease is below 10%.

5   Conclusions

In this paper we have proposed RTT-CoAP, a novel RTT-based congestion control scheme for CoAP. Our key idea was to monitor long-term and short-term RTT trends to classify network state and to proactively anticipate network congestion. Differently from other delay-based congestion control scheme our solutions doe not require to define fixed RTT thresholds that avoid congestion, but we leverage the growth of RTT variance to directly adjust the sending rate of each CoAP source. In comparison to basic CoAP and CoCoA+, RTT-CoAP ensures a significant improvement of fairness, and an increase of packet delivery ratios in presence of congestion-unaware traffic.

References

1. Borgia, E.: The Internet of Things vision: key features, applications and open issues. Comput. Commun. **54**, 1–31 (2014)
2. Hui, J., Thubert, P.: Compression format for IPv6 datagrams over IEEE 802.15.4-based networks. IETF RFC 6282, September 2011. http://www.ietf.org/rfc/rfc6282.txt
3. Winter, T., et al.: RPL: IPv6 routing protocol for low-power and lossy networks. IETF RFC 6550, March 2012
4. Shelby, Z., Hartke, K., Bormann, C.: The constrained application protocol (CoAP). IETF RFC 7252, June 2014. http://www.ietf.org/rfc/rfc7959.txt
5. Palattella, M.R., et al.: Standardized protocol stack for the internet of (important) things. IEEE Commun. Surv. Tutor. **15**(3), 1389–1406 (2013)
6. Betzler, A., Gomez, C., Demirkol, I., Paradells, J.: CoCoA+: an advanced congestion control mechanism for CoAP. Ad Hoc Netw. **33**, 126–139 (2015)
7. Bolettieri, S., Vallati, C., Tanganelli, G., Mingozzi, E.: Highlighting some shortcomings of the CoCoA+ congestion control algorithm. In: Puliafito, A., Bruneo, D., Distefano, S., Longo, F. (eds.) ADHOC-NOW 2017. LNCS, vol. 10517, pp. 213–220. Springer, Cham (2017). https://doi.org/10.1007/978-3-319-67910-5_17
8. Ancillotti, E., Bruno, R.: Comparison of CoAP and CoCoA+ congestion control mechanisms for different IoT application scenarios. In: Proceedings of IEEE ISCC 2017, pp. 1186–1192. IEEE (2017)
9. Mittal, R., et al.: TIMELY: RTT-based congestion control for the datacenter. SIGCOMM Comput. Commun. Rev. **45**(4), 537–550 (2015)
10. Liu, S., Başar, T., Srikant, R.: TCP-Illinois: a loss- and delay-based congestion control algorithm for high-speed networks. Perform. Eval. **65**(6), 417–440 (2008)
11. Afanasyev, A., Tilley, N., Reiher, P., Kleinrock, L.: Host-to-host congestion control for TCP. IEEE Commun. Surv. Tutor. **12**(3), 304–342 (2010)

12. Brakmo, L.S., Peterson, L.L.: TCP Vegas: end to end congestion avoidance on a global internet. IEEE J. Sel. Areas Commun. **13**(8), 1465–1480 (1995)
13. Paxson, V., Allman, M., Chu, J., Sargent, M.: Computing TCP's retransmission timer. IETF RFC 6298, June 2011. http://www.ietf.org/rfc/rfc6298.txt
14. Hayes, D.A., Armitage, G.: Revisiting TCP congestion control using delay gradients. In: Domingo-Pascual, J., Manzoni, P., Palazzo, S., Pont, A., Scoglio, C. (eds.) NETWORKING 2011. LNCS, vol. 6641, pp. 328–341. Springer, Heidelberg (2011). https://doi.org/10.1007/978-3-642-20798-3_25

Ranged Name Retrieval: Design and Evaluation of a Flexible Data Retrieval Approach for ICN

Konstantinos Trichias[(✉)], Lucia D'Acunto[(✉)], Floris Drijver[(✉)],
and Bastiaan Wissingh[(✉)]

TNO, The Hague, The Netherlands
{kostas.trichias,lucia.dacunto,floris.drijver,bastiaan.wissingh}@tno.nl

Abstract. In Information-Centric Networking (ICN), applications request data based on the (exact) name of the data of interest. This poses a challenge for a growing number of applications, which do not know a priori the full name of a data object they seek, or do not necessarily need a specific data object, but are interested in a certain scope (e.g. the temperature in a particular geographical area). To address this challenge, we propose the more flexible and application-agnostic *Ranged-Name Retrieval* (RNR), which allows applications to define a range within each hierarchical component of the name they are requesting, obtaining in return one of the objects within that defined range. The performance evaluation of RNR indicates that, compared to the state of the art, it improves the bandwidth utilization efficiency 16-fold when retrieving data with unknown names, and even decreases the average end-to-end (E2E) delay for data delivery, while only adding 2% overhead for the processing of ranged-names.

1 Introduction

Information-Centric Networking (ICN) aims at evolving the Internet infrastructure from a connection-oriented towards a data-oriented approach, by directly addressing data objects themselves. The name of a data object is arguably a central concept in ICN. Popular ICN architectures, such as CCN [1] and NDN [2], have hierarchically designed names. The fact that any data object can be described by a hierarchical name has many benefits, from the ability to cache the data at intermediate nodes, to security and efficient routing and forwarding [2]. However, using the same hierarchical naming mechanism to also retrieve these data objects presents some limitations, primary among which is the fact that an application is required to know the exact name of the object it wants to obtain. In order to mitigate this issue, CCN supports the concept of "manifests", while NDN supports matching of Interests to Data packets with "partially known names", but both techniques suffer from limited flexibility and scalability, and can be unpractical for a number of emerging applications, where the space of potential named objects is very large and/or where a (ultra) low latency

© IFIP International Federation for Information Processing 2018
Published by Springer Nature Switzerland AG 2018. All Rights Reserved
K. R. Chowdhury et al. (Eds.): WWIC 2018, LNCS 10866, pp. 16–28, 2018.
https://doi.org/10.1007/978-3-030-02931-9_2

response is required. One example is that of an Internet-of-Things (IoT) application interested in sensor data related to a particular geographical area, e.g. a temperature sensor between certain longitude/latitude boundaries. In this case, the application is not interested in the readings of a specific sensor within that area, and the space of potential data objects may possibly be much larger than the actual data objects available.

Easing the process of applications obtaining the data they need, through a potentially vast (and/or partially unknown) naming space within acceptable latency, becomes crucial for the success of ICN as future Internet architecture. We aim to address this challenge by increasing the flexibility of data retrieval for hierarchical names. In particular, we introduce a *Ranged-Name Retrieval* (RNR) approach, which allows applications to define a range within each hierarchical component of the name they are requesting, and obtain in return one of the objects within that defined range. An early version of RNR was demonstrated at the ACM ICN 2016 conference for a surveillance use case [3], as a proof of concept. In this paper, we expand on our previous work, and evaluate RNR's performance against legacy NDN operation via extensive large scale simulations in NS-3, as well as via small scale experiments with real nodes running a version of NDN with the RNR extension. Our experiments show that a 16-fold bandwidth utilization improvement and a decrease of the end-to-end (E2E) delay can be achieved with RNR, while only imposing a 2% increase in the computational load for realistic scenarios.

2   Related Work

The need for data retrieval mechanisms better suited to the requirements of applications has been tackled in previous work in ICN. In particular, some of the advantages of using a range in the name of the Interest to retrieve data object(s) in ICN has been advocated by both industry and academia proposals. At a first instance, the authors in [4] propose the use of ranges in Interest names for a vehicular network application, as a way for vehicles to request information about an area around specific geographical coordinates and/or between certain streets, and within certain time periods. While this is a first attempt at defining efficient name ranges, the proposed scheme is limited by its application-specific nature (i.e. ranges can only be interpreted by the nodes running the specific vehicular networking application) and by the assumption of a known name-space (known street names). Another application-specific proposal, [5], describes a method for efficiently requesting content that is segmented (e.g. a video file comprised by multiple temporal "chunks") in ICN, by means of so-called "block queries". Block queries are inserted in the header of the Interest packet and the ICN routers interpret a range as being the last part of the name, hence limiting the applicability of this solution to names with only one range and always positioned at the end of the name.

The work in [6] also addresses the issue of obtaining all the data within certain segment ranges, with multiple components of the name possibly carrying the range. To enable their solution, the authors of [6] introduce the concept of "pointers", network nodes associated to specific name components which keep track of where all content within those specific names resides. However, the knowledge base of "pointers" needs to continuously be updated (which is difficult in highly dynamic scenarios), and pointers become single points of failure, decreasing the network's robustness.

What most of these solutions seem to have in common is that (a) they propose application-specific naming schemes (only ICN nodes equipped with specific applications are able to understand/process the proposed naming scheme) and/or (b) assume the existence of a finite and well defined space of named objects for which the request will be made. Our solution builds on top of the generic lines proposed in the literature and we expand the functionality of such a ranged-name retrieval mechanism to operate in an application-agnostic manner and to account for vast (unknown) name spaces, while still relying on the distributed routing mechanisms of ICN architectures.

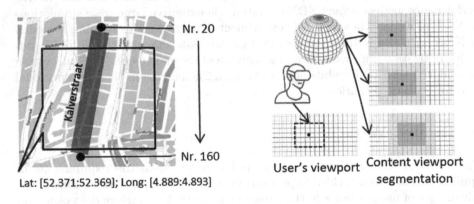

Fig. 1. Some use cases for RNR. IoT and V2X (left), VR/AR (right)

3   RNR: The Concept

3.1   Use Cases

In the era of Big Data and Internet of Things, an exploding number of devices is producing and requesting data and in a plurality of scenarios the exact name of an object is not known in advance: either because of the mobility of data producers in the network, or because of the dynamicity of certain applications (e.g. content on-demand, or within specific time frames), or simply because the exact number, type and name of all nodes (IoT devices, sensors, vehicles, etc.) deployed within a certain area, is not always known. In many of these cases, though, applications may know an approximation or part of the name, and seek to retrieve a data object within one request - either because of latency requirements, or because the specific data object to be retrieved is not important, as long as it fits within a certain "scope". The design of RNR stems from these needs. A few use cases where RNR is beneficial are outlined below.

IoT/Monitoring: Data is typically produced by (static) sensors placed in the area of interest (e.g. urban/environmental monitoring, use during festivals). In such cases, the name space of possible data objects may greatly exceed the number of actual data objects and many applications may not even be interested in the output of a specific sensor, as long as they obtain one sensor reading within a certain range. Ranges may appear in several components of the name (e.g. one indicating latitude and the other longitude), see for example Fig. 1 (left).

Vehicle-to-Everything (V2X): In this use case the sensors themselves are mobile (on the vehicles), and the data they produce may change name over time. For example, an application that may want to sample the speed of a random vehicle between street numbers 100 and 160 of the Kalverstraat in Amsterdam (Fig. 1, left), may receive a response by any vehicle situated in the area, and at different times that information may be provided by different vehicles fitting the criteria of the request.

Immersive Media (VR/AR): In Virtual or Augmented Reality (VR/AR) applications, content is commonly spatially segmented, with each spatial segment catering for a different, wide, viewport [7,8] (Fig. 1, right). Viewports for immersive media are usually centered a few degrees apart (e.g., with steps of 30–60° [7,9]), and are often partially overlapping [10]. As users move their head in the virtual world, the content matching their new orientation needs to be streamed to them. This adaptation needs to be very quick because of the extremely low latency requirements of immersive media use cases. If an application does not know the viewport segmentation used by the video source (e.g. when the content is produced *live*), it might be convenient for the application to specify a range of viewports that will cover the user's orientation (e.g. 30° clockwise from the north, within a 30° range: */WaltDisney/JungleBook/orientation/[15:45]*) and let the network fetch the closest viewport matching this orientation, in order to minimize latency.

3.2 A More Flexible Data Retrieval Approach

To cater for the different needs and use cases as described in the previous section, we have designed and built *Ranged-Name Retrieval* (RNR) as an extension to NDN. Embedding RNR at the network layer (i.e. extending the core of NDN) also makes our approach application-agnostic, since nodes on the request path can process ranged-names without needing to invoke (and have installed) a specific application to deal with it. Our approach remains compliant to the "1 Interest packet, 1 Data packet" principle: even if an Interest with a ranged-name may be potentially satisfied by multiple data objects, only one will be returned to the requester. RNR comes with two inherent advantages. On one hand, it facilitates the retrieval of data with unknown names by applications, while on the other hand its application-agnostic design also has the potential of decreasing the network traffic, since it may be used by all applications, independently of their nature, and since ICN nodes in the network understand the range and will be able to fetch the closest data matching the range. Even in cases where the application knows the exact name of a data packet, the use of an Interest with a range may result in reduced end-to-end latency for data delivery and traffic per link, since a data object that also satisfies the application and is different than the originally intended one, may be fetched by an ICN node in closer vicinity.

4   Implementation and Experimental Design

4.1   RNR Extensions to NDN

The extensions for supporting the RNR concept, implemented on NDN version 0.4.1, are described below.

A New Name Component in Interest Names: We have introduced a new type of Name Component, a Name-Range Component (NRC) [3], that includes special syntax to indicate ranges within Interest packets. The NRC is implemented as a new Type-Length-Value (TLV) type, so that NDN routers can easily distinguish them from regular name components. Only names in Interest packets are allowed to have a NRC in them.

Processing Incoming Interests: The NDN network forwarder has been extended to be able to process incoming Interests bearing NRCs name components. When a NDN node receives a new Interest, it adds it to the Pending Interest Table (PIT) and checks whether this Interest is already pending. Upon insertion in the PIT, if the Interest contains a NRC, it is flagged and its position in the PIT is saved in an additional "NRC index table" for quicker lookups on the incoming data path. If the Interest is not pending, the node performs a lookup in the Content Store (CS). When the prefix of the Interest contains a NRC, the node searches the CS for possible entries within the range of the prefix. If a match is found, the matching entry is returned, and the corresponding PIT entry is removed. If no match is found, the node looks in the Forwarding Interest Base (FIB) for possible entries within the range of the prefix. If a matching entry within range is found, it is returned and used to forward the Interest containing the NRC.

Processing Incoming Data Packets: The NDN network forwarder has also been extended in order to match incoming Data packets with PIT entries containing NRCs name components. Specifically, upon receiving an incoming Data packet, a RNR node checks the PIT for entries that match the Name of the Data packet. When searching the PIT, the node first checks for standard entries, and then proceeds to check for NRC entries, using the NRC index table.

4.2 Simulator Integration and Evaluation Scenarios

The network level performance of RNR is evaluated using version 2.3 of the ndnSIM module [11], available for the NS-3 simulator. For all nodes in NS-3 simulations (whether a consumer or a producer) caching was disabled for reasons of simplicity. In fact, for this initial evaluation, our goal is to provide a good understanding of how RNR helps with fetching content with unknown name components from the original, spatially distributed producers themselves. The introduction of caching, which is part of our future work, is not expected to alter the outcome significantly, since any node that would cache a data object could also be seen as a new producer of that same data object. The consumer nodes transmit NRC Interests following a realistic Zipf-Mandelbrot distribution.

Network Level Evaluation. To get a full picture of RNR's capabilities, we evaluated its performance in a large scale network, and performed a sensitivity study of the various network parameters that can affect its performance. For this purpose, we have used the NS-3 simulator with the ndnSIM extension and the RNR upgrades.

The performance of RNR under varying network conditions is bench marked against baseline scenarios where legacy NDN is used, applying three major Key Performance Indicators (KPIs):

- *average end-to-end delay (E2E delay)*, i.e. from the generation of the first Interest to the delivery of the corresponding Data packet;
- *bandwidth utilization*, i.e. traffic on the wire in MB (differentiating between Interest and Data traffic);
- *Interest success ratio* i.e. percentage of Interests that returned a Data packet.

Since there is no official approach in NDN on requesting data with unknown names, an assumption has been made regarding the functionality of the baseline scenarios using legacy NDN. A traditional approach would be having the consumer sending out sequential legacy NDN Interests for the names in the specific range under consideration, until a name is used that corresponds to actual existing data in the network, at which case the correct data object will be returned. As an example, in the case of a temperature reading from an unknown street number in Amsterdam in the range [20:40], the RNR scenario would use an Interest with a name such as */NL/Amsterdam/Kalverstraat/streetnr/[20:40]/temperature*, while a baseline scenario would start transmitting sequential Interests with names such as */NL/Amsterdam/Kalverstraat/streetnr/20/temperature, /NL/Amsterdam/Kalverstraat/streetnr/21/temperature*,..., etc. until it transmitted an Interest with an existing name, and the corresponding Data packet is returned. Since transmitting these Interests in a sequential fashion, and waiting for a timeout of the previous one before sending the next one, would result in unrealistic delays that no application could tolerate, we have designed the legacy NDN baseline operation to flood all individual Interests at the same time, thus keeping delays at a reasonable level. In the aforementioned example, that would mean that in the legacy NDN case the consumer would flood the network with 21 Interests at the same time, and hope that at least one of them finds a match and returns a Data packet. The *Traffic Mix (% ranged requests)* parameter (Table 1) indicates the percentage of requests where a range is used, which are implemented by means of one NRC interest for the case of the RNR implementation, and by means of the flooding approach for the case of the legacy NDN implementation. The *Range Size* parameter indicates, for the legacy NDN implementation, the amount of parallel Interests that are flooded in the network.

Table 1. RNR simulation parameter settings

Topology	Barabási–Albert
Data Availability	1%, **10%**, 25%, 50%, 75%, 100%
Consumers/Producers	90%/10%, **75%/25%**, 50%/50%, 25%/75%
Traffic Mix (% ranged requests)	0%, **10%**, 20%, ..., 100%
Range Size	5, 10, **25**, 50, 100
Number of Nodes	25, 100, **500**, 1000, 2000
Avg. Data Packet Size	10 B, 100 B, 500 B, **1 KB**, 1.5 KB

For both the legacy and RNR versions of NDN, the *"best route"* forwarding strategy is employed. Furthermore, a Zipf distribution is used for content generation and a realistic *Barabási–Albert* topology is used for the network layout, with a varying number of nodes to cover the entire range from small-scale to large-scale NDN networks, while the simulation duration was network-size dependent with a minimum requirement for 10^5 transmitted Interests per scenario. All nodes in the network were either a consumer generating Interests or a producer generating data (content randomly distributed over the available producers), while at the same time all of them could act as forwarders. Different combinations of consumer/producer ratios were evaluated as can be seen in Table 1. Finally, different Data Packet Sizes were implemented in order to cater for applications with different needs, with a maximum packet size of 1.5 KB to simulate the maximum MAC PDU size over Ethernet.

The *Data Availability* parameter indicates the actual percentage of existing data objects in relevance to the possible name space for a name component. As can be understood, Data Availability is far less than 100% in most scenarios, resulting in a lot of failed (timed-out) Interests in both legacy and RNR implementations of NDN, when looking for data with unknown names. For both implementations a "penalty" of 1 s (equal to the timeout timer) was imposed to the E2E delay for every failed Interest.

For the purposes of this evaluation, we use the "immersive media" use case described in Sect. 3 where the video content is spatially segmented into specific viewport orientations. For simplicity, we assume that the content only offers a horizontal degree of freedom (i.e. users can look around 360°, but cannot look up or down). In this case, the possible name space for the component *"orientation"* is [0–359], corresponding to degrees starting from the North. In an exemplary case where the entire 360° video would be covered by 24 viewports, equally spaced (each 15° apart), the Data Availability for such a case would be 24/360 = 6.6%. An overview of all the settings is presented in Table 1.

5   Performance Evaluation

In this section, we present the outcome of the large-scale NS-3 simulations and elaborate on the gained insights. During the evaluation while the effect of one parameter on the performance of RNR was under investigation, some default values have been selected for the rest of the parameters in Table 1, for the experiments on the simulator. The selected default values per parameter represent a realistic scenario and are indicated with bold and underlined text in Table 1.

5.1   Network Wide Evaluation

We have evaluated the network-wide performance of RNR NDN based on our NS-3 implementation (see Sect. 4.2), using the parameter values from Table 1. Figure 2 depicts the average E2E delay per Interest-Data packet pair, for various Data Availability values (a), and for different ranged request percentages within the Traffic Mix (b). In both cases there is an upper limit of the E2E delay at 1 s (1000 ms) which is caused by the high "miss" ratio of Interests and the resulting enforcement of the time-out penalty (as described in Sect. 4.2). When Data Availability is very small (Fig. 2(a), left side), or when only legacy NDN Interests are used to request data with unknown names (Fig. 2(b)), most Interests do not find an appropriate Data packet to return and hence the time-out penalty dominates the E2E delay.

From Fig. 2(a) we can observe that the average E2E delay drops significantly for higher Data Availability values (down to about 11 ms for 100% Data Availability). In these cases most Interests return a Data packet and there are almost no time-out penalties enforced, depicting the pure latency of the network. The fact that legacy NDN and RNR NDN (using the default values for RNR settings) seem to provide similar delays is attributed to the implementation of flooding for the legacy NDN as a way to request data with unknown names (see Sect. 4.2). Since legacy NDN 'floods' the network with multiple Interests at the same time, it is able to attain a similar latency as RNR NDN does by using one Interest to achieve the same 'search'. This results in a significant difference in used bandwidth, as depicted in Fig. 3.

From Fig. 2(b) we can conclude that RNR NDN is a much more efficient way of looking for data with unknown names, since the more ranged requests are used, the lower the average E2E delay. The entire range of traffic mix for the legacy NDN is dominated by the 1 s penalty (due to the default 10% Data Availability), since with higher traffic mix, more Interests are 'flooded' into the network and even though more Data packets are returned, the ratio of successful-to-failed Interests remains very low. This is not the case for the RNR NDN implementation which can achieve a search over the same range of names with only one Interest. As a result when the Traffic Mix is close to 100% (all Interests are ranged requests) most Interests are successful and there are very few time-out penalties imposed which greatly improves the performance. In a realistic scenario we expect the Traffic Mix to match the percentage of data requests with unknown names, i.e. if 10% of the requested data have unknown names then approximately 10% of NRC Interests should be used.

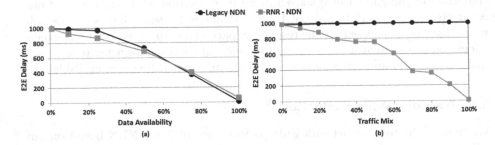

Fig. 2. Average End-to-End (E2E) Delay versus (a) Data Availability and (b) Traffic Mix (% ranged names)

Next to the average E2E delay, we have looked at the bandwidth used, in terms of MB on the wire, to achieve the same result (i.e. obtain a data object in the range) for both legacy and RNR NDN. This KPI enables us to evaluate the overall efficiency of the two solutions.

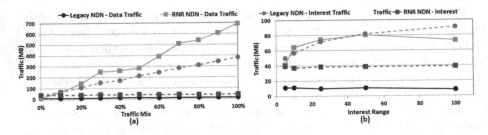

Fig. 3. Interest and Data packet bandwidth utilization vs (a) Traffic Mix, (b) Interest Range

Figure 3(a) depicts the bandwidth utilization per solution versus the Traffic Mix. This figure provides many interesting insights, foremost of which is that the bulk of the traffic in the legacy NDN case originates from the Interests while in the RNR NDN case it originates from the Data packets returned. Although the Data packets are much larger in size (default value of 1 KB) compared to the 58 Bytes of the Interest packets, in the case of legacy NDN the Interest traffic dominates the bandwidth utilization, as a result of the fact that a large number of Interest packets is transmitted while only a low number of Data packets is returned. The RNR NDN on the other hand uses a fixed amount of bandwidth for Interest traffic, while the more ranged requests that are used the better the success ratio (transmitted Interests vs Delivered Data packets) and hence more data is delivered. It is also interesting to note that the legacy NDN Interest traffic load increases with increasing range utilization since more and more Interests need to be flooded, while at the same time the increase in returned Data packets is minimal (from about 10 MB for 0% ranged requests to about 12 MB for 100% ranged requests) and remains even under the RNR NDN Interest traffic. During our experiments we also observed that for 100% ranged requests the success ratio is also 100% which serves as a good sanity check for the scenario under consideration. With the default values used here (Data Availability = 10%, NRC range = 25, name space = [0–359]) it is expected that there are about 360*10% = 36 individual data objects (VR viewports). With an approximate equal spacing among them it is expected that each viewport will be about 360/36 = 10° apart. Since the range used has a size of 25°, it is then expected that when 100% of the Interests are ranged requests there will be at least one (likely two) data object within this 25° range that satisfies each Interest and hence all Interests are successful, bringing the success ratio to 100%. The above presented analysis indicates that RNR clearly outperforms legacy NDN and operates much more efficiently in scenarios where data objects with unknown names need to be requested.

Figure 3(b) depicts the bandwidth utilization of Interest and Data traffic for various values of Range Sizes. As the Range Size increases, the Interest traffic for legacy NDN also increases while the Interest traffic for RNR NDN remains the same. This can be explained as follows: for the legacy case an increase in the Range Size from 25° to 50° means a doubling of Interest traffic since for every data object search a consumer would have to 'flood' 50 sequential legacy NDN Interests instead of 25 resulting in 50 * 58 = 2900 Bytes on the wire per search instead of 25 * 58 = 1450 Bytes per search. This phenomenon can be clearly seen in Fig. 3(b). In the case of RNR, however, an increase in the Range Size from 25° to 50° would simply mean an update of the relevant name component of the Interest from e.g. /[50–75] to e.g. /[50–100], thus keeping the Interest traffic to a minimum of 58–60 Bytes transmitted per search. As a result, the Interest traffic of RNR remains independent of the range used which is a great advantage when the possible name-space of an unknown data object is very large. It is also interesting to note that even though the data traffic of RNR increases at first with increasing Range Size, it seems to reach a maximum (truncation point) after some value of the range (around a Range Size of 25°) and after that an increase in the range has no effect on the number of returned packets. This effect is attributed to the fact that with a Data Availability of 10%, a Range Size of 25° is enough to guarantee that every NRC Interest will find at least one data object. A further increase of the range beyond that point will not result in any extra Data packets delivered.

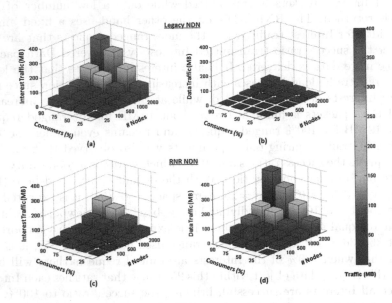

Fig. 4. Traffic on the wire versus consumer percentage and network size (number of nodes) originating from (a) Legacy NDN Interests, (b) Legacy NDN Data packets, (c) RNR NDN Interests and (d) RNR NDN Data packets

As a final step, we have investigated the effect of a varying network size and a varying mix of consumers and producers in the network on the RNR implementation, in order to establish the trade-offs of our solution against different types of networks. Figure 4 is a 3D bar graph depicting the bandwidth utilization for a variety of network sizes (number of nodes) and consumer/producer mixes showcasing (a) the legacy NDN Interest traffic, (b) the legacy NDN data traffic, (c) the RNR Interest traffic and (d) the RNR data traffic. It is evident from Fig. 4 that both Interest and Data traffics grow with increasing number of nodes and increasing number of consumers since more consumers means more Interest packets and more Data packets as a response. The corresponding decrease of producers (result of the increase of consumers) does not negatively affect the data traffic in this case, since the number of contents actually remains the same. The only difference is that the same content is now more scarcely placed within the network, evenly distributed among the decreased number of producers. This scarce distribution of content may affect other KPIs such as E2E delay (content available at a producer further away) but this effect can also be counterbalanced by the inherent NDN caching mechanism. We observe that both the legacy and RNR NDN average E2E delays are unaffected by the change in Consumer/Producer ratio for these experiments due to the fact that in both cases the E2E delay is dominated by the time-out penalties enforced. The delay is 10%

shorter for the RNR case due to the higher success ratio but in both cases there are a lot of non-ranged requests (since the default value of 10% Traffic Mix is used) which result in several time-out penalties.

The results presented in Fig. 4 also indicate that the RNR solution scales very well with network size as well as with content size and/or amount of content producers, which makes it highly adaptable and suitable for a wide range of networks and applications. The legacy NDN on the other hand shows scalability issues which would make it unsuitable, as is, to be implemented in large scale networks and/or networks with a high percentage of unknown names (e.g. massive IoT sensor networks).

6   Conclusions and Future Work

In this paper we have presented the design, implementation and performance evaluation of *Ranged-Name Retrieval*, an extension of NDN with support for names with range indications to enable the consumers to request data with partially unknown names. The direct implementation of RNR within the core of the NDN architecture enables it to operate at wire speed and on any NDN node, making it application-agnostic so that data from different applications can be cross-utilized.

Our extensive performance evaluation indicates that RNR manages to address a key issue where legacy NDN is highly inefficient (retrieval of data with unknown names), by significantly improving the network performance (up to 16-fold bandwidth utilization improvement), while at the same time exhibiting a high degree of scalability and imposing minimal overhead (2% additional computation load for realistic scenarios).

The fact that RNR can accommodate varying Range Sizes without increasing the overhead on the nodes, and support multiple ranges within the same Interest (for different name components), makes it highly scalable and adaptable to current of future networks and applications.

Our future work is planned along two main directions, (a) the further development of the RNR scheme and (b) the more detailed testing, evaluation and benchmarking of RNR. As a first step we will extend RNR to support multiple ranges within a single name, each range specifying a search space for a specific component of the name. In this way data objects with inherent tuples in their name, such as latitude and longitude, can be requested while specifying an individual search space for each attribute. New ways to increase the functionality of the range component will also be researched, e.g. combining ranges and data manipulation functions (i.e. to request data aggregates like average, minimum, etc.).

In terms of performance evaluation, a larger variety of scenarios will be tested in the simulator and more extensive KPIs will be used, such as hop count, cache hit ratio and latency, which will allow for a deeper understanding of RNR under different network conditions. Finally, a first version of RNR will be implemented in the TNO IoT testbed, currently under construction, which will consist of dozens of IoT devices/sensors spreading over multiple rooms and floors and running both IP and NDN protocol stack. Experimenting on such a real-life IoT testbed will give us new insights regarding the performance of RNR and the potential issues that may arise or be solved by it, in a true environment.

References

1. Jacobson, V., Smetters, D.K., Thornton, J.D., Plass, M.F., Briggs, N.H., Braynard, R.L.: Networking named content. In: ACM CoNEXT (2009)
2. Zhang, L., et al.: Named data networking. ACM SIGCOMM Comput. Commun. Rev. **44**, 66–73 (2014)
3. Wissingh, B., D'Acunto, L.: Extending named-data-networking with support for names with range indications. In: ACM ICN (2016)
4. Wang, L., Wakikawa, R., Kuntz, R., Vuyyuru, R., Zhang, L.: Data naming in vehicle-to-vehicle communications. In: IEEE INFOCOM WKSHPS (2012)
5. Samsung Electronics Co., Ltd.: Terminal device based on content name, and method for routing based on content name. US 20140181140 A1 (2014)
6. Varvello, M., Esteban, J., Smith, M., Greenwald, L., Guo, Y., Schurgot, M.: Range queries in MANET: can information-centric networking help? In: IEEE ICCCN (2013)
7. Corbillon, X., Devlic, A., Simon, G., Chakareski, J.: Viewport-adaptive navigable 360-degree video delivery. arXiv preprint arXiv:1609.08042 (2016)
8. D'Acunto, L., van den Berg, J., Thomas, E., Niamut, O.: Using MPEG DASH SRD for zoomable and navigable video. In: ACM MMSys (2016)
9. Next Generation Video Encoding Techniques for 360 Video and VR. https://code.facebook.com/posts/1126354007399553/next-generation-video-encoding-techniques-for-360-video-and-vr/
10. Niamut, O., Thomas, G., Thomas, E., van Brandenburg, R., D'Acunto, L., Gregory-Clarke, R.: Immersive live event experiences-interactive UHDTV on mobile devices. Technical report, British Broadcasting Corporation (2014)
11. Mastorakis, S., Afanasyev, A., Moiseenko, I., Zhang, L.: ndnSIM 2: an updated NDN simulator for ns-3. Technical report, Internet Research Lab (2016)

Distributed Path Reconfiguration and Data Forwarding in Industrial IoT Networks

Theofanis P. Raptis$^{(\boxtimes)}$ ⓘD, Andrea Passarella, and Marco Conti

Institute of Informatics and Telematics, National Research Council, Pisa, Italy
{theofanis.raptis,andrea.passarella,marco.conti}@iit.cnr.it

Abstract. In today's typical industrial environments, the computation of the data distribution schedules is highly centralised. Typically, a central entity configures the data forwarding paths so as to guarantee low delivery delays between data producers and consumers. However, these requirements might become impossible to meet later on, due to link or node failures, or excessive degradation of their performance. In this paper, we focus on maintaining the network functionality required by the applications after such events. We avoid continuously recomputing the configuration centrally, by designing an energy efficient local and distributed path reconfiguration method. Specifically, given the operational parameters required by the applications, we provide several algorithmic functions which locally reconfigure the data distribution paths, when a communication link or a network node fails. We compare our method through simulations to other state of the art methods and we demonstrate performance gains in terms of energy consumption and data delivery success rate as well as some emerging key insights which can lead to further performance gains.

Keywords: Industry 4.0 · Internet of Things · Data distribution

1 Introduction

With the introduction of Internet of Things (IoT) concepts in industrial application scenarios, industrial automation is undergoing a tremendous change. This is made possible in part by recent advances in technology that allow interconnection on a wider and more fine-grained scale [12]. The core of distributed automation systems and networks is essentially the reliable exchange of data. Any attempt to steer processes independently of continuous human interaction requires, in a very wide sense, the flow of data between some kind of sensors, controllers, and actuators [9].

In today's typical industrial configurations, the computation of the data exchange and distribution schedules is quite primitive and highly centralised. Usually, the generated data are transferred to a central network controller or

K. R. Chowdhury et al. (Eds.): WWIC 2018, LNCS 10866, pp. 29–41, 2018.
https://doi.org/10.1007/978-3-030-02931-9_3

intermediate network proxy nodes using wireless links. The controller analyses the received information and, if needed, reconfigures the network paths, the data forwarding mechanisms, the caching proxy locations and changes the behaviour of the physical environment through actuator devices. Traditional data distribution schemes can be implemented over relevant industrial protocols and standards, like IEC WirelessHART and IEEE 802.15.4e.

Those entirely centralised and offline computations regarding data distribution scheduling, can become inefficient in terms of energy, when applied in industrial IoT networks. In industrial environments, the topology and connectivity of the network may vary due to link and sensor-node failures [10]. Also, very dynamic conditions, which make communication performance much different from when the central schedule was computed, possibly causing sub-optimal performance, may result in not guaranteeing application requirements. These dynamic network topologies may cause a portion of industrial sensor nodes to malfunction. With the increasing number of involved battery-powered devices, industrial IoT networks may consume substantial amounts of energy; more than would be needed if local, distributed computations were used.

Our Contribution. In this paper we consider an industrial IoT network comprised of sensor and actuator nodes. Data consumers (actuators) and producers (sensors) are known. A number of intermediate resource-rich nodes act as proxies. We assume that applications require a certain upper bound on the data delivery delay from proxies to consumers, and that, at some point in time, a central controller computes an optimal set of multi-hop paths from producers to proxies, and from proxies to consumers, which guarantee a maximum delivery delay, while maximising the energy lifetime of the network (i.e., the time until the first node in the network exhaust energy resources). We focus on maintaining the network configuration in a way such that application requirements are met after important network operational parameters change due to some unplanned events (e.g., heavy interference, excessive energy consumption), while guaranteeing an appropriate utilisation of energy resources. We provide several efficient algorithmic functions which locally reconfigure the paths of the data distribution process, when a communication link or a network node fails. The functions regulate how the local path reconfiguration should be implemented and how a node can join a new path or modify an already existing path, ensuring that there will be no loops. The proposed method can be implemented on top of existing data forwarding schemes designed for industrial IoT networks. We demonstrate through simulations the performance gains of our method in terms of energy consumption and data delivery success rate.

2   Related Works

There are numerous relevant previous works in the literature, but due to lack of space, we provide some information about the most representative and most related ones to this paper, which are [2,3,5,6,8,11]. Although some of those works use proxy nodes for the efficient distributed management of network data, they all perform path selection computations centrally. Placement and selection strategies of caching proxies in industrial IoT networks have been investigated in [2]. Efficient proxy-consumer assignments are presented in [5]. Data re-allocation methods among proxies for better traffic balancing are presented in [11]. Scheduling of the data distribution process maximising the time until the first network node dies is suggested in [6], respecting end-to-end data access latency constraints of the order of 100 ms, as imposed by the industrial operators [1]. Delay aspects in a realistic industrial IoT network model (based on WirelessHART), and bounding of the worst case delay in the network are considered in [8]. Reliable routing, improved communication latency and stable real-time communication, at the cost of modest overhead in device configuration, are demonstrated in [3]. Different to those works, in this paper, we present a method which exploits the local knowledge of the network nodes so as to perform distributed, local path reconfiguration computations towards more efficient energy dissipation across the network.

3 The Model

We model an industrial IoT network as a graph $G = (V, E)$. Typically, the network features three types of devices [13]: resource constrained sensor and actuator nodes $u \in V$, a central network controller C, and a set of proxy nodes in a set P, with $P \subset V$, $|P| \ll |V - P|$. Every node $u \in V$, at time t, has an available amount of finite energy E_u^t. In general, normal nodes u have limited amounts of initial energy supplies E_u^0, and proxy nodes have significantly higher amounts of initial energy supplies E_p^0, with $E_p^0 \gg E_u^0, \forall u \in V, p \in P$.

A node $u \in V$ can achieve one-hop data propagation using suitable industrial wireless technologies (e.g., IEEE 802.15.4e) to a set of nodes which lie in its neighbourhood N_u. N_u contains the nodes $v \in V$ for which it holds that $\rho_u \geq \delta(u, v)$, where ρ_u is the transmission range of node u (defined by the output power of the antenna) and $\delta(u, v)$ is the Euclidean distance between u and v. The sets N_u are thus defining the set of edges E of the graph G. Each one-hop data propagation from u to v results in a latency l_{uv}. Assuming that all network nodes operate with the same output power, each one-hop data propagation from u to v requires and amount of ϵ_{uv} of energy dissipated by u so as to transmit one data piece to v. A node can also transmit control messages to the network controller C by consuming ϵ_{cc} amount of energy. For this kind of transmissions, we assume that more expensive wireless technology is needed, and thus we have that $\epsilon_{cc} \gg \epsilon_{uv}$ (for example, the former can occur over WiFi or LTE links, while the latter over 802.15.4 links).

Occasionally, data generation occurs in the network, relevant to the industrial process. The data are modelled as a set of data pieces $D = \{D_i\}$. Each data piece is defined as $D_i = (s_i, c_i, r_i)$, where $s_i \in V$ is the source of data piece D_i, $c_i \in V$ is the consumer[1] of data piece D_i, and r_i is the data generation rate of D_i.

---

[1] If the same data of a source, e.g., s_1, is requested by more than one consumers, e.g., c_1 and c_2, we have two distinct data pieces, $D_1 = (s_1, c_1, r_1)$ and $D_2 = (s_2, c_2, r_2)$, where $s_1 = s_2$.

Each data piece D_i is circulated in the network through a multi-hop path $\Pi_{s_i c_i}$. Each node $u \in \Pi_{s_i c_i}$ knows which is the previous node $previous(i, u) \in \Pi_{s_i c_i}$ and the next node $next(i, u) \in \Pi_{s_i c_i}$ in the path of data piece D_i. Without loss of generality, we divide time in time cycles τ and we assume that the data may be generated (according to rate r_i) at each source s_i at the beginning of each τ, and circulated during τ. The data generation and request patterns are not necessarily synchronous, and therefore, the data pieces need to be cached temporarily for future requests by consumers. This asynchronous data distribution is usually implemented through an industrial pub/sub system [5]. A critical aspect in the industrial operation is the timely data access by the consumers upon request, and, typically, the data distribution system must guarantee that a given maximum data access latency constraint (defined by the specific industrial process) is satisfied. We denote this threshold as $L_{\max}$.

Due to the fact that the set P of proxy nodes is strong in terms of computation, storage and energy supplies, nodes $p \in P$ can act as proxy in the network and cache data originated from the sources, for access from the consumers when needed. This relieves the IoT devices from the burden of storing data they generate (which might require excessive local storage), and helps meeting the latency constraint. Proxy selection placement strategies have been studied in recent literature [2,5]. We denote as L_{uv} the latency of the multi-hop data propagation of the path Π_{uv}, where $L_{uv} = l_{ui} + l_{i(i+1)} + \ldots + l_{(i+n)v}$. Upon a request from c_i, data piece D_i can be delivered from p via a (distinct) multi-hop path. We denote as L_{c_i} the data access latency of c_i, with $L_{c_i} = L_{c_i p} + L_{p c_i}$. We assume an existing mechanism of initial centrally computed configuration of the data forwarding paths in the network, e.g., as presented in [6]. In order to meet the industrial requirements the following constraint must be met: $L_{c_i} \leq L_{\max}, \forall c_i \in V$.

4   Network Epochs and Their Maximum Duration

In order to better formulate the data forwarding process through a lifetime-based metric, we define the network epoch. A network epoch j is characterised by the time J (τ divides J) elapsed between two consecutive, significant changes in the main network operational parameters. A characteristic example of such change is a sharp increase of ϵ_{uv} between two consecutive time cycles, due to sudden, increased interference on node u, which in turn leads to increased retransmissions on edge (u, v) and thus higher energy consumption. In other words, $\frac{\epsilon_{uv}(\tau) - \epsilon_{uv}(\tau-1)}{\epsilon_{uv}(\tau)} > \gamma$, where γ is a predefined threshold. During a network epoch, (all or some of) the nodes initially take part in a configuration phase (central or distributed), during which they acquire the plan for the data distribution process by spending an amount of e_u^{cfg} energy for communication. Then, they run the data distribution process. A network epoch is thus comprised of two phases: *Configuration phase.* During this initial phase, the nodes acquire the set of neighbours from/to which they must receive/forward data pieces in the next epoch. *Data forwarding phase.* During this phase the data pieces are circulated in the network according to the underlying network directives.

Network epochs are just an abstraction that is useful for the design and presentation of the algorithmic functions, but does not need global synchronisation. As it will be clear later on, each node locally identifies the condition for which an epoch is finished from its perspective, and acts accordingly. Different nodes "see" in general different epochs. Although some events which affect the epoch duration cannot be predicted and thus controlled, we are interested in the events which could be affected by the data distribution process and which could potentially influence the maximum epoch duration. We observe that an epoch cannot last longer than the time that the next node in the network dies. Consequently, if we manage to maximise the time until a node dies due to energy consumption, we also make a step forward for the maximisation of the epoch duration.

We now define the maximum epoch duration, as it can serve as a useful metric for the decision making process of the distributed path reconfiguration. The maximum epoch duration is the time interval between two consecutive node deaths in the network. Specifically, each epoch's duration is bounded by the lifetime of the node with the shortest lifetime in the network, given a specific data forwarding configuration. Without loss of generality, we assume that the duration of the configuration phase equals τ. We define the variables, x_{uv}^{ij} which hold the necessary information regarding the transmission of the data pieces across the edges of the graph. More specifically, for epoch j, $x_{uv}^{ij} = 1$ when edge (u, v) is activated for data piece D_i. On the contrary, $x_{uv}^{ij} = 0$ when edge (u, v) is inactive for the transmission of data piece D_i. We denote as $a_{uv}^j = \sum_{i=1}^d r_i x_{uv}^{ij}$ the aggregate data rate of (u, v) for epoch j. Stacking all a_{uv}^j together, we get $\mathbf{x}_u^j = [a_{uv}^j]$, the data rate vector of node u for every $v \in N_u$. Following this formulation (and if we assumed that $J \to \infty$) the maximum lifetime of u during epoch j can be defined as:

$$
T_u(\mathbf{x}_u^j) = \begin{cases} \dfrac{E_u^j}{\sum_{v \in N_u} \epsilon_{uv} a_{uv}^j} & \text{if } E_u^j > e_u^{\text{cfg}} \\ \tau & \text{if } E_u^j \leq e_u^{\text{cfg}} , \\ 0 & \text{if } E_u^j = 0 \end{cases} \tag{1}
$$

where e_u^{cfg} is the amount of energy that is needed by u in order to complete the configuration phase. Consequently, given an epoch j, the maximum epoch duration is $J_{\max} = \min_{u \in V} \{T_u(\mathbf{x}_u^j) \mid \sum_{v \in N_u} x_{uv}^{ij} > 0\}$.

There have already been works in the literature which identify, for each data source s_i, the proxy p where its data should be cached, in order to maximise the total lifetime of the network until the first node dies [6] (or, in other words, maximise the duration of the first epoch: $\max \min_{u \in V} \{T_u(\mathbf{x}_u^1) \mid \sum_{v \in N_u} x_{uv}^{i1} > 0\}$), and configure the data forwarding paths accordingly. Reconfigurations can be triggered also when the conditions under which a configuration has been computed, change. Therefore, (i) epoch duration can be shorter than J, and (ii) we do not need any centralised synchronisation in order to define the actual epoch duration. We consider the epoch as only an abstraction (but not a working parameter for the functions), which is defined as the time between two consecutive reconfigurations of the network, following the functions presented in Sect. 5.

5   Path Reconfiguration and Data Forwarding

The main idea behind our method is the following: the nodes are initially provided with a centralised data forwarding plan. When a significant change in the network occurs, the nodes involved are locally adjusting the paths, using lightweight communication links among them (e.g., 802.15.4) instead of communicating with the central network controller (e.g., LTE, WiFi). The main metric used for the path adjustment is the epoch-related $T_u(\mathbf{x}_u^j)$, as defined in Eq. 1. The functions' pseudocode is presented in the following subsections. Due to lack of space we omit the presentation of some functions' pseudocodes, but those can be found in the extended version of the paper [7]. The functions are presented in upright typewriter font and the messages which are being sent and received are presented in italics typewriter font. The arguments in the parentheses of the functions are the necessary information that the functions need in order to compute the desired output. The arguments in the brackets of the messages are the destination nodes of the messages and the arguments in the parentheses of the messages are the information carried by the messages. We assume that a node u complies with the following rules: u knows the positions of every $v \in N_u$, u knows the neighbourhood N_v of every node v in its own neighbourhood N_u, and u stores only local information or temporarily present data pieces in transit.

Distributed Data Forwarding. The distributed data forwarding function `DistrDataFwd`(u) pseudocode is being ran on every node u of the network and is provided in the body of Algorithm 1. At first, if $E_u^0 > 0$, the node communicates its status to the central network controller (which uses the method presented in [6] for computing the data distribution parameters (proxy allocation, data forwarding paths) in an initial setup phase of the network), it receives the data forwarding plan and it initiates the first time cycle (lines 1–4). Then, for every time cycle u repeats the following process, until either it is almost dead, or more than half of its associated wireless links spend more energy compared to the previous time cycle, according to the system parameter γ (lines 5–18): u starts the data forwarding process according to the data distribution plan received by C (line 6). Afterwards, it checks if a set of control messages have been received from any $v \in N_u$ and acts accordingly, by calling the necessary functions (lines 7–15).

If u detects that a link is consuming too much energy and has to be deactivated, it deactivates this link (by causing a path disconnection for every D_i that is using this link) and notifies the previous node in the path of every D_i that was using this link, $previous(i, u)$, by sending an alert message (lines 7–7). For a given deactivated link (u, v) for data piece D_i, alert messages contain information about D_i and about the two nodes u, v in the path prior to disconnection. Then, u checks whether there has been an alert message received (line 10), and calls function `LocalPathConfig` (displayed in Algorithm 2). Through this function the paths can be reconfigured accordingly, for all involved data pieces D_i. Due to the fact that `LocalPathConfig` sends some additional messages regarding joining a new path and modifying an existing one, u then checks

---

Algorithm 1. DistrDataFwd(u)

---

1 **if** $E_u^0 > 0$ **then**
2 $\quad$ send $status\,[C](E_u, \epsilon_{uv}, l_{uv})$
3 $\quad$ receive $plan\,[u]$
4 $\quad$ $\tau = 1$
5 $\quad$ **repeat**
6 $\quad\quad$ run DataForwarding(τ)
7 $\quad\quad$ **if** $\exists (u,v)\ with\ \frac{\epsilon_{uv}(\tau) - \epsilon_{uv}(\tau-1)}{\epsilon_{uv}(\tau)} > \gamma$ **then**
8 $\quad\quad\quad$ Deactivate($i, (u,v)$), $\forall D_i$
9 $\quad\quad\quad$ send $alert\,[previous(i,u)](u,v)$, $\forall D_i$
10 $\quad\quad$ **if** $receive\ alert[u](v, next(i,v))$ **then**
11 $\quad\quad\quad$ Deactivate($i, (u,v)$)
12 $\quad\quad\quad$ call LocalPathConfig($i, u, next(i,v)$)
13 $\quad\quad$ **if** $receive\ join[u](i, w, v)$ **then**
14 $\quad\quad\quad$ call JoinPath(i, w, v)
15 $\quad\quad$ **if** $receive\ modify\_path[u](i, w, deleteArg, dirArg)$ **then**
16 $\quad\quad\quad$ call ModifyPath($i, w, deleteArg, dirArg$)
17 $\quad\quad$ $\tau ++$
18 $\quad$ **until** $E_u = 0\ or\ \frac{\epsilon_{uv}(\tau) - \epsilon_{uv}(\tau-1)}{\epsilon_{uv}(\tau)} > \gamma\ for > 50\%\ of\ active\ edges\ (u,v)\ of\ u$
19 send $alert\,[previous(i,u)](u,v)$, $\forall D_i$, $\forall v \in N_u$
20 Disconnect(u)

---

for reception of any of those messages (lines 13 and 15) and calls the necessary functions JoinPath and ModifyPath.

Finally, u sends an alert message to the previous nodes in the existing paths prior to final disconnection due to energy supplies shortage (line 19).

Local Path Configuration. A node u calls the path configuration function LocalPathConfig when it receives an alert which signifies cease of operation of an edge (u,v) due to a sudden significant increase of energy consumption due to interference $\left(\frac{\epsilon_{uv}(\tau) - \epsilon_{uv}(\tau-1)}{\epsilon_{uv}(\tau)} > \gamma \right)$ or a cease of operation of a node v due to heavy interference in all of v's edges or due to low energy supplies (Algorithm 1, lines 7 and 19).

LocalPathConfig is inherently local and distributed. The goal of this function is to restore a functional path between nodes u and v by replacing the problematic node $previous(v)$ with a better performing node w, or if w does not exist, with a new efficient multi-hop path Π_{uv}. At first, u checks if there are nodes ι in its neighbourhood N_u which can directly connect to v and achieve a similar or better one-hop latency than the old configuration (line 1). If there are, then the w selected is the node ι which given the new data piece, will achieve a maximum lifetime compared to the rest of the possible replacements, i.e., $w = \arg\max_{\iota \in N_u} T_\iota(\mathbf{x}_u^j)$, and an acceptable latency $l_{uw} + l_{wv}$ (line 2). u then sends to w a $join$ message (line 3).

Algorithm 2. `LocalPathConfig`(i, u, v)

1 **if** $\exists \iota \in N_u$ *with* $v \in N_\iota$ *and* $l_{u\iota} + l_{\iota v} \leq l_{uprevious(i,v)} + l_{previous(i,v)v}$ **then**
2 $\quad$ $w = \arg\max_{\iota \in N_u} T_\iota(\mathbf{x}_u^j)$
3 $\quad$ send $join[w](i, u, v)$
4 $\quad$ $\Pi_{s_i c_i} \leftarrow$ replace v with w
5 **else**
6 $\quad$ run `local_aodv+`(u, v, TTL)

If such a node does not exist, then u runs `local_aodv+`, a modified, local version of AODV protocol for route discovery, between nodes u and v. `local_aodv+` is able to add more than one replacement node in the path. The main modification of `local_aodv+` with respect to the traditional AODV protocol is that `local_aodv+` selects the route which provides the maximum lifetime $T_w(\mathbf{x}_u^j)$ for the nodes w which are included in the route. Specifically, this modification with respect to the classic AODV is implemented as follows: The nodes piggyback in the route request messages the minimum lifetime $T_w(\mathbf{x}_u^j)$ that has been identified so far on the specific path. Then when the first route request message arrives at v, instead of setting this path as the new path, v waits for a predefined timeout for more route request messages to arrive. Then, v selects the path which provided the $\max \min_{w \in N_u} T_w(\mathbf{x}_u^j)$. The reader can find more details about the AODV protocol in [4].

Joining New Paths, Modifying Existing Paths and Avoiding Loops. In this subsection, we briefly describe the functions regarding joining a new path and modifying an already existing path for loop elimination. Due to lack of space, we do not include the pseudocode of those functions; however, they can be found at the extended version of this paper [7]. JoinPath(i, w, v) is the function which regulates how, for data piece D_i, a node u will join an existing path between nodes w and v and how u will trigger a path modification and avoid potential loops which could result in unnecessary traffic in the network. Due to the fact that the reconfigurations do not use global knowledge, we can have three cases of u joining a path: (i) u is not already included in the path ($u \notin \Pi_{s_i c_i}$), (ii) u is already included in the path ($u \in \Pi_{s_i c_i}$), and w is preceding u in the new path ($previous(i, u) = w$) with a new link (w, u), and (iii) u is already included in the path ($u \in \Pi_{s_i c_i}$), and u is preceding w in the new path ($previous(i, w) = u$) with a new link (u, w). In all three cases, JoinPath sends a modification message to the next node to join the path, with the appropriate arguments concerning the deletion of parts of the paths, and the direction of the deletion, for avoidance of potential loops (see [7]). This message triggers the function ModifyPath (see [7]). In case (i) it is apparent that there is no danger of loop creation, so there is no argument for deleting parts of the path. In order to better understand cases (ii) and (iii) we provide Figs. 1 and 2. In those Figures we can see how the function ModifyPath eliminates newly created loops on u from path reconfigurations which follow unplanned network changes.

Following the loop elimination process, loop freedom is guaranteed for the cases where there are available nodes $w \in N_u$ which can directly replace v. In the case where this is not true and `LocalPathConfig` calls `local_aodv+` instead (Algorithm 2, line 6), then the loop freedom is guaranteed by the AODV path configuration process, which has been proven to be loop free [14].

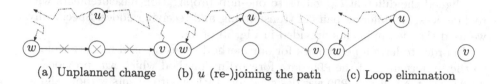

(a) Unplanned change   (b) u (re-)joining the path   (c) Loop elimination

Fig. 1. Loop avoidance - forward loop

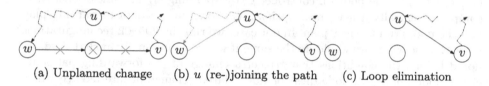

(a) Unplanned change   (b) u (re-)joining the path   (c) Loop elimination

Fig. 2. Loop avoidance - backward loop

6   Performance Evaluation

We implemented `DistrDataFwd` method and we conducted simulations in order to demonstrate its performance. We configured the simulation environment (Matlab) according to realistic parameters and assumptions. A table presenting the parameter configuration in details can be found in the extended version of the paper [7]. Briefly, we assume an industrial IoT network, comprised of devices equipped with ultra low-power MCUs like MSP430 and IEEE 802.15.4 antennae like CC2420, able to support industrial IoT standards and protocols like WirelessHART and IEEE 802.15.4e. We assume a structured topology (as in usual controlled industrial settings) of 18 nodes with 4 proxies which form a 2D grid with dimensions of 7.5 m × 16.0 m. We set the transmission power of the nodes for multi-hop communication to −25 dBm (typical low-power) which results in a transmission range of 3 m. For the more expensive communication with the network controller, we set the transmission power to 15 dBm, typical of wireless LAN settings. We set the time cycle $\tau = 1$ s, the percentage of consumers over the population $0.05 - 45\%$ and we produce $1 - 8\ D_i/\tau$ per consumer. In order to perform the simulations in the most realistic way, we align

the $L_{\max}$ value with the official requirements of future network-based communications for Industry 4.0 [1], and set the latency threshold to $L_{\max} = 100$ ms.
We set $\gamma = 50\%$, the TTL argument of local_aodv+ equal to 2, we assume a
maximum battery capacity of 830 mAh (3.7 V) and equip the nodes with energy
supplies of $E_u^0 = 0 - 1$ Wh and $E_p^0 = 3$ Wh. Last but not least, in order to have a
realistic basis for the values of the one-hop latencies l_{uv} used in the simulations,
we aligned the different l_{uv} values to one-hop propagation measurements with
real devices, for different pairs of transmitting and receiving nodes. Specifically,
we used the measurements provided in Fig. 3b of [6].

In order to have a benchmark for our method, we compared its performance
to the performance of the PDD data forwarding method which was provided in
[6]. Due to the fact that PDD was designed for static environments without significant network parameter changes, we also compare to a modified version of PDD,
which incorporates central reconfiguration when needed (we denote this version
as PDD-CR). Specifically, PDD-CR runs PDD until time t, when a significant change
in the network happens, and then, all network nodes communicate their status
(E_u^t, e_{uv}, l_{uv}) to the network controller C by spending e_{cc} amount of energy. C
computes centrally a new (near-optimal as shown in [6]) data forwarding plan
and the nodes run the new plan. In our case, we run the PDD-CR reconfigurations
for each case where we would do the same if we were running DistrDataFwd. As
noted before, the conditions that trigger a change of the forwarding paths are
either node related (a node dies) or link related (change of interference which
results in $\frac{\epsilon_{uv}(\tau) - \epsilon_{uv}(\tau-1)}{\epsilon_{uv}(\tau)} > \gamma)^2$.

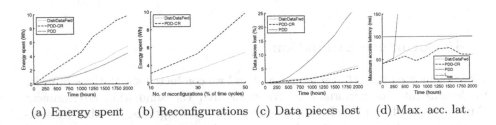

(a) Energy spent   (b) Reconfigurations   (c) Data pieces lost   (d) Max. acc. lat.

Fig. 3. Performance results.

Energy Efficiency. The energy consumption over the entire network during
2000 h of operation is depicted in Fig. 3a. The energy consumption values include
the energy consumed for both the data distribution process and the reconfiguration. Our method achieves comparable energy consumption as PDD, despite
being a local, adaptive method. This is explained by the following facts: PDD-CR
requires more energy than DistrDataFwd for the path reconfiguration process,
as during each epoch alteration every node has to spend e_{cc} amount of energy

---

^{2} The qualitative behaviour would not change in case of additional reconfiguration
events, which simply increase the number of reconfigurations.

for the configuration phase. On the contrary, in the `DistrDataFwd` case, only some of the nodes have to participate in a new configuration phase (usually the nodes in the neighbourhood of the problematic node), and spend significantly less amounts of energy. In the case of PDD, the nodes do not participate in configuration phases, so they save high amounts of energy. In Fig. 3b, we can also see the energy consumption of `DistrDataFwd` and PDD-CR for different percentages of reconfigurations (w.r.t. the number of time cycles τ). It is clear that the more the reconfigurations that we have in the network, the more the gap between the performance of `DistrDataFwd` and PDD-CR increases.

Data Delivery Rate. The data pieces lost during 2000 h of operation are depicted in Fig. 3c. We consider a data piece as lost when the required nodes or path segments are not being available anymore so as to achieve a proper delivery. When a data piece is delivered, but misses the deadline L_{max}, it is not considered as lost, but we measure the high delivery latency instead. We can see that the low energy consumption of the PDD method comes at a high cost: it achieves a significantly lower data delivery rate than the PDD-CR and the `DistrDataFwd` methods. This is natural, because as noted before, PDD computes an initial centralised paths configuration and follows it throughout the entire data distribution process. The performance of the `DistrDataFwd` method stays very close to the performance of the PDD-CR method, which demonstrates the efficiency of `DistrDataFwd` in terms of successfully delivering the data pieces.

Maximum Data Access Latency. The maximum data access latency during 2000 h of operation is depicted in Fig. 3d. The measured value is the maximum value observed among the consumers, after asynchronous data requests to the corresponding proxies. PDD does not perform well, due to the fact that it is prone to early disconnections without reconfiguration functionality. The fluctuation of PDD-CR's curve is explained by the re-computation from scratch of the data forwarding paths which might result in entirely new data distribution patterns in the network. `DistrDataFwd` respects the L_{max} threshold for most of the time, however at around 1700 h of network operation it slightly exceeds it for a single proxy-consumer pair. On the contrary, PDD-CR does not exceed the threshold. This performance is explained by the fact that `DistrDataFwd`, although efficient, does not provide any strict guarantee for respecting L_{max}, for all proxy-consumer pairs, mainly due to the absence of global knowledge on the network parameters during the local computations. PDD-CR, with the expense of additional energy for communication, is able to centrally compute near optimal paths and consequently achieve the desired latency. There are two simple ways of improving `DistrDataFwd`'s performance in terms of respecting the L_{max} threshold: (i) insert strict latency checking mechanisms in the `local_aodv+` function, with the risk of not finding appropriate (in terms of latency) path replacements, and thus lowering the data delivery ratio due to disconnected paths, and (ii) increase the TTL argument of `local_aodv+`, with the risk of circulating excessive amounts of route discovery messages, and thus increasing the energy consumption in the network. Including those mechanisms is left for future work.

7 Conclusion

We identified the need for a distributed reconfiguration method for data forwarding paths in industrial IoT networks. Given the operational parameters the network, we provided several efficient algorithmic functions which reconfigure the paths of the data distribution process, when a communication link or a network node fails. The functions regulate how the local path reconfiguration is implemented, ensuring that there will be no loops. We demonstrated the performance gains of our method in terms of energy consumption and data delivery success rate compared to other state of the art solutions.

Acknowledgments. This work was funded by the European Commission through the FoF-RIA Project *AUTOWARE: Wireless Autonomous, Reliable and Resilient Production Operation Architecture for Cognitive Manufacturing* (No. 723909).

References

1. Network-based communication for Industrie 4.0. Publications of Plattform Industrie 4.0 (2016). www.plattform-i40.de. Accessed 01 Jan 2018
2. Ha, M., Kim, D.: On-demand cache placement protocol for content delivery sensor networks. In: 2017 International Conference on Computing, Networking and Communications (ICNC), pp. 207–216, January 2017
3. Han, S., Zhu, X., Mok, A.K., Chen, D., Nixon, M.: Reliable and real-time communication in industrial wireless mesh networks. In: 2011 17th IEEE Real-Time and Embedded Technology and Applications Symposium, pp. 3–12, April 2011
4. Perkins, C., Belding-Royer, E., Das, S.: Ad hoc on-demand distance vector (AODV) routing. IETF RFC (3561), July 2003
5. Raptis, T.P., Passarella, A.: A distributed data management scheme for industrial IoT environments. In: 2017 IEEE 13th International Conference on Wireless and Mobile Computing, Networking and Communications (WiMob), pp. 196–203, October 2017
6. Raptis, T.P., Passarella, A., Conti, M.: Maximizing industrial IoT network lifetime under latency constraints through edge data distribution. In: 1st IEEE International Conference on Industrial Cyber-Physical Systems. (ICPS), May 2018
7. Raptis, T.P., Passarella, A., Conti, M.: Distributed path reconfiguration and data forwarding in industrial IoT networks. CoRR abs/1803.10971 (2018). http://arxiv.org/abs/1803.10971
8. Saifullah, A., Xu, Y., Lu, C., Chen, Y.: End-to-end communication delay analysis in industrial wireless networks. IEEE Trans. Comput. **64**(5), 1361–1374 (2015)
9. Sauter, T., Soucek, S., Kastner, W., Dietrich, D.: The evolution of factory and building automation. IEEE Ind. Electron. Mag. **5**(3), 35–48 (2011)
10. Shrouf, F., Ordieres, J., Miragliotta, G.: Smart factories in Industry 4.0: a review of the concept and of energy management approached in production based on the internet of things paradigm. In: 2014 IEEE International Conference on Industrial Engineering and Engineering Management, pp. 697–701, December 2014
11. Sun, X., Ansari, N.: Traffic load balancing among brokers at the IoT application layer. IEEE Trans. Netw. Serv. Manag. **15**(1), 489–502 (2018)

12. Wollschlaeger, M., Sauter, T., Jasperneite, J.: The future of industrial communication: automation networks in the era of the internet of things and Industry 4.0. IEEE Ind. Electron. Mag. **11**(1), 17–27 (2017)
13. Xu, L.D., He, W., Li, S.: Internet of things in industries: a survey. IEEE Trans. Ind. Inform. **10**(4), 2233–2243 (2014)
14. Zhou, M., Yang, H., Zhang, X., Wang, J.: The proof of AODV loop freedom. In: 2009 International Conference on Wireless Communications Signal Processing, pp. 1–5, November 2009

Real-World Deployments of Sensor Networks: Practical Lessons for Researchers

Marcin Brzozowski[✉], Max Frohberg[✉], and Peter Langendoerfer[✉]

IHP, Im Technologiepark 25, 15236 Frankfurt (Oder), Germany
{brzozowski,frohberg,langendoerfer}@ihp-microelectronics.com

Abstract. To prevent other research groups from making the same errors as we did in real-world deployments of sensor networks, we share our experience from previous installations and lessons learned from them.

First of all, we are finally convinced to apply the KISS principle (Keep it Simple Stupid) also to real-world deployments, especially that as researchers we tend to prefer more complex and sophisticated ideas.

Second, researchers underestimate practical issues in outdoor installations, and it may lead to unexpected and time-consuming problems. For instance, we did not notice that the selected voltage regulator works reliably only in temperatures above zero degree Celsius, leading to packet losses and a long debugging process.

Third, apart from extensive software tests before deployment, our protocols and applications include also self-healing instructions. They detect software bugs on run-time and restart motes if needed.

With all these three major steps, we were able to run real-world sensor networks for several years without major problems, even when we do not have resources for efficient testing and debugging, the problem that most research groups have.

1   Introduction

There are several ways to ensure that hard- and software is working as expected, such as various system-tests, different behavioral simulations, and also testbeds. However, researchers usually cannot carry out such extensive tests with a limited budget of research projects. Nonetheless, WSN applications should work maintenance-free and reliable for a long time in real-world scenarios. But often they failed quite early due to some unpredicted practical issues. We suffered similar problems and in this paper we share our experience on real-world WSN deployments.

The major difference between scientific and commercial sensor networks is their maturity. Commercial WSN are mostly based on thoroughly tested hardware and software, sometimes not changed significantly throughout several years.

© IFIP International Federation for Information Processing 2018
Published by Springer Nature Switzerland AG 2018. All Rights Reserved
K. R. Chowdhury et al. (Eds.): WWIC 2018, LNCS 10866, pp. 42–53, 2018.
https://doi.org/10.1007/978-3-030-02931-9_4

On the contrary, scientific WSN include novel solutions and they resemble prototypes rather than products, due to limited testing and debugging resources. Nonetheless, even such WSN prototypes should also work reliably for a long time.

In this paper we present lessons learned from our deployments: how to install and run reliably WSN regardless of limited testing resources. We hope these lessons will help other research groups to avoid the errors we did and in this way make their scientific efforts more productive and efficient.

The main lesson we learned in our WSN deployments is: keep it simple. Simple solutions tend to have fewer errors, work more reliably than complex ones, and also are easier to maintain. Therefore, we replaced our complex medium access control protocol [4], which included advanced features like clock drift prediction, with a simpler solution based on preamble sampling [5].

Another problem with testing in that some bugs are hard to spot before the real deployment, because they do not occur under testing conditions [1]. For example, our motes deployed next to a highway collected weather/traffic conditions and forwarded it to the sink. Before that, we tested the complete setup in long-time simulations and then with our testbed. It worked without problems so we decided to deploy it along the highway. However, due to some minor bugs in the radio module and the routing protocol, not spotted during in-lab tests, our motes lost plenty of frames, leading to failures. To attack such problems, we include self-healing mechanisms in our software, which detect software bugs on run-time and restart the affected mote. These mechanisms include mainly watchdogs, assertions, periodic reset, introduced later in this work.

This papers is organized as follows. Section 2 lists similar works that provide practical information about real-world deployments of sensor networks. In Sects. 3, 4, and 5 we introduce major lessons we learned during our WSN deployments, for low power radio communication, location and hardware, and for software issues respectively. Finally, we conclude this work in Sect. 6.

2   Related Work

In our previous work [3] we presented techniques to deal with software bugs in long-living sensor networks. It includes two major steps: offline bug fixing, to fix software errors before deployment, and self-healing to detect bugs on run-time and restart motes. Section 5 shortly introduces these both techniques.

Our work [2] shows several methods to efficiently debug software for sensor networks, including drivers, protocols, and applications. In that paper we evaluated several debugging techniques, mainly their memory footprint and impact on the execution time.

Other research works showed experiences from real-world deployments of sensor networks. In Ref. [1] the authors noticed that the deployment is the time to face unexpected problems. The major observation made by the authors is KISS (*"Keep it Small and Simple"* or *"Keep it Simple Stupid"*), and we fully agree. Further, the authors explained that some bugs are hard to spot before the real deployment, because they do not occur under testing conditions. Therefore, we add also self-healing code in our software for long-living WSN applications.

Other experiences from a real-world deployment, a sensor network monitoring a potato field, are presented in Ref. [7]. The authors confessed they neglected software testing, leading to huge problems in the runtime. They stressed the need of thorough testing of the sensor network, mainly using a testbed. One year later these authors started the same application again and presented results in Ref. [6]. This time, the authors kept in mind the KISS idea and made the system much simpler than before. For instance, the MAC protocol was much simpler and there was no routing protocol at all. This new, simple approach achieved much better results than a year before: the sink gathered about 51% of sensor readings this time, whereas it got only 2% readings a year before. After reading these works, we changed our attitude towards potential problems in the deployment and assumed the worst-case will happen. Therefore, we put even more effort on debugging and fixed most errors in the lab. The remaining bugs were handled with self-healing code.

3   Lessons Learned from Low-Power Wireless Communication

In this section, we present major problems we encountered in low-power wireless communication between motes and also highlight the lessons we learned from our mistakes.

3.1   Real-World Conditions Bring Scientific Results into Question

At the beginning of the project our partners selected several locations to install sensors for water monitoring (see Fig. 1). The distance between these locations span from about 200 m to about 23 km. We planned to cover the long distances between motes with multi-hop connections. Based on our RF measurements in this area, we would need about 4–5 extra motes, equipped with high-gain antennas, to support data transmission over 23 km.

Then, we learned from the operator they would rather prefer a simple solution, since the multi-hop setup includes hard accessible and insecure areas, such as top of the mountains, places without road infrastructure, and so on. It would lead to difficult maintenance works and a high risk of vandalism or stealing. Therefore, instead of providing a single multi-hop sensor network, we installed several single-hop networks, each network with its own cellular IP gateway (see Fig. 1).

Lesson Learned. Reasonable scientific ideas, a multi-hop network in this case, sometimes must not be applied to real-world applications due to external conditions, such as challenging topography or a risk of vandalism in our case.

It is better to discuss these issues with the local operators and technicians a long time before deployment.

Fig. 1. We planned to deploy a multi-hop sensor network to monitor the complete area. However, due to some practical issues (a risk of vandalism, maintenance problems) we installed several 1-hop networks, each network with its own GSM modem.

Fig. 2. Avoid hard-accessible places, if possible. To achieve this platform, the technicians needed about 45-min boat drive. They installed the platform (incl. motes and a GSM modem) but had to come back here after a few days only to update software.

3.2   Assume Hardware May Break in a Way You Do Not Expect

During the project we encountered some unexpected hardware problems. For example, we assumed that the radio used by our motes cannot be partially broken: we expected either it works or not. At a certain location the mote was placed at the bridge located about 100 m away from the sink. This setup worked without major problem over several months, and then sink stopped receiving packets from the mote. On visiting this location, we noticed that the mote and the sink were still powered on so the problem was not the battery. Since the mote provided correct debug messages, we expected that the mote or the sink radio is broken. Indeed, the problem was the radio but after examining it with a spectrum analyzer we found out the mote was sending data with a too small power. After moving the mote closer to the sink, just for debug purposes, the sink started getting data. Clearly, we replaced the mote in this location and everything worked well again. This radio problem would be much harder to spot, if the sink were closer to the mote. In this case, only some packets would not reach the sink due to too weak signal.

Lesson Learned. We learned that hardware may break in a way we do not expect and to be more open-minded for potential problems in real-world deployments. Further, we also learn that a mobile spectrum analyzer speeds up fixing radio problems in outdoor installations.

3.3   Ensure You Do Not Change Anything After Final Tests

We had to install a water sensor in a hard-accessible location (see Fig. 2): the technicians needed about 45-min of boat drive. Since there was only a single sensor there, we could install a single mote connected directly to the GSM modem. However, we installed the mote and the sink (attached to the GSM modem), since this setup worked well in other places. To protect hardware from vandalism, this equipment was installed in a secure metal box. Unfortunately, we did not know the technicians used such a box, and learn about it afterwards, leading to the following problem.

On the installation day, we were checking motes remotely in our lab located about 2000 km away from the install location. After the technicians installed our motes, we informed the technicians to leave this location, as our server received data from the motes. Shortly after that, our server stopped receiving sensor data, but it still got control packets, so the GSM connection was still working.

After that, we discussed it with technicians and found out the cause of this problem: misunderstanding. Then, we learned that the sink and the mote are very close to each other, and the technicians closed the metal box just before leaving the location. As a result, the receive signal strength at the sink was too high, leading to packet losses. To solve this problem, we reduced the transmission power of the mote/sink, and the technicians updated software a few days later, on the next visit.

Lesson Learned. We learn to be very cautious in changing the setup after final tests, so that not even a single detail will be changed, including positions and installation instructions. Further, we learned again to avoid hard accessible places if possible, even when we assume that we will not have to visit this place again, for instance to update software. Moreover, wireless code update probably makes the maintenance of sensor networks much easier, provided wireless communication is still operable.

3.4   Read Operating Conditions Carefully

To enable low-power communication over long distances, we integrated off-the-she lf transceivers on a new board (Fig. 3). Then, we made some RF measurements, in the south of Spain, and this setup worked fine. Later we started another project and installed the same type of transceivers, but from another production lot, along a motorway in Germany. During first few weeks our motes worked flawlessly, but later on some problems with unexpected packet losses occurred. We suspected our new software to cause these problems, since hardware had already been tested in the previous project. We were trying to find the cause of this problem for several weeks, and finally realized that the assembled voltage regulators used on this production batch of PCB (printed circuit board) work only above $0\,°C$. Since the temperature dropped rapidly several weeks after installation, some motes stopped working. We did not spot this problem in the previous

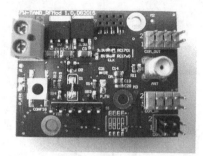

Fig. 3. Our long-range RF board worked reliably in tests in the south of Spain, but suffered from problems in the middle of Germany after several days of the deployment. Finally we found the reason: the voltage regulator did not work below 0 °C.

Fig. 4. We developed a new board for connecting SDI-12 sensors and were able to connect up to 10 sensors to it. Since SDI-12 sensors provide digital data, we did not encounter problems with analog-to-digital conversions again.

project, since the temperature in south of Spain was always above 0 °C. Further, we did not spot this problem while testing our motes for several hours in a freezer.

Finally, we replaced this voltage regulator with another one, with a much wider temperature range, and it fixed these problems.

Lesson Learned. We still cannot explain the reason for using a voltage regulator that operate only at temperatures above 0 °C. We probably did not specify the exact component, voltage regulator, and our PCB manufacturer might have selected another one, as we put an asterisk at the component name in the bill of materials (BOM).

We learn to double check the BOM and the operating conditions of all electronic parts used on our boards. Further, we must also check PCBs of newly assembled devices carefully and ask for the BOM of the components that really were used.

4 Low Power, Good Location for Hardware and Sensors

Apart from problems with low power wireless communication, we had also some issues with cellular IP modems and sensors. Here, we shortly introduce these problem and lessons we learned from them.

4.1 Standby GSM Router Is Not Low Power

To enable GSM communication at locations without mains power, we found a low-power GSM modem, which also included FTP and HTTP protocols, needed for our application.

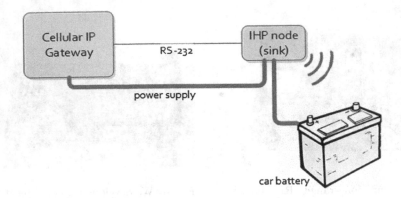

Fig. 5. The default low-power mode of the cellular IP gateway still consumes too much energy for low-power sensor application. Therefore, the sink powers down the GSM gateway completely when not used.

However, this modem still consumes too much power for our long-living application, about 21 mW, whereas our sinks needs 3000x less energy. Because of a low duty cycle of our application (about 100 kB of data transmitted every 15 min), we decided to switch off the modem completely when not used. To do so, the sink switched on the modem (see Fig. 5) only to transmit data, and switched it off afterwards. By doing so, the sink coupled with the GSM modem consumed less than 0.02 mW in standby, and achieved a lifetime of several months.

Lesson Learned. We learn that default low-power modes of various devices may still consume too much energy for long-living sensor network applications. Instead of using the device internal low power modes, switching it off completely may lead to energy savings, provided the power-down and power-up energy is not too high.

4.2 Don't Forget an Easy Accessible Placement of Hardware

At the beginning of the project, we used a GSM modem tailored for automotive application, with special antenna connectors. Since we could not find neither high-gain antennas nor cable adapters for such connectors, we installed the modem and its antenna high above the ground, on a mast. In this way, the modem benefited from a stronger GSM signal and was able to send data to the Internet. Since the modem was previously tested and used outdoors, we did not expect it to stop working, and it assured us to install the modem on the mast. Unfortunately, some problems with the modem occurred during the project, and we had to climb the mast to reach the modem. Then, we regretted we did not spend more time on looking for another antenna or connector that would allow us to install only the antenna on the mast and the modem close to the ground.

Lesson Learned. We learn that even if we are sure that nothing wrong will happen, because we tested or used our equipment previously for a long time, it may still break. Therefore, we have to keep it in mind when selecting the install location.

4.3   Periodic Reset

In our previous project, we did not have problems with limited energy and therefore the GSM modem was constantly powered on so. However, there was still a risk of power outage, up to 24 h without power, and in this time the modem should be running from an external car battery. For this scenario we selected a typical USB-dongle-based modem and connected it to the BeagleBone Black (BBB) embedded computer. In case of power shortage, this setup would work for several hours on a car battery.

Since the equipment was installed far from our office, we configured it to work autonomously. We provided several scripts that fix potential network or software problems on its own.

Again, we encountered problems that we did not foresee before. After some time, our server stopped getting data from the monitored area, although the complete setup was tested in our lab for a long time. First, it looked like the GSM connection was broken, because we could not log in remotely onto the embedded server. After examining the system on-site, we noticed that the cellular IP gateway could not be detected by the BBB, although the modem was still connected to it and nobody even touched it. We restarted the BBB computer and it detected the cellular modem without problems. We did not expect that the modem can just disappear from the system and our script could not handle this problem. Instead of adapting our script to deal also with this problem, we implemented a well-known, simple and robust solution: a watchdog[1]. In short, the hardware-based watchdog restarted the operating system of BBB once a day.

Lesson Learned. We learn that backup strategies are needed to deal with various hardware and software problems. For example, in this case a periodic reset or watchdog solves various temporary problems.

4.4   Do Not Forget About Redundancy

In the same application as in the previous paragraph, the BBB stored sensor readings on a SD card. After some time, our server was receiving some control frames from the BBB, but the sensor data was missing. We suspected the sink was broken and it did not forward sensor readings to the Internet server. After arriving to the monitored area, we examined the BBB computer and noticed that

---

[1] A watchdog is a counter that performs system reset on a certain value, mostly zero. However, if software clears the watchdog flag, the counters starts again. In our case, we did not clear the flag so the watchdog performed reset each time it finished counting.

SD card was not detected by the system anymore. Then, the BBB tried to write sensor data to the internal flash memory but it was full. After reinserting the SD card, the BBB detected it and saved sensor reading on the card. It showed us that a periodic reset, introduced in the previous paragraph, helps in various run-time problem. Further, we considered again adding an extra hardware drive to store data, in case the SD card breaks.

Lesson Learned. Here we learn not to forget to use redundant storage devices to safely save sensor readings. Further, we saw again the need of simple mechanism - a periodic reset - to deal with unpredictable problems.

4.5   Sensors: Do Not Reinvent the Wheel

During our first real-world deployment we considered how to design software and hardware to be reused among several different sensors. Then, we decided to use analog sensors, as they can easily be connected to a typical analog-to-digital converter (ADC). Further, since our mote already has an ADC available, we would not need to design new hardware for using such sensors.

Unfortunately, we suffered from some problems soon, because the embedded ADC precision was not good enough. Even by taking dozens of analog samples and averaging it, the error in digital values was higher than 10%, due to design imperfections. Further, in some locations we had to connect up to 12 sensors, but we could connect only a single analog sensor to our mote.

Nonetheless, we were still convinced to use analog sensors and developed a new board (Fig. 6) with connectors up to 12 sensors. Although this board provided more accurate results than the embedded ADC, we had to calibrate each board manually by defining some conversion constants in our application. Further, we were not sure if these constants need adapting later, for example when the outdoor temperature changes.

In the next project we got some water monitoring sensors from the project partner. We found out that most sensors provide only digital data and were afraid of writing several sensor drivers. However, it turned out that all these sensor support the SDI-12 protocol, which is quite popular in environmental monitoring. In the end, we needed only to implement this protocol and develop an SDI-12 adapter board (Fig. 4). After that, all SDI-12 based sensors can be connected to our mote, and a single mote can read data from 10 sensors. Further, we do not care about ADC conversion and calibration, we just get digital data. We can also add or remove sensors on runtime, which makes this setup even more flexible and useful.

Lesson Learned. Digital sensor readings are more reliable than our previous, ADC-based solution, and also simpler to maintain. So instead of struggling with several ADC issues, it is better to find and use standards that are already available.

Fig. 6. Since the embedded analog-to-digital converter suffered from precision problems, and could not connect several sensors, we developed our own ADC board and connected up to 12 sensor to it (showed in this photo). However, we had to still manually calibrate the new ADC and did not know if the calibration is needed after some time, e.g. when the temperature changes. Therefore, in the next project we used sensors based on the digital SDI-12 protocol.

5   Software Development

In this section, we present our major findings for software problems running in long-term outdoor applications, introduced partially in our previous work [3].

5.1   Keep It Simple

In some of our previous projects we applied our schedule-based MAC protocol [4]. To make it work reliably in long-term applications, the protocol included quite complex mechanisms to deal with problems like beacon overlap, clock drift, and so on. Although the protocol was already running in outdoor applications, we kept finding minor problems in PC simulations. Thus, we were not convinced that the protocol has no bugs, and there was a risk that some undetected bugs affect motes while running outdoors. Further, because of high complexity it was not easy to add new features to the protocol, and to maintain it.

Because of all these problems we were looking for another, a simpler MAC protocol and decided to use a protocol based on preamble sampling [5]. It took us only a few weeks to implement the new protocol from scratch, and it was much simpler indeed. According to our calculations, this simple MAC would need a bit more energy in our application, caused by idle listening. However the extra penalty was small enough to start using this protocol and benefit from its simplicity.

Lesson Learned. Although it might be tempting to make complex, sophisticated solutions, especially in scientific communities, the real-world application need simple and robust approaches. We learned to make our design simple and benefit from easier maintenance, easier testing, and high reliability compared to the complex solutions.

5.2   Some Bugs Attack Only on Run-Time

To examine the impact of weather and traffic conditions on wireless communicatio n, we deployed our motes along a highway in Germany. Before starting our application outdoors, we performed several test operations: PC simulations, hardware tests, and finally WSN testbed. After fixing some minor problems our application worked without problems in simulations and on the testbed. Therefore, we installed motes along the highway but soon after they suffered from communication problems, leading to high packet error rates.

We examined the problem in our lab and found a bug in the radio driver. In short, this driver should filter incoming messages based on the destination address. However, sometimes this filter did not work properly and it forwarded incoming packets to the upper layers. It lead to various problems with our routing protocol, and in the end to packet losses.

This problem shows the risk already mentioned in Ref. [1]: some bugs cannot be spotted in in-lab tests, because they occur only on certain conditions. Therefore, we include in our software also self-healing instructions, which detect run-time problems and reset motes if needed. It is based mainly on hardware watchdogs, available on most microcontrollers, and also on software assertions. We provided more details about that in our previous work [3].

With all these means we run various WSN applications outdoors for more than three years without major software problems. Further, in our first deployment we were aware of some bugs in our medium access control protocol, but still could run the complete application for several weeks outdoors, thanks to the self-healing mechanisms.

Lessons Learned. Although software testing for sensor networks needs plenty of time and effort, it pays off in long-running application: fewer bugs means less maintenance effort. However, some bugs cannot be spotted before deployment, since they do not occur under testing conditions. To deal with this problem, software for sensor networks should include also self-healing instructions, which recover from software errors on run time.

6   Conclusion

In research projects we mostly concentrate on scientific work and do not have enough time and resources to deal with practical problems in real-world applications. Nonetheless, these applications should operate for a long time, preferably without maintenance. In last years we learned how to achieve this goal, that is, run long-term applications with limited testing resources. In the following we summarize the lessons we learned from our previous WSN deployments:

- you must include plenty of time for test and verification into your project schedule
- apart from simulations and testbed you have to run outdoor tests with real world conditions

- do not forget backup strategy and redundancy, even when you think your components are tested
- read the hardware errata carefully and make sure you ordered the right components, for example the same revision that you tested
- make sure your project partner knows what you do and vice versa,
- close the communication and specification gap by clear and strict documentation
- for complex installations get the specification or build it up in advance
- consider how to reuse your previous work, such as implementation or hardware designs, to gain more time for testing

We hope these lessons will let other research groups to install real-world applications more efficiently by avoiding trial-and-error approach.

Acknowledgement. The research leading to these results was partly founded from the Federal Ministry of Education and Research (Germany), from the DIAMANT project.

References

1. Barrenetxea, G., Ingelrest, F., Schaefer, G., Vetterli, M.: The hitchhiker's guide to successful wireless sensor network deployments. In: Proceedings of SenSys 2008 (2008)
2. Brzozowski, M., Langendoerfer, P.: Overview and benchmarks of pragmatic debugging techniques for wireless sensor networks. In: Proceedings of SoftCOM 2013 (2013)
3. Brzozowski, M., Langendoerfer, P.: Bug-tolerant sensor networks: experiences from real-world applications. In: Mitton, N., Kantarci, M.E., Gallais, A., Papavassiliou, S. (eds.) ADHOCNETS 2015. LNICST, vol. 155, pp. 251–262. Springer, Cham (2015). https://doi.org/10.1007/978-3-319-25067-0_20
4. Brzozowski, M., Salomon, H., Langendoerfer, P.: Completely distributed low duty cycle communication for long-living sensor networks. In: Proceedings of EUC 2009 (2009)
5. El-Hoiydi, A.: Spatial TDMA and CSMA with preamble sampling for low power ad hoc wireless sensor networks. In: Proceedings of ISCC 2002 (2002)
6. Haneveld, P.K.: Evading murphy: a sensor network deployment in precision agriculture (2007). http://www.st.ewi.tudelft.nl/koen/papers/LOFAR-agro-take2.pdf
7. Langendoen, K., Baggio, A., Visser, O.: Murphy loves potatoes. In: Proceedings of IPDPS 2006 (2006)

An Obstacle-Aware Clustering Protocol for Wireless Sensor Networks with Irregular Terrain

Riham Elhabyan[✉], Wei Shi, and Marc St-Hilaire

School of Information Technology, Faculty of Engineering and Design,
Carleton University, Ottawa, ON, Canada
{riham.elhabyan,wei.shi,marc.sthilaire}@carleton.ca

Abstract. Clustering in Wireless Sensor Networks (WSNs) is considered an efficient technique to optimize the energy consumption and increase the Packet Delivery Rate (PDR). Most of the proposed clustering protocols assume that there is a Line of Sight (LOS) between all the sensors. In real situations, there are obstacles which could interfere this LOS. Moreover, most of the available WSNs simulators assume the use of optimistic path loss models that neglect the effect of the obstacles on the PDR. In this paper, we adopt an obstacle-aware path loss model to reflect the effect of the obstacles on the communication between any the sensors. The Castalia simulator is then adapted to use this the proposed path loss model. Moreover, we propose an obstacle-aware clustering protocol, the NSGA-based, Non-LOS Cluster Head selection (NSGA-NLOS-CH) protocol, to solve the CHs selection problem in WSNs with an irregular field. Simulation results have shown that the effect of the obstacles on the PDR cannot be neglected. Moreover, NSGA-NLOS-CH outperforms other competent protocols in terms of the PDR while maintaining an acceptable energy consumption at the same time.

Keywords: Obstacle-aware · Clustering · WSNs

1 Introduction

Clustering in Wireless Sensor Networks (WSNs) is considered an efficient technique to optimize the energy consumption. Many clustering protocols have been proposed in the literature to optimize the energy consumption in Wireless Sensor Networks (WSNs). Most of these protocols assume that the sensors are deployed in a Two-Dimensional (2D) network field. However, there is an increasing number of WSNs applications in which the network field is often a Three-Dimensional (3D) rolling terrains, such as volcano monitoring and landslide detection. Although recent studies have proposed clustering protocols for 3D WSNs [7], these studies assume that the field is a 3D volume where sensors can be positioned freely within the whole 3D space. Compared to this free

© IFIP International Federation for Information Processing 2018
Published by Springer Nature Switzerland AG 2018. All Rights Reserved
K. R. Chowdhury et al. (Eds.): WWIC 2018, LNCS 10866, pp. 54–66, 2018.
https://doi.org/10.1007/978-3-030-02931-9_5

deployment in 3D space, in the case of deployment on rolling fields, sensors are deployed on the exposed surface and not freely within the 3D space. Therefore, these protocols cannot be applied to the rolling terrain either. Clustering protocols developed for 2D fields cannot be applied directly in such applications because the nature of the 3D rolling field may lead to the creation of obstacles in the network field. These obstacles have a substantial impact on the link quality between the communicating sensors as they cause an increased path loss. Therefore, determining the optimal set of CHs on the 3D rolling fields is a critical task.

Data delivery reliability is considered a key requirement in WSNs. In order to realize this requirement, clustering protocols should ensure high-quality links between the cluster members and their associated Cluster Heads (CHs). The Received Signal Strength Indicator (RSSI) is considered a prominent metric to assess the link quality between the transmitter and the receiver sensors. The RSSI calculation depends mainly on the adopted path loss model. Therefore, the performance of clustering protocols critically depends on the ability to accurately model the path loss of the communication signal between the transmitter and the receiver. A common limitation in most of the previously proposed clustering protocols is assuming the free space path loss model. The fundamental assumption behind this model is that the transmitter and the receiver sensors have a Line Of Sight (LOS) communication with no obstacles of any kind [8]. In real situations, there are almost always obstacles in the path between the transmitter and the receiver. Therefore, the free space path loss model is considered ideal and optimistic for predicting the path loss between any two sensors since it does not take the obstacles effect between the transmitter and the receiver into account [10]. Most of the available WSNs simulators assume the use of the free space path loss model [9]. The log-normal shadow fading model is proposed as an attempt to construct a more realistic path loss model by simulating the path loss around the sensors. Yet, this model does not account for the effect of the obstacles on the communication signal. Another significant limitation is that most of the existing clustering protocols assume the use of the first order radio model. However, this energy model is idealized and fundamentally flawed for modeling radio power consumption in sensor networks [5].

Castalia is a popular and very efficient WSN simulator that provides a well-designed channel model [9] and adopts a realistic energy consumption model that is based on the characteristics of the Chipcon CC2420 radio transceiver data sheet. However, Castalia adopts the log-normal shadow fading model and hence shares the same drawback as most of the available WSNs simulators with regard to accurately modeling the path loss in case of No Line Of Sight (NLOS) communication, i.e. when there are obstacles between the transmitter and the receiver.

1.1   Contributions

As we discussed earlier, obstacles have a great impact on both the design of clustering protocols for WSNs and the simulation and evaluation of the performance of these protocols. Therefore, the purpose of this paper is twofold. First, to design, implement and test an obstacle-aware clustering protocol to solve the CHs selection problem in 3D rolling fields. Since the CHs selection problem has been proven to be a Non-deterministic Polynomial (NP)-hard problem with many conflicting objectives, a Pareto-based Evolutionary Algorithm (EA) is adopted to solve this problem. The proposed protocol takes into consideration the following key requirements: the network's energy efficiency, the network's data delivery reliability, and the protocol's scalability. Second, to test and investigate the performance of the proposed protocol against well-known clustering protocols, in the existence of obstacles and under a realistic energy consumption model. The main contributions of this paper are listed below:

- We adapt an obstacle-aware path loss model to evaluate the effect of the obstacles in the communication between any two sensor nodes. In order to achieve that, we implement a visibility function to find the obstacles in the path between any two sensors. This function is implemented based on the Bresenham's algorithm. Based on the adopted path loss model, a path loss map is derived. The Castalia simulator is then modified to use this map to calculate the path loss and the RSSI values between any two sensors in the network.
- We propose a new EA-based clustering protocol for 3D WSNs where the network field is a 3D rolling terrain.
- In order to realize the aforementioned contributions, the network field is modeled using the Digital Elevation Model (DEM) to account for different elevations, and hence obstacles, in the field.

The novelties of the proposed research work are as follows: (a) To the best of our knowledge, the proposed clustering protocol is the first to consider and test the obstacles' effect on the communication between the sensors, (b) Experimental validation are performed on real elevation data for 3D terrains.

1.2 Paper Organization

The remainder of this paper is organized as follows. Section 2 presents the related work on protocols designed for 3D WSNs. Section 3 presents the system model and assumptions. The design of the obstacle-aware clustering protocol and the problem formulation are provided in Sect. 4. A detailed analysis of the simulations results is provided in Sect. 5. Finally, Sect. 6 concludes this paper and highlights future research directions.

2   Related Works

The Low Energy Adaptive Clustering Hierarchy for 3D WSNs (LEACH-3D) protocol [2] is a direct extension of the original LEACH protocol and is considered the first clustering protocol designed for 3D WSNs. The first order radio model, which is initially proposed by LEACH, is extended to work for 3D WSNs. Based on this extension, the authors prove that the effect of the 3D environment on clustering protocols cannot be neglected. LEACH-3D uses a variable number of CHs and different number of CHs could be elected each round.

A Fuzzy-based Clustering Scheme for 3D WSNs (FCM-3) is proposed in [7] to apply clustering protocols in 3D WSNs. The proposed protocol assumes the radio model which is proposed in [2]. The adopted fuzzy approach optimizes one objective function which is defined as minimizing the total energy consumption and is constructed by combining the distances between sensor nodes and their corresponding CHs and between the CHs and the Base Station (BS) into the radio model. FCM-3 defines two constraints to ensures single-hop connections for the intra-cluster and inter-cluster communication. Similar to LEACH-3D, the number of CHs is variable. However, experimental results show that FCM-3 achieves the best performance when the number of CHs is from 20% to 30% of the network size, which is considered a high number.

A Particle Swarm Optimization (PSO)-based Protocol for CHs selection (PSO-CH) [5] is a centralized PSO-based protocol that is used to find the optimal set of CHs. The PSO-CH protocol considers the following properties: the network's energy efficiency, data transmission reliability, and the protocol's scalability. The objective function that is used to evaluate each candidate solution is defined as the weighted sum of three sub-objectives, each of which is related to the aforementioned properties. PSO-CH is designed and implemented under realistic networks settings and realistic energy consumption model. The link quality estimation in PSO-CH is based on the Received Signal Strength Indicator (RSSI) of received packets.

All the aforementioned protocols are applicable to 3D WSNs. However, the path loss model adapted by these protocols ignore the effect of the obstacles on the communication between the sensors. They also assume that the field is a 3D volume where the sensors can be positioned freely within the field. Moreover, all these protocols assume the use of an ideal energy consumption model.

The Surface-Level Irregular Terrain (SLIT) path loss model [4] is a semi-empirical path loss model for WSN with irregular terrain. The SLIT model uses the terrain information, expressed by the DEM data, to provide a fast and an accurate estimation of the large-scale path loss due to the obstacles existing in the field. The total path loss is expressed as a function of both the free-space path loss and the path loss due to the obstacles in the field, which is calculated using the Epstein-Peterson diffraction loss model [6]. In order to verify the SLIT model, empirical experiments are conducted and the average difference between the measured results and the predicted results from the SLIT model are recorded. Experimental results have shown that the SLIT model provides an accurate path loss model that accounts for the terrain profile.

In this paper, we adopt the SLIT path loss model [4] and propose an obstacle-aware clustering protocol for 3D WSNs to evaluate the effect of obstacles on clustering protocols.

3   The System Model

The 3D rolling field is modeled using the Digital Elevation Model (DEM). The DEM is a digital representation of a given ground surface topography or terrain. In the DEM, the network field is represented as a matrix of cells, where each cell holds a value that represents the average elevation of the area contained by that cell. DEMs are commonly built using remote sensing technology or from land surveying, and are usually available to download. For example, the geospatial data extraction tool [1] is part of Natural Resources Canada's altimetry system designed to meet the users' needs for elevation data and products. This tool provides data from seamless national datasets based on custom-defined geographic area and customized data options. The main motivation to adopt the DEM in our proposed protocol is to be able to simulate a realistic 3D rolling field and to find the obstacles between any two sensor nodes in the network. The sensors are assumed to be uniformly deployed in a 3D rolling field. Based on the DEM data, the height coordinate of a sensor located at position (x, y) is restricted to the field's elevation at that specific position.

For the energy consumption model, a discrete-based realistic model which is based on the characteristics of the Chipcon CC2420 radio transceiver data sheet [11] is used. The total energy consumed by sensor node n, $consumedE_n$, is calculated as follows [3]:

$$consumedE_n = \sum_{statej} P_{statej} \times t_{statej} + \sum_{tr} E_{transitions} \qquad (1)$$

The index $statej$ refers to the energy states of the sensor: sleep, reception, or transmission. P_{statej} is the power consumed in each $statej$, t_{statej} is the time spent in the corresponding state, and tr is the number of transitions for S. The energy spent in transitions between states, $E_{transitions}$, is also added to the node's total energy consumption. The different values of P_{statej} and $E_{transitions}$ can be found in [11].

For the path loss model, we adopt the SLIT path loss model [4] to find the path loss between any two sensors.

4   An Obstacle-Aware Clustering Protocol for WSNs with Irregular Terrain

The network operating time of the proposed protocol is divided into rounds. Each round consists of two phases, the set-up phase, and the steady-state phase. The operation of these phases is similar to that of [5]. In this paper, we focus on the protocol adopted by the BS in the set-up phase to find the optimal set of CHs and clusters. We refer to the proposed protocol as the NSGA-based, Non-LOS CH selection (NSGA-NLOS-CH) protocol which includes six different processes as illustrated below:

4.1   DEM Extraction

The geospatial data extraction tool [1] provided by Natural Resources Canada is used to extract the elevation data for a given network field. Based on the DEM data for a given network field, the BS constructs an elevation matrix that holds the elevation data for all the cells contained by the network field. The ArcGIS software package is utilized to generate and extract the elevation data given the DEM data for that field.

4.2   LOS Algorithm

A Line of Sight (LOS) algorithm is needed to find the obstacles in the communication link between any two sensors in the field. In this paper, the Bresenham LOS algorithm is utilized to implement the visibility function. The Bresenham algorithm is often used in computer graphics for line drawing on 2D surfaces. In this paper, we have modified it to be used for LOS determination on 3D rolling fields. In this algorithm, if the elevation of any corresponding points between the transmitter and the receiver does not cut the virtual line drawn between them, then there is a LOS between the transmitter and the receiver. Otherwise, it is said that there is NLOS (non-LOS) between them. In this paper, an obstacle is defined as the point which has an elevation higher than that of the transmitter or the receiver. The LOS algorithm returns a visibility matrix that has N rows and N columns, where N is the total number of sensors. This visibility matrix holds the path loss of all the obstacles between any two sensors in the network.

4.3   Path Loss Map Calculation

Based on the visibility matrix, a path loss map is generated by the BS. This map reflects that path loss between any two communicating sensors in the network and is calculated using the SLIT path loss model. The Castalia simulator is then modified to use this path loss map instead of the one provided by the log-normal shadow fading model to calculate the propagation loss and the RSSI values for the links between any two communicating sensors.

4.4   Finding the Optimal Set of CHs

Once the modified RSSI values are calculated, the BS runs an EA-based algorithm to find the optimal set of CHs. In this paper, we adopt the Non-dominated Sorting Genetic Algorithm II (NSGA-II) as an optimization tool to find the optimal set of CHs. The problem formulation for the adopted NSGA-based algorithm is provided in the next section. Table 1 presents the main notations used in this paper.

Table 1. Notations

Symbol	Definition
P	Population generated from the adopted EA
N	Total number of sensors
n	Sensor number n, $0 \leq n < N$
I_i	Individual number i of P
$X_{i,n}$	Component number n of C_i
K_i	Total number of clusters generated from C_i
CL_{k_i}	Cluster number k generated from C_i, $0 \leq k_i < K_i$
CH_{k_i}	Cluster head number k generated from C_i, $0 \leq k_i < K_i$
$|CL_{k_i}|$	Number of sensors clustered in CL_{k_i}
$E(n)$	Remaining energy of node n
$initial E(n)$	Initial energy of node n
$RSSI_{(n,CH_{k_i})}$	RSSI value for the link from n to CH_{k_i}
$LQ_{(n,CH_{k_i})}$	Link quality for the link from n to CH_{k_i} $$LQ_{(n,CH_{k_i})} = \frac{RSSI(n,CH_{k_i})}{-100}$$

Decision Variables. In the proposed protocol, a sensor node may be in one of two states: a CH, or non-CH. To find the optimal set of CHs, a random initial population P is generated and evolved by the adopted EA. Each candidate solution (chromosome) C_i in P has a dimension equal to the network size minus the BS (i.e., $N-1$). Binary encoding is adopted to represent each chromosome, where the size of each component of I_i is 1 bit.

Let, $C_i = [X_{i,1}, X_{i,2}, X_{i,3}, ..., X_{i,N-1}]$ be the i_{th} chromosome of P where each component, $X_{i,n}, 1 \leq n \leq N - 1$ maps the state of sensor n. Each component $X_{i,n}$ of chromosome C_i is initialized with either 1 to indicate that sensor n is a CH node, or 0 to indicate that n is non-CH node. It should be noted that this encoding process will result in a variable number of CHs. Table 2 shows the random sequences created for two individuals in P on a network including 10 sensor nodes other than the BS. Each row presents a solution for a chromosome in P. For example, in chromosome C_1 sensors 2, 5 and 10 are CHs while the rest of the sensors are non-CH nodes.

Table 2. Chromosomes population

Node ID	1	2	3	4	5	6	7	8	9	10
I_1	0	1	0	0	1	0	0	0	0	1
I_2	0	0	1	1	1	0	0	0	1	0

The clusters are formed by associating each non-CH node to its closest CH that has the lowest RSSI value. After the clustering process ends, each sensor node belongs to only one cluster and each cluster head node acts as the CH of exactly one cluster.

Objective Functions. Each chromosome C_i is evaluated according to four objective functions, which are briefly described in Table 3 and defined below.

Table 3. The objective functions

Objective function	Description	Goal
K_i	Minimize the total number of CHs	Save energy
U_i	Minimize the number of unclustered sensors	Enhance scalability
L_i	Maximize the link quality for the inter-cluster communication	Data delivery reliability
E_i	Maximize the total remaining energy of the CHs	Balance energy consumption

$$K_i = \sum_{n=1}^{N-1} 1, \quad \text{if } X_{i,n} = 1 \tag{2}$$

$$U_i = N - \sum_{k_i=1}^{K_i} |CL_{k_i}| \tag{3}$$

$$L_i = \max_{k=1,2,\ldots,K} \frac{\sum_{\forall n \in CL_k} LQ_{(n,CH_{k_i})}}{|CL_{k_i}|} \tag{4}$$

$$E_i = \sum_{n=1}^{N} \frac{initialE(n)}{E(n)}, \quad \text{if } X_{i,n} \neq 00 \tag{5}$$

It should be noted that the calculation for L_i in the proposed protocol depends on the newly derived RSSI values which depend on the generated path loss map.

5 Simulation Results and Analysis

The NSGA-NLOS-CH protocol and the proposed path loss model are implemented in Castalia. In addition, we have implemented both LEACH-3D and PSO-CH. The simulations are performed on elevation data from the Armadillo Peak volcano in British Columbia, as illustrated in Fig. 1. The DEM of this field is obtained using the geospatial data extraction tool [1] provided by Natural Resources Canada. In order to generate the elevation data, a 20 × 20 fishnet is constructed using the ArcGIS software on a scaled version of the network field.

The network field is scaled down to 100×100 meters. The sensors are deployed randomly and their position is restricted by the elevation of the rolling field. The initial energy of the sensors is set as 18720 J. Each round is 500s and the number of rounds is 5. We vary the total number of sensors from 100 to 500.

Fig. 1. Scaled version of the Armadillo Peak volcano in British Columbia

In this section, we consider the following objectives:

1. Investigate the effect of the obstacles on the Packet Delivery Rate (PDR).
2. Compare the performance of all the competent protocols in the existence of obstacles. The comparison is done in terms of the PDR, the number of elected CHs, the energy consumption and the average number of unclustered nodes per round.

We consider two cases to investigate the effect of the obstacles on the PDR. In the first case, we assume that there is a LOS between all the sensors and that there are no obstacles in the rolling field. For this case, the log-normal shadow fading model is used to calculate the path loss and we refer to the proposed protocol as the NSGA-LOS-CH protocol. In the second case, we use the provided elevation data to find the obstacles in the field and we use the

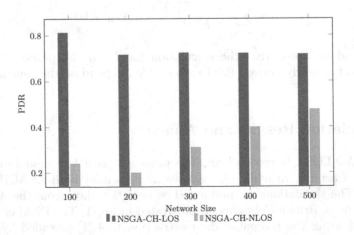

Fig. 2. PDR for NSGA-LOS-CH and NSGA-NLOS-CH

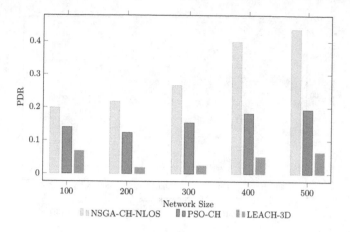

Fig. 3. PDR

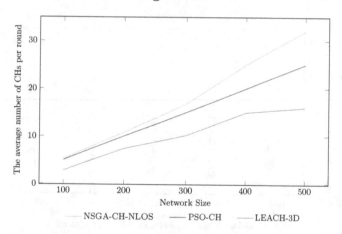

Fig. 4. The average number of CHs per round

proposed obstacle-aware path loss model. For this case, we refer to the proposed protocol as the NSGA-NLOS-CH protocol. Figure 2 shows the PDR for both of these cases.

It is clearly shown that ignoring the effect of the obstacles, as in the case of NSGA-LOS-CH, can lead to more optimistic PDR values. It is also noted that the PDR of NSGA-NLOS-CH increases with the increase in the number of sensors. Increasing the number of sensors in the same network field area leads to constructing shorter links for communication with a lower probability of obstacles that could interfere those links. Next, the performance of all the competent protocols is compared in the existence of obstacles. Figure 3 shows the PDR for all the protocols. It is clearly shown that NSGA-NLOS-CH outperforms the other protocols in terms of the PDR. This is due to the fact that NSGA-NLOS-CH clusters the network based on the RSSI values that are derived from the

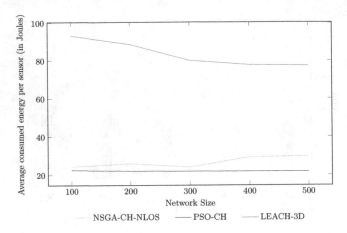

Fig. 5. The average consumed energy per sensor (in Joules)

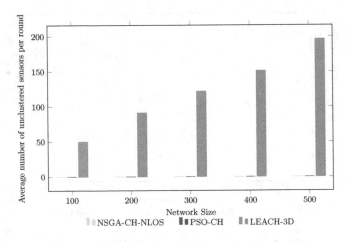

Fig. 6. The average number of unclustered sensors per round

proposed path loss model. This leads to creating clusters that are adopted for the field profile. While PSO-CH uses the RSSI values as criteria for clustering the network, the way the RSSI calculated does not take into consideration the obstacles in the field. LEACH-3D uses a totally random mechanism when electing the CHs and this, in turn, does not guarantee a high PDR.

Figure 4 shows the average number of CHs per round for all the protocols. It is noted that the NSGA-NLOS-CH protocol results in a higher number of CHs. Unlike PSO-CH, the number of CHs in NSGA-NLOS-CH is variable. Moreover, NSGA-NLOS-CH uses a Pareto-based approach to optimize all of its objectives concurrently. In the existence of obstacles, a higher number of CHs needs to cluster the whole network in order to achieve the scalability objective.

The average consumed energy per sensor is shown in Fig. 5. NSGA-CH-NLOS has a slightly higher energy consumption than that of PSO-CH because NSGA-CH-NLOS elects a higher number of CHs as shown in Fig. 4. These CHs have to stay active during the whole round which leads to a higher level of energy consumption. On the other hand, LEACH-3D has a very high energy consumption level. Experimental results have shown that LEACH-3D results in a very high number of unclustered sensors. These unclustered sensors stay active during the whole round and consume more energy. On the other hand, both NSGA-CH-NLOS and PSO-CH are able to cluster all the sensors. The average number of unclustered sensors per round is shown in Fig. 6.

6   Conclusions and Future Work

In this paper, we adopt an obstacle-aware path loss model to account for the effect of the obstacles in the network field. In order to locate those obstacles, the 3D rolling field is modeled using the DEM. Based on the adopted path loss model, an obstacle-aware clustering protocol, NSGA-NLOS-CH, is proposed. Simulation results have shown that the effect of the obstacle on the PDR cannot be neglected. Moreover, NSGA-NLOS-CH outperforms both PSO-CH and LEACH-3D in terms of the PDR while maintaining an acceptable energy consumption at the same time.

The coverage problem in 3D WSNs with a rolling field is another fundamental problem. As a future research direction, an integrated solution for both the clustering and coverage problems in an irregular field should be investigated.

References

1. Geospatial data extraction. http://maps.canada.ca/czs/index-en.html. Accessed 15 Aug 2017
2. Baghouri, M., Hajraoui, A., Chakkor, S.: Low energy adaptive clustering hierarchy for three-dimensional wireless sensor network. In: Recent Advances in Communications, pp. 214–218 (2015)
3. Barberis, A., Barboni, L., Valle, M.: Evaluating energy consumption in wireless sensor networks applications. In: 10th Euromicro Conference on Digital System Design Architectures, Methods and Tools, 2007. DSD 2007, pp. 455–462, August 2007. https://doi.org/10.1109/DSD.2007.4341509
4. Chong, P.K., Kim, D.: Surface-level path loss modeling for sensor networks in flat and irregular terrain. ACM Trans. Sens. Netw. 9(2), 15:1–15:32 (2013). https://doi.org/10.1145/2422966.2422972
5. Elhabyan, R.S., Yagoub, M.C.E.: Particle swarm optimization protocol for clustering in wireless sensor networks: a realistic approach. In: Proceedings of the 2014 IEEE 15th International Conference on Information Reuse and Integration (IEEE IRI 2014), pp. 345–350, August 2014. https://doi.org/10.1109/IRI.2014.7051910
6. Epstein, J., Peterson, D.W.: An experimental study of wave propagation at 850 MC. Proc. IRE 41(5), 595–611 (1953)

7. Hai, D.T., Son, L.H., Vinh, T.L.: Novel fuzzy clustering scheme for 3D wireless sensor networks. Appl. Soft Comput. **54**, 141–149 (2017). https://doi.org/10.1016/j.asoc.2017.01.021
8. Kurt, S., Tavli, B.: Path-loss modeling for wireless sensor networks: a review of models and comparative evaluations. IEEE Antennas Propag. Mag. **59**(1), 18–37 (2017). https://doi.org/10.1109/MAP.2016.2630035
9. Minakov, I., Passerone, R., Rizzardi, A., Sicari, S.: A comparative study of recent wireless sensor network simulators. ACM Trans. Sens. Netw. **12**(3), 20:1–20:39 (2016). https://doi.org/10.1145/2903144
10. Raheemah, A., Sabri, N., Salim, M., Ehkan, P., Ahmad, R.B.: New empirical path loss model for wireless sensor networks in mango greenhouses. Comput. Electron. Agric. **127**, 553–560 (2016). https://doi.org/10.1016/j.compag.2016.07.011
11. Texas Instruments: Chipcon CC2420 radio transceiver data sheet (2013). http://www.ti.com/lit/ds/symlink/cc2420.pdf. Accessed 25 Sep 2014

Evolutionary-Based Coverage Control Mechanism for Clustered Wireless Sensor Networks

Riham Elhabyan[✉], Wei Shi, and Marc St-Hilaire

School of Information Technology, Faculty of Engineering and Design,
Carleton University, Ottawa, ON, Canada
{riham.elhabyan,wei.shi,marc.sthilaire}@carleton.ca

Abstract. Many clustering protocols have been proposed for Wireless Sensor Networks (WSNs). However, most of these protocols focus on selecting the optimal set of Cluster Heads (CHs) in order to reduce or balance the network's energy consumption and unfortunately, how to effectively cover the network area is often overlooked. Coverage optimization in WSNs is a well-known Non-deterministic Polynomial (NP)-hard optimization problem. In this paper, we propose a Genetic Algorithm (GA)-based Coverage Control Mechanism (GA-CCM) for clustered WSNs. GA-CCM provides an add-on mechanism that is designed to be integrated with any centralized clustering protocol to enhance its energy efficiency. GA-CCM finds the optimal set of active nodes that provides full area coverage and puts the redundant sensors into sleep mode to save energy. Extensive simulations of GA-CCM on 25 different WSNs topologies are conducted. Performance results are evaluated and compared against several well-known clustering protocols as well as a coverage-aware clustering protocol. Results show that GA-CCM always achieves full area coverage while minimizing the redundancy degree and the number of active nodes. To further evaluate the performance of GA-CCM as an add-on to existing clustering protocols, we integrate it with a Particle Swarm Optimization based CH selection protocol (PSO-CH), a comprehensive clustering protocol that considers many clustering objectives. To the best of our knowledge, PSO-CH has the lowest overall energy consumption among well-known clustering protocols. Experimental results show that this integration of GA-CCM to PSO-CH further improves its performance in terms of energy efficiency and packets delivery rate.

Keywords: Sleep scheduling · Clustering · WSNs

1 Introduction

Wireless Sensor Networks (WSNs) are frequently used, among other applications, in environmental monitoring, industry and disaster management. In these

K. R. Chowdhury et al. (Eds.): WWIC 2018, LNCS 10866, pp. 67–80, 2018.
https://doi.org/10.1007/978-3-030-02931-9_6

applications, a large number of sensors with limited battery capacity and communication capabilities are usually deployed randomly and in high density in order to observe/measure a certain phenomenon or to detect the occurrence of an event in the network field. Such random and dense deployment is unavoidable due to the hazardous environment, in which WSN application needs to be implemented. Consequently, maintaining connectivity and coverage ratio while maximizing the network lifetime constitutes the biggest challenge on the wide spread of WSNs usage. This is because due to the random and dense deployment of the sensors, there may exist many redundant sensors covering the same area and therefore causing unnecessary energy consumption. Therefore, the intuitive solution is to have a set of sensors activated while keeping redundant nodes in sleep mode periodically. The Optimal Coverage Problem (OCP) in WSNs is defined as finding the smallest number of sensors to monitor the network area while maintaining the coverage ratio requirement of the application. The main approach to solve such problem is to employ sleep scheduling protocols, in which the redundant sensors are scheduled to be asleep/deactivated alternately to minimize the energy consumption, hence, increase the overall network lifetime while meeting the connectivity and coverage requirement. On the other hand, clustering protocols provide efficient methods to achieve energy-efficient communication, namely, connectivity in WSNs. However, most existing clustering protocols overlook this redundant sensors fact. Despite the close relationship between the clustering problem and the sleep scheduling problem, they are studied separately and very few works consider a joint solution for both problems. To enhance the energy efficiency of WSNs, integrated protocols that solve both of these problems are highly recommended. As both of these problems are well-known Non-deterministic Polynomial (NP)-hard optimization problems, Evolutionary Algorithms (EA) can be used to solve such problems.

1.1   Contributions of This Paper

In this paper, we propose a GA-based Coverage Control Mechanism (GA-CCM) for clustered WSNs. We assume that the network operating time is divided into rounds and the network is clustered using [3]. In each round, GA-CCM is executed to find an optimal set of active nodes to provide full area coverage. Redundant sensors are put into sleep mode to save energy. The main contributions are listed below:

- We formulate the OCP in clustered WSNs as an optimization problem. Up to our best knowledge, the proposed formulation is the first to consider the OCP problem in a clustered WSN. The proposed formulation ensures that the network area is fully covered by the least number of sensor nodes. To do so, the sub-objective functions of GA-CCM aim at minimizing the sensors' redundancy while balancing the energy consumption of the active sensors to avoid selecting the same set of active nodes in each round. Most importantly, GA-CCM is designed and developed as an add-on mechanism which can be integrated to any centralized clustering protocol in order to achieve a better energy efficiency.

- We introduce new ways to assess the level of coverage in WSNs. Most of the previously proposed protocols assume that the number of active nodes and/or the coverage ratio are useful metrics to assess the coverage performance of their proposed protocols [9]. The coverage ratio is defined as the ratio of the covered area to the whole network area [13]. The covered area is calculated as the product of the number of active nodes and the sensing area of each active node. However, these two metrics ignore the overlaps in the sensing areas, hence, do not reflect the real coverage degree. According to the current definition of coverage ratio, two sets of active nodes may result in the same coverage ratio but not necessarily the same redundancy degree, that is defined as the number of sensors monitoring a Point of Interest (PoI). In this paper, we redefine a new coverage ratio in order to assess the coverage more accurately. Furthermore, we also measure the redundancy degree using different metrics.
- Contrary to other coverage protocols, we test and examine the performance of the proposed protocol against other protocols under a more realistic energy consumption model that is based on the characteristics of the Chipcon CC2420 radio transceiver data sheet.

Extensive simulations of GA-CCM on 25 different WSNs topologies are conducted, evaluated and compared against several well-known clustering protocols as well as a coverage-aware clustering protocol. To further evaluate the performance of GA-CCM as an add-on to the existing clustering protocols, we integrate it with the Particle Swarm Optimization based cluster head selection (PSO-CH) protocol, a comprehensive clustering protocol that considers many clustering objectives. It is also known to have the lowest overall energy consumption among well-known clustering protocols [4].

1.2   Paper Organization

The remainder of this paper is organized as follows: Sect. 2 presents the related work on clustering protocols and coverage-aware clustering protocols. Section 3 presents the system model. The general design and the problem formulation are provided in Sect. 4. A detailed analysis of the simulation results is provided in Sect. 5. Finally, Sect. 6 concludes this paper.

2   Related Work

Many probability-based clustering algorithms have been proposed in the literature. In such algorithms, the Cluster Heads (CHs) are elected based on a probability function in a random fashion. Examples of such algorithms include: Low Energy Adaptive Clustering Hierarchy (LEACH) [5]; Energy Efficient Heterogeneous Clustered (EEHC) scheme [7] and Multi-hop Overlapping Clustering Algorithm (MOCA) [14]. All these algorithms are distributed, self-organized and have low overhead. However, these algorithms have some problems in terms of the form and distribution of the clusters [1]. These algorithms do not consider the residual energy of the sensors. Moreover, the random mechanism of selecting the CHs does not guarantee the selection of the optimal set of CHs [4]. This, in turn, will reduce the reliability of these algorithms [1].

In order to select the optimal set of CHs, many research works propose centralized EA-based clustering algorithms. In these algorithms, the Base Station (BS) adopts an EA to find the optimal set of CHs based on a set of predefined objective functions. An Example of such algorithms is the GA-based Clustering (GA-C) algorithm [10] which define one objective function as the minimization of the total distance from cluster members to their respective CHs in addition to the distance from the CHs to the BS. However, GA-C does not consider the energy efficiency of the selected CHs. A PSO-based Clustering (PSO-C) protocol [8] defines two objective functions which consider both the residual energy of the sensor nodes and the physical distances between the CHs and their associated cluster members. However, the objective functions are not scaled, hence the final solution is biased towards one of them. Another PSO-based CH (PSO-CH) selection algorithm is proposed in [3]. PSO-CH considers the following properties: the network's energy efficiency, data transmission reliability, and the protocol's scalability. The objective function is defined as the weighted sum of three sub-objectives, each of which is related to the aforementioned properties. The sub-objectives are scaled to avoid any bias.

All the aforementioned clustering protocols focus only on selecting CHs to reduce or to balance the network's energy consumption, without adopting any sleep scheduling mechanism for the redundant sensors. Only a few integrated protocols consider them in a joint way. An example of such protocols is the Coverage-Preserving Clustering Protocol (CPCP) [11]. CPCP is a distributed coverage-aware clustering protocol which defines different cost metrics for each sensor. The minimum-weight coverage cost metric is defined such that sensors deployed in densely populated network areas and that has higher remaining energy are better candidates to act as CHs and/or to stay active. The main operation of CPCP depends mainly on the values of activation timers. Although the authors of CPCP recommend the activation time to be proportional to the coverage cost, no specific recommendation is given on how to set this value. CPCP provides an integrated protocol to solve both the clustering and sleep scheduling problems in WSNs, it lacks a redundancy check mechanism and since it is a distributed protocol, there is no guarantee it will find the optimal status of the nodes. PSO-CH is a comprehensive clustering protocol that adopts a realistic energy consumption model and has well-defined objective functions. Experimental results of PSO-CH have proven that it has higher Packet Delivery Rate (PDR) at the CHs and at the same time has low energy consumption. However, PSO-CH lacks a mechanism for detecting the redundant sensors in the network and no sleep scheduling mechanism is adopted to put the redundant sensors into sleep mode.

In this paper, we address the aforementioned concerns by extending the PSO-CH protocol with a sleep scheduling mechanism.

3   The System Model

We consider a two-tiered WSNs with N sensors randomly and uniformly deployed. There are K cluster heads and 1 BS among N sensors. Each sensor has a unique ID, and the BS ID is 0. In the cluster formation process, each sensor node (including a CH) belongs to only one cluster. We assume that all nodes are stationary after deployment and that the sensors are aware of their location.

The Boolean sensing model [2] is assumed in this paper as it is the most commonly used sensing model. In this model, if a point p in the network field is located within the sensing range r of sensor node n, then it is assumed that p is covered/detected by n. The sensing area of n is defined as a disk centred at n with a radius of the sensing range r. In this model, the coverage function, $C(n,p)$, of sensor node n and point p is given by the following equation, where $d(n,p)$ is the euclidean distance between sensor node n and point p:

$$C(n,p) = \begin{cases} 1, & \text{if } d(n,p) \leq r \\ 0, & \text{otherwise} \end{cases} \tag{1}$$

For the energy consumption model, a realistic model which is based on the characteristics of the Chipcon CC2420 radio transceiver data sheet [12] is used. The total energy consumed by sensor node n, E_n, is calculated as follows [3]:

$$E_n = \sum_{statej} P_{statej} \times t_{statej} + \sum_{tr} E_{transitions} \tag{2}$$

Where $statej$ refers to the energy states of a sensor: sleep, reception, or transmission. P_{statej} is the power consumed in each $statej$, t_{statej} is the time spent in the corresponding state, and tr is the number of transitions for S. The energy spent in transitions between states, $E_{transitions}$, is also added to the node's total energy consumption. The different values of P_{statej} and $E_{transitions}$ can be found in [12].

4   General Design and Problem Formulation

First, the optimal set of CHs is determined using the PSO-CH protocol described in [3]. Then, the GA-CCM is adopted to solve the OCP in the clustered network. We choose the PSO-CH protocol as it has high PDR at the CHs and at the same time maintains reasonable energy consumption. We refer to the integrated protocol as EA-based Coverage-aware, Clustering Protocol (EA-CCP). The formulation of the OCP in clustered WSNs is given below.

In this paper, we assume that the network area A is divided into M virtual cells. At the start of EA-CCP, the BS constructs a coverage matrix CM that has $N-1$ rows and M columns as follows, where $CM(n,m) = 1$ when sensor $n, 1 \leq n \leq N-1$ covers cell $m, 0 \leq m \leq M$ and $CM(n,m) = 0$ otherwise:

$$CM = \begin{pmatrix} CM(1,1) & CM(1,2) & \cdots & CM(1,M) \\ CM(2,1) & CM(2,2) & \cdots & CM(2,M) \\ \vdots & \vdots & \ddots & \vdots \\ CM(N-1,1) & CM(N-1,2) & \cdots & CM(N-1,M) \end{pmatrix}$$

According to the boolean sensing model 1, sensor n is said to cover cell m if the distance between sensor n and cell m is less than the sensing range of sensor n. Unlike other coverage protocols, we measure the distance from the farthest corner of cell m rather than its center to ensure that cell m is totally covered by sensor n.

In GA-CCM, the dimension of each potential solution is equal to the number of sensor nodes in the network minus the BS (i.e., $N-1$). Let, $C_i = [X_{i,1}, X_{i,2}, X_{i,3}, \ldots, X_{i,N-1}]$ be the i_{th} chromosome of the population where each gene, $X_{i,d}, 1 \leq d \leq N-1$ maps the status of the sensor node with the ID n_d. Each gene $X_{i,d}$ of chromosome C_i is initialized with either 0 to indicate that sensor n_d is in inactive mode, or 1 to indicate that n_d is in active mode. Due to this problem formulation, GA is used instead of PSO since the velocity and position updates in PSO result in real values.

Each chromosome C_i is evaluated as follows:

- Create a new coverage matrix $UpdatedCM_i$ as a copy of CM.
- Update $UpdatedCM_i$ as follows: if $X_{i,d} = 0$ then $UpdatedCM_i(d,m) = 0$ for $m, 0 \leq m \leq M$.
- Based on the updated $UpdatedCM_i$, evaluate C_i using the below-mentioned objective functions.

In order to save more energy, fewer sensor nodes need to be active during each round. The main approach of GA-CCM to achieve that is to minimize the average number of redundant nodes per cell, $avgRedNodes$ which is calculated for chromosome C_i as follows:

$$avgRedNodes_{C_i} = \frac{\sum_{m=1}^{M} \sum_{n=1}^{N-1} UpdatedCM_i(n,m)}{M} \tag{3}$$

Furthermore, sensor nodes with higher level of energy are better candidates for activation during each round. Let the number $K = \sum_{n=1}^{N-1} X_{i,d}$ represents the number of active nodes for chromosome C_i. The remaining energy ratio for sensor node n with ID d, is $E(n_d) = \frac{Remaining\,energy\,of\,n_d}{Initial\,energy\,of\,n_d}$. Then, the average remaining energy per an active node in chromosome C_i is calculated as follows:

$$avgRemEnergy_{C_i} = \frac{\sum_{n=1}^{N-1} E(n_d), if\, X_{i,d} = 1}{K} \tag{4}$$

It should be noted that both $avgRedNodes_{C_i}$ and $avgRemainingEnergy_{C_i}$ are not scaled and may lead to values that are not in the same range. This will cause the final objective function to be biased towards one sub-objective. Moreover, it can be very difficult to precisely and accurately select the final objective function weights, even for domain experts [6]. In order to avoid this drawback, each sub-objective is scaled to result in the scaled values $sAvgRedNodes_{C_i}$ and $sAvgRemEnergy_{C_i}$, respectively. Therefore, the final objective function to be minimized, assuming each sub-objective is equally important, is expressed as follows:

$$Fitness_{C_i} = sAvgRedNodes_{C_i} + (1 - sAvgRemEnergy_{C_i}) \tag{5}$$

In the case that a CH is set to inactive in C_i or that a covered cell becomes uncovered, the final objective function is assigned a high penalty value to narrow the search to optimal valid solutions only.

5   Simulations and Results

The performance of EA-CCP is investigated against CPCP in terms of the number of active nodes, the minimum, maximum and average number of sensors monitoring a cell, and the coverage ratio. We choose the CPCP for comparison as it can provide full area coverage. Authors of CPCP claim that the minimum-weight coverage cost provides the best results where the sensor network has to provide complete (100%) coverage of the monitored area [11]. Moreover, the performance of EA-CCP is investigated against CPCP, LEACH, PSO-C, GA-C, and PSO-CH in terms of the average consumed energy per node and the Packet Delivery Rate (PDR). Although LEACH, PSO-C, GA-C, and PSO-CH do not use any coverage control, we choose them for comparison as they are well-known clustering protocols and experimental results have shown that they have high PDR and low energy consumption due to their adapted cluster-based sleep scheduling mechanism [3].

Simulations are carried on Castalia, which is based on the OMNeT++ platform. The simulations are performed on a group of homogeneous sensor networks consisted of 5 different network sizes ranging from 100 to 500 sensor nodes. Overall, the simulation results are averaged over five simulation runs for a total of 25 different playground topologies. Table 1 summarizes the configuration of the network's simulation environment.

The CHs selection problem is solved using PSO while the OCP is solved using GA. Table 2 summarizes the configuration of the different EAs parameters.

5.1   Coverage Performance

In this section, we compare between CPCP and EA-CCP in terms of their coverage performance. We choose these two particular protocols since they provide a coverage control mechanism and assume that they can provide full area coverage. The results presented in this section represent the average of 5 different runs for 5 different network sizes and for one round of operation.

The coverage ratio for both CPCP and EA-CCP is assessed and the results are shown in Table 3. We define the coverage ratio as the ratio of the number

Table 1. Summary of the WSNs simulation settings for EA-CCP

Parameter	Value
BS location	$(0,0)$
Data transmission rate	1 packet/s
Network size	(100–500) sensor nodes
Field size	$100\,\text{m} \times 100\,\text{m}$
MAC protocol	TMAC
Simulation time	2500 s
Round length	500 s
Slot length	1 s
Initial energy	18,720 J
Sensing range	20 m
Cell width	5 m

Table 2. The EAs parameters settings for EA-CCP

Parameter	Value
PSO-CH	
Problem dimension (number of CHs)	[5–25]
Population size	50
Number of iterations	500
Learning factor $c1$	2
Learning factor $c2$	2
Interia weight w	0.9
GA-CCM	
Problem dimension (network size - 1)	[99–455]
Population size	100
Number of iterations	25000
Mutation probability, p_m	1/problem dimension
Crossover probability, p_c	0.9

of covered cells to the total number of cells. Column 2 in Table 3 shows the coverage ratio before applying any Coverage Control (CC), i.e. before running any of the protocols. Table 3 shows that EA-CCP achieves higher coverage ratio than CPCP. In most of the cases, EA-CCP achieve full area coverage. In the case of 100 nodes, the network area is not fully covered even before applying any CC, as shown in the second column. That is why EA-CCP did not provide full coverage in that case. Although we are assuming uniform sensors deployment, the cell width determines the granularity of the network area. Choosing smaller cell width may have led to higher coverage ratio for both protocols and full coverage in EA-CCP.

Table 3. Coverage ratio

Network size	No CC	CPCP	EA-CCP
100	0.999	0.645	0.999
200	1	0.7365	1
300	1	0.803	1
400	1	0.8375	1
500	1	0.8495	1

To assess the redundancy degree, Table 4 shows the minimum (MIN), maximum (MAX) and average (AVG) number of sensors, including the CHs, monitoring a cell for both EA-CCP and CPCP. In Table 4, columns 2, 3 and 4 show the same values before applying any Coverage Control (CC), i.e. before running any of the protocols. In CPCP, the MIN column shows that, in all the networks, there are cells that are not monitored by any sensor. Hence, CPCP fail to provide full area coverage. Moreover, the MAX column shows that there is a high degree of redundancy in monitoring a cell. This degree of redundancy increases as the network density increases. Therefore, the average number of sensors monitoring a cell increases too. On the other hand, EA-CCP shows more stable and consistent performance, regardless of the network density. EA-CCP always succeeded in providing full area coverage and all the cells has at least 1 sensor monitoring it. The reason for the lower value in case of 100 nodes is justified in the results of Table 3. Furthermore, EA-CCP has much lower redundancy degree. Regardless of the network density, EA-CCP has on average around 1 node monitoring each cell.

Table 4. Average number of sensors monitoring a cell

Network size	No CC			CPCP			EA-CCP		
	MIN	MAX	AVG	MIN	MAX	AVG	MIN	MAX	AVG
100	1.2	15.8	7.406	0	5.4	1.5524	0.8	3.2	1.602
200	3.8	28	14.76	0	10.6	2.5642	1	3.4	1.6307
300	6.4	37.4	22.09	0	23.8	3.6861	1	3.6	1.6503
400	9.2	47	29.417	0	28	5.1626	1	3.4	1.6329
500	12.4	58	36.6315	0	34.6	6.7182	1	3.8	1.7172

Table 5 shows the average number of active nodes per round (Ns). This number represents both the CHs and other Active Nodes (ANs) involved in the communication. The main operation of CPCP depends mainly on the values of the activation timers. Hence, it is more likely that more than one sensor with the same timer value will announce themselves as CHs at the same time which will lead to a higher number of CHs. These CHs mark their sensing areas as covered areas. In CPCP, the activation stage occurs after the CH selection which leads to activating less number of sensor nodes.

Table 5. Average number of active nodes per round

Network size	CPCP			EA-CCP		
	Ns	CHs	ANs	Ns	CHs	ANs
100	21.4	15.8	5.6	25.2	5	20.2
200	30	24.8	5.2	33	10	23
300	70.2	64.6	5.6	38.2	15	23.2
400	80.8	75.6	5.2	41.8	20	21.8
500	95	90.6	4.4	48.6	25	23.6

5.2 Clustering Performance

Figure 1 records the average consumed energy per node for the different protocols. The results presented here represent the average of 5 different runs, for each network size, with a confidence level of 0.99. It can be clearly shown that EA-CCP protocol outperforms the other protocols in terms of energy efficiency. This is due to minimizing the number of active nodes by minimizing the nodes redundancy as illustrated in Tables 5 and 4, respectivly. Although CPCP also minimizes the number of active nodes, a higher number of CHs are selected as shown in Table 5. Higher levels of energy consumptions are recorded in CPCP because the CHs stay active for the whole round. Moreover, the decision of whether a sensor will stay active or not in CPCP is not taken at the beginning of the round. This decision could be taken by the node anytime during the round, depending on its activation time. This will lead to unnecessary consumed energy by the redundant nodes who are waiting for their timer to expire to take the decision to be inactive. In EA-CCP, a centralized approach is adopted so each node knows its status at the start of each round. The clustering process in EA-CCP employs the PSO-CH protocol which leads to less number of CHs (5% of network size) and more scalable clusters [3]. The results obtained in Fig. 1 are also confirmed by Fig. 2 which shows the average consumed energy per node for a different number of rounds in case of a 300 sensors networks. Figure 2 shows that EA-CCP consistently outperforms the other protocols in terms of energy efficiency for different network operation time.

Figure 3 shows the average PDR for the different protocols. The PDR is calculated as the ratio of the total packets received by all the cluster heads

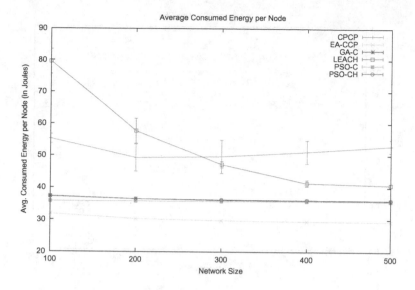

Fig. 1. Average consumed energy per node for different network sizes

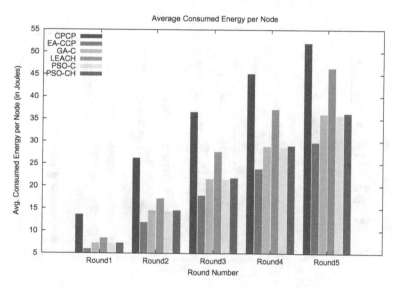

Fig. 2. Average consumed energy per node for different number of rounds

against all the packets sent by all the active nodes. Figure 3 clearly shows that
the EA-CCP protocol significantly outperforms the other protocols in terms of
PDR. Minimizing the number of redundant nodes enhances the network topology
and minimize the network collisions, which in turn enhances the PDR. Although
the CPCP also reduces the number of redundant nodes, there are no link quality
measures taken when the clusters are constructed. This is also confirmed by Fig. 4

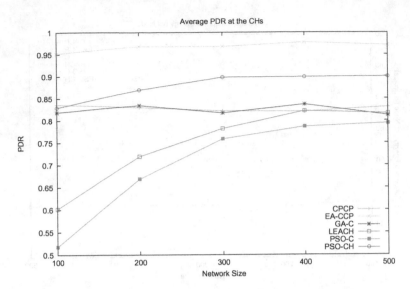

Fig. 3. Average PDR at the CHs for different network sizes

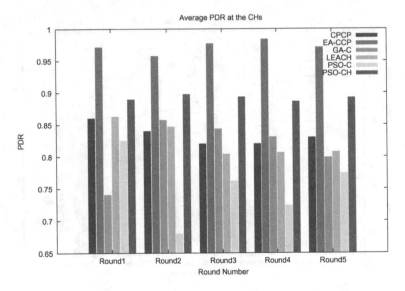

Fig. 4. Average PDR at the CHs for different number of rounds

which shows the average PDR for a different number of rounds, when network size is 300. The results Fig. 4 represent the average of 5 different runs for one round of operation, for each network size. Figure 4 shows that the EA-CCP protocol consistently outperforms the other protocols in terms of the PDR for different network operation time.

6 Conclusions

Both network clustering and coverage optimization can help to conserve energy. In this paper, we propose GA-CCM as an add-on mechanism that can be adopted by any centralized clustering protocol to solve the OCP. Simulation results show that integrating GA-CCM into PSO-CH results in better energy consumption and PDR comparing to other popular clustering protocols. Moreover, the proposed mechanism greatly enhances the coverage ratio, reduces redundancy degree and the number of active nodes.

References

1. Afsar, M.M., Tayarani-N, M.H.: Clustering in sensor networks: a literature survey. J. Netw. Comput. Appl. **46**, 198–226 (2014)
2. Boudaren, M.E.Y., Senouci, M.R., Senouci, M.A., Mellouk, A.: New trends in sensor coverage modeling and related techniques: a brief synthesis. In: 2014 International Conference on Smart Communications in Network Technologies (SaCoNeT), pp. 1–6, June 2014
3. Elhabyan, R.S., Yagoub, M.C.E.: Particle swarm optimization protocol for clustering in wireless sensor networks: a realistic approach. In: Proceedings of the 2014 IEEE 15th International Conference on Information Reuse and Integration (IEEE IRI 2014), pp. 345–350, August 2014
4. Elhabyan, R.S., Yagoub, M.C.: Two-tier particle swarm optimization protocol for clustering and routing in wireless sensor network. J. Netw. Comput. Appl. **52**, 116–128 (2015). https://doi.org/10.1016/j.jnca.2015.02.004
5. Heinzelman, W., Chandrakasan, A., Balakrishnan, H.: An application-specific protocol architecture for wireless microsensor networks. IEEE Trans. Wirel. Commun. **1**(4), 660–670 (2002)
6. Konak, A., Coit, D.W., Smith, A.E.: Multi-objective optimization using genetic algorithms: a tutorial. Reliab. Eng. Syst. Saf. **91**(9), 992–1007 (2006)
7. Kumar, D., Aseri, T.C., Patel, R.: Eehc: Energy efficient heterogeneous clustered scheme for wireless sensor networks. Comput. Commun. **32**(4), 662–667 (2009). https://doi.org/10.1016/j.comcom.2008.11.025
8. Latiff, N., Tsimenidis, C., Sharif, B.: Energy-aware clustering for wireless sensor networks using particle swarm optimization. In: IEEE 18th International Symposium on Personal, Indoor and Mobile Radio Communications (PIMRC 2007), pp. 1–5, September 2007
9. Mostafaei, H., Montieri, A., Persico, V., Pescapé, A.: A sleep scheduling approach based on learning automata for WSN partialcoverage. J. Netw. Comput. Appl. **80**, 67–78 (2017)
10. Rahmanian, A., Omranpour, H., Akbari, M., Raahemifar, K.: A novel genetic algorithm in LEACH-C routing protocol for sensor networks. In: 2011 24th Canadian Conference on Electrical and Computer Engineering (CCECE), pp. 001096–001100, May 2011
11. Soro, S., Heinzelman, W.B.: Cluster head election techniques for coverage preservation in wireless sensor networks. Ad Hoc Netw. **7**(5), 955–972 (2009)
12. Texas Instruments: Chipcon CC2420 radio transceiver data sheet (2013). http://www.ti.com/lit/ds/symlink/cc2420.pdf. Accessed 25 September 2014

13. Wu, Y., Ai, C., Gao, S., Li, Y.: p-percent coverage in wireless sensor networks. In: Li, Y., Huynh, D.T., Das, S.K., Du, D.-Z. (eds.) WASA 2008. LNCS, vol. 5258, pp. 200–211. Springer, Heidelberg (2008). https://doi.org/10.1007/978-3-540-88582-5_21
14. Youssef, A., Younis, M., Youssef, M., Agrawala, A.: WSN16-5: distributed formation of overlapping multi-hop clusters in wireless sensor networks. IEEE Globecom **2006**, 1–6 (2006)

Learning-Based Networking

Toward Resilient Smart Grid Communications Using Distributed SDN with ML-Based Anomaly Detection

Allen Starke[✉], Janise McNair, Rodrigo Trevizan, Arturo Bretas,
Joshua Peeples, and Alina Zare

University of Florida, Gainesville, FL 32611, USA
{allen1.starke,rodtrevizan,jpeeples}@ufl.edu,
{mcnair,arturo,azare}@ece.ufl.edu

Abstract. Next generation "Smart" systems, including cyber-physical systems like smart grid and Internet-of-Things, integrate control, communication and computation to achieve stability, efficiency and robustness of physical processes. While a great amount of research has gone towards building these systems, security in the form of resilient and fault-tolerant communications for smart grid systems is still immature. In this paper, we propose a hybrid, distributed and decentralized (HDD) SDN architecture for resilient Smart Systems. It provides a redundant controller design for fault-tolerance and fail-over operation, as well as parallel execution of multiple anomaly detection algorithms. Using the k-means clustering algorithm from the machine learning literature, it is shown that k-means can be used to produce a high accuracy (96.9%) of identifying anomalies within normal traffic. Furthermore, incremental k-means produces a slightly lower accuracy (95.6%) but demonstrated an increased speed with respect to k-means and fewer CPU and memory resources needed, indicating a possibility for scaling the system to much larger networks.

Keywords: Software defined networks · Anomaly detection
Machine learning · Security · Resilience

1   Introduction

The next-generation power grid, named the Smart Grid, has drawn the attention of academia, industry and government agencies due to the great impact of such systems on the distribution of power within and between various regions. These next generation systems integrate control, communication and computation to achieve stability, efficiency and robustness of the physical processes. While a great amount of research has addressed these objectives, science and technology related to secure SG communications is still relatively immature. Additionally,

K. R. Chowdhury et al. (Eds.): WWIC 2018, LNCS 10866, pp. 83–94, 2018.
https://doi.org/10.1007/978-3-030-02931-9_7

many critical cyber-physical infrastructures are increasing dependency of control of physical processes on communication networks, thus becoming exposed to various cyber-threats or faulty operation. An example is the network of smart grid subsystems shown in Fig. 1. The smart grid subsystems are local agents, composed of Distributed Energy Storage Systems (DESS), such as flywheels and grid-connected batteries, a Synchronous Generator, a Phasor Measurement Unit (PMU) and a Distributed State Estimator (DSE). The PMUs in the smart grid form a communication network, where smart grid data is regularly exchanged with other PMUs to coordinate and analyze energy performance measures. In the attack model considered, a PMU subsystem may be attacked in order to disable it or to inject faulty data; or a PMU element may fail, generating faulty data as a result of the failure. If a PMU subsystem is attacked or fails, the communication of invalid data may introduce substantial errors when exchanged with the other connected PMU subsystems, creating an avalanche effect. We propose to secure the PMU subsystem network by introducing a hybrid distributed and decentralized (HDD) software-defined network (SDN). The HDD-SDN architecture will leverage data and statistics from PMU communications to gain situational awareness and will provide machine intelligence to detect and protect against abnormal network behavior within the distributed PMU communication network. SDN is a networking paradigm in which the forwarding hardware is decoupled from the control decisions. The network intelligence is logically centralized in software-based controllers (the control plane), and the network devices become simple packet forwarding devices (the data plane) that can be programmed via an open interface [1]. The controller is the only source responsible for determining routing paths, developing policies, partitioning the network, as well as other network administrative functionality. The traditional SDN operation is a centralized, global controller. While the centralized approach does strengthen the capability of the controller to manage the entire network, it is well known that a centralized approach also creates a vulnerability for a single point of failure. This is a significant barrier to using SDN for large-scale cyber-physical networks. New approaches must ensure that SDN controllers are fault tolerant on a larger scale and retain the advantages of the centralized perspective (global view) even while the implementation takes a distributed approach.

1.1 Related Work and Contributions of This Work

To this point, there has been limited research on SDN for monitoring of smart grid communications. Previously, SDN for Smart Grid has been proposed using centralized, non-real-time network monitoring and control. For example, the work of [2], presents a self-healing PMU smart grid network using SDN. When a cyber-attack takes place on a PMU then that node is isolated and reconfigured to a previous stable state. These works do not consider cyber-attacks on the centralized SDN architecture itself nor the restoration and reconfiguration of the SDN controllers in a distributed SDN design. Very recently, distributed SDN (D-SDN) solutions have been proposed for specific categories of Smart Grid, including (PEVs) [3]. A few works proposed a distributed architecture for cyber-

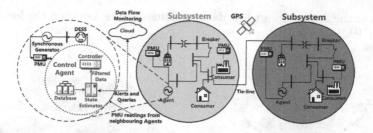

Fig. 1. Distributed PMUs in the Smart Grid. The distributed PMUs form a communication network, where smart grid data is regularly exchanged with other PMUs to coordinate and analyze energy performance measures. If a PMU subsystem is attacked or fails, the communication of invalid data may introduce substantial errors when exchanged with the other connected PMU subsystems.

security [4]. The work in [5], provides detailed insights on various approaches for developing a distributed SDN architecture.

Our proposed HDD-SDN is a real-time, distributed approach that uses current information available at the PMUs and can respond in real-time to failures and attacks. HDD-SDN analyzes traffic flow as well as smart grid measurement data and use machine learning techniques to identify, fix, and then attempt to prevent similar cyber-attacks, while continuing to detect anomalous behavior in the future. Our work will leverage the *physically distributed controller approach* described in [5] and employs machine intelligence-based anomalous flow detection to increase resilience of smart grid systems as well as the underlying SDN communication network.

The rest of the paper is divided as follows. Section 2 introduces the hybrid distributed and decentralized controller software-defined network architecture for smart grid systems. Section 3 describes the execution of multiple anomaly detection algorithms to be able to maintain reliability while reducing latency and CPU/memory use. Section 4 provides the experimental setup, a combination of Smart Grid test bed and SDN network simulation. Section 4 also provides results on the machine learning clustering algorithms that were evaluated for anomaly detection in network traffic and generated PMU data. Finally, Sect. 5 provides conclusions and future work.

2   Network Architecture

As mentioned previously, Fig. 1 shows an example application for the HDD-SDN architecture, namely the control and monitoring of PMU communications in a smart grid system. The problem of protecting and controlling the power grid is reduced into simpler, more tractable engineering problems by subdividing the power system into small regions or zones. For example, a fault in a transmission line or a fault in the control of the power output of a generator are problems solved locally by monitoring the variables measured by local sensors. The proliferation of the fault comes when data exchange begins between the local PMU and other PMUs.

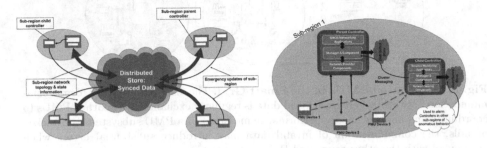

Fig. 2. Distributed SDN architecture and store

Fig. 3. Sub-region operations - decentralized controller architecture

The proposed HDD-SDN architecture is shown in Fig. 2. The network consists of a collection of sub-regions, which can represent the PMU sub-systems within the smart grid architecture. In the hierarchical architecture, multiple controllers share their sub-region network topology and state information with their neighbors in the distributed system. This is accomplished using the distributed store function of the open-source network operating system ONOS [6]. The distributed store provides a global view of the entire networking system, and ensures sub-systems are performing as efficiently as possible. Each controller is responsible for managing the nodes under its sub-region/domain, and for updating important information from their sub-region to the distributed system. In this sense, the controllers are connected in a mesh using a specific TCP port for interactions and using keep-alive messages to monitor each controller's status. Consistency levels among the users can be "strongly consistent", which in ONOS indicates frequent updates of network topology state to the distributed stores using the RAFT protocol, or "eventually consistent", which implies less frequent updates using the Anti-Entropy protocol [7]. In the case of this project, we use an "eventually consistent" model for updating the distributed store of anomalous behavior taking place in a region. More information about the types of stores used in ONOS can be found here: [7]. Multiple controller support, introduced in OpenFlow 1.2 [8], allows a switch to connect to multiple controllers simultaneously. Each controller has either a MASTER role, EQUAL role, or a SLAVE role to each switch in the network. Next, we describe the decentralized approach that provides the SDN and Smart Grid network with additional benefits compared to a centralized strategy.

2.1 Decentralized SDN Architecture

The sub-region operation for the proposed HDD-SDN architecture is shown in Fig. 3. Child controllers are placed in each sub-region to monitor data and control planes. This provides a redundant, decentralized SDN architecture for each sub-region. The primary tasks of the child controller are to intercept: (1) network data packets relayed in the data plane between PMU devices, and (2) network control packets transmitted from the parent controller to the PMU's switching devices. The child controller cannot make changes to the network it is monitoring. It is only allowed to communicate with the distributed store (hierarchical distributed controller cluster) if its parent controller demonstrates anomalous behavior to the network. If this condition is detected, the child controller can flag the parent's anomalous behavior and relay the indication to its neighboring parent controllers. A neighbor parent controller can then take control of the affected sub-region, and the faulty controller can be reconfigured.

The proposed approach also allows the parent controller to offload security features, such as firewalls, deep packet inspection (DPI), or anomaly detection techniques to the child controller, since the logical decentralized child controller can be aware of all statistics in the network. Delegating jobs to separate controllers releases the burden placed on one controller, and allows room for numerous possibilities for managing or reconfiguring the network. Further details about the parent and child controller roles and operation are shown in Fig. 4 and described below. We depend on network statistics from the entire system to identify anomalous behavior, including (1) anomalous behavior in the network traffic and payload content, i.e. control data sent between the SDN controller and PMU devices, network data with current and voltages reading exchanged between PMU devices and a state estimator, (2) anomalous behavior in topology changes, i.e. additional node changes within the network, such as new addition of external nodes and unwanted changes within network configurations; and (3) a variety of network performance changes, i.e. broken links, lost connections, and performance decreases.

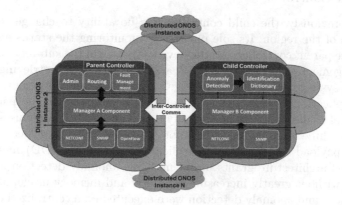

Fig. 4. Decentralized sub-regional architecture details

2.2   Parent Controller

Efficient resource allocation and management takes place on the parent controller to provide congestion control, load balancing, and traffic engineering for the smart grid and to distribute the computation load among the PMUs. The parent controller is also responsible for reconfiguring the network when the child controller demonstrates anomalous behavior in the system. The parent controller interacts with the devices in the region using the Openflow protocol for updating flows, while simple network management protocol (SNMP) and NETCONF are used for gaining statistical information and reconfiguring devices when necessary. Each parent controller of each sub-region allocates enough memory to store the network states of their neighboring regions, allowing for each controller to monitor the network performance of the neighboring regions.

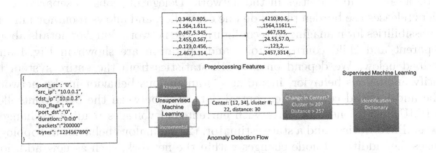

Fig. 5. Example flow diagram of applications in child controller

2.3   Child Controller

As stated previously, the child controller has no ability to change topological information of the region. Its sole purpose is monitoring the status and performance of the parent controller and the devices that form the sub-regions network using management protocols like SNMP, and NETCONF for retrieving information of the system. As indicated in Fig. 2, the child controller contains a few security applications specifically for determining anomalies of the packets sent in the control or data plane. The anomaly detection (AD) module uses a combination of machine learning algorithms for clustering different types of network traffic and payload data, and an identification dictionary (IDD) module. The decentralized architecture grants use of multiple anomaly detection algorithms in parallel, without greatly increasing the CPU and memory usage, as it would if management and anomaly detection were executed on a centralized controller.

Feature Scaling and Preprocessing. The application flow of the child controller is described in Fig. 5. Preprocessing features is a standard step for implementing machine learning algorithms for anomaly detection [9]. However, while most techniques attempt to normalized a wide range of different features into a standard range of 0 to 1 [9], in this approach, we increased the scaling factor by 1000 while incrementing through the columns. This granted a substantial change in the calculation of centers when certain features are present and allowed the clustering algorithm to better distinguish between different cluster groups.

3   Anomaly Detection in the HDD-SDN Child Controller

Various machine learning techniques can be implemented in parallel to detect anomalous behavior. A commonly used clustering algorithm, *k-means*, is implemented, along side a sparse clustering extension called *incremental k-means* [10]. The k-means algorithm clusters data points by alternatively assigning data points to clusters and updating cluster representatives. Data points are assigned to the cluster in which they have the minimum Euclidean distance to cluster centers computed using Eq. 1:

$$d(\mathbf{p}_n, \mathbf{c}_k) = \left(\sum_{d=1}^{D} (\mathbf{p}_n - \mathbf{c}_k)^2 \right)^{1/2}$$

(1)

where $\mathbf{p}_n = [p_1, p_2, \ldots, p_D] \in R^D$ is a D dimensional vector containing the features associated with the nth data point (in our case, a network packet) and $\mathbf{c}_k = [c_1, c_2, \ldots, d_D] \in R^D$ is a D dimensional vector of the kth cluster representative. Cluster representatives are using the vector mean of the data points assigned to that cluster. Since the k-means algorithm requires repeated pair-wise distance computations between each data point and each cluster representative, the computational load is significant for large data sets. Incremental k-means is a k-means approximation that is applicable to large scale sparse dynamic datasets (such as network traffic). During each iteration, the standard k-means algorithm uses the entire dataset for recalculating cluster centers. In contrast, Incremental k-means updates the previous centers with only newly input data [10].

The k-means approach and its extensions have an obvious limitation in that the number of clusters must be known before executing the algorithm. However, the number of clusters are rarely known in advance, particularly for dynamic datasets containing anomalies. Cluster validity metrics are one mechanism to address this issue. Cluster validity metrics provide a quantitative measure of clustering effectiveness for a particular data set. Thus, a data set can be repeatedly clustered with a different number of clusters and, then, each result evaluated using a validity metric to determine the appropriate number of clusters. Validity metrics appropriate for the k-means algorithm include Dunn's index and the Davies-Bouldin index [11,12]. A draw-back of this potential approach is the need to repeatedly cluster the data using a different number of clusters each time. Alternatively, the number of clusters can be adapted in real time with incoming data by generating new clusters when data points appear that are far from all current cluster representatives (similar to approaches used to generate new clusters in Dirichlet Process Mixture Modeling) [13]. These new clusters could then be evaluated and tagged as corresponding to anomalous behaviors when appropriate. When anomalous behavior is identified, short-term mitigation techniques can take place for a quick response to the problem. For example, a firewall can be activated on an infected IP address.

Identification and Detection Dictionary in the HDD-SDN Child Controller. Figure 4 also shows the Identification and Detection Dictionary (IDD) process in the Child Controller. The IDD uses a simple logical algorithm for comparing extracted features from the anomalous traffic to features associated with different types of cyber-attacks as identified during a training phase. Different types of cyber-attacks affect different features of network traffic. If the anomalous behavior is completely different from what is stored and cannot be identified, then the system has learned a new type of cyber-attack or a new type of fault in the system. This information will be recorded and classified as a new anomaly. Then it is sent to the distributed store for the other regions to be able to take action in mitigating that type of attack or fault, or tagging reported data with the current attack or fault. After an anomaly is identified, the ONOS system can now produce long-term changes in the network configuration to prevent future attacks of this type,such as changing flows, reconfiguring the attacked device, rerouting around the offending sub-region, etc.

The extracted features from the anomalous traffic in a sub-region sometimes cannot be directly used in another sub-region. Different regions may have different network topology and configurations. An abnormal traffic pattern in one region may be normal in another region. We envision the child controller to be able to develop mitigation schemes for their respective sub-domains in which they reside. For instance if anomalous behavior is detected in sub-region 1, the child controller (monitor controller) in that region will develop a mitigation scheme for its sub-region only. This information is transmitted to it's respective parent controller to take action. The child controller will then relay information about the type of attac, what network features were affected, feature threshold values to be used by other child controllers in separate sub-regions. It is up to the other sub-regions to monitor their network features and determine if they are being changed in a similar manner. If their thresholds aren't met then no change will take place for the other regions. If their thresholds are met then the child controllers of those regions will develop their own mitigation scheme to correct the anomalous behavior.

4   Experimental Results

The proposed HDD-SDN environment was simulated in Mininet using the wireless devices environment. The SDN controller used was the open-source network operating system ONOS [6]. ONOS provides a large API for users to develop their own networking applications to meet requirements of custom networking scenarios.

Kmeans of Network Traffic (n = 277950)				Incremental Kmeans of Network Traffic (n = 277950)			
	Predicted Normal	Predicted Anomaly			Predicted Normal	Predicted Anomaly	
Actual Normal	TP = 28345	FN = 8214	36559	Actual Normal	TP = 27283	FN = 10875	38158
Actual Anomaly	FP = 233	TN = 241158	241391	Actual Anomaly	FP = 632	TN = 239160	239792
	28578	249372			27915	250035	

Fig. 6. Kmeans and incremental kmeans confusion matrix for network traffic

4.1   Simulation Setup

Using Mininet, we developed networking scenarios and topologies similar to real-istic smart grid environments. In addition, we deployed an instant virtual net-work on a stand-alone computer and were able to expand this network by allow-ing the connection of multiple external nodes and other computation resources, including other PCs, mobile devices, VMs, etc. In this environment the state estimator was the client node connected to multiple PMUs setup as servers or client nodes.

We are developing our testbed to integrate a smart grid network emulator called OPAL-RT to generate the smart grid information. Virtual measurements of the smart grid emulator are taken from OPAL-RT, streamed from the server to the clients, and analyzed by the HDD-SDN application in ONOS. Network state information (i.e. number of devices, number of links, flow information, net-work traffic, etc.) collected by the external SDN parent and child controllers were stored in a database (InfluxDB, AWS, etc.) to be analyzed by an instance AD module operating in the child controller. Any necessary network reconfigura-tions were sent back to the parent SDN controller for the proper actions to take place. For experimentation purposes, the cluster algorithms were trained using the KDD CUP 1999 dataset that contains a standard set of data, which includes a wide variety of classified intrusions emulated in a military network environ-ment [14]. With this data we extracted key features of network traffic identical to features which can be obtained using ONOS controller during network mon-itoring to compare anomaly detection techniques. We simulated measurements of the recorded and exchanged measurements by PMUs using MATLAB.

4.2   Performance Evaluation

For this experiment, we executed both k-means and incremental k-means for clustering and, subsequently, anomaly detection on network traffic data and PMU measurement data. In order to evaluate how well the network traffic was classified, the data was separated into training and testing sets. The training set is used to generate cluster centers for the k-means and incremental k-means

Data type	Clustering Algorithm	True Positive Rate (%)	True Negative Rate (%)	Positive Predictive Value (%)	Negative Predictive Value (%)	False Positive Rate (%)	False Negative Rate (%)	False Discovery Rate (%)	Overall Accuracy (%)	Execution Time (s)	CPU Usage (%)	Mem Usage (%)
Network Traffic	Kmeans	77.5	99.9	99.4	96.6	0.096	22.5	0.586	96.9	25.505	99.2 – 100	19.2 – 24.3
	Incremental Kmeans	71.5	95.9	97.7	95.6	0.26	28.5	2.26	95.6	2.646	99.5 – 100	6.7 – 19.5
Generated PMU Data	Kmeans	100	89.4	15.9	100	10.6	0	84.1	89.6	.4812	99.7	2.7
	Incremental Kmeans	100	92.8	21.6	100	7.2	0	78.4	92.9	.1203	99.2	2.7

Fig. 7. Table showing accuracy of anomaly detection algorithms for network traffic and PMU data

algorithms. Once the cluster centers are calculated, a label (normal or anomaly) is manually assigned to each cluster based on the IDD approach described above. The testing set is then added to the dataset and assigned the label of the cluster center closest to that data point. The size of the training set was n = 194,565 (70%) and the size of the testing set was n = 83385 (30%). The results of the classification of the network traffic are shown in Fig. 6. We recorded true positive (TP), true negative (TN), false positive (FP), and false negative (FN) results. Using these values we calculated true positive rate, TPR (sensitivity), true negative rate, TNR (specificity), positive predictive value PPV (precision), negative predictive value, NPR, false positive rate FPR (fallout), false negative rate, FNR, false discovery rate FDR, and overall accuracy, ACC, with the inclusion of execution time, CPU and memory usage as follows:

$$TPR = TP/(TN + FP)$$
$$TNR = TN/(TN + FP)$$
$$PPV = TP/(TP + FP)$$
$$NPV = TN/(TN + FN)$$
$$FPR = FP/(FP + TN)$$
$$FNR = FN/(TP + FN)$$
$$FDR = FP/(TP + FP)$$
$$ACC = (TP + TN)/(TP + FP + FN + TN)$$

$$(2)$$

As shown in Fig. 6, we observed that k-means produces a high accuracy (96.9%) of identifying anomalies within network traffic. Incremental k-means produces a slightly lower accuracy (95.6%), but demonstrated an increased speed with respect to the k-means by approximately 22 s. For the CPU and memory usage, k-means used more resources than incremental kmeans. This is likely due to the fact that kmeans is a batch algorithm, using the entire dataset during every iteration to recalculate cluster centers.

On the other hand, it was observed that the accuracy of anomaly detection for the OPAL-RT generated PMU data is lower than the accuracies provided when clustering network traffic. This is possibly because features of the PMU data are not as readily distinguishable from each other as expected, causing a higher false positive rating than expected. The proposed anomaly detection technique using clustering still preserves approximately 90% accuracy, mostly due to the true negative value exceeding others. It can be seen that CPU and memory usage are much lower for this data type, due to use of fewer features when clustering. This is a positive indicator for scaling the system to larger PMU networks (Fig. 7).

For performance overhead, we implemented a single ONOS controller with network management applications running on a device with the following specs: Ubuntu OS 14.04 (64-bit), AMD A6-6310 APU processor, 3.3 GiB memory, Java version 1.7.0 to manage a simple network consisting of 5 switches and 10 hosts. CPU usage for this system ranged from 1.3–17.3% of the device. We predict adding an additional controller on the same device to manage the same network will double this usage. With the ONOS system we can deploy separate controllers as VMs operating on different servers if need be. The research in [7] highlights the amount of increased bandwidth between decentralized controllers communication as the number of nodes controlled is increased.

5   Conclusion and Future Work

In conclusion, the benefits of implementing an adaptive distributed and decentralized SDN in place of the common networking or in place of traditional SDN strategy has been discussed. It was shown that implementing the HDD-SDN architecture can provide safe fail-over using redundant systems and additional resilience in the presence of faulty or attacked data or communication nodes in the smart grid system. The paper also evaluated the use of a combination of machine learning clustering algorithms for parallel processing of anomaly detection and discussed potential approaches for automated determination of the number of clusters needed. K-means produced a high accuracy for identifying anomalies within normal traffic and incremental k-means produced a slightly lower accuracy with increased speed and fewer CPU and memory resources, indicating a possibility for scaling the system to much larger networks. In future work, the process for preprocessing of the features before executing the machine learning will be examined. In addition, we continue to develop the SDN architecture integration with the OPAL-RT Smart Grid test bed.

Acknowledgment. The authors would like to thank the Harris Corporation Excellence in Research program for providing funding for this research.

References

1. Monsanto, C., Reich, J., Foster, N., Rexford, J., Walker, D.: Composing software defined networks. In: The 10th USENIX Symposium on Networked Systems Design and Implementation (NSDI 2013), pp. 1–13. IEEE (2013)

2. Lin, H., Chen, C., Wang, J., Qi, J., Jin, D.: Self-healing attack-resilient PMU network for power system operation. IEEE Trans. Smart Grid 1 (2016)
3. Chen, N., Wang, M., Zhang, N., Shen, X.: SDN-based framework for the PEV integrated smart grid. IEEE Netw. **31**(2), 14–21 (2014)
4. Pisharody, S., Natarajan, J., Chowdhary, A., Alshalan, A., Huang, D.: Brew: a security policy analysis framework for distributed sdn-based cloud environments. IEEE Trans. Dependable Secur. Comput. **PP**(99), 87–93 (2017). https://doi.org/10.1109/TDSC.2017.2726066
5. Nkosi, M., Lysko, A., Ravhuanzwo, L., Nandeni, T., Engelberencht, A.: Classification of SDN distributed controller approaches: a brief overview. In: 2016 International Conference on Advances in Computing and Communication Engineering (ICACCE), ICACCE, pp. 342–344 (2016)
6. ONOS-Open Network Operating System, March 2018. https://wiki.onosproject.org/. Accessed 4 Mar 2018
7. Muqaddas, A., Giaccone, P., Bianco, A., Maier, G.: Inter-controller traffic to support consistency in ONOS clusters. IEEE Trans. Netw. Serv. Manag. **14**(11), 126–133 (2017)
8. Kopeikin, A., Ponda, S.S., Johnson, L.B., How, J.P.: Multi-UAV network control through dynamic task allocation: ensuring data-rate and bit-error-rate support. In: 2012 IEEE Globecom Workshops, pp. 1579–1584. IEEE (2012)
9. Limthong, K.: Real-time computer network anomaly detection using machine learning techniques. J. Adv. Comput. Netw. **1**(1), 126–133 (2013)
10. Yadav, A.: Incremental k-means clustering algorithms: a review. Int. J. Latest Trends Eng. Technol. (IJLTET) **5**(4), 126–133 (2015)
11. Dunn, J.C.: Well-seperated clusters and optimal fuzzy partitions. Cybernetics **4**(1), 95–104 (1974)
12. Davies, D.L., Bouldin, D.W.: A cluster seperation measure. IEEE Trans. Pattern Anal. Mach. Intell. **1**(2), 224–227 (1979)
13. Neal, R.M.: Markov chain sampling methods for Dirichlet process mixture models. Comput. Graph. Stat. **9**(2), 249–265 (2000)
14. KDD Cup 1999 Data, March 1999. http://kdd.ics.uci.edu/databases/kddcup99/kddcup99.html. Accessed 4 Mar 2018

Machine Learning-Based Real-Time Indoor Landmark Localization

Zhongliang Zhao$^{(\boxtimes)}$, Jose Carrera, Joel Niklaus, and Torsten Braun

Institute of Computer Science, University of Bern, 3012 Bern, Switzerland
{zhao,carrera,braun}@inf.unibe.ch, joel.niklaus@students.unibe.ch

Abstract. Nowadays, smartphones can collect huge amounts of data from their surroundings with the help of highly accurate sensors. Since the combination of the Received Signal Strengths of surrounding access points and sensor data is assumed to be unique in some locations, it is possible to use this information to accurately predict smartphones' indoor locations. In this work, we apply machine learning methods to derive the correlation between smartphones' locations and the received Wi-Fi signal strength and sensor values. We have developed an Android application that is able to distinguish between rooms on a floor, and special landmarks within the detected room. Our real-world experiment results show that the Voting ensemble predictor outperforms individual machine learning algorithms and it achieves the best indoor landmark localization accuracy of 94% in office-like environments. This work provides a coarse-grained indoor room recognition and landmark localization within rooms, which can be envisioned as a basis for accurate indoor positioning.

Keywords: Machine learning · Indoor localization
Real-time landmark detection

1 Introduction

High localization accuracy within buildings would be very useful - in particular, large complex buildings like shopping malls, airports and hospitals would be well served by this feature. It would make orientation within these highly complicated structures much easier and would diminish the need for big floor maps scattered all around these buildings. However, walls, roofs, windows and doors of the buildings greatly reduce the GPS signals carried by radio waves, which leads to a severe accuracy loss of GPS inside buildings.

Different solutions already exist for indoor localization of mobile devices such as Pedestrian Dead Reckoning (PDR) and Wi-Fi fingerprinting based methods [1, 2]. In PDR the future location of a smartphone user is predicted based on the current location, and the movement information derived from the inertial sensor

© IFIP International Federation for Information Processing 2018
Published by Springer Nature Switzerland AG 2018. All Rights Reserved
K. R. Chowdhury et al. (Eds.): WWIC 2018, LNCS 10866, pp. 95–106, 2018.
https://doi.org/10.1007/978-3-030-02931-9_8

measurements. In Wi-Fi fingerprinting, the Received Signal Strength (RSS) values of several access points in range are collected and stored together with the coordinates of the location. A new set of RSS values is then compared with the stored fingerprints and the location of the closest match is returned.

In contrast to outdoors, building interiors normally have a large number of different Wi-Fi access points constantly emitting signals. By scanning the area around the device, we can measure the received signal strength of each of the nearby access points. Because there are typically so many of them, we presume that the list of all these values combined is unique at every distinct point in the building. Furthermore, we can strongly assume that these values are also constant over time as the access points are fixed in place and are constantly emitting signals of the same strength. Of course, there may be occasional changes, for instance if the network is remodeled, but we expect these changes to be infrequent.

In this way, we can collect lots of labeled location data of the building. However, because each data point may contain a very large number of Wi-Fi access point RSS measurements and magnetic field measurements, the data is very complex. Therefore, we propose using supervised Machine Learning (ML) methods to process this large amount of collected data. By training a classifier (supervised learning algorithm such as K-Nearest-Neighbor) on the collected labeled data, rules can be extracted. Feeding in the actual live data (RSS values, magnetic field values, illuminance level, etc.) of a moving user, the trained classifier can then predict the user's location on a coarse-grained level. We propose to apply machine learning methods, both individual predictors and ensemble predictors, to solve this task due to the large amount of features that are available in indoor environments, such as Wi-Fi RSS values, magnetic field values, and other sensor data. We expect that ensemble predictors can outperform the individual machine learning algorithms to discover patterns in the data, which can then be used to differentiate between different rooms and regions within the detected rooms.

The rest of the paper is organized as follows. In Sect. 2 we present some related work in indoor localization and landmark detection. Section 3 describes the used machine learning models, including the individual and ensemble ones, as well as the considered features to conduct the indoor landmark localization task. Section 4 presents implementation and experiment details. Section 5 discusses the performance results of our approach. Section 6 concludes the paper.

2   Related Work

Various machine learning-based approaches that use fingerprinting to estimate user indoor locations have been proposed. Machine learning-based indoor localization can be classified into generative or discriminative methods, which build the machine learning model using a joint probability or conditional probability respectively [1,2]. K-Nearest-Neighbor (KNN) is the most basic and popular discriminative technique. Based on a similarity measure such as a distance function, the KNN algorithm determines the k closest matches in the signal space to the target. Then, the location of the target can be estimated by the average of the coordinates of the k neighbors [3]. Generative localization methods apply statistical approaches, e.g., Hidden Markov Model [4], Bayesian Inference [5], Gaussian Processes [6], on the Wi-Fi fingerprint database. Thus, the accuracy can obviously be improved by adding more measurements. In [6] for instance, Gaussian Processes are used to estimate the signal propagation model through an indoor environment. There is a limited number of works that have focused in reducing off-line efforts in learning-based approaches for indoor localization [7–9]. These approaches reduce the off-line effort by reducing either the number of samples collected at each survey point or the number of survey points or both of them. Then, a generative model is applied to reinforce the sample collection data. In [7] for instance, a linear interpolation method is used. In [8], a Bayesian model is applied. In [9], authors propose a propagation method to generate data from collected samples. In [2], authors combine characteristics of generative and discriminative models in a hybrid model. Although this hybrid model reduces offline efforts, it still relies on a number of samples collected from fixed survey points (i.e., labeled samples) along the environment. Therefore, to maintain high accuracy, the number of survey points shall be increased in larger environments. Thus, collecting samples from numerous survey points will become a demanding process, which makes the system unsuitable to large environments. In [10], authors validated the performance of different individual machine learning approaches for indoor positioning systems. However, they rather compare the results without any deep analysis of the performance difference. Moreover, they did not discuss how ensemble learning approaches could be used to enhance system performance.

In this work we present and analyze the performance of different individual predictors as well as ensemble predictors for the indoor landmark localization problem. This work could also be used as a basis of indoor tracking systems to firstly locate the target with a coarse-grained accuracy using indoor landmark localization, which then triggers the real-time localization algorithm to locate the object around the detected landmarks. The located landmark can also be used to correct the localization failures like the kidnapped robot problem [11].

3   Machine Learning-Based Indoor Landmark Localization

An indoor landmark is defined as a small area within a room. The aim of the indoor landmark localization system presented in this work is to improve the accuracy of indoor landmark recognition using machine learning approaches. We do this by excluding all the possible locations of the user within the room if the system predicts the others by using landmarks. Thus, when a landmark has been recognized, the indoor positioning system can use the identified coarse-grained locations to optimize the positioning accuracy, such as revising positioning errors.

3.1 Algorithms

In this section, we shortly describe the machine learning algorithms that are used in this work to perform the room landmark localizations.

Naive Bayes (NB) classifiers are a family of simple probabilistic classifiers based on applying Bayes' theorem with strong (naive) independence assumptions between the features.

K-Nearest Neighbors (KNN) is a non-parametric method used for classification and regression. In both cases, the input consists of the k closest training examples in the feature space.

Support Vector Machine (SVM) is a supervised learning model with associated learning algorithms that analyze data used for classification and regression. Given a set of training examples, each is marked as belonging to one or the other category. An SVM training algorithm builds a model that assigns new data measurements to one category or the other, making it a non-probabilistic binary linear classifier.

Multilayer Perceptron (MLP) is a class of feed-forward artificial neural network. An MLP consists of at least three layers of nodes. Except for the input nodes, each node is a neuron that uses a nonlinear activation function.

Voting is one of the simplest ensemble predictors. It combines the predictions from multiple individual machine learning algorithms. It works by first creating two or more standalone prediction models from the training dataset. A Voting classifier can then be used to wrap the models and average the predictions of the sub-models when asked to make predictions for new data.

3.2 Features

In a machine learning-based classification task, the attributes of the classes are denoted as features. Each feature is describing an aspect of the classes. In our case features are our measurements, for instance an RSS value. To deliver good machine learning prediction accuracy it is very important to select the right attributes/features and to also modify certain features or even create new features out of existing features.

Wi-Fi RSS values provide the core data as they contribute the most to the performance of the ML methods. The smartphone scans the surrounding Wi-Fi access points, obtains and registers the RSS values of each access point. Wi-Fi RSS values depend on the distance between the smartphone and the Wi-Fi access points. Normally, the Wi-Fi RSS values in our datasets were between $-20\,\mathrm{dBm}$ and $-90\,\mathrm{dBm}$.

Magnetic Field (MF). The device's sensors measure the magnetic field in the device's coordinate system. As the user walks around, the orientation of the device may change all the time. Therefore, we have to collect all possible values from every orientation in every point in the training phase. This would result in a huge amount of data and the training performance would be inaccurate.

Light sensors might also be helpful to identify rooms. For instance, a room facing a window will clearly be brighter than one surrounded by walls only. As shown in Sect. 5 this does improve the prediction accuracy. However, these assumptions are not stable, as the illuminance level might change over time. Therefore, it is better to work with light differences instead of absolute values.

4   Implementation and Experiments

This section explains how the indoor room landmarks are defined and presents details about how to make the room landmark localization using ML algorithms.

4.1   Room and Landmark Recognition

A room landmark is defined as a small area within a room, and room landmark fingerprint database includes the Wi-FI RSS, MF measurements, and illuminance level data measured within that small area. In the room recognition phase we distinguish several rooms on the same floor. In the landmark recognition phase we distinguish several landmarks inside the detected room. Therefore, we define two landmarks in a small room with size of 3×3 m, and four landmarks in a normal office-sized room (5×5 m). In a big room (7×7 m) we define five landmarks, one in each corner and one in the center, as shown in Fig. 1.

4.2   System Architecture

Figure 2 shows the data flow and the different components of our developed Android app. Sensor and Wi-Fi RSS values are measured by the smartphone and received by the app. We then perform the data training process offline in a PC to pass the collected data to the Model Training component, which applies different machine learning algorithms to build the models. The trained models are then optimized and transfered to the app on the smartphone for online experiments.

Considering that the landmark detection accuracy can be influenced by some environmental parameters, we conduct some experiments to determine how parameters such as AP position or number of APs influence the accuracy of the Wi-Fi-based fingerprinting landmark detection approach. Additionally, we perform experiments to show how the accuracy is improved by considering additional features such as magnetic field (MF) values and light illuminance level readings. As shown in Fig. 3, we define 9 wall separated areas in our experiment

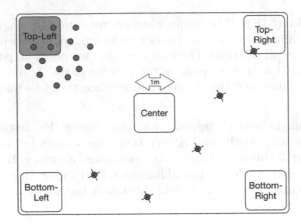

Fig. 1. Five landmarks and the collection of red points (location examples) predicted by the indoor landmark localization system. (Color figure online)

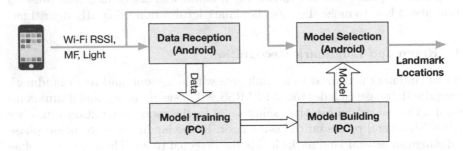

Fig. 2. The architecture of the implemented Android app.

environment. Hereafter, we refer to these areas as rooms. In our experiments, we do not need to know the locations of the APs, while only the fingerprints of Wi-Fi RSSI, MF readings, and illuminance level readings are recorded during the data collection process.

Parameters of learning-based algorithms are optimized from training data. Additionally, certain algorithms also have parameters that are not optimized during the training process. These parameters are called hyperparameters, which have significant impact on the performance of the learning-based algorithm. Therefore, we use a nested cross validation technique to adjust them. The nested cross validation technique defines an inner and outer cross validation. The inner cross validation is intended to select the model with optimized hyperparameters, whereas outer cross validation is used to obtain an estimation of the generalization error. Ten-fold cross validation was applied on both inner and outer cross validation. The classifiers were optimized over a set of hyperparameters. We optimized the global blend percentage ratio hyperparameter for KNN, kernel type function for SVM, number of hidden layers and neurons per layer for MLP. Based on the parameter optimization process, we established the optimal hyper-

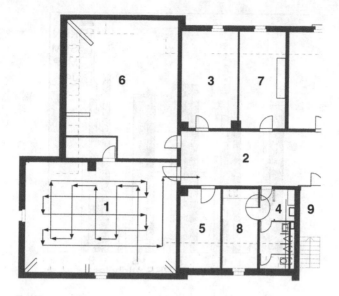

Fig. 3. Experiment scenario and data collection path.

parameter values for the classifiers as follows: global blend percent ratio of 30% for KNN, single order polynomial kernel, $c = 1$, $\gamma = 0.0$ for SVM, and single hidden layer with 10 neurons for MLP.

4.3 Datasets

To test the room landmark detection performance, we performed experiments on the third floor of the Computer Science building of the University of Bern, as shown in Fig. 3. During the experiments, we collected 14569 data points in total, 3061 data points were collected from the biggest room (1) and 514 data points were from the smallest room (4). Collecting the training dataset takes around 50 min. With the collected data, we build models with different data: the first one builds the fingerprint using only collected Wi-Fi RSSI data, the second one using Wi-Fi RSS together with MF readings, and the third one with Wi-Fi RSS, MF readings, and illuminance level readings.

As described before, to build the landmark fingerprint database, we ask a person to walk randomly around each room holding the phone in his/her hand. Landmark fingerprint database entries must be collected equally distributed along the whole area in each room. The data collection rate is only constrained by computational capabilities of the Wi-Fi sensor of the smartphone. Thus, in our experiments every data measurement was collected at a rate of 3 entries/second. Because our approach does not need to predefine any survey point, the time needed to build the landmark fingerprint database is proportional to the number of collected instances multiplied by the instance collection rate.

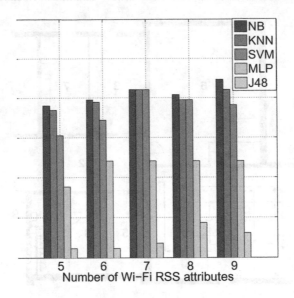

Fig. 4. Landmark prediction performance with different numbers of Wi-Fi RSS values.

5 Results

5.1 Indoor Landmark Localization Accuracy

This section discusses the accuracy of the landmark detection model when different classifiers and features are used. When comparing their performance, it is impossible to define a single metric that provides a fair comparison in all possible applications. We focus on the metrics of prediction accuracy, which refers to the percentages of correct room recognition and landmark localization within the detected room. Landmark definition is described in Sect. 4.1.

At first we use only Wi-Fi RSS values as inputs to machine learning algorithms. Figure 4 shows the classification accuracy of different predictors when different numbers of Wi-Fi RSS values are used. As we can see, starting from 5 RSS values, more RSS inputs increase the prediction accuracy for most of the predictors. Nevertheless, after 7 Wi-Fi RSS values are used, the improvement of adding more RSS values is almost negligible in all tested classifiers, and some of the predictors even got reduced accuracy when additional RSS values are considered. We think that the signal interferences may be the reason for the worse performance when more than 7 Wi-Fi RSS values are utilized. Therefore, we take 7 Wi-Fi RSS as the default configuration for the following experiments.

Next, we compare the classification accuracy when using only Wi-Fi RSS, Wi-Fi RSS plus MF, and Wi-Fi RSS plus MF and illuminance levels. Figure 5 shows the performance evaluation of the selected classifiers obtained with different feature combinations. The best performance is reached by the Naive Bayes classifier, which achieves 90.13% of instances correctly classified if the fingerprint is composed by Wi-Fi RSS, MF readings, and illuminance levels. By using Wi-Fi

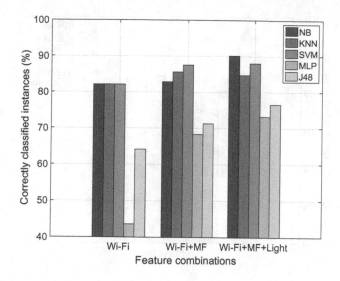

Fig. 5. Landmark prediction performance when using different features.

RSS, MF readings, and illuminance levels in the room landmark recognition, the accuracy is improved in all tested classifiers.

As mentioned before, hyperparameters have significant impacts on the performance of the learning-based algorithm. Figure 6 shows the performance of the selected classifiers with the hyperparameters optimized. The classifiers are all fed with Wi-Fi RSS plus MF and illuminance levels. As we can see, compared to results in Fig. 5, all the classifiers have improved performance, and MLP even reaches an accuracy of 92.08%. We also include the results of Voting, which combines the prediction results of MLP, Naive Bayes, KNN, and SVM using majority vote. It shows that Voting can reach an accuracy of 94.04%.

5.2 Result Analysis

In indoor environments, Wi-Fi RSSI and MF measurement vary dependent on locations. However, these values will remain similar on nearby positions. For example, on locations close to landmark borders, high similarities will be observed on the RSS values. These similarities could lead to misclassification problems. From Fig. 5 we can see that KNN and SVM outperform others in terms of accuracy when Wi-Fi RSS and MF readings are used. This is because KNN is an instance-based learning algorithm, which uses entropy as a distance measure to determine how similar two instances are. Thus, this method is more sensitive to slight variations upon the instance as unity. J48 builds the classification model by parsing the entropy of information at attribute level. It means that J48 measures entropy in the attribute domain to decide which attribute goes into a decision node. Therefore, the classification model is prone to misclassification in the landmark detection problem. When the illuminance level is included

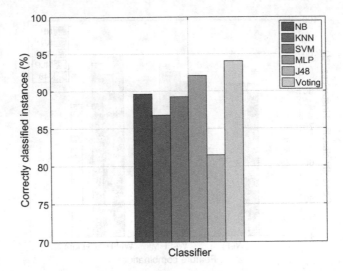

Fig. 6. Landmark prediction performance of individual predictors with optimized hyperparameters and Voting ensemble predictor.

as input feature to predictors, Naive Bayes outperforms others. This is because the feature of illuminance level is completely independent from other radio signal measurements, which fits with Naive Bayes' strong assumptions about the independence of each input variable.

Table 1. The confusion matrix for MLP with optimized hyperparameters.

a	b	c	d	e	f	g	h	i	<-- classified as
2164	0	0	0	0	0	0	0	0	a = 1
0	527	0	0	0	0	0	0	138	b = 2
0	25	865	0	0	0	0	0	0	c = 3
0	9	0	154	0	0	0	128	0	d = 4
0	43	0	0	642	0	0	0	0	e = 5
0	25	0	0	44	1249	0	0	0	f = 6
0	6	0	0	0	0	1064	0	1	g = 7
0	0	0	149	0	0	0	498	0	h = 8
0	0	0	51	0	0	0	64	778	i = 9

To further explain how the Voting predictor improves the performance of individual predictors, we show the confusion matrix of room recognition using MLP, SVM, Naive Bayes (NB), and Voting in Tables 1, 2 and 3. We can observe that room 2 is correctly identified 527 times by MLP, 632 times by SVM and 393 times by NB. As a consequence, SVM seems to be better in predicting room 2 as compared to other two predictors. Furthermore, NB does not seem to have less misclassification of class b compared to other two predictors. Analyzing the results from the above-mentioned tables, MLP has misclassified class b 138 times, NB 272 times, and SVM only 33 times. From the confusion matrix of

Table 2. The confusion matrix for SVM with optimized hyperparameters.

a	b	c	d	e	f	g	h	i	<-- classified as
2164	0	0	0	0	0	0	0	0	a = 1
10	632	0	0	0	0	0	0	23	b = 2
0	55	799	0	0	36	0	0	0	c = 3
0	147	0	144	0	0	0	0	0	d = 4
0	43	0	0	642	0	0	0	0	e = 5
204	69	32	0	0	1013	0	0	0	f = 6
0	126	0	0	0	0	945	0	0	g = 7
0	0	0	119	0	0	0	528	0	h = 8
0	0	0	57	0	0	0	7	829	i = 9

Table 3. The confusion matrix for Naive Bayes with optimized hyperparameters.

a	b	c	d	e	f	g	h	i	<-- classified as
2149	0	0	0	15	0	0	0	0	a = 1
0	393	9	153	0	0	0	110	0	b = 2
0	0	876	0	0	14	0	0	0	c = 3
0	130	0	135	0	0	0	26	0	d = 4
1	0	44	0	628	0	0	12	0	e = 5
0	0	101	0	0	1217	0	0	0	f = 6
0	59	12	0	0	0	973	0	27	g = 7
0	0	0	119	0	0	0	528	0	h = 8
0	0	0	0	0	0	0	64	829	i = 9

Table 4. The confusion matrix for the Voting ensemble classifier.

a	b	c	d	e	f	g	h	i	<-- classified as
2164	0	0	0	0	0	0	0	0	a = 1
0	663	0	0	0	0	0	0	2	b = 2
0	25	865	0	0	0	0	0	0	c = 3
0	32	0	143	0	0	0	116	0	d = 4
0	43	0	0	642	0	0	0	0	e = 5
0	69	0	0	0	1249	0	0	0	f = 6
0	43	0	0	0	0	1027	0	1	g = 7
0	0	0	119	0	0	0	528	0	h = 8
0	0	0	0	0	0	0	64	829	i = 9

Voting, as shown in Table 4, we can see that the Voting ensemble predictor adopts behaviors of different individual predictors. For instance, it adopts the good behavior of MLP and Naive Bayes, which leads to a much better prediction accuracy for room 2. This can be observed from the only two misclassifications of room 2 as room 9 as shown in Table 4. Unfortunately, it still has problems in some classifications. For instance, there are 116 misclassification of room 8 as room 4, which is probably due to a higher weight assigned to MLP instead of SVM. In general, it can be observed that the Voting ensemble predictor improves the accuracy, while there are still difficulties to distinguish small rooms that are next to each other, as room 8 and 4 depicted in Fig. 3.

6   Conclusions and Future Work

This work analyzes the performance of 5 common individual predictors and 1 ensemble predictor in indoor landmark localization to distinguish rooms on a floor and special landmarks using machine learning methods. We have validated the performance of the system using different smartphone sensor measurements, such as Wi-Fi RSS, MF readings, and illuminance levels. Evaluation results show that the Voting ensemble predictor achieves the best indoor landmark localization accuracy of 94%. In the future, we will further optimize the hyperparameter cross-validation procedure and integrate this work with an indoor tracking system to firstly locate the target with a coarse-grained accuracy, which then triggers the tracking algorithm to track the object around the located landmarks.

Acknowledgements. This work was supported by the Swiss National Science Foundation #154458.

References

1. He, S., Chan, S.: Wi-Fi fingerprint-based indoor positioning: recent advances and comparisons. IEEE Commun. Surv. Tutor. **18**, 466–490 (2016)
2. Ouyang, R.W., Wong, A.K.S., Lea, C.T., Chiang, M.: Indoor location estimation with reduced calibration exploiting unlabeled data via hybrid generative/discriminative learning. IEEE Trans. Mob. Comput. **11**, 1613–1626 (2012)
3. Lakmali, B., Wijesinghe, W., de SIva, K., Liyanagama, K., Dias, S.: Design, implementation & testing of positioning techniques in mobile networks. In: The 3rd International Conference on Information and Automation for Sustainability
4. Ghahramani, Z.: An introduction to hidden Markov models and Bayesian networks. Int. J. Pattern Recognit. Artif. Intell. **15**, 9–42 (2001)
5. Bousquet, O., von Luxburg, U., Ratsch, G.: Bayesian inference: an introduction to principles and practice in machine learning. Fresenius Environ. Bull. 20(5) (2004)
6. Ferris, B., Hahnel, D., Fox, D.: Gaussian processes for signal strength-based location estimation. In: Procedures of Robotics Science and Systems (2006)
7. Chai, X., Yang, Q.: Reducing the calibration effort for probabilistic indoor location estimation. IEEE Trans. Mob. Comput. **6**(6), 649–662 (2016)
8. Madigan, D., Einahrawy, E., Martin, R.,Ju, W., krishnan, P., Krishnakumar, A.:Bayesian indoor positioning systems. In: IEEE INFOCOM, vol. 2, pp. 1217–1227 (2005)
9. Liu, S., Luo, H., Zou, S.: A low-cost and accurate indoor localization algorithm using label propagation based semi supervised learning. In: Fifth International Conference Mobile Ad-Hoc and Sensor Networks, pp. 108–111 (2009)
10. Mascharka, D., Manley, E.: LIPS: learning based indoor positioning system using mobile phone-based sensors. In: 2016 13th IEEE Annual Consumer Communications and Networking Conference (CCNC), Las Vegas, NV, pp. 968–971 (2016)
11. Carrera, J., Zhao, Z., Braun, T., Li, Z., Neto, A.: A real-time robust indoor tracking system in smartphones. J. Comput. Commun. https://doi.org/10.1016/j.comcom.2017.09.004

An Intelligent Defense and Filtration Platform for Network Traffic

Mehrnoosh Monshizadeh[1,2]([✉]), Vikramajeet Khatri[1] [iD], Buse Atli[2], and Raimo Kantola[2]

[1] Nokia Bell Labs, Espoo, Finland
{mehrnoosh.monshizadeh,
vikramajeet.khatri}@nokia-bell-labs.com
[2] Department of Comnet, Aalto University, Espoo, Finland
{mehrnoosh.monshizadeh, buse.atli,
raimo.kantola}@aalto.fi

Abstract. Hybrid Anomaly Detection Model (HADM) is a security platform to detect and prevent cyber-attacks on communication networks. The platform uses a combination of linear and learning algorithms combined with protocol analyzer. The linear algorithms filter and extract distinctive attributes and features of the cyber-attacks while the learning algorithms use these attributes and features to identify new types of cyber-attacks. The protocol analyzer in this platform classifies and filters vulnerable protocols to avoid unnecessary computation load. The use of linear algorithms in conjunction with learning algorithms allows the HADM to achieve improved efficiency in terms of accuracy and computation time in order to detect cyber-attacks over existing solutions.

Keywords: Security · Cloud computing · Internet of things · Machine learning Anomaly detection

1 Introduction

Although the Intrusion Detection System (IDS) is considered as a well-known mechanism to monitor and detect malicious traffic in communication networks, the cost and high processing time is a challenge to handle large amount of data. Moreover, IDSs and all other detection systems or mechanisms are applicable for known attacks rather than unknown or new attacks.

Data Mining (DM) is a technology that uses highly developed and complex algorithms for processing large volume of data [1]. However, complexity of mentioned algorithms in [1] results to high computation time. In order to solve this problem, network traffic flow control in combination with DM techniques are proposed in this paper. The protocol analyzer in this platform classifies and filters vulnerable protocols to avoid unnecessary computation load. On the other hand, each data set includes hundreds of features that may cause performance degradation in detection process. To overcome this problem, feature selection methods are used to select less number of features and reduce the dimensions of the dataset [1]. In addition, the use of linear algorithms in conjunction with learning algorithms improves accuracy and computation

© IFIP International Federation for Information Processing 2018
Published by Springer Nature Switzerland AG 2018. All Rights Reserved
K. R. Chowdhury et al. (Eds.): WWIC 2018, LNCS 10866, pp. 107–118, 2018.
https://doi.org/10.1007/978-3-030-02931-9_9

time. Linear algorithms will detect the attack in general level regardless of their types while learning algorithms cluster the attacks in different categories. This mechanism decreases the load of input data for the learning algorithm that is the most time consuming part because of its complex structure [2].

The rest of the paper is organized as follows. Section 2 briefly reviews related work and research motivation. Section 3 describes the Hybrid Anomaly Detection Model (HADM) architecture. Section 4 discusses the implementation and results. The discussion on future work presented in Sect. 5 and last section concludes the paper.

2 Related Work and Research Motivation

Di Pietro et al. [3] proposes anomaly detection using Deep Packet Inspection (DPI) and machine learning methods upon selected captured packets. Based on output from machine learning method, the packet capture criterion is adjusted again to capture further packets and again fed into DPI and machine learning methods. The machine learning model may use k-Nearest Neighbor (k-NN), replicator nearest neighbor, Bayesian networks, k-means, Artificial Neural Networks (ANN) and Support Vector Machines (SVM) algorithms. However, the learning process of algorithm is not explained and packet capture criterion does not consider taking all packets for one or more protocols.

Vasseur et al. [4] proposes an approach for training supervised learning classifiers for effective detection and cites Deep Neural Networks (DNN) classifier as an example. The study mentions Distributed Denial of Service (DDoS) attacks. Security device in this study refers to firewall, IDS, Intrusion Prevention System (IPS) etc.; which use traffic signatures to access traffic in the network. Distributed learning agents refer to components or modules which use machine learning based anomaly detection to analyze or access traffic in the network. A supervisory device in the network receives traffic from both security device and distributed learning agent; and combines the received traffic to train the classifier. Then, the supervisory device assigns the trained classifier to one or more distributed learning agents. Since, the challenge in the supervised learning classifiers is the labelled training data, this study aims to optimize training by continuously providing the labelled data. However, this study does not consider other machine learning methods, does not use protocol analyzer for filtering the traffic to be analyzed considering the traffic bandwidth and traffic collection period in order to reduce the load.

In the study by Pietro et al. [5], a network trains and generates an expected traffic model based on a set of training data. The device receives an unexpected behavior notification from a particular node based on a comparison between the expected traffic model and an observed traffic behavior by the node. The particular node also prevents the machine learning attack detector from analyzing the observed traffic behavior. The device updates the machine learning attack detector to account for the observed traffic behavior. This method receives a model of normal traffic behavior. The Signature Generator Entity (SGE) compares the input data with the expected normal traffic models. If they are different, SGE generates a signature for the attack class and trains the ANN accordingly with new information for the next detection phase. This model may have high false positive rate since it compares input traffic only with an expected model.

In the study by Yadav et al. [6], network traffic data is collected from several sensors, distributed and installed into network components. The network traffic data comprises process, user and host information. The analytics module inside a network device or Virtual Machine (VM) identifies anomalies within the network traffic data based on dynamic modeling of network behavior. The anomaly detection in this study is based on the honeypot to collect labelled malicious network traffic as an input to the anomaly detection unit comprising of unsupervised and supervised machine learning algorithms. The honeypot relies only on received attacks and not the other attacks. This study points in general dynamic machine learning.

In this study we propose a platform compromises of two main parts where each part independently increases the efficiency of attack detection based on the factors such as precision, recall, accuracy and computation time. While part 1 of the model utilizes some algorithms and the protocol analyzer for traffic filtration, reducing the processing time and increasing the accuracy, the part 2 applies a dynamic feature selection with genetic algorithm to classify unknown attacks and increase the accuracy as well.

The HADM model comprises a protocol analyzer, linear and learning algorithms as well as other modules. Since some protocols such as streaming protocols are not vulnerable and attackers usually target specific protocols, protocol analyzer in this platform classifies and filters vulnerable protocols to avoid unnecessary computation load. Protocol analyzer forwards the filtered traffic either to a linear algorithm only for Denial of Service (DoS) detection or to a combination of a linear and a learning algorithm for other types of attacks. The linear algorithm initially defines if the traffic is secure or unsecure regardless of the attack type. In addition, it extracts the proper features in order to provide them to a learning algorithm in order to classify already known attacks and detect unknown attacks. The other counter measurement located after the learning algorithm extracts information for known attacks (which network is already protected against them) from other deployed security mechanisms in the network e.g., firewall, IDS, DPI etc. It compares the extracted information with the attack received from the linear algorithm and drops the similar attacks. In each step, a feedback is sent to a database for next level detection. In the learning algorithm, the received attack is assigned to one of the attack clusters. In addition, algorithm changes its structure and input weights dynamically based on the received feedback. If the attack does not belong to any of the mentioned clusters, it is assigned to a totally new cluster. This novel mechanism dynamically defines new features in order to detect new types of attack.

3   Architecture

As it is shown in Fig. 1, the HADM functionality is divided into three phases: protocol analyzer, dynamic machine learning and validator & database.

3.1 Protocol Analyzer

The first phase of the proposed HADM is called protocol analyzer which filters vulnerable protocols. The protocol refers to communication protocol over which the traffic is carried on such as HyperText Transfer Protocol (HTTP) and Transmission Control Protocol (TCP). As it is shown in Fig. 2, protocol analyzer consists of five modules.

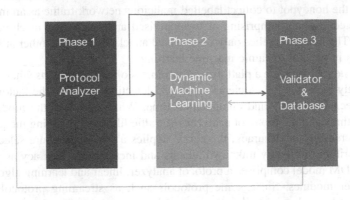

Fig. 1. HADM on operational level in brief

Decision Module. This module includes a list of vulnerable protocols which are predefined and also dynamically updated based on the received feedback from log file via database. Some protocols such as HTTP and TCP are well known vulnerable protocols while others like Real Time Streaming Protocol (RTSP) could be a safe protocol. It checks whether traffic is carried on any of the listed vulnerable protocol.

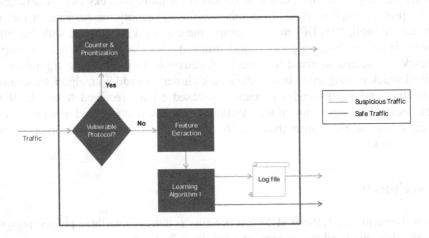

Fig. 2. Protocol analyzer

Counter and Prioritization Module. The function of this module is based on the occurrence threshold (n) and prioritization. It means that if the vulnerable protocol carries suspected traffic for n times, then this module will forward the suspicious traffic to the next layer for detection and labelling. The idea is to cycle all possible vulnerable protocols over an agreed time window (1 h, 1 day etc.). The module only keeps a certain number of vulnerable protocol in the list which is based on prioritization. For example, if we already have 20 vulnerable protocols and 21st comes up, then the counter must prioritize only 20 of these protocols. The prioritization is based on the counting occurrence over the time window. The sole purpose of this technique is to reduce the computation load of traffic analysis.

Feature Extraction. It extracts the best features from the suspicious protocol. This module is utilized in second phase as well.

Learning Algorithm I. If the protocol (that carries the input traffic) is not listed as vulnerable, traffic is still sent to this learning algorithm for analysis and reconfirmation. The learning algorithm I will check whether the protocol is vulnerable or not. Our proposed platform is tested with Extreme Learning Machines (ELM), Self-Organizing Map (SOM) and MultiLayer Perceptron (MLP) algorithms.

Log file. Every time the learning algorithm I in the protocol analyzer detects a new vulnerable protocol, it is recorded into the log file and a feedback will be sent to decision module via database. The log file records packet features such as time stamp, packet size, Internet Protocol (IP) header and information on other layers (Ethernet, TCP, application layer).

3.2 Dynamic Machine Learning

The second phase of the proposed HADM combines linear and learning algorithms for efficient attack detection. As it is illustrated in Fig. 3, dynamic machine learning consists of the following modules in addition to feature extraction that has been explained earlier.

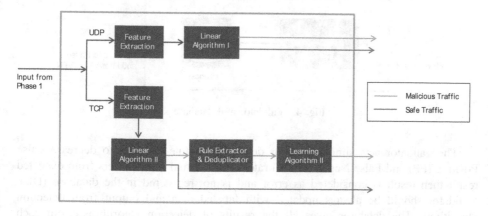

Fig. 3. Dynamic machine learning

Linear Algorithm I. This module analyzes User Datagram Protocol (UDP) traffic to detect UDP DoS attacks. Therefore, a separate algorithm such as Decision Tree (DT) is considered for this module in order to avoid overloading the rest of the proposed hybrid model. However, the decision tree algorithm can be replaced based on the operator demand, we have considered it due to its low processing time.

Rule Extractor and Deduplicator. This module filters the known attacks that system is already protected against, by using other deployed security mechanisms and forwards other attacks to learning algorithm II for labelling. A set of rules are extracted from those deployed security mechanisms in the network, the extracted information is compared with received attack from linear algorithm I and is dropped if it is similar. Rules in this module are updated dynamically based on input from the parallel security mechanisms.

Learning Algorithm II. This module is the last detection layer. Initial features and clusters are defined for the algorithm during the training process in order to cluster different attacks such as Botnet attack (B) and Malicious codes (M). At first, the traffic is labelled to one of the clusters based on their similarity or distance. Since the traffic that arrives to this module has been already identified as attack, if it does not belong to any of the mentioned clusters then it is considered as new type of attack (N) and a cluster will be created for it. The features of the new type of attack (N) must be added to the algorithm accordingly. The implementation of the proposed platform with Artificial Neural Networks (ANN) and Genetic Algorithm (GA) is already ongoing by authors and results will be presented in future paper. Other potential unsupervised algorithms can be SOM and hierarchical clustering.

3.3   Validator and Database

The last phase of the proposed HADM validates detected attacks, stores them into the database and shares the updates to all relevant modules. It consists of following modules as shown in Fig. 4.

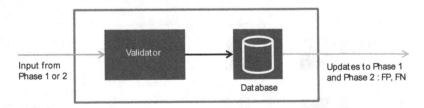

Fig. 4. Validator and database

The validator acts similar to error detection module in order to decrease False Positive (FP) and False Negative (FN) rates. If the actual result differs from expected result then result is considered as error and is not registered in the database (DB). Validator should be always updated with labeled data and output from detection algorithms. The database saves all the results of detection algorithms; from each algorithm, a sample of the outcome (feedback) is sent to database that will be used in the future detection. A database contains known attacks, new attacks and dropped attacks.

4   Implementation Phases

As it is shown in Fig. 5, the implementation of HADM platform is divided into two parts. Due to space limitation, the part 1 is presented in this paper while the implementation and experimental results of part 2 will be published in a separate paper. In this section, we first introduce the algorithms and feature extraction methods that are applied for mentioned algorithms. Next, we describe the selected datasets for the experimental study. Finally, we present the measures employed to evaluate the performance of each algorithm independently and also for the integrated scenario.

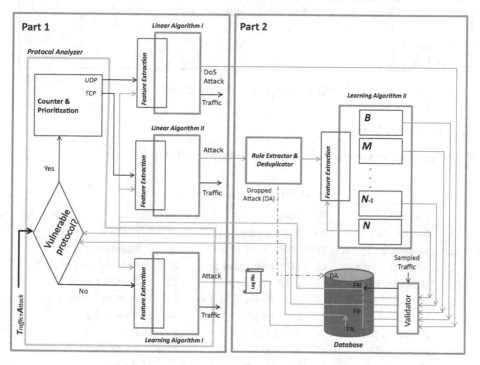

Fig. 5. Hybrid Anomaly Detection Model (HADM)

4.1   Applied Algorithms

In order to evaluate HADM, different algorithms including ELM, MLP (with 10 and 50 hidden nodes), k-Nearest Neighbor (k-NN), Support Vector Machine (SVM), Decision Tree (DT) and Logistic Regression (LR) are applied. In addition, our simple Decision maker algorithm (Algorithm D) is used in protocol analyzer to filter vulnerable protocol. The algorithm D is shown in Fig. 6.

```
for each packet do:
    if packet is encapsulated then
        decapsulate packet
    else
        if packet contains vulnerable protocol then
            if packet is carried over UDP then
                forward packet to Linear Algorithm I
            elseif packet is carried over TCP then
                forward packet to Linear Algorithm II
            end if
        elseif packet does not contain vulnerable protocol then
            forward packet to Learning Algorithm I
        end if
    end if
end for
```

Fig. 6. Pseudocode for algorithm D

4.2   Feature Selection

The original dataset contains 27 features as shown in Table 1.

Table 1. Features in datasets

No.	Feature	No.	Feature	No.	Feature
1	Ethernet size	10	IP destination	19	Connection starting time
2	Ethernet destination	11	TCP source port	20	IP fragmentation flag
3	Ethernet source	12	TCP destination port	21	IP fragmentation overlap
4	IP header length	13	UDP source port	22	TCP ACK flag
5	IP type of service	14	UDP destination port	23	TCP retransmission
6	IP length	15	UDP length	24	TCP push flag
7	IP time to live	16	ICMP type	25	TCP SYN flag
8	IP protocol	17	ICMP code	26	TCP FIN flag
9	IP source	18	Duration of connection	27	TCP urgent flag

Since there are not many variations on features related to protocol, for learning algorithm I in protocol analyzer module, we considered 9 fixed features including source IP address (saddr1, saddr2, saddr3, saddr4), destination IP address (daddr1, daddr2, daddr3, daddr4) and time to live (ip.ttl). Three different feature selection methods including Chi2, FScore and SVMonline have been applied on linear algorithm

I and II and the best combinations for both feature selection methods and algorithms have been selected based on the achieved efficiency. The final combinations include FScore for LR and Chi2 for k-NN. The selected best features for these algorithms can be seen in Table 2.

Table 2. Selected features for each algorithm

Linear algorithm I (k-NN)				Linear algorithm II (LR)			
No.	Feature	No.	Feature	No.	Feature	No.	Feature
1	SDC2	6	dstport	1	daddr4	6	saddr2
2	daddr2	7	srcport	2	SMC3	7	saddr4
3	SMC1	8	daddr4	3	ip.len	8	SDC1
4	saddr2	9	saddr4	4	frame.len	9	daddr2
5	SMC3	10	ip.ttl	5	daddr3	10	SMC2

4.3 Data Preprocessing

The ISCX-2012 dataset exhibits realistic network behavior and contains diverse intrusion scenarios. The dataset includes network traffic on HTTP, SMTP, SSH, IMAP, POP3, and FTP protocols with FTP and SSH password brute force, Java based Meterpreter, Add new Superuser, Linux Meterpreter payload and C100Webshel attacks [7]. To evaluate HADM efficiency, the modified version of the ISCX-2012 [8] dataset with diverse attacks have been used. Since the ISCX-2012 dataset lacks the DoS attack on UDP protocol, we extracted the UDP DoS from UNSW-NB15 dataset [9] and injected to the ISCX-2012 dataset. The final dataset is classified in three categories: normal, attack and unknown. The IP address and hex MAC address of the applied dataset are transformed into separate numeric attributes to improve the performance of the algorithms.

Table 3 shows the distribution of each intrusion type in the training and testing data.

Table 3. Distribution of packets in dataset

Data	Normal	DoS	Other attacks	Unknown	Total
Training (2/3)	1419441	47198	131713	2359518	3957870
Testing (1/3)	709723	23599	65856	1179763	1978941

4.4 Experimental Results

All the experiments are carried out on a workstation with Intel core i5 Quad @2.6 GHz, 16 GB RAM, 500 GB HDD. The scripts were developed in Python in a Linux environment. All applied algorithms in the evaluation process of HADM are trained once and saved for the future tests. However, currently platform is tested on single workstation, the whole functionality can be installed on several VMs for load balancing and decentralized monitoring purposes in order to handle large amount of traffic at core network. The similar mechanism has been explained in other papers presented by authors on SDN security [10].

As it is shown in Table 4, for learning algorithm I, testing time, total accuracy score, binary cross entropy error and false negative score are compared and MLP methods outperforms the ELM approach.

Table 4. Learning algorithm I performance evaluation

Data	Accuracy score	Cross entropy error	False negative score	Testing time (s)
ELM 10	0.80	0.84	12.35	0.72
ELM 50	0.58	3.01	30.95	1.06
MLP 10	0.87	0.66	00.11	0.09
MLP 50	0.88	0.57	00.12	0.34

The binary cross entropy error and the false negative score of ELM is quite high, which means that in most cases, it fails to give alarm when an intrusion occurs. If MLP with 10 and 50 hidden layer neurons are compared, it can be seen that MLP with 50 hidden layer neurons performs slightly better than the MLP with 10 hidden layer neurons in terms of differentiating the normal and attack traffic, although the time complexity for the testing is smaller with MLP with 10 hidden layer neurons. Since the overall architecture has a high time and model complexity with many preprocessing (protocol analyzer) and post-processing (genetic algorithm etc.) steps, we have chosen MLP with 10 hidden layer neurons for this module to reduce the overall processing time for labelling an incoming network packet and the model complexity.

To evaluate part 1 of HADM as whole and with protocol analyzer functionality, the traffic carried on vulnerable protocol will be directed to k-NN and LR and the rest of the traffic to ELM/MLP. Training in this phase is covered in two scenarios. In the scenario I, the incoming traffic to k-NN includes: $UDP_{DoS} + TCP_{DoS}$ while the LR algorithm processes the rest of the traffic (TCP-TCP_{DoS}). In Scenario II, all UDP traffic will be forwarded to k-NN algorithm and all TCP traffic to LR algorithm. Tables 5 and 6 show the performance evaluation for testing scenario I and II based on three metrics. The precision and recall values are measured for attack class.

As it is shown in Tables 5, 6 and 7, the computation time decreased greatly in scenario II, while the accuracy, precision and recall factors also improved. That means the HADM outperforms considerably while UDP DoS is separated from attacks carried over TCP (applying protocol analyzer). However, in this study, we only classified our input data to three categories of normal, attack and unknown and have not applied the part II of HADM yet to categorize different types of attacks, which is a factor to consider in our future work.

Table 5. k-NN and LR detection performance for scenario I

Input data	Accuracy	Precision	Recall
k-NN	0.94	0.95	0.93
LR	0.92	0.95	0.06

Table 6. k-NN and LR detection performance for scenario II

Input data	Accuracy	Precision	Recall
k-NN	0.99	0.97	0.97
LR	0.92	0.63	0.20

Table 7. Computation time

Input data	MLP 10		k-NN		LR	
	Training	Testing	Training	Testing	Training	Testing
Scenario I	158.08	0.24	10926.64	5766.36	80.63	0.62
Scenario II	158.08	0.24	284.63	105.23	80.6	0.44

5 Discussion on Future Work

The proposed model compromises of two main parts where each part independently increases the efficiency of attack detection based on the factors such as precision, recall, accuracy and computation time. While part 1 of the model utilizes the protocol analyzer and mentioned algorithms are implemented for traffic filtration, reducing the processing time and increasing the accuracy, the part 2 applies a dynamic feature selection with genetic algorithm in order to classify unknown attacks and increase the accuracy as well. In current paper, in order to evaluate the performance of the part 1, the modified version of ISCX-2012 and UNSW-N15 datasets with diverse attacks have been used. The performance of the part 1 is compared for two scenarios where UDP DoS is separated from other protocols and where it is not.

In order to evaluate the model robustness and scalability, we will also test the model against five different latest datasets to cover also the new protocols that are missed from ISCX-2012 [11]. Furthermore, for each algorithm, we applied other feature selection methods such as FScore, Chi2 and SVM_{online} to find the best features [12]. On the other hand, we applied three more different algorithms including Multi-Layer Perceptron (MLP), SVM and Decision Tree (DT). The best algorithms were selected through a benchmark on applied datasets and based on the achieved accuracy, FP, FN, training and testing time.

6 Conclusion

This paper reviewed current mechanisms such as Data Mining (DM) techniques for security purposes and their limitations to defend networks against cyber-attacks. While learning algorithms may have high accuracy in general and longer computation time in comparison to linear algorithms, they may give unexpected responses to a specific type of attack. Therefore, this paper proposed a security platform called Hybrid Anomaly Detection Model (HADM) that uses a combination of linear and learning algorithms along with protocol analyzer. The linear algorithms filter and extract distinctive attributes and features of the cyber-attacks, while the learning algorithms use these attributes and features to identify new types of cyber-attacks. The protocol analyzer classifies and filters vulnerable protocols to avoid unnecessary computation load. The use of linear algorithms in conjunction with learning algorithms allows the HADM to achieve improved efficiency in terms of the accuracy and computation time to detect cyber-attacks over existing solutions.

We also described testing scenarios and concluded that the proposed protocol analyzer filters the vulnerable protocols such as UDP and TCP to decrease the computation load, processing time and accuracy for applied algorithms. Our future work concentrates on applying extra datasets, feature selection methods and algorithms to evaluate the model robustness and scalability.

References

1. Desale, K., Ade, R.: Genetic algorithm based feature selection approach for effective intrusion detection system. In: 2015 International Conference on Computer Communication and Informatics (ICCCI), Coimbatore, pp. 1–6 (2015)
2. Monshizadeh, M., Yan, Z.: Security related data mining. In: IEEE International Conference on Computer and Information Technology, Xi'an, pp. 775–782 (2014)
3. Di Pietro, A., et al.: Dynamic deep packet inspection for anomaly detection. US Patent 2017099310 (A1), 6 April 2017
4. Vasseur, J., et al.: Anomaly detection in a network coupling state information with machine learning outputs. US Patent 20170104774 (A1), 13 April 2017
5. Di Pietro, A., et al.: Signature creation for unknown attacks. US Patent 20160028750 (A1), 28 January 2016
6. Yadav, N., et al.: Network behavior data collection and analytics for anomaly detection. US Patent 20160359695 (A1), 8 December 2016
7. Atli, B.: Anomaly-based intrusion detection by modeling probability distributions of flow characteristics. MS thesis, Aalto University (2017)
8. ISCX-2012: University of New Brunswick. http://www.unb.ca/cic/datasets/ids.html
9. The UNSW-NB15 data set. https://www.unsw.adfa.edu.au/australian-centre-for-cyber-security/cybersecurity/ADFA-NB15-Datasets/
10. Monshizadeh, M., Khatri, V., Kantola, R.: Detection as a service: an SDN application. In: 19th International Conference on Advanced Communication Technology (ICACT), Bongpyeong, pp. 285–290 (2017)
11. Sharafaldin, I., et al.: Toward generating a new intrusion detection dataset and intrusion traffic characterization. In: 4th International Conference on Information Systems Security and Privacy (ICISSP), Portugal, January 2018
12. Yann, L., et al.: Deep learning. Nature **521**(7553), 436 (2015)

Network Deployment

Implementation and Evaluation
of Distributed Geographical Routing

Bernd Meijerink$^{(\boxtimes)}$ and Geert Heijenk

University of Twente, Enschede, The Netherlands
{bernd.meijerink,geert.heijenk}@utwente.nl

Abstract. Geocast has the potential to facilitate message delivering for geographically scoped information in many future scenarios such as vehicular networking and crisis control. An efficient geographic routing protocol is needed to enable Internet-wide geocast on the network level. In this paper we evaluate an implementation of a path based geographic routing protocol. We specifically look at the behavior and performance of this protocol during network convergence. We show that our implementation constructs forwarding trees that are close to a shortest path tree in link cost. We also show that our algorithm converges relatively quickly in case the network changes.

Keywords: Geocast · Routing · Route distribution

1 Introduction

Due to the increase in networked devices, vehicular networks in particular, we believe that location based packet delivery or geocast will become an important method of data distribution in the future. It could provide benefits for vehicular networks in the form of location dependent weather warnings or, on a more local level, information on traffic incidents or road conditions [3].

Geocast, first introduced by Navas and Imielinski [12], is a transmission method where packets are sent to a location or area rather than an IP-address. It can be seen as a one-to-many or many-to-many system like multicast with the main difference that devices receive packets based on their location rather then a subscription model.

While geocast might seem similar to multicast in some ways, multicast-like routing will not be sufficient in a geocast environment for scalability reasons. Multicast routing algorithms are mostly designed to route packets to predefined multicast groups that are relatively static. Geocast packets on the other hand will have to be routed to a set of routers based on an arbitrary destination area that could contain several or even no routers.

Most research around geocast has been centered on mobile and ad-hoc applications [6] and mainly in the area of vehicular networking [1]. We believe that enabling geocast on an Internet-wide scale would make even more applications

© IFIP International Federation for Information Processing 2018
Published by Springer Nature Switzerland AG 2018. All Rights Reserved
K. R. Chowdhury et al. (Eds.): WWIC 2018, LNCS 10866, pp. 121–133, 2018.
https://doi.org/10.1007/978-3-030-02931-9_10

feasible. To reach such a deployment geocast would need to be enabled in the network layer [3]. Network layer solutions have the benefit that any application can benefit, possibly leading to applications not considered before. Application layer solutions already exist [2] but they have scalability problems [11] that might prove difficult to overcome in a global scenario. Previous proposals for Internet-wide geocast, such as GeoNode [12] relied on modified IP packets, while unicast based concepts [7] rely on partially unicasting a message to a covering router and special servers.

In our previous work we designed and evaluated a path based geographic routing algorithm. In this paper we describe our implementation of this algorithm and evaluate its performance during network convergence. In our previous work we have evaluated the link cost of the algorithm after convergence compared to a perfect shortest path tree. This previous evaluation was done in a static environment. In this paper we answer the question how our routing protocol behaves during convergence, by evaluating the performance of our geographic routing implementation in a simulated network environment.

The main contributions of this paper are: (1) validation of our geographic routing protocol by means of an implementation; (2) evaluation of the convergence speed of the protocol; (3) evaluation of the link usage and packet loss during convergence.

This remainder of this paper is structured as follows: In Sect. 2 we describe our routing protocol, followed by a description of our implementation in Sect. 3. In Sect. 4 we describe our evaluation approach followed by the actual results in Sect. 5. We conclude the paper in Sect. 6.

2   Geographic Routing

In this section we will shortly describe the addressing system that is the basis of our routing system followed by a high level overview of the algorithm that makes the routing decision.

2.1   Addressing

The addressing system our routing system is based on divides the world into 4 rectangles. We then divide these rectangles into increasingly smaller nested rectangles. These rectangles are numbered in such a way, that neighboring rectangles that are at the same depth but have different parents share the same number [9]. An example of this scheme applied to the world with rectangles up to a depth of 3 can be seen in Fig. 1. In this figure we have highlighted an area encompassing much of northern Europe and the UK. Individually these can be addressed as 3.4.2 and 4.4.2, but taken together we can address them as [3, 4].4.2.

We can map this representation to a binary format by using 4 bits per depth level, where we set the bits in the order 1, 2, 3, 4 with a bit set to 1 indicating that rectangle is included. The example used before would translate to

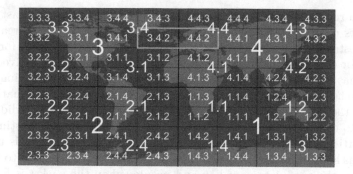

Fig. 1. Geographic addressing up to a depth of 3

0011.0001.0100. By using 4 bits per level we can combine any neighboring rectangles into the area we wish to describe. Using this representation we could use this geographic address as a destination IPv6 address. Given that we use 4 bits per level and assuming the first 2 bytes of the IPv6 address are needed to distinguish geocast from unicast or multicast, we are left with $112/4 = 28$ levels. This gives us a worst case rectangle size of 7 by 3.5 cm on the equator.

2.2 Routing

We have developed a geographic routing protocol on the basis of the following assumptions: All routers know the area (if any) that they service specified in the form of the addressing system described above. Destinations are addressed using the same addressing format. Routers know the (unicast) shortest path to every other router in the network. Links in the network are symmetrical.

Our geographic routing algorithm is based on path information, somewhat like BGP [13]. A complete specification of our algorithm including a discussion on the design choices made can be found in [8]. The main idea is that every router knows the shortest path to every other router and can use this information to find the next hop(s) that will lead to a (close to optimal) shortest path tree from the source to all destination routers that cover part of a packet's destination area. Packets are always forwarded over the least cost path, if there are multiple such paths the path with the lowest next hop id is chosen. This guarantees paths are chosen in a deterministic manner, which leads to shared paths to destination routers located close together.

To perform packet forwarding each router keeps track of 4 types of information essential to the routing process: (1) The two best paths it knows from every other router in the network (this corresponds to the path packets would take coming from those routers). (2) A mapping of destination routers to next hops based on our lowest next hop id rule (this corresponds to the path a packet will take going to that router). (3) The shortest path to all other routers for each of its neighbors. (4) The coverage area(s) of each router in the network.

When a router receives a packet it looks at the destination geocast address and uses its coverage table to lookup the routers who's coverage area overlap with the destination area. On a high level each router will evaluate a forwarding next hop for each destination router a packet has if this packet arrived on the link that has the shortest path back to the source. For every destination the router will choose a candidate next hop from its best next hop information. The router will then use the path information from the interface the candidate next hop is on to calculate the shortest path from the source to that destination as seen (advertised) by the candidate next hop. A similar calculation is made for the previous hop. If the path through the router is better or identical to the path as seen from the candidate next hop and previous hop the packet is forwarded to that next hop. If multiple destinations have the same next hop the packet is only forwarded once.

This forwarding operation might seem overly complicated, but using a more simple approach like forwarding packets on the shortest path to all destinations will lead to a form of limited flooding where packets are forwarded over multiple paths to the same destination. In our previous work [8] we have shown that simpler algorithms all show this limited flooding effect to some extent.

3   Implementation

In order to validate the proposed algorithm we have implemented the path based geographic routing algorithm and protocol for advertising paths presented in our previous work [8] and briefly described in Sect. 2.2. First we will present the general structure of the software followed by our information distribution, information tracking and forwarding approach.

3.1   Software Structure

Our software consists of 8 main components: The Packet receiver, Advertisement parser, Packet forwarding, Link path table, General path table, Coverage table, Route advertisement generator and Packet sender. These components and their mutual relationships can be seen in Fig. 2.

The packet receiver handles all incoming packets. Packets that have a geocast destination address are passed to the packet forwarding system while advertisement packets are passed to the advertisement parser.

The route advertisement (RA) parser parses the advertisement packet into path data and coverage data. Path data consists of a path for each router included in the advertisement. This data is given to the per link path table and the general path table. Coverage information consists of a geographic address of the coverage area and the id of the covering router. This information is passed to the coverage table.

The per link path table is a table of all path advertisements received on a link. It is essentially the best path table of the router on the other side of the

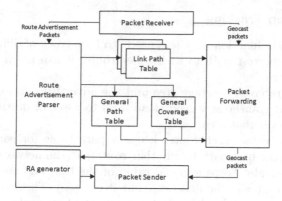

Fig. 2. Global structure of the routing software

link, with the possible exception of paths that include the current router unless no other path was available.

The global path table contains the best and second best known path from all other routers in the network to a router. It also includes the best next hop for each destination. Due to our lowest id next hop choice this is not necessarily the same as the best known incoming path.

The coverage table is simply a mapping of coverage areas to the router id of the routers covering those areas. The Packet forwarding system receives geocast packets and actually runs the forwarding algorithm based on the information it receives from the coverage, path and per link tables. It gives the packet including a list of links to forward it on to the Packet sender.

The RA generator uses the information from the path and coverage table to generate a route advertisement for each link the router has. When a neighboring router is included in a path the second best known path is sent when available.

Finally the Packet sender, as its name implies, sends out all packets on the correct interface.

3.2 Route Distribution

Routers periodically send route advertisements consisting of all shortest paths and coverage areas known to the router. They take the following form: Advertising router ID (1 byte), Number of advertisements in packet (1 byte) followed by the actual advertisements. A single route advertisement consists of: the coverage area (16 bytes: an IPv6 address), the path length (1 byte), the covering router id (1 byte) and the advertised path (of path length bytes, with a minimum of 1).

The time needed for every node to have at least one path to each other node is given by $t_c = t_{ra} \cdot d$ where t_c is the time needed to converge (in seconds), t_{ra} the time between route advertisements and d the diameter of the network (the maximum distance, or hops, between any two nodes).

3.3 Information Tracking

To perform its main function a routers needs to keep track of different information, mainly the shortest path to each other router it can reach and the areas these routers cover.

Based on the received coverage area and the advertising router, each router keeps a table that translates a geocast address to a set of destination routers that (partially) cover that area.

As mentioned before, each router keeps a path table for each link it has. This table tracks the best path to all other routers in the network reachable on that link. A router also keeps a global table of the best and second best path it knows to each router in the network (that it can see). The second best route is needed for the routing algorithm to function. The best route table is used to generate the route advertisement packets, unless the path contains the router it is transmitted to. If this happens the second best route is used if it exists, letting the neighbor know that there is another path. If there is no such path the best link is used, this lets the receiving router know there is no other known path except the return path to a certain other router.

3.4 Forwarding

The forwarding procedure is based on the known paths to the source and destination(s). When a geocast packet is received the router checks its destination address against its coverage table leading to a set of destination routers D. If the current router is in D it is removed as the packet already reached that destination.

For each destination d in D we evaluate the forwarding path. We combine our best paths to the source and d into a candidate forwarding path. We compare this path to a similar combination of paths reported by the candidate next hop and the previous hop (this is the main reason we keep a path table for each interface). If our candidate path is better than the other two options the packet is forwarded on this path. This approach ensures that our path is indeed the shortest path from source to destination based on our limited knowledge. Using this method we can construct close to optimal shortest path trees through a network.

4 Evaluation Approach

We want to evaluate our protocol during different convergence scenarios. In this section we will describe the metrics we are interested in, the exact scenario that will be used for the evaluation, and present overview of the tools used and our method of variable selection.

4.1   Evaluation Metrics

Our evaluation is focused on protocol convergence times and the behavior of the system during convergence following a link drop or restore. We evaluate our system on the following timing values related to convergence: Initial convergence time, convergence time following a link drop, convergence time following a restored link, and packet delivery restoration time following a link drop.

We further evaluate the number of packets that are lost during network convergence. For this last metric we take into account the number of destinations that did not receive a packet. Using this method we hope to accurately represent the number of deliveries that were missed during convergence.

We will also look at the possible multi path issues during a convergence phase, in which packets are delivered to a router over multiple paths. Ideally this should never occur, but it is likely unavoidable during network convergence due to incomplete or outdated networks knowledge in different routers.

4.2   Evaluation Scenario

We start each simulation run by giving the routing algorithm time to converge. We have set this waiting time to 25 s as we have not observed the convergence taking longer than this time. After this initial wait we start transmitting packets from our randomly selected source to a randomly selected area. 10 s after the transmissions start we drop a randomly chosen link on the routing tree for those packets. We measure how long it takes the network to converge again and the effect this has on the packets that were in transit during this time. 50 s after the link drop we restore the link. We measure how long it takes for the network to converge again and the number of packets lost during the entire run.

4.3   Networks and Variable Selection

We use real world network graphs taken from the Topologyzoo project [4] to evaluate our protocol on a set of realistic networks. We used a total of 162 ranging in size from 6 to 51 routers, with an average of 26 routers. We import these networks into a Mininet virtual network [10] by generating a new node running our routing implementation for each Vertex in the graph and establishing a link (1 gbit/s Ethernet) between nodes if the corresponding graph has an edge.

The latitude and longitude location of the node is used to generate a coverage area of a size corresponding to depth 10 of our addressing scheme (Sect. 2.1) to ensure routers cover reasonable portions of a network. For each run within a network a destination area is randomly generated. This area can cover between 10% and 95% of the bounding box containing all nodes in the network. We also randomly select a source node for each run, this node can be inside or outside the destination area.

To simulate a link drop we set both ends of a link to have a 100% packet loss rate using the Linux network emulator [5] functionality. The link to drop is chosen from the set of links on the shortest path tree from the source to

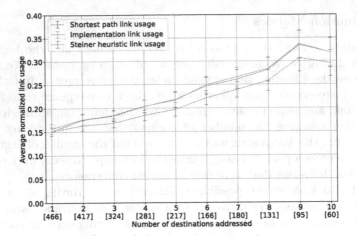

Fig. 3. Normalized link usage in a converged network

the destination. With this link selection we try to guarantee that the dropped link will at least have some effect on the forwarding situation. The dropped link is chosen in such a way that is does not lead to a disconnected network, so the algorithm can actually converge to the new situation and still reach all destinations. Later in the run we restore this link by returning the loss rate on both ends to 0%.

Routers are configured to exchange route advertisements every 0.5 s. Route entries expire after two seconds, leading to a relatively fast update time.

5   Evaluation

We evaluate our networks in the way described in the previous section. In this section we will present our results. We start with an overview of our algorithm's performance in a converged state and continue with the convergence time of the protocol in different network states. We end the section with the performance during different convergence situations.

5.1   General Link Usage

In general our algorithm establishes forwarding trees that use a comparable number of links compared to a shortest path tree. The routing stretch factor for single destinations is on average 1.046.

In Fig. 3 we plot the link usage of our implementation against the shortest path tree and a Steiner tree for the same (source, destination) tuples. On the y-axis we show an average of the normalized value of the link usage, meaning the number of links used to reach all destinations divided by the number of links in the network. The x-axis shows the number of destinations addressed and below that, the number of runs with this number of destinations in brackets. The difference in number of runs is a consequence of our destination area generation system, which chooses areas with a small number of routers in geographically large networks. The error bars show the 95% confidence interval for that value. Runs with more than 10 destination were not numerous enough to provide significant results.

In our 2505 runs there were 375 runs where the algorithm established a path with a different number of links than the shortest path tree. In most of these cases this path was one link longer, and in some rare cases one shorter. The former can in some cases be explained by minor inefficiencies while most cases, and the latter difference can be explained by situations where there are multiple shortest paths from the source to a single destination. If the chosen path overlaps with that of another destination the resulting link usage can be lower compared to the situation where the other path was taken.

We can conclude that our protocol performs mostly as expected with respect to the number of links used to construct a forwarding tree.

5.2   Convergence Time

One of the more important aspects of any routing protocol is the time it takes to converge following a change in the network. The correlation between the network size (the amount of routers in the network) and the time convergence takes during the evaluation is shown in Fig. 4. We can see that the initial convergence time (blue line) of the network shows a strong correlation to the network size. As a larger network mostly corresponds to more possible paths it correlates with the time it takes for the algorithm to converge. On average the convergence time after a link drop (red line) is significantly larger than that of adding or restoring a link (green line) to the network. As noted before this can be explained by the timeout of 2 s that needs to occur before link loss is propagated while new links are advertised with at most a 0.5 s delay. The time it takes for full packet delivery to be restored after a link drop (orange line) follows a similar pattern as the convergence time but takes less time overall. This is likely caused by the locality of the destination area, where especially in larger networks the area is contains less routers relative to the number of routers in the entire network. The most interesting thing to note in this graph is the time to convergence after a link restoration is significantly lower than the initial convergence time for larger networks. We expect this is caused by the locality of the change. In larger networks a single link drop is not likely to affect path entries further away in the network, although this does strongly depend on how well connected the network is.

5.3   Behavior During Convergence

In Fig. 5 we show the convergence behavior in two different networks. On the left y-axis (blue line) we show the normalized distribution tree cost where 100% corresponds to the link usage of the initial distribution tree. On the right y-axis

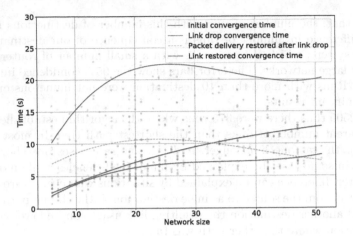

Fig. 4. Convergence times of all runs in the evaluation (Color figure online)

(yellow line) we show packet loss as the number of destination routers that did not receive a packet at a certain time. The x-axis shows the elapsed time from the start of the packet transmissions in seconds. The time of the link drop is marked as a dotted red vertical line and the link restore time with a dotted green vertical line. The dotted blue vertical lines mark the time the network had converged to the new situation. We can see that immediately following the loss of a link there is a period of packet loss, but packet delivery is restored before the network has fully converged. This can be explained by the fact that the link loss occurs on a path that is used, resulting in local convergence before the entire network has had time to converge. A similar pattern can be seen following the link restore, but the packet loss is minimal here. This is likely caused by the fact that information about new link propagates faster compared to information of lost links due to the way that timeouts function. The small red lines that can be seen following the link restoration represent packets that arrived multiple times at a router in the network. Packets are sometimes routed over multiple paths during convergence, temporarily increasing link usage as can be seen in the graphs.

As can be expected, during the convergence directly following a link drop a number of packets is not delivered to the destination routers. We plot these losses in Fig. 6a. In this figure the red dots represent the number of routers that did not receive a packet in a certain simulation run at that time. The intensity of the red color corresponds to the number of runs in which this number of packets was lost for that particular time, with the barely visible dots representing a single occurrence. The blue line represents the percentage of runs in which packet loss occurred at that time. Note that while we plot the red and green dotted line to represent the link drop and restore this does not correspond to the exact drop time in all simulation runs, as can be seen by dropped packets that occur earlier than expected. This is caused by varying startup time in the emulation, mostly

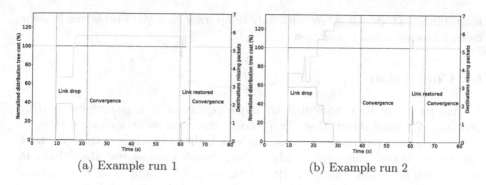

(a) Example run 1   (b) Example run 2

Fig. 5. Examples of convergence behavior on different networks (Color figure online)

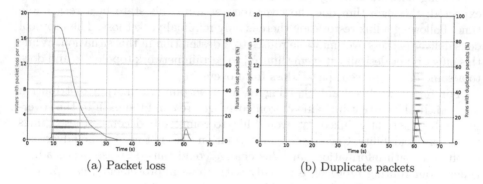

(a) Packet loss   (b) Duplicate packets

Fig. 6. Loss and duplicate delivery data over all simulation runs (Color figure online)

depending on network size. Note that packet loss mainly occurs after a link drop, and link restoration barely leads to any lost packets.

While our routing system should not route packets in a loop it does in some specific conditions route packets to a single router through multiple paths. This effect can occur during convergence when the network is temporarily in a configuration that allows a multi path situation to occur. This effect can be observed in Fig. 5a and b as a solid red line. We can see this line corresponds to the small peak in path cost directly following the restoration of a link. We show the overall duplicate packet delivery rate in Fig. 6b. In this figure the red dots represent the number of routers in a certain run that received a certain packet twice, or more times. The time represents the time at which the packet was sent from the source router. The blue line represents the percentage of runs in which a packet was received multiple times by any router. As we can see this effect mainly occurs when a link is restored (or added) to the network.

Compared to unicast routing we avoid certain issues, like the count to infinity problem, by relying only on path information. Packets are simply not forwarded anymore if a router finds itself on anything but the shortest path from its point of view. On the topic of network change we can conclude that our protocol correctly reestablishes a forwarding tree with only temporary multipath problems in some cases following a link restoration.

6   Conclusion

In this paper we have presented an implementation of a geographic routing protocol. We have shown that the protocol forwards packets along a close to optimal shortest path tree in situations where the network is stable. We have also shown that during periods where the network changes our algorithm can recover in a reasonable time. The time it takes our algorithm to recover depends on factors like network size and how well connected the network is.

During network convergence due to link failure we lose packets as can be expected, the algorithm does however recover from this state in a reasonable time. Following a link restoration there is only minimal packet loss. The protocol does deliver packets over multiple routes to a destination in this situation. While this effect is not desirable it seems limited to certain network topologies and does to a some degree prevent packet loss from occurring.

For future work we are planning to improve our information distribution method. In the current implementation coverage area and the path to the covering router are tightly linked. We would like to completely decouple these things to increase scalability. Coverage area information does not need to be advertised as often as path information, and this change could thus decrease overhead. In general our routing protocol, especially with these improvements, can provide another step in enabling Internet-wide geocast in the future.

References

1. Di Felice, M., Bedogni, L., Bononi, L.: Group communication on highways: an evaluation study of geocast protocols and applications. Ad Hoc Netw. **11**(3), 818–832 (2013)
2. Fioreze, T., Heijenk, G.J.: Extending DNS to support geocasting towards VANETs: a proposal. In: VNC, pp. 271–277. IEEE (2010)
3. Karagiannis, G., Heijenk, G., Festag, A., Petrescu, A., Chaiken, A.: Internet-wide geo-networking problem statement (2013). https://tools.ietf.org/html/draft-karagiannis-problem-statement-geonetworking-01
4. Knight, S., Nguyen, H., Falkner, N., Bowden, R., Roughan, M.: The internet topology zoo. IEEE J. Sel. Areas Commun. **29**(9), 1765–1775 (2011). https://doi.org/10.1109/JSAC.2011.111002
5. Linux Foundation: netem (2009). http://www.linuxfoundation.org/collaborate/workgroups/networking/netem
6. Liu, J., Wan, J., Wang, Q., Deng, P., Zhou, K., Qiao, Y.: A survey on position-based routing for vehicular ad hoc networks. Telecommun. Syst. **62**(1), 15–30 (2016)
7. Maihöfer, C., Franz, W., Eberhardt, R.: Stored geocast. In: Irmscher, K., Fähnrich, K.P. (eds.) Kommunikation in Verteilten Systemen (KiVS), pp. 257–268. Springer, Heidelberg (2003). https://doi.org/10.1007/978-3-642-55569-5_21

8. Meijerink, B., Baratchi, M., Heijenk, G.: A distributed routing algorithm for internet-wide geocast, May 2018. https://arxiv.org/abs/1805.01690, under submission, pre-publication: arXiv:1805.01690
9. Meijerink, B., Baratchi, M., Heijenk, G.: An efficient geographical addressing scheme for the internet. In: Mamatas, L., Matta, I., Papadimitriou, P., Koucheryavy, Y. (eds.) WWIC 2016. LNCS, vol. 9674, pp. 78–90. Springer, Cham (2016). https://doi.org/10.1007/978-3-319-33936-8_7
10. Mininet Project: Mininet. http://mininet.org
11. Moscoviter, D., Gholibeigi, M., Meijerink, B., Kooijman, R., Krijger, P., Heijenk, G.: Improving spatial indexing and searching for location-based DNS queries. In: Mamatas, L., Matta, I., Papadimitriou, P., Koucheryavy, Y. (eds.) WWIC 2016. LNCS, vol. 9674, pp. 187–198. Springer, Cham (2016). https://doi.org/10.1007/978-3-319-33936-8_15
12. Navas, J.C., Imielinski, T.: GeoCast - geographic addressing and routing. In: Pap, L., Sohraby, K., Johnson, D.B., Rose, C. (eds.) MOBICOM, pp. 66–76. ACM (1997)
13. Rekhter, Y., Li, T., Hares, S.: A border gateway protocol 4 (BGP-4). Technical report (2005)

Testbed Evaluation of Optimized REACT over Multi-hop Paths

Matthew J. Mellott[1]($\boxtimes$), Charles J. Colbourn[1], Violet R. Syrotiuk[1], and Ilenia Tinnirello[2]

[1] School of Computing, Informatics, and Decision Systems Engineering, Arizona State University, P.O. Box 878809, Tempe, AZ 85287, USA
{mmellott,colbourn,syrotiuk}@asu.edu
[2] Department of Electrical Engineering, University of Palermo, Viale delle Scienze, Parco D'Orleans, 90128 Palermo, Italy
ilenia.tinnirello@unipa.it

Abstract. REACT is a distributed resource allocation protocol that computes a max-min allocation of airtime for mesh networks. The allocation adapts automatically to changes in local traffic load and in local network views. SALT, a new contention window tuning algorithm, ensures that each node secures the airtime allocated to it by REACT. REACT and SALT are extended to the multi-hop flow scenario with the introduction of a new airtime reservation algorithm. With a reservation in place, multi-hop TCP flows show increased throughput when running over SALT and REACT compared to running over 802.11 DCF. All results are obtained from experimentation on the w-iLab.t wireless network testbed in Belgium.

1 Introduction

Wi-Fi network performance is known to degrade dramatically when node density is high, and when flows are sustained over multiple hops. These conditions arise when multiple networks coexist [10,21] and when large access infrastructure is deployed [3,17]. The degradation results from the starvation and unfairness associated with carrier sense multiple access (CSMA) based protocols. This is attributed to a mismatch in the local views of the wireless medium among the nodes, and due to high levels of contention when the network is congested [12].

To mitigate such problems several approaches have been proposed. These include adopting rate limiters on nodes [4,7], using multi-hop reservations [16], using different access priorities for data and control traffic [8], and exploiting admission control [22].

Airtime measures the channel time in which a link is sensed busy because of frame transmissions. Airtime measurements are position-dependent, because channel attenuation differs for each transmitter-receiver pair. Airtime has been applied in routing in mesh networks [7,9], and in admission control [18].

This paper makes two contributions. First, we use a measurement driven approach to control the airtime allocated to each node in a wireless network

© IFIP International Federation for Information Processing 2018
Published by Springer Nature Switzerland AG 2018. All Rights Reserved
K. R. Chowdhury et al. (Eds.): WWIC 2018, LNCS 10866, pp. 134–145, 2018.
https://doi.org/10.1007/978-3-030-02931-9_11

computed by the REACT protocol [19]. REACT negotiates airtime allocations among the nodes on the basis of traffic requirements and local views of the network. In order to achieve its allocated airtime we develop SALT, a mechanism for dynamically tuning the contention window of each node.

There has been much work on contention window tuning but with different objectives. Among the first may be MACAW [1], replacing the binary exponential backoff with a multiplicative increase and linear decrease (MILD) of the contention window (CW) size to improve fairness. Other work tunes the CW to achieve a theoretical throughput limit [6]. Our goal here is different: Our aim is to tune the contention window at each node to realize a specific airtime allocation.

REACT and SALT are both compatible with the 802.11 standard [15] and have been implemented on legacy devices. Extensive experimentation in the w.i-Lab.t wireless network testbed [5] shows that the tuning approach is able to align allocations to those negotiated.

The second contribution is an extension of REACT to reserve an allocation along the path of a multi-hop TCP flow. This requires that neighbours of the nodes along the forwarding path take the reservation into account as part of their own allocations so that they do not interfere with the multi-hop flow. Multi-hop wireless mesh networks present many challenges for TCP. In addition to the unreliable wireless transmission at each hop, contention from hidden and exposed nodes in a wireless network constrain the TCP throughput achievable over a multi-hop path [11]. To the best of our knowledge, Gupta et al. [14] is one of the few works conducting experimentation with TCP in a physical wireless network. However, their emphasis is on how TCP throughput is affected by routing, user mobility, and the number of hops in the network rather than on the impact of the MAC protocol. While no performance advantages for TCP were found in their results [14], we have achieved higher TCP throughput in running the flow over REACT combined with SALT, than over 802.11.

The rest of this paper is organized as follows. In Sect. 2, we describe the REACT protocol for negotiating channel airtime. Section 3 presents SALT, a new tuning algorithm, its implementation in legacy commercial Wi-Fi cards, and an evaluation of how well it achieves the airtime allocation. Section 4 provides an algorithm to reserve airtime for a multi-hop flow over the REACT/SALT framework and evaluates the algorithm using a multi-hop TCP flow. Finally, we summarize and propose future work in Sect. 5.

2   Realizing a REACT Allocation

REACT is a distributed resource allocation protocol that uses the metaphor of an auction [19]. When used in the context of mesh wireless networks, the resource being allocated (or put up for "auction") is *airtime*, the percentage of time a node controls the medium over a given period. Each node runs an auctioneer and a bidder algorithm concurrently; auctioneers offer capacity while bidders claim capacity at adjacent auctions to satisfy their own airtime demand. Auctioneers update their offers to satisfy all nodes bidding at their auction while also ensuring that all nodes receive a fair allocation of the resource. Bidders update their claims to ensure that they are not consuming any more airtime than can be offered at any adjacent auction. Nodes participating in REACT converge to a lexicographic max-min airtime allocation [19]. A change in the local network view or traffic load triggers REACT to run and adapt the allocation.

Lutz et al. [19] realize the REACT allocation in a schedule-based MAC protocol, in which a number of transmission slots at each node are selected at random to correspond to its allocation. A node can recompute its schedule immediately upon receiving a new allocation from REACT, rather than waiting for the end of a frame, making it competitive with contention-based protocols. Their initial evaluation was conducted in simulation where synchronization is not a challenge.

Hence, Garlisi et al. [13] instead realize the REACT allocation in a contention-based MAC protocol. Because the channel access probability depends on the average contention window (CW) size [2], a node's REACT allocation is realized by tuning the CW size. A legacy Wi-Fi node i can estimate its current allocation s_i as a function of the total number n_i of channel accesses it makes, the total time F_i that its backoff is frozen, and the total airtime A_i in an observation interval C:

$$s_i = \frac{A_i}{C} = \frac{A_i}{A_i + F_i + W_i/2 \cdot \sigma \cdot n_i} \tag{1}$$

where $W_i/2 \cdot \sigma \cdot n_i$ is an approximation of the total time required for the backoff countdown. This suggests how the contention window can be tuned.

3   REACT Implementation with SALT Tuning

Different from [13], rather than modify 802.11 packet headers, we send control messages to implement REACT periodically. The time period must be longer than the amount of time it takes to update bids and offers. With this method the overhead for control traffic does not increase when the data rate increases.

Our implementation of REACT is paired with a new contention window tuning approach, described next.

3.1   Smoothed Airtime Linear Tuning (SALT)

Smoothed Airtime Linear Tuning (SALT) is a new contention window tuning technique. As in [13], the contention window size is *fixed* unless and until a new airtime is allocated to node i by REACT. The intuition is that a node's channel access behaviour should depend on its allocation, not on the packet outcome.

SALT measures airtime a_i^t at node i over observation interval t and uses it to set W_i^{t+1}, the contention window size for the next interval $t + 1$. However a_i^t is not passed directly to the tuning component of SALT. Its value is first smoothed, using an exponentially weighted moving average in Eq. (2) with parameter

$0 \leq \beta \leq 1$, to produce S_i^t which is then used for tuning. Smoothing is done to reduce the effect of random background noise.

$$S_i^t = \begin{cases} a_i^1 & \text{if } t = 1 \\ \beta a_i^t + (1 - \beta)S_i^{t-1} & \text{if } t > 1 \end{cases} \tag{2}$$

SALT's tuning component is given in Eq. (3); s_i^t is the airtime allocation for node i from REACT, k is a constant scaling factor, and the maximum CW size is 1024. The difference between S_i^t and s_i^t is scaled by k to convert the difference of unit-less airtime ratios into a contention window size value.

$$W_i^t = \begin{cases} 0 & \text{if } t = 0 \\ \lfloor S_i^t - s_i^t \rfloor k + W_i^{t-1} & \text{if } t > 0 \text{ and } 0 \leq \lfloor S_i^t - s_i^t \rfloor k + W_i^{t-1} < 1024 \\ 1023 & \text{if } t > 0 \text{ and } \lfloor S_i^t - s_i^t \rfloor k + W_i^{t-1} \geq 1024 \\ 0 & \text{if } t > 0 \text{ and } \lfloor S_i^t - s_i^t \rfloor k + W_i^{t-1} < 0 \end{cases} \tag{3}$$

3.2 SALT Implementation

SALT is implemented as a Python program running at user level on each Linux testbed node in an experiment. It is part of the same program that is running REACT, and the airtime allocation is passed from the thread running REACT to the thread running SALT. The airtime measurement interval used is one second. SALT is invoked after each of these one second intervals and uses data collected by the networking subsystem to determine the airtime during the last interval.

The Linux kernel is modified to expose the minimum W_{min} and maximum W_{max} contention window size to user level programs. The interface allows a user level program to set these parameters; we set $W_{min} = W_{max} = W_i^t$. The wireless subsystem is also patched to accept CW sizes that are not powers of two.

3.3 SALT Evaluation

To evaluate SALT, we use the IMEC advanced w-iLab.t testbed, located in Zwijnaarde, Belgium [5]. It is pseudo-shielded from external interference and is equipped with various wireless technologies, including IEEE 802.11, IEEE 802.15.4, Bluetooth dongles, Software Defined Radios (SDRs), LTE femto cells, among others. The w-iLab.t testbed uses the cOntrol Management Framework (OMF) for resource allocation, hardware and software configuration, and the orchestration of experiments. Measurement data are collected and stored in a central database over a wired control network for further processing.

Configuring wireless topologies in such an indoor controlled environment is important for benchmarking and for the reproducibility of the results. However, it is a non-trivial task, because the distance at which nodes are able to interfere can be much farther than the transmission range. In order to limit the physical visibility of the nodes, we use the 802.11a PHY, at the central frequency of 5180 MHz with a transmission power of 1 dBm.

Tests are conducted to identify "zotac" nodes among the more than 90 available to match the logical topologies in Fig. 1. Each node is programmed to send

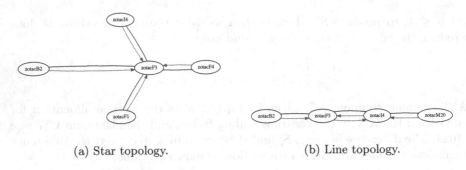

(a) Star topology.   (b) Line topology.

Fig. 1. Logical testbed topologies used to evaluate SALT. Black lines correspond to bidirectional links while blue arrows denote single-hop flows. (Color figure online)

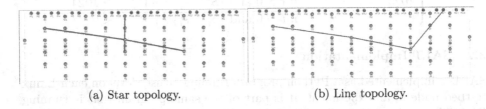

(a) Star topology.   (b) Line topology.

Fig. 2. Logical topologies from Fig. 1 mapped onto physical nodes in `w-iLab.t`.

broadcast `pings` in a dedicated time interval when all the other nodes are silent. Nodes that can decode the `ping` (`ICMP Echo Request` and `Response`) are neighbours connected by a bidirectional link. At the end of these tests, we build the network topologies in Fig. 1; see [20] for more topologies. The physical location of the nodes in `w-iLab.t` is shown in Fig. 2.

In each topology, each experiment conducted uses greedy UDP flows. These flows are set up with a target 1 Gbps UDP bandwidth, far beyond the capabilities of the wireless link (i.e., the channel is saturated).

Experiments to Select the Values of β and k. In order to determine values for β and k in Eqs. 2 and 3, we conduct an experiment where we varied their values over their range; we vary β from 0.1 to 1.0 in steps of 0.1 and k from 250 to 5000 in steps of 250, making for 120 trials on each of the topologies. Each trial lasts 15 s and we measure airtime for each node in the trial over that time. The heat maps in Fig. 3 show the convergence results for each topology and each combination of β and k. The darker the square in the heat map the faster the trial converged. We average the convergence time for each trial on each topology for the same β and k and select the lowest average. This results in a $\beta = 0.6$ and $k = 500$, for the best average convergence time of 7.44 s; these values of β and k are used in all subsequent experiments.

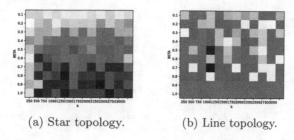

(a) Star topology.   (b) Line topology.

Fig. 3. β versus k "heat maps" by topology. The darker the square in the heat map the faster the trial converged.

3.4 Experiment to Compare Tuning Algorithms

We conduct an experiment to compare SALT and the original tuning algorithm [13], running along with REACT; 802.11 DCF is included as a control. The flows in this experiment are greedy UDP flows set up as described in Sect. 3.3.

We present the results for the star topology in Figs. 4 and 5 because they are representative; see [20] for more detail. Figure 4 plots airtime as a function of time. As expected, the airtime of nodes running 802.11 is unequal and highly variable for each node. In this topology, the allocation computed by REACT for each node is 20%. The original tuning algorithm converges more quickly than SALT but not as tightly. Moreover, each node running SALT oscillates around the allocated airtime whereas in the original tuning algorithm some nodes are unable to reach their allocated airtime of 20%.

Figure 5 plots per-node throughput, jitter, drop rate, and aggregate throughput for the star topology. The high variability in airtime for 802.11 is reflected in the per-node results: The throughput, jitter, and drop rates from node to node are also highly variable. The tighter convergence of SALT leads to the higher throughput and lower jitter than the original tuning algorithm. Both tuning algorithms have a near zero drop rate while 802.11's drop rate is extremely high, well above 90% for three of the four nodes. Despite the high drop rate for 802.11, it still leads in aggregate throughput of 67.96 MiB; one node (zotacF4), which obtains around 60% of the airtime, is almost solely responsible for the higher aggregate throughput achieved. SALT has throughput of 55.57 MiB with the original tuning algorithm achieving 49.72 MiB.

We now examine a more challenging multi-hop scenario.

4   Multi-hop REACT and Multi-hop Reservations

Until now, nodes running REACT have only taken into account their own traffic needs. In the auction a node's bid secures airtime for itself, but if there are multi-hop flows in a network this is insufficient because it does not take into account the fact that a node might need to forward traffic ultimately destined to other nodes. We present a multi-hop airtime reservation protocol that addresses this issue.

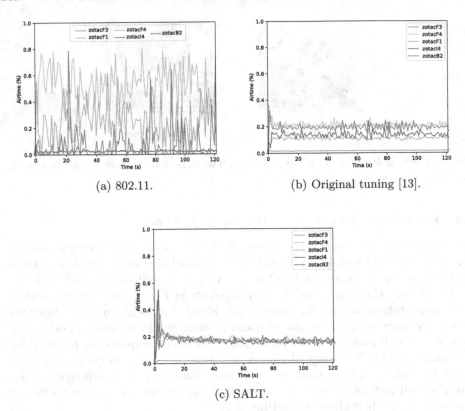

(a) 802.11.   (b) Original tuning [13].

(c) SALT.

Fig. 4. Airtime versus time for the star topology for 802.11, the original tuning algorithm, and SALT.

Without a reservation algorithm a node could try to predict how much airtime to reserve for multi-hop flows passing through it. Nodes store each of their neighbour's claims and could speculate how their demand should reflect the possibility of multi-hop flows. Unfortunately claims provide no information on the directionality of flows, multi-hop or not. A claim is sent to every node within broadcast range and only informs the receiver that the sender is currently expecting to utilize the amount of airtime claimed. Claims also do not tell a node anything about the demands of nodes beyond their one-hop neighbourhood, where the multi-hop flow could be originating. Multi-hop reservations allow the originators of multi-hop flows to inform nodes of the additional traffic they are expected to forward. Nodes along the reservation path can also inform the originator of resource saturation. The REACT auction itself is a convenient mechanism that can be used for the purpose of making these reservations.

Each auction in the REACT protocol allocates the channel capacity. In our multi-hop reservation algorithm, a reservation is made by reducing this capacity by the reservation amount at nodes along the path and at their neighbours. Once the reservation is placed nodes along the reservation path they each increase their

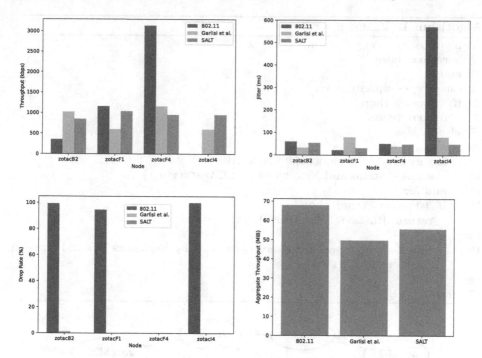

Fig. 5. Per-node throughput, jitter, and drop rate for each of 802.11 (in blue), the original tuning algorithm (in green), and SALT (in red), in addition to aggregate throughput, for the star topology. (Color figure online)

allocation by the reservation amount. This secures airtime for the flows that will be passing through the node while still maintaining the standard REACT auction for allocating airtime in the neighbourhood. Section 4.1 provides a more precise description of this process and Sect. 4.2 presents our evaluation of it.

4.1 Multi-hop Reservation Algorithm

The RESERVE algorithm is recursive, with parameters s, r and d, where s and d are the source and destination of the multi-hop flow, requiring a reservation of r. First, the source reserves r for the multi-hop flow. If it is unable, the reservation fails. If it is successful, then it requests each of its one-hop neighbours, except the next-hop along the multi-hop path, to reserve r for the multi-hop flow. If any neighbour cannot reserve r it returns failure, causing the reservation to fail and recursively release the reserved resources. However, if all neighbours succeed in making a reservation, then RESERVE is called recursively with the source equal to the next-hop node along the multi-hop path. If the next hop is the destination, then the reservation has succeeded at each node along the path, and the success propagates back to the source of the multi-hop flow. The pseudocode for the RESERVE algorithm is provided in Algorithm 1.

Algorithm 1. RESERVE(s, r, d)

1: **if** (capacity$_s - r$) ≤ 0 **then**
2:     **return false**
3: **end if**
4: capacity$_s \leftarrow$ capacity$_s - r$
5: **if** ($s == d$) **then**
6:     **return true**
7: **else**
8:     status $\leftarrow$ **true**
9:     **for** each $n \in$ (NEIGHBOURS(s) \ NEXT_HOP(s)) **do**
10:         status $\leftarrow$ status **and** NEIGHBOUR_HAS_CAPACITY(n, r)
11:     **end for**
12:     **if** (status == **true**) **then**
13:         **return** RESERVE(NEXT_HOP(s), r, d)
14:     **else**
15:         tear down any completed reservations made by neighbours of s and s itself
            for this multi-hop flow
16:     **end if**
17: **end if**

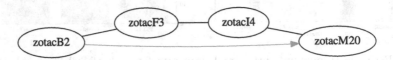

Fig. 6. A three-hop line topology used in the multi-hop reservation experiment. (Color figure online)

4.2   Multi-hop Reservation Evaluation

To evaluate the reservation process, experiments were conducted on the line topology with a multi-hop TCP flow. Figure 6 shows the line topology used with the multi-hop flow indicated in green. In the trials that used REACT, the TCP flow is started only after successful reservation along the path. In our experiments, we auction 80% of the channel, not 100%, leaving 20% for the control traffic; this is the same data/control traffic split used in [13]. The interior nodes of the line (e.g., zotacF4), must split 80% of the channel among three nodes (itself, and its previous and its next hop along the line). The reservation is placed for $\frac{80}{3} \approx 26.6\%$ airtime, which is close to the maximum amount of airtime that can be reserved in this scenario, assuming no other traffic flows. The TCP flow lasts for 120 s in both the REACT and 802.11 trials. Multi-hop routing is static with each node having neighbour information before the flow starts.

Figure 7 plots the airtime graphs for both REACT and 802.11 in the multi-hop scenario. The reservation of 26.6% airtime was placed after 0.9063 s and REACT converged after 9.041 s. Line topologies suffer both hidden and exposed node problems, with the airtime of 802.11 being highly unstable; in a multi-hop

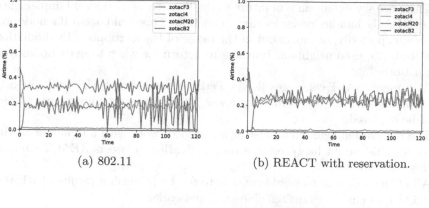

(a) 802.11

(b) REACT with reservation.

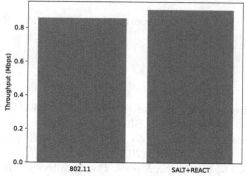

(c) Multi-hop TCP throughput comparison.

Fig. 7. Multi-hop TCP results: The airtime of 802.11 and of REACT with reservation over the life of the multi-hop flow, and the multi-hop TCP throughput.

flow, the relatively high airtime of `zotacF3` cannot help the throughput of the multi-hop flow. The more consistent airtime and lower jitter for REACT leads to higher TCP throughput over REACT than over standard 802.11. Specifically, 802.11 achieved throughput of 0.86 Mbps, while multi-hop REACT achieved 0.91 Mbps.

5   Summary and Future Work

A new tuning algorithm, SALT, converges more tightly to REACT's airtime allocations, and tighter convergence leads to reductions in unfairness and jitter compared to 802.11 DCF. A new multi-hop reservation algorithm that leverages the airtime allocation and realization capabilities of this combination was proposed. With a reservation in place we have shown that REACT and SALT achieve higher throughput in a multi-hop TCP flow than in one that runs over 802.11 DCF.

There are several avenues of future work. To date, no real-world implementation of REACT handles nodes leaving an auction. This could occur if a node goes offline unexpectedly, or moves out of the range of the auctioneer. In simulation, Lutz et al. [19] used neighbour timeouts to determine when to evict nodes from the auction.

At present, SALT converges slowly. Perhaps combining SALT with the original tuning algorithm to leverage the lower jitter and faster convergence of each could be explored.

The reservation algorithm must be adapted to work with a dynamic routing protocol. This would likely require communication between REACT and the routing software.

All of these directions would contribute to the promising results of REACT with SALT to enabling fair, scalable mesh networks.

Acknowledgements. This work is supported in part by the U.S. National Science Foundation under Grant No. 1421058.

References

1. Bharghavan, V., Demers, A., Shenker, S., Zhang, L.: MACAW: a media access protocol for wireless LANs. In: ACM SIGCOMM (1994)
2. Bianchi, G., Tinnirello, I.: Remarks on IEEE 802.11 DCF performance analysis. IEEE Commun. Lett. **9**(8), 765–767 (2005)
3. Bicket, J., Aguayo, D., Biswas, S., Morris, R.: Architecture and evaluation of an unplanned 802.11b mesh network. In: Proceedings of the 11th Annual ACM Mobi-Com, pp. 31–42 (2005). https://doi.org/10.1145/1080829.1080833
4. Blefari-Melazzi, N., Detti, A., Habib, I., Ordine, A., Salsano, S.: TCP fairness issues in IEEE 802.11 networks: problem analysis and solutions based on rate control. IEEE Trans. Wirel. Commun. **6**(4), 1346–1355 (2007)
5. Bouckaert, S., Vandenberghe, W., Jooris, B., Moerman, I., Demeester, P.: The w-iLab.t testbed. In: Magedanz, T., Gavras, A., Thanh, N.H., Chase, J.S. (eds.) TridentCom 2010. LNICST, vol. 46, pp. 145–154. Springer, Heidelberg (2011). https://doi.org/10.1007/978-3-642-17851-1_11
6. Cali, F., Conti, M., Gregori, E.: Dynamic tuning of the IEEE 802.11 protocol to achieve a theoretical throughput limit. IEEE/ACM Trans. Netw. **8**(6), 785–799 (2000)
7. Camp, J., Robinson, J., Steger, C., Knightly, E.: Measurement driven deployment of a two-tier urban mesh access network. In: Proceedings of the 4th ACM Mobisys, pp. 96–109 (2006)
8. Carlson, E., Prehofer, C., Bettstetter, C., Karl, H., Wolisz, A.: A distributed end-to-end reservation protocol for IEEE 802.11-based wireless mesh networks. IEEE J. Sel. Areas Commun. **24**(11), 2018–2027 (2006)
9. Carrano, R., Magalhaes, L., Saade, D., Albuquerque, C.: IEEE 802.11s multihop MAC: a tutorial. IEEE Commun. Surv. Tutor. **13**(1), 52–67 (2011)
10. Ergin, M.A., Ramachandran, K., Gruteser, M.: An experimental study of inter-cell interference effects on system performance in unplanned wireless LAN deployments. Comput. Netw. **52**(14), 2728–2744 (2008)

11. Fu, Z., Zerfos, P., Luo, H., Lu, S., Zhang, L., Gerla, M.: The impact of multi-hop wireless channel on TCP throughput and loss. In: Proceedings of IEEE INFOCOM, April 2003
12. Garetto, M., Salonidis, T., Knightly, E.: Modeling per-flow throughput and capturing starvation in CSMA multi-hop wireless networks. IEEE/ACM Trans. Netw. **16**(4), 864–877 (2008)
13. Garlisi, D., Giuliano, F., Lo Valvo, A., Lutz, J., Syrotiuk, V.R., Tinnirello, I.: Making Wi-Fi work in multi-hop topologies: automatic negotiation and allocation of airtime. In: Proceedings of IEEE CNERT, pp. 48–55 (2015)
14. Gupta, A., Wormsbecker, I., Williamson, C.: Experimental evaluation of TCP performance in multi-hop wireless ad hoc networks. In: Proceedings of the 12th Annual IEEE International Symposium on MASCOTS, pp. 3–11 (2004)
15. IEEE standard 802.11: W-LAN medium access control & physical layer specifications, December 1999
16. Imboden, T., Akkaya, K., Moore, Z.: Performance evaluation of wireless mesh networks using IEEE 802.11s and IEEE 802.11n. In: Proceedings of the IEEE ICC, pp. 5675–5679, June 2012
17. Jardosh, A.P., Mittal, K., Ramachandran, K.N., Belding, E.M., Almeroth, K.C.: IQU: practical queue-based user association management for WLANs. In: Proceedings of the 12th ACM MobiCom, pp. 158–169 (2006)
18. Kosek-Szott, K., et al.: What's new for QoS in IEEE 802.11? IEEE Netw. **27**(6), 95–104 (2013)
19. Lutz, J., Colbourn, C.J., Syrotiuk, V.R.: ATLAS: adaptive topology-and load-aware scheduling. IEEE Trans. Mob. Comput. **13**(10), 2255–2268 (2014)
20. Mellott, M.J.: Smoothed airtime linear tuning and optimized REACT with multi-hop extensions. Master's thesis, Arizona State University (2018)
21. Papagiannaki, K., Yarvis, M., Conner, W.: Experimental characterization of home wireless networks and design implications. In: Proceedings of the 25th IEEE INFOCOM, pp. 1–13, April 2006
22. Shen, Q., Fang, X., Li, P., Fang, Y.: Admission control based on available bandwidth estimation for wireless mesh networks. IEEE Trans. Veh. Technol. **58**(5), 2519–2528 (2009)

Segmented Source Routing for Handling Link Failures in Software Defined Network

Sharvari Komajwar[(⊠)] and Turgay Korkmaz

Department of Computer Science, The University of Texas at San Antonio,
San Antonio, TX 78249, USA
{sharvari.komajwar,turgay.korkmaz}@utsa.edu

Abstract. When a link fails in Software Defined Networks (SDN), the flows that use the failed link need to be rerouted over other paths. To achieve this rerouting task, researchers have proposed reactive and proactive recovery approaches. In reactive approach, upon failure, SDN controller computes new paths for the affected flows and installs them on demand. In proactive approach, the SDN controller pre-calculates backup paths and installs them on the switches in advance. While proactive approach minimizes packet loss and delay, it introduces a new problem, namely excessive usage of limited TCAM memory at SDN switches. In this paper, we consider two promising techniques (namely source routing and segment routing), and propose a new proactive technique called Segmented Source Routing (SSR). SSR uses source routing but in a segmented manner: one from the failure detecting node to an emergency node and one from emergency node to the destination. After addressing various challenges in placing emergency nodes and assigning emergency nodes to flows, our simulations shows that SSR maintains the same level of performance of pure source routing while significantly reducing the memory overhead, computation overhead, and the packet sizes as it shortens the source routes and avoids storing them at every node.

Keywords: SDN · Link failure · Source routing · Segment routing

1 Introduction

One of the key issues in SDN is how to re-route the flows on a failed link through other paths. Formally, this problem can be stated as follows.

Definition 1. *Link Failure Handling (LFH) Problem:* Consider a network that is represented by a directed graph $G = (V, E)$, where V is the set of nodes/switches and E is the set of links. Let $n = |V|$ be the number of nodes in the network and $m = |E|$ be the number of edges in the network. Each link $(u, v) \in E$ is associated with a cost parameter $c(u, v)$. Suppose the SDN controller accurately maintains this network state information and uses it to

© IFIP International Federation for Information Processing 2018
Published by Springer Nature Switzerland AG 2018. All Rights Reserved
K. R. Chowdhury et al. (Eds.): WWIC 2018, LNCS 10866, pp. 146–158, 2018.
https://doi.org/10.1007/978-3-030-02931-9_12

compute the shortest paths for each flow request that goes from a source node s to a destination node d. Suppose there are F flows passing through a link (u, v). If that link fails, all the flows using the failed link (u, v) will be affected as the packets belonging to these flows get lost and/or delayed. Given a failed link (u, v), the LFH problem is how to quickly and efficiently reroute all the affected F flows to other paths so that we can avoid or minimize the packet loss and delay.

In response to addressing the LFH problem, researchers have proposed various recovery mechanisms in the literature [1,6–12]. The existing techniques are mainly of two types: Reactive (or path restoration) [12] and Proactive (or path protection) [1,7–11]. In the case of *reactive* solutions, the controller needs to be informed about the link failure. Upon receiving link failure notification, the controller determines a new path and updates all the switches related to the new path. The main advantage of the reactive approach is the fact that the underlying switches do not need to store any extra backup paths or state information besides the primary paths. Moreover, the found path will be the best one under the given network state information. However, due to the extra times required for conveying the link failure information to the controller, computing new paths, and consistently updating/installing new forwarding rules [4,5], the reactive techniques loose and/or delay many packets until the recovery is completed. To minimize the recovery time, Sharma et al. in [12] have proposed an improvement where the controller pre-calculates all the backup paths and use them on demand to reroute the affected flows. However, due the dominance of delays in conveying link failure and updating new rules consistently, reactive techniques would be still very slow to avoid packet loss and/or delay in practice. As a mater of fact, Sharma et al. demonstrates that it is hard to obtain less than 50 ms recovery times when using a controller-based restoration approach [13].

To avoid (or minimize) packet loss and delay during recovery time, the researchers have considered *proactive* techniques [1,7–11]. The basic idea here is to have a backup path readily available so that the packets from the affected flows can quickly be re-routed without waiting for the controller's intervention. The performance and the cost of this approach depends on how to determine and maintain backup paths. At one extreme, while installing the primary path for a flow, the controller computes and installs a backup path per flow from every node on the primary path to the destination. Clearly, this extreme version of proactive approach significantly speeds up the response time and thus totally avoids the packet loss and delay as the backup path is readily available at each node. However, this improvement comes at the cost of excessive memory usage for storing and maintaining additional backup paths per flow on the underlying switches, where the TCAM memory is limited and consumes significant amount of energy [7–10]. For example, if we have F flows going through a link (u, v), then we have to maintain at least $2F$ flow entries at node u, which will be a significant memory overhead as F increases. Therefore, it is deemed necessary to limit the number of backup paths for efficient use of memory space while being able to quickly reroute the affected flows.

With this in mind, researchers have investigated different proactive techniques. For example, Capone et al. have considered utilizing the cranckback routing idea to avoid maintaining backup paths at each node [1]. In this case, some backup paths are computed from some selected nodes and installed through the network. Upon a link failure, the failure detecting node uses cranckback routing to send the packets back. When the packets reach a node with a backup path, that node re-routes the traffic. While this reduces the number of backup paths, the reverse paths might be longer or congested, causing delays and loss. Sgambelluri et al. have proposed to use backup paths per destination rather than per flow [11]. While these approaches reduce the number of backup paths and saves some memory, they may still use significant amount of TCAM space for storing and maintaining the backup paths or the backup path might not be the best one.

To minimize the excessive TCAM memory overhead while using better paths, researchers have considered new techniques based on *source routing* [8,10] and *segment routing* [6]. In source routing, the controller calculates the shortest paths from each source node to all other destination nodes and stores the complete paths at each source node. When a particular flow is created, its source node checks the destination and inserts the whole path to that destination into the packet header. In SDN, VLAN tags can be pushed into the header to store the whole path information, which contains either the IDs of nodes along the path or just port IDs on each node of the path [8,14].

In [8], Liaoruo et al. have proposed to use source routing for maintaining backup paths. In source routing, every switch u on the primary path of a flow stores the complete backup paths to its destination rather than installing it throughout the network. To do this, the controller eliminates each link (u,v) on the primary path at a time, and computes the shortest paths from u to the destination of the flow. It then stores the corresponding path on switch u. So, if F flows are passing through u, then that switch has to store F source routes (note that these backup paths are not installed throughout the network). When there is a failure on link (u,v), node u will quickly detect the link failure and (without waiting for the controller) it will reroute the incoming packets by inserting the pre-stored source route from u to the destination into the packet header and forward it to the next node. Clearly, source routing minimizes the number of flow entries in the switches. But the length of each entry increases since the whole backup path is stored per flow [8]. Effectively, each switch needs to maintain F many backup paths, which will be costly as F increases. Moreover, the authors in [8] propose to update these backup paths after some interval of time based on the current status of the network, which further increases the computation overhead on the controller. Another issue with pure source routing is that it increases the packet size as the whole backup path is included into the packets.

Segment routing (SR) [3] is similar to loose source routing (an IP option to record the set of routers that a packet must visit). In contrast to the pure source routing, SR inserts the IDs of a few nodes into the packet header and then tries to send a packet to the next node by using the paths determined and maintained by the underlying routing protocol. The path between the consecutive nodes in the header is called a segment. In [6], authors have considered using 2-segment routing to deal with LFH problem. This approach limits the number of node IDs in the header and the number of entries in the SDN flow tables. However, it relies on the underlying protocol to compute new paths for the segments to deal with the link failure. Unfortunately, when the failed link is on the segment that needs to be used, this approach can still cause packet loss and delay until the underlying routing protocol finds new paths, as in the reactive approach. Moreover, in segment routing when link fails, all the paths on intermediate nodes need to be updated consistently to guarantee loop-free and black-hole-free routing.

In this paper, we propose a new link failure handling technique called Segmented Source Routing (SSR) by merging the best of the source routing and segment routing. As in the source routing, SSR includes the path information into the packet headers so that we can avoid memory overhead by not installing backup paths through the network. However, to further minimize the number of source routes maintained at each node and to minimize the length of the paths included in the packet headers, SSR does this in a segmented manner and per destination rather than per flow. In SSR, we first identify some nodes as emergency nodes. The controller then pre-computes the shortest paths from every node to the emergency nodes and from emergency nodes to every node. We store these paths at their respective source nodes. When a flow request arrives, the controller determines a primary path and installs it as usual. In contrast to the pure source routing, which computes a backup path from each node on that primary path [8], our SSR approach simply determines which emergency node (say node e) to use at each node u. For each flow, this information is maintained in the flow table at node u. Upon detecting a link failure, node u simply inserts the source route from u to e into the packet headers of the affected flows and sends them towards the corresponding emergency node e. Upon receiving such a packet, emergency node e inserts the source route from e to d and sends it towards d. In contrast to the pure segment routing, we do not rely on the underlying routing protocols to find paths for segments. Instead, we determine each segment using source routing. In the following sections, we will further describe the proposed SSR framework and address the challenges in it.

The rest of the paper is organized as follows. Section 2 gives the overview of the proposed SSR framework. Section 3 addresses the challenges in SSR. Section 4 presents the performance evaluation using simulation. Section 5 talks about future work and concludes the paper.

2   The Proposed Segmented Source Routing Framework

To quickly and efficiently respond to the link failures, we propose a new technique called Segmented Source Routing (SSR). In essence, SSR is similar to source routing. However, instead of including the whole source route into packet headers, SSR divides the path into two segments and include the source route for each segment into packet headers one at a time. To be able to that, SSR designates some nodes in the network as the *emergency* nodes. Then, SSR makes every emergency node store the list of source routes to all destinations while making every other switch/node store only the source routes to all the emergency nodes. Since the number of emergency nodes is expected to be significantly less than n, we will avoid significant memory overhead when storing source routes. Moreover, instead of storing source routes per flow as in [8], SSR stores source routes per destination. This way SSR minimizes both the length of the path information included into packet headers and the number of source routes stored. This will significantly reduce memory overhead, particularly when the number of flows F increases.

When installing the primary path for a particular flow, the SDN controller needs to determine which emergency nodes to contact from each node on the primary path. Emergency node information is included as part of the flow entry at each node on the primary path. So when link (u, v) fails, node u can detect the failure and identify the emergency node for each flow passing through this link. Accordingly, node u inserts the first segmented source route from u to the corresponding emergency node e into the packet header and sends it. Upon receiving such a packet, the emergency node e inserts the second segmented source route from the emergency node to the destination.

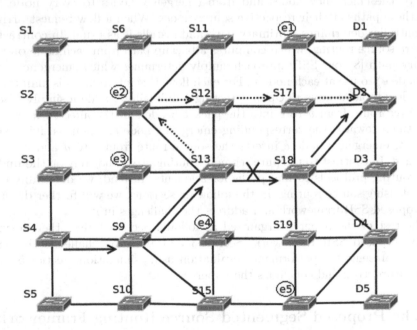

Fig. 1. An example for link failure handling.

For example, Fig. 1 shows a link failure scenario where primary shortest path from the source $S4$ to destination $D2$ is $\{S4, S9, S13, S18, D2\}$. Suppose node

$e2$ is the emergency node for that flow at node $S13$ and the link $(S13, S18)$ fails. In this case, the switch $S13$ detects the link failure and inserts the first segmented source route $\{S13, e2\}$ into the packets of that flow and sends them to the emergency node $e2$. Upon receiving these packets, the emergency node $e2$ inserts the second segmented source route $\{e2, S12, S17, D2\}$ into the packets and sends them to the destination node $D2$.

Instead of using pure source routing per flow as in [8] or the pure segment routing as in [3], we combine the best of these two mechanisms as segmented source routing, which pre-computes and installs two segments of source routes: $segment(u, e)$ from every node u to each emergency node e; $segment(e, d)$ from every emergency node e to every destination node d. Then, when installing a primary path, the SDN controller decides which emergency node to use for each node on the primary path, and includes the ID of the selected emergence node in the flow entry. So, when a link fails, the failure detecting node u simply includes the corresponding $segment(u, e)$ into the packets of the affected flows. Receiving emergency nodes include the corresponding $segment(e, d)$ into the packets and send them.

The key goals of SSR are to (a) reduce the packet size by including shorter source routes into the packets, (b) minimize the number of source routes maintained at each node, and (c) avoid the unnecessary path computations during the installation of the primary path. While achieving these goals, the proposed SSR method should maintain the same level of performance as the pure source routing. Using simulations, we show that SSR has almost the same performance in terms of the cost of the backup paths used and the link utilization, while significantly reducing the packet size, minimizing the number of source routes at each node, and avoiding the unnecessary path computations. We should also note that segmented-source routes are computed in a loop-free and black-hole-free manner and can be changed independently without worrying about a network wide convergence of the underlying routing protocol that maintains the paths for the segments in the pure segment routing.

3   Challenges and Solutions in SSR

In this section, we discuss three crucial challenges that need to be addressed for the SSR technique to efficiently handle link failures. Specifically, we consider: (a) how to select and place emergency nodes, (b) how to compute the segmented source routes from each node to emergency nodes and from each emergency node to all destinations, and (c) which emergency node to assign to which flow at each node on the primary path.

3.1   Emergency Node Selection and Placement Problem

Selection of emergency nodes and their placement play an important role in improving the performance of proposed SSR technique. Intuitively, emergency nodes need to be distributed evenly in the network so that a given node can access one of the emergency nodes with minimum number of hops. At the same time, the emergency node should be able to access the destination with minimum number of hops. In this paper, we will content with randomly selecting the desired number of nodes as emergency nodes to achieve even distribution. In the future, we will investigate how to optimally place them to further improve the performance.

3.2   Segmented Source Route Calculation

Once the controller selects emergency nodes in the network, it calculates the shortest paths for two segments. For the first segment, it computes the shortest paths from every node to emergency nodes and stores these as source routes at each node. For the second segment, it computes the shortest paths from every emergency node to all destinations and stores these as source routes at each emergency node.

We compute the shortest paths based on the same cost parameter used for the pure source routing in [8]. Specifically, the cost of a link (u, v) is determined as follows:

$$c(u, v) = \frac{1}{1 - \rho(u, v)} \tag{1}$$

where $\rho(u, v)$ represents the utilization of link (u, v) and computed using

$$\rho(u, v) = \frac{D(u, v)}{B(u, v)} \tag{2}$$

where $B(u, v)$ is the bandwidth capacity of link (u, v) and $D(u, v)$ is the total demand of the flows using link (u, v). In the future, we plan to also consider different cost parameters that take into account the interference of backup paths on the primary paths.

3.3   Per Flow Emergency Node Assignment

In the case of a link failure, the failure detecting node needs to know which emergency node to contact for each affected flow passing through the failed link. This decision should be made by the SDN controller, which determines a primary path and installs the necessary flow table entries as usual. In the pure source routing, the controller computes the shortest path from each node u on the primary path to destination d as a backup path per flow, and stores that path as the source route at node u. In contrast, SSR assigns an emergency node for each node u on the primary path and saves this information as part of the flow entry at node u. Since our segmented-source routes are pre-computed and stored at each node per destination, the controller is not overloaded with backup path computations per flow or sending these paths to each node while installing the primary path. This way SSR significantly reduces the memory requirements at each node while also decreasing the computation and communication overheads at the controller. Such reductions in the computational load and chattiness of the controller will significantly improve its responsiveness and performance.

The selection of emergency node at each node is an important decision as it will impact the overall performance when there is a link failure. So the controller needs to carefully select the emergency node at each node on the primary path. We formally define this problem as follows:

Definition 2. *Emergency Node Assignment (ENA) Problem*: Consider the network model given in Definition 1. Let R be the set of emergency nodes, where $R \subseteq V$. Suppose the controller has already computed and stored the shortest paths (source routes) from each node $u \in V$ to the emergency node $e \in R$; and from each emergency node $e \in V$ to every node $u \in V$. Upon receiving a request for a flow going from s to d, the controller finds the shortest path (the primary path) p_{sd} as usual. Given R, p_{sd} and the pre-computed segmented-source routes, the EAN problem is to find/assign the best emergency node $e \in R$ for each node $u \in p_{sd} = \{s, \ldots, u, v, \ldots, d\}$ such that the link (u, v) is not included in source routes denoted by $segment(u, e)$ or $segment(e, d)$.

Ideally, we would like to select an emergency node $e \in R$ for each node $u \in p_{sd}$ such that the sum of the cost of $segment(u, e)$ and the cost of $segment(e, d)$ is minimum. However, since we would like to also minimize the packet size by including a source route with minimum number of hop IDs, we should select the segments containing less number of hops. To minimize both hop count and the cost, we propose to select the emergency node $e \in R$ for each node $u \in p_{sd}$ based on the following objective function:

$$\min_{\forall e \in R}\{C(u, e) * H(u, e) + C(e, d) * H(e, d)\} \tag{3}$$

where $C(u, e)$ and $C(e, d)$ represent the total costs and $H(u, e)$ and $H(e, d)$ represents the hop counts of $segment(u, e)$ and $segment(e, d)$, respectively.

Regarding computational complexity, for each node u, this optimization can simply be done in $O(|R|)$ while the pure source routing requires the execution of the shortest path algorithm with $O(|E| + |V|log|V|)$. Note that $|R| << |V|$.

While the above heuristic finds an emergency node quickly in most cases, it is possible that the source path from u to e or the source path from e to d might include the failed link. We call such a path as a non-safe path. So, the controller needs to eliminate such non-safe paths by simply checking it as follows. Suppose we have a link (u, v) on the computed primary path. So when selecting the emergency node e for node u, the controller needs to make sure that the link (u, v) is not part of the source route from u to e or from e to d. Note that since the controller has all the source routes that are stored in the switches, it can do this locally. There is no communication between the controller and switches. In our simulations, we always find a safe path. But in a rare case, if there is no safe path through any emergency node, then we can use the pure source routing for that case only.

3.4   Computation Overhead and Memory Consumption

The major goals of the proposed SSR method is to reduce the computation overhead on the controller and memory consumption on the switches. In [8], while installing the flow entries for a flow, the controller calculates a backup path (source route) for the possible failure of each link (u, v) on the primary path and stores that source route from u to the destination d on the switch u. Moreover, to keep these backup paths up-to-date, the controller runs a modified Dijkstra for each switch after a particular interval, which further increases the computation overhead on the controller and the chattiness between the controller and the switches. Since the backup paths are maintained per flow, each flow entry at node u has to contain the full source route from u to d, causing significant memory overhead. In contrast, the proposed SSR method pre-computes the shortest path per destination as in the segment routing. In contrast to segment routing, SSR stores the shortest paths as source routes. So these source routes can be independently computed or updated without relying on the underlying routing protocols to determine and install them in a consistent manner as the pure segment routing does.

Compared to the pure source routing, the proposed SSR approach involves much less computation overhead and memory consumption. Another key advantage of SSR is that since it includes a segment rather than the whole source route into the packets, it decreases the packet size, resulting in efficient use of resources and faster transfer. Despite these advantages, one natural question is to find out how SSR performs in terms of other measures. In the next section, we compare SSR against the pure source routing in terms of the cost of the backup paths used and the level of increase in link utilization after the link failure. Clearly, the pure source routing would be better as it uses per flow backup paths. However, our simulations show that the proposed SSR closely achieves the same performance while using less resources and computation time.

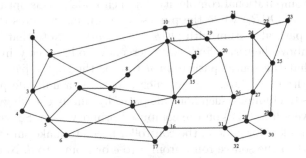

Fig. 2. Topology with n = 32, m = 110

4 Performance Evaluation

4.1 Simulation Setup

We compared our proposed SSR method against the pure source routing (PSR) in [8]. We implemented both methods in Python and compared them by using the realistic network topology shown in Fig. 2, which is modified from ANSNET [2].

Our topology (shown in Fig. 2) has $n = 32$ nodes and $m = 110$ directed edges. We first randomly select the bandwidth for each link from uniform (10, 20). We randomly select the source node s from uniform (1, 6), the nodes on the left, while selecting the destination d from uniform (23, 32), the nodes in the right. To test different load, we used two set of experiments with 20 flows and 40 flows. Respectively, the demand of each flow is randomly selected from the range uniform (1, 6) and uniform (1, 4). For the proposed SSR, we varied the number of emergency nodes as 3, 6, 12 and selected the given number of emergency nodes randomly. After installing the given set of flows, we do not generate any new flow. But we fail randomly selected links one at a time and re-route the affected flows through backup paths.

As the performance measures, we consider (a) the cost of the backup paths at the time of link failures, (b) the increase in link utilization because of using backup paths, and (c) the number of hop IDs included into the packets (hop count). We repeated each experiments 10 times and took their averages.

Average Cost. Figure 3 shows the average cost of the backup paths used by SSR and PSR with different number of flows while varying the number of emergency nodes. The cost of a backup path is calculated using (1) at the time of using that backup path. As shown in Fig. 3, the performance of SSR gets very close to that of PSR as the number of emergency nodes increase from 3 ($\approx$10% of all nodes) to 6 ($\approx$20% all nodes). With 12 emergency nodes ($\approx$40% all nodes), the average cost of backup paths provided by SSR is almost the same as that of PSR.

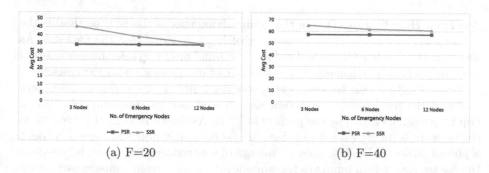

(a) F=20   (b) F=40

Fig. 3. Average cost of backup paths at the time of link failures.

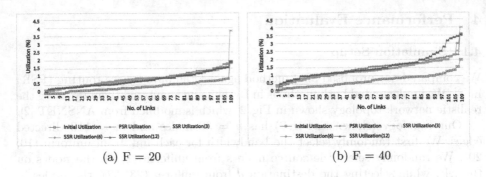

(a) F = 20   (b) F = 40

Fig. 4. Link utilization distribution before and after link failures.

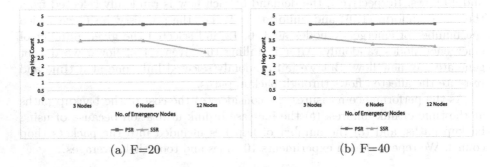

(a) F=20   (b) F=40

Fig. 5. Average number of hops carried by the packet

Utilization. Figure 4 shows the increase in link utilization for PSR and SSR with 3, 6 and 12 emergency nodes after a failure happens. In the case of 3 emergency nodes, since all the traffic of backup paths goes through these 3 emergency nodes, SSR with 3 emergency nodes makes a few links heavily loaded. But as the number of emergency nodes increases, SSR is able to distribute the load as the PSR does and provide similar link utilization distributions.

Average Hop Count. One of the main advantages of the SSR method is the reduction of hop count (i.e., the number of hops included into the packets). As shown in the Fig. 5, SSR method reduces the number of hop information inserted into the packets, particularly as the number of emergency nodes increases.

From Fig. 5, it can be seen that when the number of emergency nodes are ≈40% of the total number of nodes, each packet carries approximately 50% of hop information carried by the packets in PSR. As shown in Fig. 5(b), even when the network is highly loaded and there are 6 emergency nodes average hop count is almost 50% of PSR. The main advantage of this reduced hop count is to reduce the packet size, which improves transmission time and avoids unnecessary usage of resources.

5 Conclusion and Future Work

We proposed a failure handling method in SDN based on the best features of source routing and segment routing. Through simulations, we showed that proposed SSR method reduces memory overhead on the switches, computation time at the controller, and the packet size while providing almost the same performance of pure source routing in terms of the cost of the backup paths and the link utilization increase after the failure.

To demonstrate the potential benefits of the proposed SSR framework, we used simple heuristics in addressing various challenges in SSR. We now plan to further investigate new algorithms to address these challenges. Both PSR and our SSR simply computes the shortest path as a backup path. We plan to develop new cost parameters that can take into account the interference of backup paths on the primary paths.

References

1. Capone, A., Cascone, C., Nguyen, A.Q.T., Sansò, B.: Detour planning for fast and reliable failure recovery in SDN with OpenState. CoRR, abs/1411.7711 (2014)
2. Comer, D.E.: Internetworking with TCP/IP, vol. 1, 3rd edn. Prentice Hall Inc., Upper Saddle River (1995)
3. Filsfils, C., Nainar, N.K., Pignataro, C., Cardona, J.C., Francois, P.: The segment routing architecture. In: IEEE Global Communications Conference (GLOBE-COM), pp. 1–6, December 2015
4. Foerster, K.-T., Schmid, S., Vissicchio, S.: Survey of consistent network updates. CoRR, abs/1609.02305 (2016)
5. Frster, K.T., Mahajan, R., Wattenhofer, R.: Consistent updates in software defined networks: on dependencies, loop freedom, and blackholes. In: IFIP Networking Conference (IFIP Networking) and Workshops, pp. 1–9, May 2016
6. Hao, F., Kodialam, M., Lakshman, T.V.: Optimizing restoration with segment routing. In: IEEE INFOCOM 2016 - The 35th Annual IEEE International Conference on Computer Communications, pp. 1–9, April 2016
7. Kitsuwan, N., Payne, D.B., Ruffini, M.: A novel protection design for OpenFlow-based networks. In: The 16th International Conference on Transparent Optical Networks (ICTON), pp. 1–5, July 2014
8. Liaoruo, H., Qingguo, S., Wenjuan, S.: A source routing based link protection method for link failure in SDN. In: The 2nd IEEE International Conference on Computer and Communications (ICCC), pp. 2588–2594, October 2016
9. Lin, Y.D., Teng, H.Y., Hsu, C.R., Liao, C.C., Lai, Y.C.: Fast failover and switchover for link failures and congestion in software defined networks. In: IEEE International Conference on Communications (ICC), pp. 1–6, May 2016
10. Ramos, R.M., Martinello, M., Esteve Rothenberg, C.: SlickFlow: resilient source routing in data center networks unlocked by OpenFlow. In: The 38th Annual IEEE Conference on Local Computer Networks, pp. 606–613, October 2013
11. Sgambelluri, A., Giorgetti, A., Cugini, F., Paolucci, F., Castoldi, P.: Openflow-based segment protection in ethernet networks. IEEE/OSA J. Opt. Commun. Netw. 5(9), 1066–1075 (2013)

12. Sharma, S., Staessens, D., Colle, D., Pickavet, M., Demeester, P.: Enabling fast failure recovery in OpenFlow networks. In: The 8th International Workshop on the Design of Reliable Communication Networks (DRCN), pp. 164–171, October 2011
13. Sharma, S., Staessens, D., Colle, D., Pickavet, M., Demeester, P.: OpenFlow: meeting carrier-grade recovery requirements. Comput. Commun. **36**(6), 656–665 (2013)
14. Soliman, M., Nandy, B., Lambadaris, I., Ashwood-Smith, P.: Exploring source routed forwarding in SDN-based WANs. In: IEEE International Conference on Communications (ICC), pp. 3070–3075, June 2014

Protocol Heterogeneity Issues of Incremental High-Density Wi-Fi Deployment

Haymanot Gebre-Amlak[✉], Md Tajul Islam, Daniel Cummins,
Mohammed Al Mansoori, and Baek-Young Choi

Department of Computer Science and Electrical Engineering,
University of Missouri-Kansas City, 5100 Rockhill Rd., Kansas City, MO, USA
{hhgc77,mi8rd,cumminsdm,mkakh3,choiby}@umkc.edu

Abstract. Going beyond the traditional coverage-oriented Wi-Fi network design, the recent Wi-Fi networks are designed for high traffic demand with high density deployments. A university campus environment is particularly unique in that a large number of users with multiple heterogeneous devices demand high capacity and performance from a wireless network over a wide geographical area. From a network management perspective, not only should the network support heterogeneous Wi-Fi protocols and devices, but high-density access points (APs) are needed to handle the high traffic demands. To meet the rising demands Wi-Fi AP upgrades are deployed incrementally over an extended period to cover the vast area found in a campus setting, which is different from a building-level Wi-Fi network.

In this paper, we present a measurement study to bring forth wireless network management issues faced during incremental Wi-Fi deployment on a university campus network. We discuss various design considerations given to incremental deployments of Wi-Fi 802.11 (ac) including replacing older Wi-Fi versions, and addressing compatibility, data rate, coverage, and performance concerns. In addition, we perform pre-and-post upgrade evaluations using different network performance analysis tools. This study will shed light on heterogeneous large-scale Wi-Fi network management issues, as these will become applicable with the increasing prevalence of large metro area wireless networks.

1 Introduction

The availability of versatile and resilient wireless networks with high-speed performance and Wi-Fi on-the-go service with always-connected features for bandwidth-intensive applications is considered a basic necessity these days. Faster connection and speedy performance are the bare requirements for emerging bandwidth intensive services like high resolution video uploading (i.e., YouTube), video streaming (i.e., Netflix), virtual reality, augmented reality,

© IFIP International Federation for Information Processing 2018
Published by Springer Nature Switzerland AG 2018. All Rights Reserved
K. R. Chowdhury et al. (Eds.): WWIC 2018, LNCS 10866, pp. 159–170, 2018.
https://doi.org/10.1007/978-3-030-02931-9_13

real-time updating data (i.e., Facebook), online gaming, and live stream video (i.e. surveillance camera data). For example, Cisco announced [11] that it is expecting the global traffic to extend to 3.3 ZB per year by 2021 or 278 EB per month [11]. Devices and connections are growing at a 10 percent compound annual growth rate (CAGR) [5], and North American growth is expected to be the highest rate in the world [11]. Adaptation of IPv6 throughout the Internet allows for an effortless interaction among the Internet of Things (IoT) [12]. Internet traffic is increased by internet video, video-streaming, gaming, video-conferencing, and video specific applications. Most internet users use the internet on their mobile devices such as tablets, phone, laptop, etc., and they get their connection through wireless data services. They require high throughput and seamless connectivity without outage from their network services. IEEE 802.11 [25] wireless network standards, which is the most publicly used, have evolved to meet these growing requirements in terms of features like extended channel binding, multi-user Multiple In Multiple Out (MIMO) [26] ability, wide range of modulation, beam-forming, MAC modification, coexistence mechanisms, throughput and much more [16].

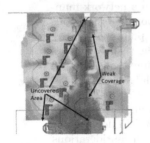

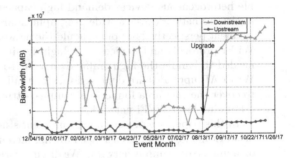

Fig. 1. An example of coverage map

Fig. 2. Network traffic

University Wi-Fi network accommodate thousands of mobile and wireless devices being used on a campus network. Multiple features of network utilization such as device variation, bandwidth requirements, application variability, operating system variability, user authentication and data off-loading, can be observed in a campus network. Each university strives to provide the best network service to its users despite the challenge of a fixed budget. To support the growing demand, it was necessary to upgrade the Wi-Fi network to improve coverage area, network speed, and throughput. The network team has taken two major steps for this enhancement. First, increase the number of access points (APs) to address the coverage gap. Second, upgrade the Wi-Fi network to 802.11 (ac) protocol to increase performance. In this paper, we conduct an extensive measurement analysis of the Wi-Fi network condition throughout the access layer of a university campus network, the University of Missouri - Kansas City (UMKC). We found some interesting phenomena like the variety of user density in the different locations with diversified bandwidth demands, lacking coverage in some area resulting in coverage gap, data rate degradation in certain points, and protocol compatibility issues. Figure 1 represents the signal strength and coverage map of a floor in a campus building prior to the upgrade. Furthermore, our observation indicates that between December 2016 and October 2017, the network's traffic (upstream and downstream) has increased by up to 20%, even though the number of clients has decreased, as illustrated in Fig. 2.

The remainder of the paper is organized as follows. Section 2 discusses the related work. Section 3 outlines the deployment consideration and design. Section 4 presents our evaluation of measurement and analysis. We conclude the paper in Sect. 5.

2   Related Work

2.1   Wi-Fi Performance

Performance measurement analysis research done by [24] on IEEE 802.11 (ac) Wi-Fi in a large 24-node indoor test-bed reveals the impact of channel width, network deployment density, and type/volume of traffic on the achieved network performance in dense indoor deployments [27]. A Framework of Heterogeneous Network(HetNet) for Mobile cloud computing (MCC) has been introduced by [21], and they discuss the challenges for supporting MCC applications in HetNet. A focused study of dual-band APs performance in heterogeneous client adapter was done in [14] with a goal to understand the characteristics of 802.11 (n) networks in heterogeneous deployments. Their result reveals that dual band routers can effectively help in reducing the negative effects of adapters heterogeneity as well as providing backward compatibility.

Wi-Fi network supports varying levels of performance, depending on the technology standard. Research [22] introduces a key mandatory and optional PHY features, as well as the MAC enhancements of 802.11 (ac) over the existing 802.11 (n) standard in the evolution towards higher data rates. They compare the MAC performance between 802.11 (ac) and 802.11 (n) over three different frame aggregation mechanisms, viz., aggregate MAC service data unit (A-MSDU), aggregate MAC protocol data unit (A-MPDU), and hybrid A-MSDU/A-MPDU aggregation through numerical analysis and simulations. The result showed 802.11 (ac) outperforms 802.11 (n) with maximum throughput by 28% (84%).

2.2   Wi-Fi Usage

Study on the usage of the Google Wi-Fi network deployed in Mountain View, CA has been done by [15]. Their finding showed that usage naturally falls into three categories based almost entirely on client device type, traditional laptop users, fixed-location access devices, and PDA-like smart-phone devices and they have a diverse set of mobility patterns that map well to the archetypal use cases for traditional access technologies. In a study done by [19], for mobile clients to evaluate and select both APs and spectral bands in wide-spectrum networks that provide access to four bands at 700 MHz, 900 MHz, 2.4 GHz and 5 GHz by a single operational access network. Their finding showed under a diverse set of operating conditions, mobile clients can accurately predict their performance without a direct measurement at their current location and spectral bands. The challenge to provide seamless mobility emerges as a key topic in various standardization bodies as explored by [18] discusses the support of seamless handover between homogeneous networks. The continued effort in pursuit of gigabit wireless communications has been most noticeable in the IEEE 802.11 WLAN [20] in recent years. In 2010, the Wireless Gigabit (WiGig) Alliance, formed by a consortium of industry leaders, has completed the defined first draft of a unified architecture to enable tri-band communications over the frequency bands of 2.4, 5, and 60 GHz in their WiGig specification [23].

Our research differs from these authors; we focused on usage behavior measurement study of the access layer to bring light to the management issue discovered during incremental Wi-Fi deployment. We analyze less known network management issues such as coverage gap, bandwidth overload, and association/authentication failures due to roaming in a campus network.

Note that while there are a number of Wi-Fi measurement works available little studies have been done to provide insight on network management issues resulting from incremental, heterogeneous high-density [8] Wi-Fi deployment.

3   Wi-Fi Deployment Design

Incremental deployments were done over four years period. How to design heterogeneous compatibility, data rate, coverage, and performance were factored into the deployment plan and roll-out schedules [17].

Table 1. Data sets used

Data source	Data size	Duration
Syslog	15.3 billion records	Jan 2014–Jan 2018
Cisco Prime	(14 categories)/(126 items) report	Oct 2016–Jan 2018
Ekahau survey map	41 buildings blue print & signals of 1137 access points	Jan 2014–Jan 2018

Table 2. Data source and tools used for analyzing coverage, authentication and bandwidth issues

Issues	Coverage gaps	Authentication failure	BW overload
Analysis	Ekahau	Splunk & Syslog	Cisco Prime & WLC
Data sources	Survey map & Syslog	Netflow	Radius Logs
Tools	Ekahau & Splunk	Cisco Prime	Ekahau

3.1   Analysis Tool

Wireless devices need to be compatible with most of the wireless protocols and decide to select the best channel and wireless protocol based on wide range of parameters. The upgrade had to be backward compatible to accommodate heterogeneous devices [27]. The University Information Services department use network log events with Splunk and Ekahau Spectrum Analyzers to locate the coverage gaps through out the campus Wi-Fi network. There were many errors from re-authentication failure, and co-channel interference due to the wide range of the 2.4 GHz APs. Additionally, Wi-Fi network faced bandwidth overload in most of the 2.4 GHz APs due to the extensive coverage area which reaches too many clients far more than the APs' capacity. Deploying an upgrade to replace the older APs which supported 802.11 (b/g/n) [13] with newer APs that supports both 802.11 (b/g/n/ac) and the adaptive 802.11 (r) [3] with FT feature would address these rising concerns. There are several tools used for the analysis of the upgrade and the different issues resolved by the upgrade as listed in Table 2. Table 1 discusses the data set used for our analysis. We had 15.3 billion records generated by Syslog server over four years period. The second data source is Cisco Prime consisting of 1 h, 1 week, 1 month and/or 1 year reports data from 14 different Categories, Autonomous AP, Clean Air, Clients, Compliance, Composite, Device, Guests, Identity Service Engin, Mesh, Network Summary, Performance, Raw NetFlow, Security and System Monitoring. There are 126 items reports under these categories.

3.2   Channel Planning and Band Select Feature

Several questions came to mind while planning the Wi-Fi protocol. What channels do the heterogeneous devices in the campus network support? Many older devices may not support the Extended channels and when that happens, the upgrade should only be providing redundant coverage. What is the student capacity in each class rooms? High density deployments were needed in some of the large auditoriums, which required increasing the number of APs in addition to the Wi-Fi upgrade. Consideration was given for APs to be allocated where coverage is optimized with minimum number of APs. Clients inside a pair of APs need to be within coverage distance from at least one of APs.

The 2.4 GHz band covers a larger range than 5 GHz and is commonly used on the campus network. Cisco APs by default send quicker probe response from 2.4 GHz band, resulting in more connection to 2.4 GHz band until the AP is overloaded and can no longer accept new connections. To overcome this crowding issue, Cisco introduced a feature called 'Band Select' [4], which allows dual-band clients to prefer the 5 GHz band over the 2.4 GHz. Band selection works by regulating probe responses to clients by making 5 GHz channels more attractive to dual-band clients from delaying 2.4 GHz probe responses. For example, the number of device association that is higher than N (our network set N to be 12) will have 2.4 GHz response suppressed M (our network set M to be 4) times before allowing the clients to receive Probe Response from 2.4 GHz wireless band.

This may cause a small delay for non-dual band 2.4 GHz only devices, however, will alleviate the crowding issue of 2.4 GHz wireless band and send dual-band clients to 5 GHz wireless band creating a more balanced network.

3.3   Addressing Roaming Issue

Wi-Fi 802.11 (ac) has the fastest data rate, 1300 Megabits per second (Mbps) and compared to 802.11 (n) [25] typically 450 Mbps, it is 3x faster. Fast Transition(FT) [1], a feature of 802.11 (ac), makes roaming between two adjacent 5 GHz band seamless. However, if a client roams outside of 802.11 (ac) or even between two adjacent 5 GHz band and 2.4 GHz band, there is bound to be a delay. FT feature, included in the Wi-Fi deployment, permit continuous connectivity aboard wireless devices in motion, with fast and secure hand-offs from one base station to another while the client is roaming. FT will not be explored in this work. However, it will be scoped as part of future works.

3.4   Managing Coverage Gap

It is part of the design process to locate the holes in the existing Wi-Fi coverage area in order to identify the precise locations to place the new APs to provide the ultimate coverage. The initial installation had the APs stacked in one location of the building providing inefficiency and weak coverage to no coverage outside of the stacked APs coverage area. The current design fans out these APs to maximize the coverage area with minimum number of APs. Additional APs were placed throughout the campus locations to manage the load capacity for high-density areas.

Table 3. 802.11 (ac) wireless upgrade summary

Model	Desc	AP Count
1810	802.11 (ac) Wave 2 MU-MIMO	735
3802 I	Decisions based on Wave 1 end-device activities	65
3702	Wave 1 150 Mbps	199
3602 Radio	Dual-band 2.4/5-GHz - Wave 1 integrated radios	130

3.5   Wi-Fi Upgrade Summary

The incremental Wi-Fi upgrade targeted the wireless infrastructure of several buildings including the university dormitories, and an off-campus network. There were 1187 APs upgraded to 802.11 (ac). Several of the old APs were replaced by the new APs with updated features. Majority of the APs (735), had Model 1810 Wave 2 with feature MU-MIMO [26]. MU-MIMO provides concurrent downstream communications to multiple wireless devices allowing client devices to get on and off the network faster, enabling more clients to use the network. 199

of the APs were with Model 3702 Wave 1 dual-band radios with a data rate of 150 Mbps. Table 3 lists the model and the number of AP which were deployed over the summer/winter weeks targeting minimal impact to clients.

4 Evaluation

In this section we perform pre-and-post upgrade evaluation using different network performance analysis tools. Cisco Prime Infrastructure reporting [9] is a tools used by network team to help monitor the system and network health and is used for troubleshooting network problems. To evaluate the sheer volume of Syslog messages generated from the Wi-Fi network during the upgrade period between 2015 and 2018, we use Big Data analytic tool named Splunk. We used Ekahau Wi-Fi Site Survey tool to capture the coverage map before and after the deployment. We used Wireshark to capture the packets of the roaming clients and FT authentications. We also used Wireless LAN Controller (WLC) and Radius logs to gather the Wi-Fi traffic activities.

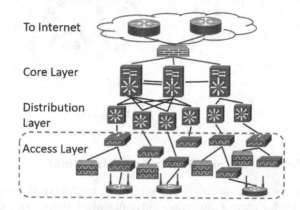

Fig. 3. Campus network architecture with three layers: core, distribution, and access layers

4.1 Campus Network Setup

The campus network is hierarchical with three layers which is a common practice for campus or enterprise networks, illustrated by Fig. 3. UMKC network's core routing depends mainly on two core routers, one as primary and the second as fail-over and load-balance. There is a third core router that is dedicated to the University housing and eduroam network. The second or middle layer is the distribution layer, connects the core layer (using routers) to the access layer (using switches). The lower layer includes all the edge switches, and APs which connect to the end users. The Wi-Fi network extends from our main university campus to nearby campus in downtown Kansas City, to Union Station of Kansas City, which is about 15 miles away. Within our university network, there are many networks, each serving a specific service. UMKCWPA is the main SSID for the UMKC wireless network. The eduroam is the network SSID for the educational network access for all the eduroam [6] parties. eduroam (education roaming) is an international roaming service for users in research, higher education and further education. It provides a single authentication access for all the mobile connectivity requirements of an institution across 78 countries in thousands of locations. The Wi-Fi network is primarily accessed by students, faculty, staff. Guest accounts use the guest network, which is dedicated for guests with very limited temporary access. The media network is the network that connects the media devices such as ROKUs [10], Firesticks [7], Chromecast [2], and Digital Video Recorder (DVR) boxes.

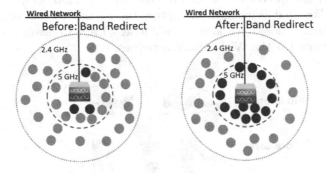

Fig. 4. Impact of band redirection

4.2   Client Redirection of 2.4 GHz to 5 GHz Band

5 GHz band offers a lot more space compared to 2.4 GHz, though it is not always fully utilized. Figure 4 illustrates authentication before and after the Band Select Feature suppresses client's association request to 2.4 GHz multiple times guiding the requests to 5 GHz band. We can see that "Before: Band Redirect" most clients where connecting to 2.4 GHz band by default. However, "After: Band Redirect", the dual band clients are guided toward the 5 GHz band. Our campus analysis indicated that there we more 5 GHz band authentication than 2.4 GHz as most laptops are only 5 GHz enabled. Between October 2016 and 2017 we observe the gradual decline in use of 2.4 GHz band and increase in 5 GHz band as illustrated by Fig. 6. Each dot on the graph represents the aggregated authentication count for a week. The lower peaks are due to holiday seasons, such as season break where student attendance is low. Comparing the first five weeks of the graph with the last five weeks, we can see that the client using 5 GHz band increased by up to 1150 count a week while clients using 2.4 GHz band decreased by up to 750 counts a week.

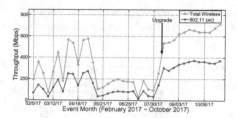
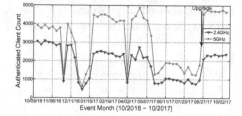

Fig. 5. 802.11 total vs 802.11(ac) throughput

Fig. 6. 2.4 GHz vs 5 GHz authentication

4.3 Throughput: Total 802.11 vs 802.11 (ac)

There were several activities during the last year that impacted the throughput to fluctuate during the Spring semester. The week of February 27th the WiFi network faced brief outage causing a dip in the traffic report. However, the controller/fail-over instantly corrected itself and traffic resumed. The week of April 2nd following spring break, our campus network upgraded to a new router resulting in short interruption. The third dip during April 23rd was due to performance issue which caused the router to reboot. Total Wireless network vs. 802.11 (ac) illustrated by Fig. 5 shows the weekly aggregated throughput in Mbps (Mega bit per second) between February 2017 and October 2017, with an increase in throughput for both Wi-Fi 802.11 (ac) and Total wireless (Wi-Fi 802.11) between spring and fall semester. Each dot on the graph represents the value of aggregated throughput for one week. Shortly after the Wi-Fi upgrade, throughput increased for both Wi-Fi 802.11 as a whole and 802.11(ac).

4.4 Coverage Gap

After the recent implementation in January 2018 which included installation of several new APs to provide coverage to the red zone, the coverage improved significantly. Figure 7 represents the initial coverage with 9 APs in 2014, where the majority of the area was red and orange indicating coverage gaps. Figure 8 illustrates the coverage map in 2016 after 2 additional APs were installed and

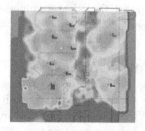
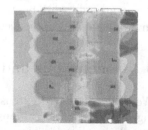

Fig. 7. Coverage in 2014 (Color figure online)

Fig. 8. Coverage in 2016 (Color figure online)

Fig. 9. Coverage 2018 (Color figure online)

coverage showed improvement. Figure 9, recent coverage representation January 2018, with total of 19 APs and majority of them were dual band high-density.

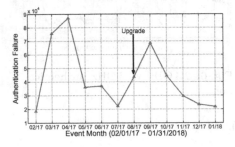

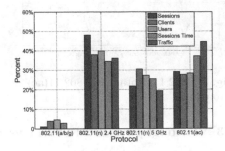

Fig. 10. Authentication failure due to roaming

Fig. 11. Usage summary by protocol

4.5   Authentication Failure Due to Roaming

Figure 10 illustrates authentication failure due to roaming between February 2017 and January 2018. The highest failure event in the spring semester happened in April with the total of 87K messages. In the fall semester, the peak month was September total failure message of 68.7K, showing a decrease of 18K compared to the spring semester. The upgraded feature enables fast and smooth roaming transition between 802.11 (ac), decreasing the authentication failure caused by roaming clients.

4.6   Heterogeneous Protocols

Figure 11 illustrates the percentage of all the protocols used in the campus network over a 31 days period grouped by sessions, clients, users, session time and traffic. Although, the top three protocols were 802.11 (n) 2.4 GHz, 802.11 (ac) and 802.11 (n) 5 GHz in respective order. Protocol 802.11 (ac) shows the highest Session to Traffic ratio and the most Session Time with the least clients. Protocols 802.11 (a/b/g) are the least used protocol in the campus network. However, the campus network has to support these heterogeneous protocols to provide the environment for all devices needing Wi-Fi access.

5   Conclusions and Future Work

We have conducted extensive analysis of heterogeneity issues encountered during an incremental campus Wi-Fi protocol deployment. We have explored various design considerations for heterogeneous compatibility, data rate, coverage, and performance. Furthermore, we discussed the issues around coverage gap, load balance, and roaming. This study of a campus incremental Wi-Fi deployment provides insights on the behaviors of Wi-Fi access network availability, and potential end-to-end expectations for high-speed and bandwidth-intensive clients. After the deployment, the most traffic is generated by 802.11 (ac) protocol. However, heterogeneous protocols such as 802.11 (a/b/g/n) still need to coexist until all devices are 802.11 (ac) compatible.

In the future, we plan to explore fast transition, performance enhancement, power saving, and time improvement benefits gained from upgrading to Wi-Fi 802.11 (ac) protocol.

References

1. 802.11r Vulnerability (CVE: 2017–13082) FAQ. https://documentation.meraki.com/zGeneral_Administration/Support/802.11r_Vulnerability_(CVE%3A_2017-13082)_FAQ. Accessed Oct 2017
2. Chromecast. https://store.google.com/product/chromecast_2015. Accessed Mar 2018
3. Cisco 802.11r. https://www.cisco.com/c/en/us/td/docs/wireless/controller/8-1/Enterprise-Mobility-8-1-Design-Guide/Enterprise_Mobility_8-1_Deployment_Guide/Chapter-11.html. Accessed Oct 2017
4. Cisco Band Select. https://www.cisco.com/c/en/us/td/docs/switches/lan/catalyst3850/software/release/3se/system_management/configuration_guide/b_sm_3se_3850_cg/b_sm_3se_3850_cg_chapter_0110.html. Accessed Feb 2018
5. Compound Annual Growth Rate - CAGR. http://www.investopedia.com/terms/c/cagr.asp. Accessed Oct 2017
6. eduroam blog. https://www.eduroam.org/?p=where. Accessed Oct 2017
7. FireStick. https://www.amazon.com/amazon-fire-tv-stick-with-alexa-voice-remote-streaming-media-player/dp/b00zv9rdkk. Accessed Mar 2018
8. High-Density Wi-Fi Design Principles. https://media.aerohive.com/documents/2034844328_Aerohive-Whitepaper-Hi-Density_Principles.pdf. Accessed Sep 2017
9. Prime Report. https://www.cisco.com/c/en/us/td/docs/net_mgmt/prime/infrastructure/3-0/user/guide/pi_ug/reps.html. Accessed Oct 2017
10. Roku. https://www.roku.com/. Accessed Mar 2018
11. The Zettabyte Era: Trends and Analysis. https://www.cisco.com/c/en/us/solutions/collateral/service-provider/visual-networking-index-vni/vni-hyperconnectivity-wp.html. Accessed Oct 2017
12. What is IoT? http://internetofthingsagenda.techtarget.com/definition/Internet-of-Things-IoT. Accessed Oct 2017
13. Bellalta, B., Bononi, L., Bruno, R., Kassler, A.: Next generation IEEE 802.11 wireless local area networks: current status, future directions and open challenges. Comput. Commun. **75**(C), 1–25 (2016)
14. Abusubaih, M.A., Najem Eddin, S., Khamayseh, A.: IEEE 802.11n dual band access points for boosting the performance of heterogeneous WiFi networks. In: Proceedings of the 8th ACM Workshop on Performance Monitoring and Measurement of Heterogeneous Wireless and Wired Networks, PM2HW2N 2013, pp. 1–4. ACM, New York (2013)
15. Afanasyev, M., Chen, T., Voelker, G.M., Snoeren, A.C.: Usage patterns in an urban wiFi network. IEEE/ACM Trans. Netw. **18**(5), 1359–1372 (2010)

16. Chou, C.T., Misra, A., Qadir, J.: Low-latency broadcast in multirate wireless mesh networks. IEEE J. Sel. Areas Commun. **24**(11), 2081–2091 (2006)
17. Dubey, A., Hudepohl, J.: Towards global deployment of software engineering tools. In: 2013 IEEE 8th International Conference on Global Software Engineering, pp. 129–133, August 2013
18. Emmelmann, M., Wiethoelter, S., Koepsel, A., Kappler, C., Wolisz, A.: Moving toward seamless mobility: state of the art and emerging aspects in standardization bodies. Wirel. Pers. Commun. **43**(3), 803–816 (2007)
19. Giannoulis, A., Patras, P., Knightly, E.W.: Mobile access of wide-spectrum networks: design, deployment and experimental evaluation. In: 2013 Proceedings IEEE INFOCOM, pp. 1708–1716, April 2013
20. Hiertz, G.R., Denteneer, D., Stibor, L., Zang, Y., Costa, X.P., Walke, B.: The IEEE 802.11 universe. IEEE Commun. Mag. **48**(1), 62–70 (2010)
21. Lei, L., Zhong, Z., Zheng, K., Chen, J., Meng, H.: Challenges on wireless heterogeneous networks for mobile cloud computing. IEEE Wirel. Commun. **20**(3), 34–44 (2013)
22. Ong, E.H., Kneckt, J., Alanen, O., Chang, Z., Huovinen, T., Nihtilä, T.: IEEE 802.11ac: enhancements for very high throughput WLANs. In: 2011 IEEE 22nd International Symposium on Personal, Indoor and Mobile Radio Communications, pp. 849–853, September 2011
23. Sadri, A.S.: Defining the future of multi-gigabit mmWave wireless communications. In: Proceedings of the 2010 ACM International Workshop on mmWave Communications: From Circuits to Networks, mmCom 2010, pp. 1–2. ACM, New York (2010)
24. Simić, L., Riihijärvi, J., Mähönen, P.: Measurement study of IEEE 802.11ac Wi-Fi performance in high density indoor deployments: are wider channels always better? In: 2017 IEEE 18th International Symposium on a World of Wireless, Mobile and Multimedia Networks (WoWMoM), pp. 1–9, June 2017
25. Wang, C.-Y., Wei, H.-Y.: IEEE 802.11n MAC enhancement and performance evaluation. Mob. Netw. Appl. **14**(6), 760–771 (2009)
26. Xiong, J., Sundaresan, K., Jamieson, K., Khojastepour, M.A., Rangarajan, S.: MIDAS: empowering 802.11ac networks with multiple-input distributed antenna systems. In: Proceedings of the 10th ACM International on Conference on Emerging Networking Experiments and Technologies, CoNEXT 2014, pp. 29–40. ACM, New York (2014)
27. Zubow, A., Sombrutzki, R.: Adjacent channel interference in IEEE 802.11n. In: 2012 IEEE Wireless Communications and Networking Conference (WCNC), pp. 1163–1168, April 2012

How to Quantify *Trust* in Your Network Emulator?

Domenico Capriglione[1] , Gianni Cerro[2(✉)] , Luigi Ferrigno[2] ,
and Gianfranco Miele[2]

[1] DIIN, University of Salerno, Via Giovanni Paolo II 132,
84084 Fisciano, SA, Italy
dcapriglione@unisa.it
[2] DIEI, University of Cassino and Southern Lazio,
Via G. Di Biasio 43, 03043 Cassino, FR, Italy
{g.cerro,ferrigno,g.miele}@unicas.it

Abstract. Network emulators are used in many contexts of communication
networks for the design and the development of network management and
routing strategies as well as for the tuning of multimedia services as Voice
Over IP, video streaming, TV on-demand, to cite a few. These devices are
generally used for modifying, in a controlled way, data traffic flows by
changing, in real time, several critical parameters as delay, packet loss percentage, throughput, and so on. Due to very attractive features as high versatility
and configurability and low cost, the solutions based on general purpose hardware platforms and free/open-source software are the most ones adopted in the
practice for implementing network emulators. Nevertheless, in such architectures the complex interaction of software and hardware sections should affect the
accuracy and repeatability of such systems in correctly emulating the desired
network behaviors. Consequently, a suitable pre-characterization stage of such
kind of network emulators should be performed before they are used. In this
framework, the paper describes a methodological approach for designing suitable test-bed and measurement procedure able to reliably characterize the performance of such systems. The final aim of the research activity is to provide a
suitable uncertainty model and a confidence level for the parameters provided by
network emulators, which can drive the final users in more reliably analyzing the
experimental results coming from their test campaigns and which involve the
network emulators.

Keywords: Network emulators · Delay · Packet loss · Network measurements
Metrological performance

1 Introduction

Computer and telecommunication networks are today involved in all main worldwide
applications as telephony, financial transactions, banking, TV, on-demand entertainment services, Internet of Things, to cite a few [1–3]. In addition, the fourth industrial
revolution, also known as Industry 4.0, pushes for bonding communication networks

© IFIP International Federation for Information Processing 2018
Published by Springer Nature Switzerland AG 2018. All Rights Reserved
K. R. Chowdhury et al. (Eds.): WWIC 2018, LNCS 10866, pp. 171–182, 2018.
https://doi.org/10.1007/978-3-030-02931-9_14

with the industrial ones with the general aims of improving the performance, the level of automation, the level of efficiency and quality of process and final products [4].

In these contexts, the design and management of communication networks are very important tasks because they straight affect the correctness, the quality and the reliability of the final services. Network active devices, algorithm routing strategies, communication protocols performance assessment are fundamental in order to assure that these services are correctly delivered to the final user by warranting the required level of expectation. These aspects are crucial also in modern and very promising Software Defined Networks (SDNs) [5].

Of course, due the complexity of the modern networks and the impracticability to make both development and testing on real scenarios, a widely used approach for these activities involves the use of suitable network emulators [6–8].

Unlike network simulation, where fixed models running on powerful computing devices try to evaluate complex systems behavior and to simulate real scenarios, the network emulation is able to introduce, in a controlled way, data traffic variations in real time [9, 10] for changing critical parameters as delay, packet loss percentage, throughput, and so on. By this way, performance devices/algorithms should be more reliably assessed before their deployment in actual networks. Obviously, the expected reliability improvement (with respect to simulators) can be achieved only if the emulator is able to accurately reproduce the desired network scenarios.

As for network emulators, on the basis of the architecture they can be divided in two main categories: Special Purpose Network Emulators (hereinafter SPNE) and General-Purpose Network Emulators (GPNE). The devices belonging to the former category are typically standalone devices, implemented on special purpose optimized and customized hardware and software platforms. Thanks to these characteristics, these solutions usually warrant very good performance, accuracy and repeatability even if they are characterized by high costs.

On the contrary, GPNE are based on computer programs to be run on general purpose hardware (i.e. Personal Computer) equipped with commercial interface cards and common operating systems. Among devices belonging to this category we can find both commercial and free/open-source software. Due to their cheapness and high degree of flexibility and versatility, the second ones are very widespread in practice [11] and, mainly thanks to the open-source feature, their employment is even more increasing also in the field of research. However, since they are based on general purpose platforms, their working strictly depends on the interaction of hardware and software sections of the hosting platform and their performance cannot be *a priori* guaranteed, as also proved in [12–15]. Therefore, prior to use such systems, a performance characterization and validation should be made for certifying the ability of these software to accurately reproduce the wanted network conditions. To this aim, a methodological approach for metrological performance evaluation of network emulators has not been adequately dealt in literature.

In this framework, focusing the attention on GPNE, starting from the past experiences in metrological characterization of computer networks devices and services [9, 15–18], a methodological approach is proposed to measure and analyze the performance of such systems. In a more detail, a suitable measurement setup is designed and characterized for analyzing the performance of GPNE. In order to show the application of the proposed methodology, two very popular network emulators, i.e. NetEM [11] and DummyNET [19] have been considered.

The paper is organized as follows: the proposed approach is reported in Sect. 2. The main features of the considered network emulators are described in Sect. 3 and an application example of the proposed approach is shown in Sect. 4. Finally, conclusions are provided in Sect. 5.

2 The Proposed Approach

To characterize the emulating ability of a GPNE, it is necessary to analyze the output of the network emulator when it is stressed with several inputs characterized by different traffic settings. To this aim a proper measurement set-up and measurement procedure are as illustrated in the next paragraphs. In particular, a three-step procedure is proposed (see Fig. 1).

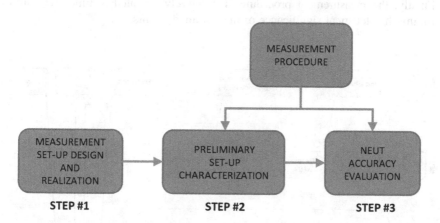

Fig. 1. The block diagram of the three-step procedure.

2.1 Measurement Set-Up Design and Realization

The proposed measurement set-up (i.e. step #1) is composed of three elements: a Reference Generator (RG), a Measurement Receiver (MR) and the network emulator under test (NEUT). As illustrated in Fig. 2, RG is connected to MR through the NEUT. RG provides a continuous service that creates a stream of packets towards the RG that acts as a sink. The characteristics of the traffic, like packet rate, packet loss, throughput and so on, can be selected by the user with aim of creating a stimulus for the NEUT. RM receives this stream of packets and measures the parameters of interest in order to quantify the accuracy of the NEUT in emulating a specific network characteristic.

2.2 Measurement Procedure

A sketch of the block diagram of the proposed measurement procedure is reported in Fig. 2. It represents the logical sequence of the operations executed during both preliminary set-up characterization (step #2) and NEUT accuracy evaluation (step #3).

Considering the importance of the clock synchronization of the host machine of the RG and MR, to avoid errors in the measurement of important parameters like packet delay, IPDV and so on, after a common initialization stage, NEUT is disabled, if it is operative.

After this operation, a clock synchronization procedure is executed between RG and MR inner clocks.

Once clock synchronization is over, NEUT is enabled. After this operation, MR is active in order to acquire and measure the incoming packets.

In the next step RG is enabled starting to generate a packet stream addressed to MR.

MR stores measurement data when RG has finished to generate the packet stream. The stored measurement data will be used to evaluate the parameters of interest related to the accuracy of the NEUT.

Finally, the measurement procedure is iteratively repeated K times with aim of improving the statistical significance of the obtained results.

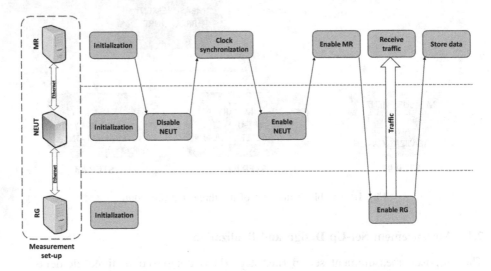

Fig. 2. Sketch of the proposed measurement set-up and procedure.

2.3 Preliminary Set-Up Characterization

To preliminary characterize the system (i.e. step #2), some tests with the emulators off have to be carried out. In particular, once selected the parameter to be tested by adopting the figures of merit described in the following subsection, the intrinsic nonidealities of the set-up itself and that cannot be imputable to the emulator capabilities are evaluated. This step allows evaluating the systematic effects introduced by the measurement set-up.

2.4 NEUT Accuracy Evaluation

To evaluate the accuracy of a NEUT in emulating a specific network condition (i.e. step #3), it is important to perform a statistical analysis of the parameters of interest, for example the experienced delay, the measured IPDV, packet loss and so on.

As a consequence, denoting with N the number of packets received during a test and $\xi_{i,j}$ the parameter of interest measured and related to the to the packet j in the i-th stream, the following quantities are evaluated:

$$\xi_i = \sum_{j=1}^{N} \frac{\xi_{i,j}}{N} \tag{1}$$

$$\mu_\xi = \sum_{i=1}^{K} \frac{\xi_i}{K} \tag{2}$$

$$\sigma_\xi = \sqrt{\frac{1}{K} \sum_{i=1}^{K} \left(\xi_i - \mu_\xi\right)^2} \tag{3}$$

$$m = \min \xi_i \tag{4}$$

$$M = \max \xi_i \tag{5}$$

where

- ξ_i is the average of the measures executed during the i-th test;
- μ_ξ is the mean value evaluated considering all the acquisitions;
- σ_ξ is the variability (standard deviation) of the mean value.

3 Considered NEUTs

In this paper we have considered two widely used GPNEs. They are free and open-source, namely NetEM and DummyNET.

3.1 NetEM

NetEM is the acronym of Network Emulator. It is a software tool, developed by Linux foundation, able to emulate the characteristics of a wide area network (WAN) such as delay, packet loss, etc. [10, 11]. It is in most Linux distributions with Kernels version 2.6 and higher and it is an extension of Linux traffic control. It allows to control and set the following traffic parameters: delay, packet loss, packet duplication, packet corruption and packet reordering.

Concerning delay, it can emulate fixed and random delay following different distributions (uniform, normal, Pareto and Pareto normal) and correlate successive delay values, trying to perform an imitation of congestion effects [10].

As packet loss regards, random loss of packets can be set by the user.

3.2   DummyNET

It is a tool developed at University of Pisa and originally designed for testing network protocols. It can emulate, delays, packet losses, multipath effects and bandwidth limitations. It runs on different operating systems like Windows, Linux and Mac OS.

It intercepts packets and passes them to object structures called *pipes*. A pipe represents a communication channel with a fixed-bandwidth and it implements a set of queues. Each queue emulates a packet queue in a network which delay or drop packets when congestion occurs [10].

4   An Application Example

In this section, with reference to the proposed three-step procedure described in Sect. 2, an application example is shown for analyzing and comparing the performance of the NEUTs described in Sect. 3. The obtained performance of adopted network emulators is provided as concerns the capability of emulating static delays and random packet losses. In detail, results are provided in terms of mean and standard deviation of the considered quantities over many trials for each test condition.

4.1   Measurement Set-Up Design and Realization

The hardware specifications of the proposed set-up are:

- RG and MR are PCs composed of: CPU Intel Pentium Dual Core E5400 @ 2.700 GHz, 4 GB RAM and a Network Interface Card (NIC) Atheros AR8121/AR8113/AR8114.
- NEUT is still a PC emulating a WAN having the same hardware characteristics of the former two PCs, but it is furthermore equipped with a second NIC Realtek RTL8169/8110.

The operating system (OS) installed on them is Scientific Linux 6.6. Each PC is connected to the WAN emulator through a 1.5 m length UTP category 5 cable. The network data rate has been set-up at 1000 Mb/s full duplex. To improve delay measurements accuracy, a NTP-based synchronization has been adopted.

4.2   Measurement Procedure

This subsection reports the measurement procedure parameters. Some details about their values (described in Sect. 2.2) are reported in Table 1.

Table 1. Numeric values of the experimental campaign parameters.

Feature	Type	Min	Max	Step
UDP traffic	Packet rate	100 pkt/s	5000 pkt/s	Logarithmic
UDP traffic	Duration	15 s	/	/
Delay	Static	1 ms	100 ms	Logarithmic
Packet loss	Random	1%	10%	Logarithmic
Test repetitions	No. of tests	50	/	/

In summary, traffic packets have been sent through the network with UDP protocol, the streaming transmission for each test lasted 15 s; different packet rates have been adopted to test the reliability of the NEUT under different stress conditions; during the tests, the NEUT has introduced several non-idealities, as described in Table 1, in terms of static delays and random packet losses. Delay and Packet Loss performance have been tested independently.

Furthermore, traffic generation, reception and packet feature extraction has been carried out by using software D-ITG [20].

4.3   Preliminary Set-Up Characterization

As described in Sect. 2.3 some tests with the emulators off have been carried out. The obtained delays and packet losses (i.e. the parameters to be tested) have been measured and reported. Such values constitute the intrinsic non-ideality of the set-up itself and they cannot be imputable to the emulator capabilities.

In Fig. 3, evaluation of experimental set-up intrinsic delay is reported. In particular, an error-bar-plot has been adopted to represent both the mean values (central points of each vertical bar, joint by an interpolating line) and standard deviations (the half of each vertical bar length), computed over the 50 trials for each test condition. It can be stated that the intrinsic delay introduced by the system itself is quantifiable in about 80 µs and the standard deviation is about 10 µs, if the worst case is considered. A decreasing trend is generally appreciable with respect to the packet rates. Best condition is achieved at packet rate equal to 2000 pkt/s, where the mean value is 71 µs and the standard deviation is equal to 5 µs. Anyway, by exploiting the concept of measurement compatibility, stating that two different measures are compatible if the intersection of their measurement intervals (evaluated as the numeric set obtained by adding and subtracting the extended measurement uncertainty to its mean value [21]) is not empty, it is possible to affirm that the intrinsic delay is not systematically changing at different packet rates and it can be considered constant and taken as the mean value

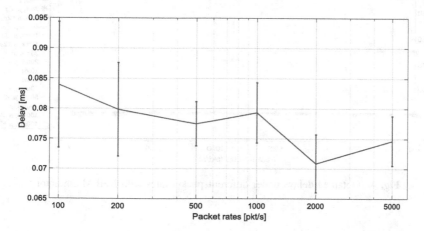

Fig. 3. Obtained delays under different packet rates with disabled emulator.

of delays obtained at different packet rates. This value should be generally taken into account (and eventually compensated) when testing the delays introduced by the NEUTs.

As for packet losses without emulator effect, we verified that the measurement system does not intrinsically introduce any problem related to packet loss, since no packets are lost in all tested conditions; therefore, following results, obtained with active emulator action, do not need to be normalized in terms of lost packets, unlike what happened for delay case.

4.4   NEUTs Accuracy Evaluation

In this section, results obtained by using the two considered emulators are reported. In particular, the emulators have both been set to introduce the same delays and packet losses to the network. Results are depicted in Figs. 4, 5, 6 and 7, and their presentation is carried out by reporting the mean values (μ in the graph legends) and the 2-coverage-factor curves ($\mu - 2\sigma$, $\mu + 2\sigma$), representing the trend of the mean values plus or minus the double of standard deviation values. Such boundary curves define the measurement interval where, under Gaussian hypothesis of the measurement distribution, the actual value resides with 95% probability.

4.4.1   Delay Related Results

In Figs. 4 and 5, the obtained delays with NetEM and DummyNET emulators are respectively reported. As stated in the introduction to this subsection, three curves for each imposed delay condition are shown in the figures. Due to the small values of standard deviations, in most cases such curves are superimposed, and a single curve is visible.

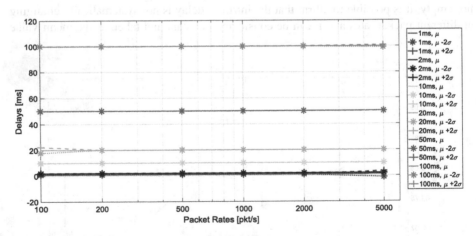

Fig. 4. Obtained delays under different packet rates with NetEM emulator.

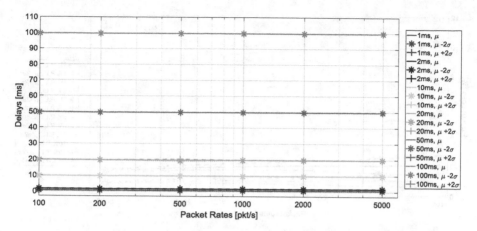

Fig. 5. Obtained delays under different packet rates with DummyNET emulator.

As expected, the mean values for each test condition are correctly reproduced, and they are pretty constant with respect to the packet rate. As regards NetEM (see Fig. 4), some particular behaviors can be observed for very low packet rate (100 pkt/s) at 20 ms imposed delay (green line) and at very high packet rate (5000 pkt/s) at 1 ms and 100 ms delay conditions (percentage standard deviations close to 5, 50 and 0.5%, respectively). In these cases, the repeatability of the measurement (intended as the capability to exhibit the same value under the same working conditions in repeated trials) is slightly worse than in other situations, where no distance among coverage and mean curves can be appreciated. Concerning DummyNET (Fig. 5), results are fully aligned with the expected values, and measurements are also highly repeatable (percentage standard deviations always lower than 0.5%), for all analyzed situations.

4.4.2 Packet Loss Related Results

Unlike delay performance, results concerning packet loss, reported in Figs. 6 and 7, show a particular behavior both with respect to the packet rate variation and repeatability. In detail, a common trend of both emulators is the poor capability to keep the packet loss constant and aligned with the imposed values, especially for high value of packet rates and required packet loss. The observed decreasing trend leads to have a measured packet loss equal to 8%, whilst the imposed one is 10% both for NetEM and DummyNET. Such phenomenon is not appreciable for lower values of packet losses, where the constant trend is kept for all packet rates condition. The second particular phenomenon related to packet loss is the very poor repeatability of the measurement results, revealed by the distance of the mean value and coverage curves, especially visible in low packet rates conditions. The standard deviations become lower in high packet rate cases.

This behavior has an important consequence: when packet rate is set to 100 pkt/s and imposed packet loss is 1 or 2%, the obtained measurement intervals are partially superimposed, thus providing compatibility among such measurements. This result

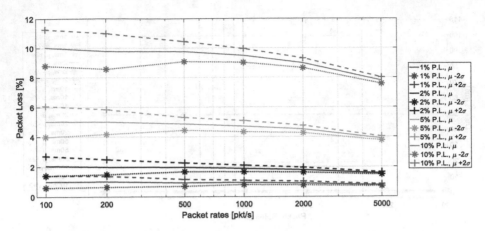

Fig. 6. Obtained packet losses under different packet rates with NetEM emulator.

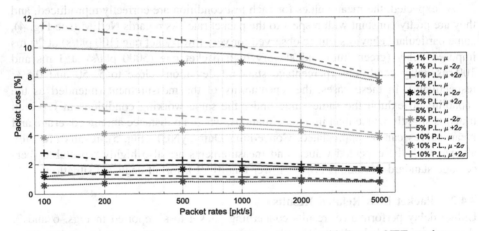

Fig. 7. Obtained packet losses under different packet rates with DummyNET emulator.

implies that if one takes the measurement in those points cannot predict if the imposed packet loss was 1 or 2%, because obtained behaviors are similar.

5   Conclusions

In this paper, a methodological approach for characterizing the performance of network emulators based on general purpose platforms and free/open source software is described. In particular, the measurement setup, the procedures for its preliminary characterization and for carrying out the performance measurements are explained. To show the application of the proposal, it has been applied to real case studies for analyzing the performance of two popular network emulators, very widespread in the academic research context. In particular, their ability in providing reliable packet loss percentages and delays has been evaluated for different values of such quantities (i.e. different imposed settings) and working conditions in terms of packet rate. The proposed approach reveals as useful also for comparing in a systematic way the metrological performance of such kind of network emulators.

Further developments will concern with the extension of the proposed approach to further parameters typically considered in network emulation, as Throughput and Internet Packet Delay Variation (together with their probability density functions) and further network emulators with the aim of better identifying factors that influence the accuracy of the emulated traffic. In addition, the possibility of providing a simple accuracy model of the parameter emulated as a function of quantities of influence will be investigated as well.

References

1. Coyle, C.L., Vaughn, H.: Social networking: communication revolution or evolution? Bell Labs Tech. J. **13**, 13–17 (2008). https://doi.org/10.1002/bltj.20298
2. Angrisani, L., Narduzzi, C.: Testing communication and computer networks: an overview. IEEE Instrum. Meas. Mag. **11**(5), 12–24 (2008). https://doi.org/10.1109/MIM.2008.4630738
3. Ayele, E.D., Meratnia, N., Havinga, P.J.M.: Towards a new opportunistic IoT network architecture for wildlife monitoring system. In: 9th IFIP International Conference on New Technologies, Mobility and Security (NTMS), Paris, France, pp. 1–5 (2018). https://doi.org/10.1109/NTMS.2018.8328721
4. Lucas-Estañ, M.C., Raptis, T.P., Sepulcre, M., Passarella, A., Regueiro, C., Lazaro, O.: A software defined hierarchical communication and data management architecture for Industry 4.0. In: 14th Annual Conference on Wireless On-demand Network Systems and Services (WONS), Isola 2000, France, pp. 37–44 (2018). https://doi.org/10.23919/WONS.2018.8311660
5. Abdallah, S., Elhajj, I.H., Chehab A., Kayssi, A.: A network management framework for SDN. In: 9th IFIP International Conference on New Technologies, Mobility and Security (NTMS), Paris, France, pp. 1–4 (2018). https://doi.org/10.1109/NTMS.2018.8328672
6. Koshimura, R., Ito, Y.: Development of Web-QoE evaluation system for wireless LAN with combination of simulator and network emulator. In: IEEE 2nd Global Conference on Consumer Electronics (GCCE), Tokyo, pp. 431–432 (2013). https://doi.org/10.1109/GCCE.2013.6664879
7. Holt, C., Kong, A., Leger, A.S., Bennett, D.: Communications network emulation for smart grid test-bed. In: IEEE Power and Energy Society General Meeting (PESGM), Boston, MA, pp. 1–5 (2016). https://doi.org/10.1109/PESGM.2016.7741999
8. Lal, C., Laxmi V., Gaur, M.S.: Video streaming over MANETs: testing and analysis using real-time emulation. In: 19th Asia-Pacific Conference on Communications (APCC), Denpasar, pp. 190–195 (2013). https://doi.org/10.1109/APCC.2013.6765940
9. Angrisani, L., Capriglione, D., Cerro, G., Ferrigno, L., Miele, G.: Experimental analysis of software network emulators in packet delay emulation. In: IEEE International Workshop on Measurement and Networking (M&N), Naples, pp. 1–6 (2017). https://doi.org/10.1109/IWMN.2017.8078382
10. Beuran, R.: Introduction to Network Emulation. Pan Stanford Publishing Pte. Ltd .(2013). ISBN: 9789814364096

11. Hemminger, S.: Network Emulation with NetEm (2005). Inlinux.conf.au
12. Hoßfeld, T., Fiedler, M.: The unexpected QoE killer: when the network emulator misshapes traffic and QoE. In: Seventh International Workshop on Quality of Multimedia Experience (QoMEX), Pylos-Nestoras, pp. 1–6 (2015). https://doi.org/10.1109/QoMEX.2015.7148093
13. Beshay, J.D., Francini, A., Prakash, R.: On the fidelity of single-machine network emulation in linux. In: IEEE 23rd International Symposium on Modeling, Analysis, and Simulation of Computer and Telecommunication Systems, Atlanta, GA, pp. 19–22 (2015)
14. Betta, G., Capriglione, D., Ferrigno, L., Laracca, M.: A Measurement driven approach to design an efficient test methodology for PLT network QoS performance parameters assessment. Meas. Sci. Technol. (2009). https://doi.org/10.1088/0957-0233/20/10/105101
15. Angrisani, L., Botta, A., Miele, G., Pescapé, A., Vadursi, M.: Experiment-driven modeling of open-source internet traffic generators. IEEE Trans. Instrum. Meas. 63(11), 2529–2538 (2014). https://doi.org/10.1109/TIM.2014.2348633
16. Angrisani, L., Capriglione, D., Ferrigno, L., Miele, G.: Internet Protocol Packet Delay Variation measurements in communication networks: how to evaluate measurement uncertainty? Measurement 46(7), 2099–2109 (2013). https://doi.org/10.1016/j.measurement.2013.03.007
17. Angrisani, L., Capriglione, D., Ferrigno, L., Miele, G.: A methodological approach for estimating protocol analyzer instrumental measurement uncertainty in packet jitter evaluation. IEEE Trans. Instrum. Meas. 61(5), 1405–1416 (2012). https://doi.org/10.1109/TIM.2012.2186478
18. Angrisani, L., Capriglione, D., Ferrigno, L., Miele, G.: An internet protocol packet delay variation estimator for reliable quality assessment of video-streaming services. IEEE Trans. Instrum. Meas. 62(5), 914–923 (2013). https://doi.org/10.1109/TIM.2013.2245051
19. Carbone, M., Rizzo, L.: DummyNet revisited. SIGCOMM Comput. Commun. 40(2), 12–20 (2010). https://doi.org/10.1145/1764873.1764876
20. Botta, A., Dainotti, A., Pescapé, A.: A tool for the generation of realistic network workload for emerging networking scenarios. Comput. Netw. 56(15), 3531–3547 (2012). https://doi.org/10.1016/j.comnet.2012.02.019
21. JCGM: Evaluation of measurement data—guide to the expression of uncertainty in measurement. JCGM 100 (2008)

On the Fraction of LoS Blockage Time in mmWave Systems with Mobile Users and Blockers

Dmitri Moltchanov[1] and Aleksandr Ometov[2(✉)]

[1] Tampere University of Technology, Tampere, Finland
[2] National Research University Higher School of Economics, Moscow, Russia
aleksandr.ometov@tut.fi

Abstract. Today, one of the emerging trends for the next generation (5G) networks is utilizing higher frequencies in closer premises. As
one of the enablers, small cells appear as a cost-effective way to reliably
expand network coverage and provide significantly increased capacity for
end users. The ultra-high bandwidth available at millimeter (mmWave,
30–300 GHz) and Terahertz (THz, 0.3–3 THz) frequencies can effectively
realize short-range wireless access links in small cells. Those technologies
could also be utilized for direct communications for users in proximity. At
the same time, the performance of mobile wireless systems operating in
those frequency bands depends on the availability of line-of-sight (LoS)
between communicating entities. In this paper, we estimate the fraction
of LoS time for randomly chosen node moving according to different
mobility models in a field of N moving blocking nodes for both base
station and device-to-device (D2D) connectivity scenarios. We also provide an extension to the case of a random number of moving blockers.
The reported results can be further used to assess the amount of traffic
offloaded to other technologies having greater coverage, e.g., LTE.

1 Background and Motivation

Due to tremendous increase in traffic demand, researchers in both industry and
academia already focus on numerous advanced networking solutions such as
client-relaying [1], heterogeneous networking [2], the use of micro/pico/femto
cells [3] and Device-to-Device (D2D) communications [4–6] to satisfy the requirements of fifth generation (5G) mobile wireless systems. These mechanisms alone,
however, are limited in achieving the required data rates.

One of the initial steps forward is moving up in the frequencies from microwaves
to millimeter waves (mmWave, 30–300 GHz) [7] and further to the terahertz (THz,
0.3–3 THz) band [8] is considered as a viable solution to principally increase the
capacity of wireless channels and eventually satisfy the requirements of 5G-grade
networks. Operating at those frequencies could be described by the following

K. R. Chowdhury et al. (Eds.): WWIC 2018, LNCS 10866, pp. 183–192, 2018.
https://doi.org/10.1007/978-3-030-02931-9_15

features: (i) higher throughput; (ii) shorter propagation distances due to higher attenuation; (iii) better spatial resolution due to smaller beamwidth; (iv) smaller antenna size in general; and (v) higher blockage affection.

The principle discord between mmWave/THz systems, compared to microwaves, is that there is an extreme difference in the received signal strength in line-of-sight (LoS) and nLoS conditions [9, 10]. Such systems are expected to be installed in open indoor and outdoor environments such as conference halls, lobbies, squares, crossroads, parks [11]. Nevertheless, as electromagnetic waves cannot "travel around" the objects whose size is smaller than their wavelengths while the human bodies serve as perfect absorbers [12], the crowd around the receiver blocks the LoS. To understand performance bounds of mmWave and THz systems, it is essential to predict the probability of having LoS at a particular instant of time as well as the fraction of time there is a LoS between communicating entities in crowded mobile environments.

The question of the LoS propagation blockage has recently received particular attention from the research and standardization community [13, 14]. As demonstrated by field measurements in [15], the loss of LoS path in mmWave systems may result in sharp drops of the (up to 30–40 dB) in the received signal strength. The first analytical studies on this topic addressed the question of LoS blockage in environments with static users and static blockers [16, 17]. These results have been recently extended to the case of moving blockers and static users in [18] as well as static blockers and moving users in [19]. In these studies, it has been shown that the mobility of both blockers and users drastically affect the blockage statistics leading to additional uncertainly in channel state. However, to the best of the authors' knowledge, there have been no studies addressing the case when both blockers and users are simultaneously mobile.

In this paper, we derive the probability of having nLoS at a random instant of time as well as the fraction of LoS for a user in a group of $N + 1$ blockers moving around in closed indoor compartment according to the random direction mobility (RDM) and random waypoint (RWP) models. We consider mmWave access point (AP) and D2D scenarios and also sketch the extension to the open outdoor scenarios, where a user and blockers may freely enter and leave the service area of interest. The presented results can further be used to assess the amount of traffic that needs to be offloaded to another type of connection.

The rest of the manuscript is organized as follows. Section 2 provides the system model and depicts the scenarios of interest. Next, we elaborate on the applicability of the model to dynamic conditions and extend it in Sect. 3. The numerical examples are given in Sect. 4. The last section concludes the manuscript.

2   Indoor Closed Compartment Scenario

Two scenarios of interest are described in this section. We focus on both conventional infrastructure-based case, where AP serves the tagged user and the remaining ones act as potential blockers, and D2D scenario, where two users are attempting to initiate direct link that could be blocked by other users. Both users and blockers are mobile and move according to a RDM mobility model [20]. Recall that according to RDM a point first randomly chooses the direction of movement uniformly in $(0, 2\pi)$. Then, it moves in the chosen direction for exponentially distributed time with constant speed v. The process is restarted at the stopping point.

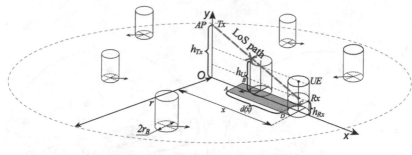

(a) LoS blocking zone for BS scenario.

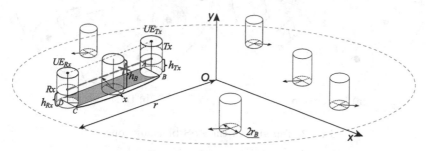

(b) LoS blocking zone for D2D scenario.

Fig. 1. Considered scenarios.

2.1 Access Point Scenario

In the first scenario, we assume $N + 1$ mobile users (UEs), acting as blockers, that randomly move according to RDM in the coverage area with radius r of a mmWave or THz AP, which height is h_{Tx} (AP is selected as transmitter (Tx)). The height of the blockers is assumed to be the constant and equal to h_B. The radius of a blocker is r_B. The height of the receiver (Rx) associated with the tagged UE is $h_{Rx} < h_B$. We are interested in the probability of nLoS at the arbitrary time instant and the fraction of nLoS. Note that these metrics are symmetric irrespective of which entity (AP or UE) acts as Tx or Rx correspondingly.

We assume that UE is located at the distance x from the AP at time t, as shown in Fig. 1(a). The LoS to the UE could be blocked by the blockers that are located in the so-called *LoS blocking zone*, marked in gray. The length of this zone is

$$d(x) = \frac{x(h_B - h_{Rx})}{h_{Tx} - h_{Rx}}. \tag{1}$$

Observing the top view of the scenario, Fig. 2(a), notice that the area of the LoS blocking zone is more complicated than a rectangle. To prevent overlapping there cannot be a blocker located closer than at $2r_B$ to the user. The area of the LoS blocking zone is

$$S_B = 2r_B[x - d(x)] - 2r_B^2 - \frac{1}{2}\pi r_B^2. \tag{2}$$

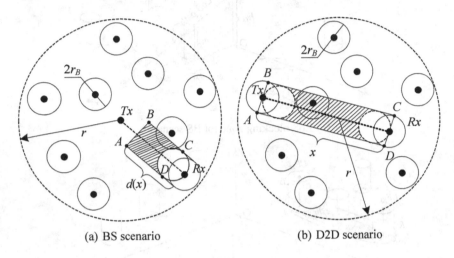

(a) BS scenario   (b) D2D scenario

Fig. 2. Top view of the LoS blocking zone.

The existence of the zone around the UE prohibiting the presence of blockers implies that the minimum distance from the AP resulting in non-zero LoS blocking zone is $2r_B$. Recall that the limiting distribution of the RDM is uniform over the area of interest [20]. Observing the system in stationary regime, the probability of a point uniformly distributed in the circle hitting an LoS blocking area is given by the ratio $S_B/\pi r^2$. Generalizing to N blockers, we arrive at

$$p_B(N) = 1 - \left(1 - \frac{2r_B[x - d(x)] - 2r_B^2 - \frac{1}{2}\pi r_B^2}{\pi r^2}\right)^N. \tag{3}$$

The probability density function (pdf) of a point uniformly distributed in a circle of radius r is given by $f(x) = 2x/r^2$. Thus, the probability of having nLoS at a random instant of time, p_{nL}, coinciding with the fraction of nLoS, f_{nL}, is

$$f_{nL} = \int_{2r_B}^{r} \frac{2x}{r^2}\left(1 - \left[1 - \frac{2r_B[x - d(x)] - 2r_B^2 - \frac{1}{2}\pi r_B^2}{\pi r^2}\right]^N\right)dx. \tag{4}$$

Integrating (4) we arrived at the final result in the following closed-form

$$f_{nL} = 1 - \frac{4r_B^2}{r^2} - \frac{\left[\frac{4(A-1)r_B^2+B+\pi r^2}{r^2}\right]^{N+1}\left[\pi r^2 - 4(A-1)(N+1)r_B^2 + B\right]}{2\pi^N(A-1)^2(N+1)(N+2)r_B^2} \tag{5}$$

$$+ \frac{\left[\frac{r(2(A-1)r_B+\pi r)+B}{r^2}\right]^{N+1}\left[r(\pi r - 2(A-1)(N+1)r_B) + B\right]}{2\pi^N(A-1)^2(N+1)(N+2)r_B^2}, \tag{6}$$

where the shortcuts are

$$A = \frac{(h_B - h_{Rx})}{h_{Tx} - h_{Rx}}, \quad B = 2r_B^2 - \frac{\pi r_B^2}{2}. \tag{7}$$

2.2 D2D Scenario

Since the height of Tx and Rx is assumed to be the same, $h_{Tx} = h_{Rx} < h_B$, it suffices to consider two dimensional case, as shown in Fig. 2(b). Given the distance x between Tx and Rx the area of the LoS blocking zone is

$$S_B(x) = 2r_Bx - 4r_B^2 - \pi r_B^2. \tag{8}$$

Similarly to the AP blocking model, there is no blocking when Tx and Rx are closer than $4r_B$. Recalling the stationary property of RDM model and the fact that the distance between two points uniformly distributed in the circle of radius πr^2 is given by [21]

$$f(x) = \frac{2x}{r^2}\left(\frac{2}{\pi}\arccos\left(\frac{x}{2r}\right) - \frac{x}{r\pi}\sqrt{1 - \frac{x^2}{4r^2}}\right), \quad 0 < x < 2r, \tag{9}$$

we have the following for the fraction of nLoS

$$f_{nL} = \int_{4r_B}^{r} f(x)\left(1 - \left(1 - \frac{2r_Bx - 4r_B^2 - \pi r_B^2}{\pi r^2}\right)^N\right)dx, \tag{10}$$

that also coincides with the nLoS blocking probability. Note that the integral cannot be expressed in elementary functions but can be computed numerically.

3 Extensions and Applications

3.1 Outdoor Environment

The scenarios considered previously are unrealistic for outdoor deployments, where blockers/user may freely enter and leave an area of interest. For AP scenario this area coincides with the service area of aN AP while for the D2D case this is the area, where D2D connectivity is feasible, e.g., UE proximity characterized by the short-range radio coverage area. In this section, we address this by introducing dynamics to the model.

Let A_0 be the circular service area of an AP and let A_1 be the greater circular area where N blockers are allowed to move according to RDM. We are interested in the probability that a randomly chosen node currently located in the AP service area is in nLoS state. This probability no longer coincides with the fraction of nLoS as the latter needs to be obtained knowing the AP service area residence time of a user.

Recall that in the stationary regime N nodes moving in A_1 are uniformly distributed in A_1 [20]. Thus, the number of nodes in A_0 follow binomial distribution with parameter A_0/A_1 and these nodes are all uniformly distributed in A_0. Increasing A_1 and N such that $\lambda = N/S_{A_1}$ is kept constant $p = A_0/A_1 \to 0$ and the binomial distribution approaches the Poisson one with parameter λ. Thus, the probability of having LoS at the distance x, $p_L(x)$, is given by the void probability of a Poisson process with the area estimated in (2), i.e.,

$$p_L(x) = \exp\left(-\lambda\left[2r_B[x - d(x)] - 2r_B^2 - \frac{1}{2}\pi r_B^2\right]\right), \tag{11}$$

where $d(x)$ is provided in (1).

The probability that a node is moving according to RDM and located in A_0 at time t experiences nLoS conditions is obtained similarly to (4) with exponential blocking probability replacing the binomial one. It is provided in (12). For D2D scenario the integral for nLoS probability is similar to (10), with $1 - p_L(x)$ from (11) replacing the binomial blocking. It also cannot be solved in elementary functions but can be numerically evaluated with any given accuracy.

$$
\begin{aligned}
p_{nL} &= \int_{2r_B}^{r} \frac{2x}{r^2}\left(1 - e^{-\lambda\left[2r_B[x-d(x)]-2r_B^2-\pi/2r_B^2\right]}\right) = \\
&= 1 - \frac{e^{\lambda r_B([\pi+4]r_B-2r)}(2\lambda r r_B + 1) - 32\lambda^2 r_B^4}{2\lambda^2 r^2 r_B^2} + \frac{e^{(\pi-4)\lambda r_B^2}\left(8\lambda r_B^2 + 1\right)}{2\lambda^2 r^2 r_B^2}.
\end{aligned} \tag{12}
$$

To evaluate the fraction of nLoS for outdoor deployment, it is necessary to obtain the time corresponding to the UE staying in the service area A_0. This is a first passage time in a circle for a random point moving according to RDM with some initial position that depends on the size of A_0 and parameters of RDM model. Neither pdf nor mean of this metric can be obtained analytically [22]. Nevertheless, one could always use computer simulations or Brownian motion approximation of RDM (see [22], Chap. 4) to quantify this metric.

3.2   Further Extensions

We specifically note that the the model proposed in this paper can be extended in many different ways. First of all, one can use any mobility model having well-defined stationary distribution, for example, random waypoint (RWP) mobility model whose distribution in a square with side A is available in closed form [23], i.e.,

$$f_{X,Y}(x,y) = \frac{36}{A^6}\left(x^2 - \frac{A^2}{4}\right)\left(y^2 - \frac{A^2}{4}\right). \tag{13}$$

The only additional step compared to the presented model is to determine the distance to the mmWave AP or the distance between two nodes. This can be done applying the random variables transformation technique. Notably, for the AP to UE case, the transformation of interest reads as $r(x,y) = \sqrt{x^2 + y^2}$ and the procedure is reduced to finding the Jacobian of the transformation [24].

We also would like to specifically note that LoS blockage does not always lead to the outage event, i.e., for a given propagation model the outage even may only occur when the current distance between communicating nodes is higher than the specific value. The result for a fraction of time can be extended to this case as well. Considering AP to UE scenario as an example, we first obtain the fraction of time UE is farther than a certain propagation distance D, then observe that the UE position conditional on being farther than D is still uniformly distributed in the ring (D, R) with density $f(x) = 2x/(R^2 - D^2)$ and then determine the fraction of LoS blockage time using $f(x)$.

4   Numerical Illustrations

In this section, we illustrate the obtained numerical results. First, we consider the LoS blockage probability for AP to UE communications scenario. We then address D2D communications case. Finally, we consider the outdoor scenario with a Poisson distribution of the number of blockers.

Consider first the AP to UE indoor communications scenario. Figure 4 illustrates the fraction of LoS blockage time as a function of systems parameters including mmWave AP height, h_A, and UE height, h_U for a range of the number of blockers in the compartment. In these illustrations, the height of Rx is set to 1.2 m, and the height of blockers is 1.7 m. The radius of the coverage is 30 m. Expectedly, as the number of blockers increases the probability of LoS blockage increases. Further, it is essential to observe that the change in AP and UE heights does not drastically affect the blockage probability. The most significant effect stems from the number of blockers in the area.

The effect of input parameters on the fraction of LoS blockage time for the D2D scenario is illustrated in Fig. 4 as the function of the number of blockers for different radii of the service area. Recall that in this scenario the height of communicating entities is the same. Logically, by keeping the number of blockers constant and increasing the service area of interest the fraction of LoS blockage time increases. Finally, by comparing the results in Fig. 4 with Fig. 3(a) and (b), we observe that the fraction of the LoS blockage time for the D2D scenario is significantly bigger. The rationale is that in the case of D2D communications the heights of entities are all the same implying that the area of the LoS blockage zone is significantly larger.

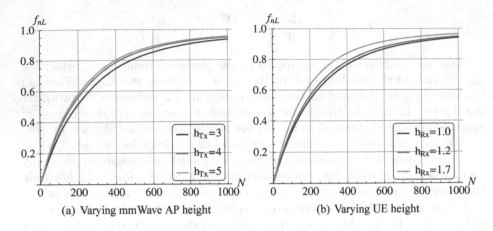

Fig. 3. Fraction of LoS blockage time in AP to UE scenario.

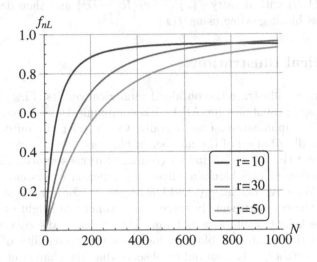

Fig. 4. The fraction of nLoS for D2D scenario.

Finally, we compare the fraction of LoS blockage time in indoor and outdoor scenarios for AP to UE case. The comparison is facilitated by parameterizing indoor model with the number of blockers corresponding to λS_A, where S_A is the service area of interest, where λ is the density of blockers in the Poisson model. The results are demonstrated in Fig. 5. As one may observe, the outdoor model with a Poisson distribution of a number of blockers is characterized by a much higher value of the fraction of the blockage time. The difference is maximized for medium values of the blockers density in the range (0.10–0.25) blockers per squared meter.

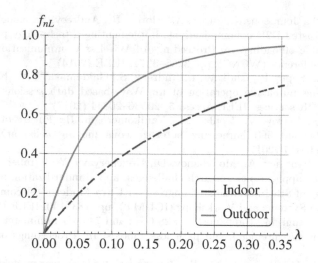

Fig. 5. Fraction of LoS blockage time in indoor and outdoor scenarios.

5   Conclusions

In this manuscript, we derived the probability of nLoS and the fraction of time a user spends in nLoS state in a group of N blockers moving according to RDM in the indoor closed compartment for both AP and D2D connectivity cases. We then provided the extension to the case for outdoor deployment, where UEs freely enter and leave the service area. Our results apply to performance analysis of mmWave and THz wireless systems.

The central application area of the proposed model is performance analysis of traffic offloading in heterogeneous multi-layer wireless access networks featuring mmWave and/or terahertz APs. Notably, the fraction of LoS blockage and/or outage time characterize the amount of time resources of systems have larger coverage, and usually smaller capacity needs to be used.

References

1. Deng, J., Tirkkonen, O., Freij-Hollanti, R., Chen, T., Nikaein, N.: Resource allocation and interference management for opportunistic relaying in integrated mmWave/sub-6 GHz 5G networks. IEEE Commun. Mag. **55**(6), 94–101 (2017)
2. Galinina, O., et al.: Capturing spatial randomness of heterogeneous cellular/WLAN deployments with dynamic traffic. IEEE J. Sel. Areas Commun. **32**(6), 1083–1099 (2014)
3. Prasad, K.S.V., Hossain, E., Bhargava, V.K.: Energy efficiency in massive MIMO-based 5G networks: opportunities and challenges. IEEE Wirel. Commun. **24**(3), 86–94 (2017)
4. Ometov, A., et al.: Toward trusted, social-aware D2D connectivity: bridging across the technology and sociality realms. IEEE Wirel. Commun. **23**(4), 103–111 (2016)

5. Pyattaev, A., Johnsson, K., Surak, A., Florea, R., Andreev, S., Koucheryavy, Y.: Network-assisted D2D communications: implementing a technology prototype for cellular traffic offloading. In: Proceedings of Wireless Communications and Networking Conference (WCNC), pp. 3266–3271. IEEE (2014)
6. Ometov, A., Sopin, E., Gudkova, I., Andreev, S., Gaidamaka, Y.V., Koucheryavy, Y.: Modeling unreliable operation of mmWave-based data sessions in mission-critical PPDR services. IEEE Access 5, 20536–20544 (2017)
7. Andreev, S., Petrov, V., Dohler, M., Yanikomeroglu, H.: Future of ultra-dense networks beyond 5G: harnessing heterogeneous moving cells. arXiv preprint arXiv:1706.05197 (2017)
8. Petrov, V., Pyattaev, A., Moltchanov, D., Koucheryavy, Y.: Terahertz band communications: applications, research challenges, and standardization activities. In: Proceedings of 8th International Congress on Ultra Modern Telecommunications and Control Systems and Workshops (ICUMT), pp. 183–190. IEEE (2016)
9. Deng, S., Samimi, M., Rappaport, T.: 28 GHz and 73 GHz millimeter-wave indoor propagation measurements and path loss models. In: Proceedings of IEEE ICC (2015)
10. MacCartney, G., Zhang, J., Nie, S., Rappaport, T.: Path loss models for 5G millimeter wave propagation channels in urban microcells. In: Proceedings of IEEE GLOBECOM, pp. 3948–3953, December 2013
11. Zeman, K., et al.: Emerging 5G applications over mmWave: hands-on assessment of WiGig radios. In: Proceedings of 40th International Conference on Telecommunications and Signal Processing (TSP), pp. 86–90. IEEE (2017)
12. Yang, K., Pellegrini, A., Munoz, M., Brizzi, A., Alomainy, A., Hao, Y.: Numerical analysis and characterisation of THz propagation channel for body-centric nano-communications. IEEE Trans. THz Sci. Technol. 5(3), 419–426 (2015)
13. METIS: Initial channel models based on measurements. METIS deliverable D1.2, April 2014
14. 3GPP: Channel model for frequency spectrum above 6 GHz (Release 14). 3GPP TR 38.900 V2.0.0 (2016)
15. Haneda, K., et al.: 5G 3GPP-like channel models for outdoor urban microcellular and macrocellular environments. In: IEEE Vehicular Technology Conference (VTC 2016-Spring), May 2016
16. Gapeyenko, M., et al.: Analysis of human body blockage in millimeter-wave wireless communications systems. In: Proceedings of IEEE ICC, May 2016
17. Bai, T., Vaze, R., Heath Jr., R.W.: Analysis of blockage effects on urban cellular networks. IEEE Trans. Wirel. Commun. 13, 5070–5083 (2014)
18. Gapeyenko, M., et al.: On the temporal effects of mobile blockers in urban millimeter-wave cellular scenarios. IEEE Trans. Veh. Technol. (2017)
19. Samuylov, A., et al.: Characterizing spatial correlation of blockage statistics in urban mmWave systems. In: 2016 IEEE Globecom Workshops (GC Wkshps), pp. 1–7. IEEE (2016)
20. Nain, P., Towsley, D., Liu, B., Liu, Z.: Properties of random direction models. In: Proceedings of IEEE INFOCOM, pp. 1897–1907, March 2005
21. Moltchanov, D.: Distance distributions in random networks. Ad Hoc Netw. 10(6), 1146–1166 (2012)
22. Weiss, G.: Aspects and Applications of the Random Walk. North Holland Press, New York (1994)
23. Bettstetter, C., Hartenstein, H., Prez-Costa, X.: Stochastic properties of the random waypoint mobility model. Wirel. Netw. 10(5), 555–567 (2004)
24. Ross, S.: Introduction to Probability Models. Academic Press, Boston (2010)

Network Security

An Anti-jamming Strategy When it Is Unknown Which Receivers Will Face with Smart Interference

Andrey Garnaev[1,3]([✉]), Wade Trappe[1], and Athina Petropulu[2]

[1] WINLAB, Rutgers University, North Brunswick, USA
garnaev@yahoo.com, trappe@winlab.rutgers.edu
[2] Department of Electrical and Computer Engineering, Rutgers University,
Piscataway, USA
athinap@rutgers.edu
[3] Saint Petersburg State University, Saint Petersburg, Russia

Abstract. The paper considers a communication system consisting of a communication node utilizing multiple antennas in order to communicate with a group of receivers, while potentially facing interference from one or more jammers. The jammers impact the scenario by possibly interfering some of the receivers. The objective of the jammers is to reduce the throughput of nearby receivers, while taking into account the cost/risk of jamming. The fact that jammers face a cost implies that they might not choose to interfere, and thus the communication node faces uncertainty about which of its receivers will be jammed. This uncertainty is modeled by the communicator having only a priori probabilities about whether each receiver will face hostile interference or not, and if he does face such jamming, whether the jamming attack is smart or not. The goal of the communication node is to distribute total power resources to maximize the total throughput associated with communicating with all of the receivers. The problem is formulated as a Bayesian game between the communication system and the jammers. A waterfilling equation to find the equilibrium is derived, and its uniqueness is proven. The threshold value on the power budget is established for the receivers to be non-altruistic.

Keywords: Multicast communication · Jamming · Bayesian game

1 Introduction

Due to the openness of the wireless channel, wireless networks are vulnerable to a variety of physical layer security threats, including interference in the form of jamming attacks. For this reason, wireless security has continued to receive considerable attention by the research community and one can find a comprehensive survey of security threats in cognitive radio networks [1,2], particular, jamming

© IFIP International Federation for Information Processing 2018
Published by Springer Nature Switzerland AG 2018. All Rights Reserved
K. R. Chowdhury et al. (Eds.): WWIC 2018, LNCS 10866, pp. 195–206, 2018.
https://doi.org/10.1007/978-3-030-02931-9_16

threats, in [3]. One of the challenges in dealing with interference attacks is to develop a strategy to cope with such interference, i.e. an anti-jamming strategy. A popular tool to design anti-jamming strategies is game theory [4] since it gives a framework involving competitive agents from which solutions can be formulated. In game theory, the agents (say, a user and a jammer) are considered as active, i.e., they respond to a variety of environmental parameters as well as to the rival's action. The main aim of such active jammers is to magnify their jamming effect in the network they intend to jam, while also balancing the costs associated with their efforts (e.g. they might aim to conserve their energy).

The term *smart jammer* is used to label jammers that aim to balance their efforts against costs/risks, while *naive jammer* is used to for jammers that do not consider their costs/risks. We now provide a quick, and wide sampling of the research literature involving smart jammers. For example, in [5], applying a Stackelberg game approach, the problem of maximizing the secure transmission rate between sensors and a controller while in the presence of a malicious eavesdropper and smart jammer was investigated. In [6], interactions between the user and a smart jammer with SNR as the user's utility was modeled as an anti-jamming Bayesian Stackelberg game involving uncertainties for the channel gain and transmission cost, and in which the user acted as the game's leader. In [7], a modified Q-learning algorithm against a user's fixed strategy and a smart jammer for multi-channel transmission was developed and compared with the corresponding Nash equilibrium. In [8], a jamming defense problem, in which the jammer can quickly learn the transmission power for the user and adaptively adjust its transmission power to maximize the damaging effect, was investigated. In [9], an adaptive rapid channel-hopping scheme was introduced using the notion of a dwell window and a deception mechanism to mitigate smart jammer attacks. In [10], a smart jammer suppression algorithm for a GPS receiver was designed combining spatial amplitude and phase estimation method and high resolution coherent subspace estimation method. In [11], the interactions between a user and a smart jammer regarding their respective transmit power choices was studied using prospect theory. In [12], the optimal user's strategy is designed when unknown whether the user faces with jamming or eavesdropping attack. In [13], a jamming attack against an LTE network was modeled by a repeated game where a smart adversary can be a cheater or a saboteur. The cheater intends to gain more resources for itself, and thus the adversary's intent is not to damage the channel resources, but rather jams the network as a side effect of its malicious activity by reducing competition among the other users, while the saboteur intends to cause the most possible damage to the network resources. In [14], the optimal bandwidth scanning strategy facing interference attacks aimed at reducing spectrum opportunities is designed. In [15], the interactions between a jammer and a communication node that exploits a timing channel to improve resilience to jamming attacks is studied in a game-theoretic framework involving a smart jammer who starts transmitting its interference signal only after detecting activity by the node. In [16], an evolutionary algorithm is proposed to find the equilibrium strategy of a collection of IoT devices seeking to thwart a jamming attack by distributing power among communication subcarries in a smart way so as to decrease the aggregate bit error rate caused by the jammer. In [17], the problem of secure multicast communications was formulated as Stackelberg game where smart private jammers were allocated nearby to eavesdroppers to increase the secrecy capacity of multicast communication.

In all of these papers, the players are assumed to be smart, i.e., rational, which is reflected by employing the best response strategy in the actions taken by the rivals. Recently, behavioral economics has challenged such rational and selfish individual behavior [18]. It has suggested that human decisions vary across time and space, and is subject to cognitive biases, emotions, and thus there may actually be uncertainty regarding the motivations of the rivals. Thus, some players, for whatever reason might not apply the best response strategy in response to their rival's strategies, and thus can be considered as non-rational strategies.

In this paper, we explore *a complementary aspect* of designing anti-jamming strategies for physical layer, multicast communication systems by recognizing a new challenge for such a system that is motivated by the observation, inherited from behavioral economics, that there may be non-rational behavior by the agents. Namely, we investigate the impact that incomplete information regarding a communication node (CN), whether its receivers face jamming attacks, and whether these attacks are smart or not can have on the anti-jamming strategy.

In order to explore this impact, we examine the specific case of a multicast system consisting of a CN employing multiple antennas to communicate with a group of receivers. The communication with some of the receivers might be targeted by jammers, and the CN knows only a priori probabilities about whether each receiver will face hostile interference or not, and if he does face such jamming, whether the jamming attack is smart or not. We formulate this problem as a Bayesian game between the CN and several jammers that might be allocated near the receivers. Existence and uniqueness of the equilibrium strategies are proven, and a waterfilling equation to find the equilibrium strategies is formulated.

The organization of this paper is as follows: in Sect. 2, the model is described. In Sect. 3, auxiliary notation and results are given. In Sect. 4, uniqueness of the equilibrium is proven, and then the waterfilling equation to find the equilibrium is derived. Finally, in Sect. 5, conclusions are given.

2   Communication Model

We begin our formulation by considering an operational scenario involving a *communication node* (CN) that is capable of supporting multiple antenna communication [19]. The multiple antenna interfaces allow this node to operate in a P2P fashion with many receivers simultaneously. We suppose the CN is equipped with n antennas allowing it to communicate with n receivers. We assume that the signals employed are orthogonal, and, thus, they do not interfere each other [20,21]. There is the possibility that a jammer might be present near each receiver, with the intent to jam the communication. Thus, the number of jammers is at most n. In our scenario, we assume each of the jammers is equipped with a single antenna, and he can jam only its neighboring receiver. We portray this scenario in Fig. 1. In order to maintain the reliable communication with the receivers, the CN has to allocate its total power $\overline{P}$ across the orthogonal signals so as to maximize the total throughput. Thus, a strategy of the CN is a vector $\boldsymbol{P} = (P_1, \ldots, P_n)$ with P_i being the power assigned to communicate with receiver i. Let Π be the set of feasible strategies for the CN.

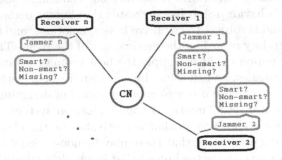

Fig. 1. The CN, receivers and jammers.

The strategy for jammer i is a power J employed to jam communication with receiver i. Let q_i be a priori probability that the jammer i is *smart*. Under the case of a smart jammer, we assume that he employs the best response strategy, i.e. he is focused on getting the best result. Thus, for a smart jammer the set of feasible strategies is $\mathbb{R}_+$. In contrast, a naive jammer, which employs a constant jamming strategy, i.e., *a constant* jammer, will be considered as our *non-smart* jammer since he does not adapt, and in particular does not use the best response strategy. Thus, for the non-smart jammer the set of feasible strategies is reduced to the single point $\{J\}$. Let $\overline{q}_i = 1 - q_i$ be the probability that the jammer i is non-smart. Let $\mathcal{G}_i(J)$ be the probability distribution function associated with applying jamming power J by the non-smart jammer i. We include here also an important particular case $J = 0$ which reflects the possibility that the jammer might be *missing* (or not active), and thus communication with the receiver might not suffer from hostile interference. Let $\boldsymbol{J} = (J_1, \ldots, J_n)$. Then, the payoff to the CN is the expected total throughput, i.e.,

$$v_{CN}(\boldsymbol{P}, \boldsymbol{J}) = \sum_{i=1}^{n} \left(q_i \ln \left(1 + \frac{h_i P_i}{\sigma_i^2 + g_i J_i} \right) + \overline{q}_i \int_{\mathbb{R}_+} \ln \left(1 + \frac{h_i P_i}{\sigma_i^2 + g_i J} \right) d\mathcal{G}_i(J) \right),$$

(1)

where h_i and g_i are fading channel gains, while σ_i^2 is the background noise.

For a boundary scenario, where the feasible strategy for each non-smart jammer is $J = 0$, the a priori probability $\overline{q}_i$ is defined as the probability that the jammer for receiver i is missing. Then, the payoff (1) can be simplified as follows:

$$v_{CN}(\boldsymbol{P}, \boldsymbol{J}) = \sum_{i=1}^{n} \left(q_i \ln \left(1 + h_i P_i / (\sigma_i^2 + g_i J_i) \right) + \overline{q}_i \ln \left(1 + h_i P_i / \sigma_i^2 \right) \right). \quad (2)$$

Since the smart jammer i intends to harm communication with receiver i, this throughput can be considered as the smart jammer's cost utility. Hence, as payoff to the smart jammer i, we consider the difference between his payoff utility (which is his cost utility multiplied by minus one) and the cost of the employed jamming efforts, i.e.,

$$v_i(P_i, J_i) = -\ln\left(1 + h_i P_i/(\sigma_i^2 + g_i J_i)\right) - C_i J_i, \qquad (3)$$

where C_i is the jamming cost per power unit. Note that (3) is a classical payoff for the jammer in CDMA-style transmission problems with resource power costs, which has been studied in literature for different scenarios [8, 22].

Each of the rivals wants to maximize its payoff, and thus we look for the Nash equilibrium [4]. Recall that $(\boldsymbol{P_*}, \boldsymbol{J_*})$ is an equilibrium if and only if, for any $(\boldsymbol{P}, \boldsymbol{J})$, the following inequalities hold:

$$v_{CN}(\boldsymbol{P}, \boldsymbol{J_*}) \le v_{CN}(\boldsymbol{P_*}, \boldsymbol{J_*}), \qquad (4)$$

$$v_i(P_{*i}, J_i) \le v_i(P_{*i}, J_{*i}) \text{ for } i = 1, \ldots, n. \qquad (5)$$

We may consider the smart jammer and non-smart jammer as a single jammer, but able to have different types. From this perspective, the CN knows only a priori probability about type of the jammer it faces with, and this allows us to interpret the game as a Bayesian game between the CN and several jammers [4].

Theorem 1. *The considered game has at least one equilibrium.*

Proof. It is clear that $v_{CN}(\boldsymbol{P}, \boldsymbol{J})$ is concave in $\boldsymbol{P}$, and $v_i(P_i, J_i)$ is concave in J_i. Also, the set Π of feasible strategies for the CN is compact. To be in the framework of Nash's theorem for the existence of equilibrium [4], the set of feasible strategies for each jammer also has to be compact, while it is $\mathbb{R}_+$. Note that

$$\frac{\partial v_i(P_i, J_i)}{\partial J_i} = \frac{h_i P_i}{\sigma_i^2 + g_i J_i + h_i P_i} \frac{g_i}{\sigma_i^2 + g_i J_i} - C_i \le \frac{g_i}{\sigma_i^2 + g_i J_i} - C_i.$$

Thus, $\partial v_i(P_i, J_i)/\partial J_i < 0$ for $J_i > 1/C_i - \sigma_i^2/g_i$. This means that none of the strategies $J_i > 1/C_i - \sigma_i^2/g_i$ can be an equilibrium strategy. Thus, the set of feasible strategies for the jammer i can be reduced to the compact set $[0, \max\{0, 1/C_i - \sigma_i^2/g_i\}]$, and the result follows. ∎

3   Auxiliary Notations and Results

Let us introduce auxiliary notations:

$$L_i(P_i, J_i) := \frac{q_i h_i}{\sigma_i^2 + g_i J_i + h_i P_i} + \int_{\mathbb{R}_+} \frac{\overline{q}_i h_i}{\sigma_i^2 + h_i P_i + g_i J} \, d\mathcal{G}_i(J), \qquad (6)$$

$$M_i(P_i, J_i) := h_i g_i P_i/((\sigma_i^2 + g_i J_i + h_i P_i)(\sigma_i^2 + g_i J_i)). \qquad (7)$$

In the next two propositions, important properties of these functions L_i and M_i, which will be employed further to design the equilibrium strategy, are gathered.

Proposition 1. *(a)* $L_i(P_i, J_i)$ *is decreasing in* P_i *and* J_i.
(b) $L_i(P_i, J_i)$ *tends to zero, while* P_i *tends to infinity.*
(c) Let $0 < \omega \leq L_i(0,0)$. *Then*

$$L_i(P_i, \mathcal{J}_i(P_i)) = \omega \text{ for } P_i \in [\underline{P}_i, \overline{P}_i], \qquad (8)$$

where

$$\mathcal{J}_i(x) := \frac{h_i}{g_i} \frac{q_i}{\omega - \int_{\mathbb{R}_+} \overline{q}_i h_i/(\sigma_i^2 + h_i x + g_i J)\, d\mathcal{G}(J)} - \frac{\sigma_i^2 + h_i x}{g_i}, \qquad (9)$$

and $\underline{P}_i = \underline{P}_i(\omega)$ *and* $\overline{P}_i = \overline{P}_i(\omega)$ *are unique positive roots of the equations:*

$$L_i(\overline{P}_i(\omega), 0) = \omega,$$
$$L_i(\underline{P}_i(\omega), \infty) := \int_{\mathbb{R}_+} \overline{q}_i h_i/(\sigma_i^2 + h_i \underline{P}_i(\omega) + g_i J)\, d\mathcal{G}_i(J) = \omega. \qquad (10)$$

(d) $\mathcal{J}_i(P_i)$ *is strictly decreasing from infinity for* $P_i \downarrow \underline{P}_i$ *to zero for* $P_i = \overline{P}_i$.
(e) $\overline{P}_i(\omega)$ *is continuous and decreasing from infinity for* $\omega \downarrow 0$ *to zero for* $\omega = L_i(0,0)$.

Proof. (a) and (b) follow directly from (6). (a) and (b) jointly with (8) imply (c). (a), (8) and (10) yield (d). (a), (6) and (10) imply (e), and the result follows. ∎

Proposition 2. *(a)* $M_i(P_i, J_i)$ *is increasing in* P_i *and decreasing in* J_i.
(b) $M_i(\overline{P}_i(\omega), 0)$ *is decreasing from* g_i/σ_i^2 *for* $\omega \downarrow 0$ *to zero for* $\omega = L_i(0,0)$.
(c) If $g_i/\sigma_i^2 \leq C_i$ *then* $M_i(\overline{P}_i(\omega), 0) < C_i$ *for* $\omega < L_i(0,0)$, *while if* $g_i/\sigma_i^2 > C_i$ *then is a unique* $\omega_i \in (0, L_i(0,0))$ *such that*

$$M_i(\overline{P}_i(\omega), 0) \begin{cases} > C_i, & 0 < \omega < \omega_i, \\ = C_i, & \omega = \omega_i, \\ < C_i, & \omega_i < \omega < L_i(0,0). \end{cases} \qquad (11)$$

Let $\Omega_i = 0$ *for* $g_i/\sigma_i^2 \leq C_i$ *and* $\Omega_i = \omega_i$ *for* $g_i/\sigma_i^2 \leq C_i$.

Proof. (a) follows from (7). Proposition 1, (a) and (7) imply (b). (b) yields (c), and the result follows. ∎

4   Equilibrium Strategies

In this section, to find the equilibrium and prove its uniqueness, we employ a *constructive* approach. We first use a parameter (Lagrange multiplier) to describe the form each equilibrium must have. This allows us to obtain a continuum of candidates for the equilibrium. Then, we prove that only one of them is the equilibrium.

Proposition 3. *Each equilibrium has to have the following form* $(\boldsymbol{P}(\omega), \boldsymbol{J}(\omega))$ *where* $\omega > 0$ *is a parameter:*

(a) If

$$i \in I_a(\omega) := \{i : L_i(0,0) \leq \omega\} \tag{12}$$

then

$$P_i(\omega) := 0 \text{ and } J_i(\omega) := 0, \tag{13}$$

(b) If

$$i \in I_b(\omega) := \{i : \Omega_i \leq \omega < L_i(0,0)\} \tag{14}$$

then

$$P_i(\omega) := \overline{P}_i(\omega) \text{ and } J_i(\omega) := 0, \tag{15}$$

(c) If

$$i \in I_c(\omega) := \{i : \omega < \Omega_i\} \tag{16}$$

then $P_i(\omega)$ *is the unique root in* $[\underline{P}_i(\omega), \overline{P}_i(\omega)]$ *of the equation*

$$\mathcal{F}_i(P_i(\omega)) = C_i \tag{17}$$

while

$$J_i(\omega) := \mathcal{J}_i(P_i(\omega)), \tag{18}$$

with

$$\mathcal{F}_i(x) := M_i(x, \mathcal{J}_i(x)). \tag{19}$$

Moreover, $J_i(\omega)$ *and* $P_i(\omega)$ *have the following monotonic properties on* ω:

Property $(\Pi - J)$: $J_i(\omega)$ *is continuous and decreasing to zero* $\omega = \Omega_i$.
Property $(\Pi - P)$: $P_i(\omega)$ *is continuous and decreasing on* ω *from infinity for* $\omega \downarrow 0$ *to* $\overline{P}_i(\omega)$ *for* $\omega = \Omega_i$.

Proof. By (4) and (5), $(\boldsymbol{P}, \boldsymbol{J})$ is an equilibrium if and only if these strategies are the best response to each other, i.e., they are solutions of the following best response equations:

$$\boldsymbol{P} = \mathrm{BR}_{CN}(\boldsymbol{J}) := \mathrm{argmax}\{v_{CN}(\boldsymbol{P}, \boldsymbol{J}) : \boldsymbol{P} \in \Pi\}, \tag{20}$$

$$J_i = \mathrm{BR}_{J,i}(\boldsymbol{P}) := \mathrm{argmax}\{v_i(P_i, J_i) : J_i \in \mathbb{R}_+\} \text{ for } i = 1, \ldots, n. \tag{21}$$

Since (20) is a concave NLP problem, to solve it we have to introduce a Lagrangian depending on a Lagrange multiplier ω as follows: $\mathcal{L}_\omega(\boldsymbol{P}) := v_{CN}(\boldsymbol{P}, \boldsymbol{J}) + \omega(\overline{P} - \sum_{i=1}^{n} P_i)$. Then, taking into account notation (8), KKT Theorem implies that $\boldsymbol{P} \in \Pi$ is the best response strategy if and only if the following condition holds:

$$\frac{\partial \mathcal{L}_\omega(\boldsymbol{P})}{\partial P_i} = L_i(P_i, J_i) - \omega \begin{cases} = 0, & P_i > 0, \\ \leq 0, & P_i = 0. \end{cases} \tag{22}$$

Since (21) is an optimization problem involving one real variable J_i and v_i is concave in J_i, in notation (7), J_i is the best response strategy if and only if the following relations hold:

$$\frac{\partial v_i(P_i, J_i)}{\partial J_i} = M_i(P_i, J_i) - C_i \begin{cases} = 0, & J_i > 0, \\ \leq 0, & J_i = 0. \end{cases} \tag{23}$$

By (23), if $P_i = 0$ then $J_i = 0$. Substituting both of them into (22) implies that $i \in I_a(\omega)$ given by (12), and (a) follows. Thus, we have only to consider separately two cases: (A) $P_i > 0$, $J_i = 0$ and (B) $P_i > 0$, $J_i > 0$.
    (A) Let $P_i > 0$ and $J_i = 0$. Then, by (22) and (23),

$$L_i(P_i, 0) = \omega, \tag{24}$$
$$M_i(P_i, 0) \leq C_i. \tag{25}$$

By Proposition 1(d), the Eq. (24) has a positive root if and only if

$$\omega < L_i(0, 0), \tag{26}$$

and, moreover, it is equal to $\overline{P}_i(\omega)$. This implies (15). Substituting this $P_i = \overline{P}_i(\omega)$ into (27) implies that the following inequality must hold:

$$M_i(\overline{P}_i(\omega), 0) \leq C_i. \tag{27}$$

By Proposition 2(b) and (c), (27) holds if and only if $\Omega_i \leq \omega \leq L_i(0, 0)$. This and (26) yield that $i \in I_b(\omega)$ given by (14), and thus (b) follows.
    (B) Let $P_i > 0$ and $J_i > 0$. Then, by (22) and (23),

$$L_i(P_i, J_i) = \omega, \tag{28}$$
$$M_i(P_i, J_i) = C_i. \tag{29}$$

Solving (28) on J_i implies that $J_i = \mathcal{J}_i(P_i)$ with $\mathcal{J}_i$ given by (9). By (28), P_i and J_i are functions of ω, i.e., $P_i = P_i(\omega)$ and $J_i = J_i(\omega)$. By (8) and (28),

$$\lim_{\omega \downarrow 0} P_i(\omega) = \infty. \tag{30}$$

By Proposition 2(a), the left side of (29) is increasing in P_i and decreasing in J_i. Thus, to be a solution for (29), these $P_i(\omega)$ and $J_i(\omega)$ have to be either decreasing or increasing simultaneously on ω. This and (30) imply that $P_i(\omega)$ and $J_i(\omega)$ are decreasing on ω. By (8), (11), (28) and (29), $J_i(\Omega_i) = 0$ and $P_i(\Omega_i) = \overline{P}_i(\Omega_i)$. This, jointly with (30) yield properties $(\Pi - J)$ and $(\Pi - P)$.
    For a fixed ω, by (28), J_i is a function on P_i, namely, $J_i = \mathcal{J}_i(P_i)$. Substituting this J_i into (28) implies that P_i has to be the root of equation (17). By Proposition 1(d), $\mathcal{J}_i(P_i)$ is decreasing from infinity for $P_i \downarrow \underline{P}_i$ to zero for $P_i = \overline{P}_i$ with $\underline{P}_i$ and small $\overline{P}_i$ given by (10). Thus, by Proposition 2(a), we have that $\mathcal{F}_i(P_i)$ is increasing on P_i. Moreover, since $\lim_{J_i \uparrow \infty} M_i(P_i, J_i) = 0$ for each fixed P_i then

$$\mathcal{F}_i(\underline{P}_i) = M_i(\underline{P}_i, \infty) = 0, \tag{31}$$

$$\mathcal{F}_i(\overline{P}_i) = M_i(\overline{P}_i, 0). \tag{32}$$

Thus, since $\mathcal{F}_i$ is increasing, (17) has root if and only if $M_i(\overline{P}_i, 0) > C_i$. By (11), this is equivalent to $\omega < \Omega_i$, i.e., $i \in I_c(\omega)$ given by (16), and (c) follows. ∎

Proposition 4. (a) The function $H(\omega) := \sum_{i=1}^{n} P_i(\omega)$ is continuous and decreasing from infinity for $\omega \downarrow 0$ to zero for $\overline{L} := \max_i L_i(0,0)$.

(b) The following water-filling equation has the unique root in $(0, \overline{L})$:

$$H(\omega) = \overline{P}. \tag{33}$$

Proof. The result follows directly from Proposition 3. ∎

Theorem 2. The game has a unique equilibrium, namely $(\boldsymbol{P}, \boldsymbol{J}) = (\boldsymbol{P}(\omega), \boldsymbol{J}(\omega))$, with $\boldsymbol{P}(\omega)$ and $\boldsymbol{J}(\omega)$ given by Proposition 3 and ω given by (33).

Proof. Proposition 3 describes such a parameterized set of functions $\boldsymbol{P} \colon \mathbb{R}_+ \to \mathbb{R}_+^n$ that each CN equilibrium strategy belongs to. To ascertain whether each of them is an equilibrium, we have to verify whether it utilizes all of the power resource, i.e., whether (33) holds. By Proposition 4, (33) has the unique root, and the result follows. ∎

If the total power budget is enough large then the CN can maintain communication with all the receivers, namely, the following result holds.

Corollary 1. $P_i > 0$ for all i if and only if $\overline{P} \geq H(\underline{L})$ where $\underline{L} := \min_i L_i(0,0)$.

Proof. By Proposition 3, $P_i(\omega) > 0$ for any i if and only if $\omega < \underline{L}$. Then, Theorem 2 straightforward implies the result. ∎

Finally, the two boundary cases of Theorem 2: (a) none of the jammers are smart, and (b) each of the jammers is smart, can be simplified as follows:

Corollary 2. (a) Let $q_i = 0, \forall i$, i.e., none of the jammers is smart. Then, the CN optimal strategy $\boldsymbol{P} = \boldsymbol{P}(\omega)$ is

$$P_i(\omega) \text{ is } \begin{cases} \int_{\mathbb{R}_+} h_i/(\sigma_i^2 + h_i P_i(\omega) + g_i J)\, d\mathcal{G}_i(J) = \omega, & \int_{\mathbb{R}_+} h_i/(\sigma_i^2 + g_i J) d\mathcal{G}_i(J) > \omega, \\ 0, & \text{otherwise.} \end{cases}$$

(b) Let $q_i = 1, \forall i$, i.e., each jammer is smart. Then, the equilibrium strategies $\boldsymbol{P} = \boldsymbol{P}(\omega)$ and $\boldsymbol{J} = \boldsymbol{J}(\omega)$ are:

$$P_i(\omega) = \begin{cases} C_i h_i / ((C_i h_i + \omega g_i)\omega), & \omega < h_i/\sigma_i^2 - h_i C_i/g_i, \\ 1/\omega - \sigma_i^2/h_i, & h_i/\sigma_i^2 - h_i C_i/g_i \leq \omega < h_i/\sigma_i^2, \\ 0, & h_i/\sigma_i^2 \leq \omega, \end{cases}$$

$$J_i(\omega) = \begin{cases} (h_i/g_i)\left(1/\omega - (\sigma_i^2 + h_i P_i(\omega))/h_i\right), & \omega < h_i/\sigma_i^2 - h_i C_i/g_i, \\ 0, & \omega \geq h_i/\sigma_i^2 - h_i C_i/g_i. \end{cases}$$

In both cases, (a) and (b), ω is given as the unique root of water-filling equation $\sum_{i=1}^{n} P_i(\omega) = \overline{P}$.

5 Discussion of Results and Conclusions

In this paper, we formulated and solved a Bayesian game between a communicating node and several jammers that might be allocated near several receivers. Our model also allowed for jammers to be smart (i.e. follow equilibrium strategy), or non-smart. The considered game combines two types of strategies: (a) *power allocation* akin to OFDM style for the CN, and (b) *power assigning* akin to CDMA style for each jammer. It is interesting that the obtained equilibrium strategies have a hierarchical structure although we look for the Nash equilibrium. Namely, in the first step, the CN equilibrium strategy is found by solving the water-filling Eq. (33). In the second step, the jamming strategies J are designed as the derivative of P. In particular, it allows to establish the threshold value on the power budget to maintain non-altruistic communication with all the receivers. This makes the problem completely different from the OFDM jamming problem in the general SNR regime, where a system of two water-filling equations must be solved simultaneously [23], i.e., user and jammer strategies have to be designed simultaneously. The equilibrium strategy of the considered game coincides with the equilibrium in OFDM jamming problem only for a boundary case where all the smart jammers are non-active due to high jamming costs, i.e., when the CN strategy is classical OFDM transmission strategy [24]. It is interesting that although in OFDM jamming problem for the low SNR regime the equilibrium jammer's strategy also can be found in one step, multiple user equilibrium strategies might arise [25], while in the considered game the equilibrium is always unique. Figure 2(a) and (b) illustrate the dependence of the equilibrium strategies on a priori probabilities for the case when non-smart jammers employ jamming power according to uniform distribution in $[0, b]$ with $b = 0.1$, and $n = 5$, $\overline{P} = 1$, $\sigma^2 = (1,1,1,1,1)$, $h = (0.5, 0.9, 0.6, 0.9, 0.7)$, $g = (1, 2, 1.3, 1.8, 0.9)$, $C = (0.1, 0.04, 0.03, 0.05, 0.02)$, while a priori probabilities are given as follows: $q = (Q, Q, Q, Q, Q)$ with $Q \in \{0.2, 0.4, 0.6, 0.8\}$. Fig. 2(c) illustrates zone in plane (b, Q) where the total power budget is enough for the CN to maintain communication with all the receivers, i.e., when the CN strategy does not assume altruistic behaviour for none of the receivers.

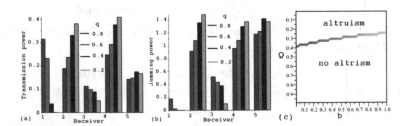

Fig. 2. (a) Equilibrium strategy of the CN, (b) equilibrium strategies of the jammers and (c) zone where none of the receivers is altruistic.

References

1. Sharma, R.K., Rawat, D.B.: Advances on security threats and countermeasures for cognitive radio networks: a survey. IEEE Commun. Surv. Tutor. **17**, 1023–1043 (2015)
2. Zou, Y., Zhu, J., Hanzo, X.W.L.: A survey on wireless security: technical challenges, recent advances, and future trends. Proc. IEEE **104**, 1727–1765 (2016)
3. Grover, K., Lim, A., Yang, Q.: Jamming and anti-jamming techniques in wireless networks: a survey. J. Int. J. Ad Hoc Ubiquitous Comput. **17**, 197–215 (2014)
4. Han, Z., Niyato, D., Saad, W., Basar, T., Hjrungnes, A.: Game Theory in Wireless and Communication Networks: Theory, Models, and Applications. Cambridge University Press, New York (2012)
5. Yuan, L., Wang, K., Miyazaki, T., Guo, S., Wu, M.: Optimal transmission strategy for sensors to defend against eavesdropping and jamming attack. In: IEEE International Conference on Communications (ICC), Paris, France (2017)
6. Jia, L., Yao, F., Sun, Y., Niu, Y., Zhu, Y.: Bayesian Stackelberg game for antijamming transmission with incomplete information. IEEE Commun. Lett. **20**, 1991–1994 (2016)
7. Slimeni, F., Scheers, B., Le Nir, V., Chtourou, Z., Attia, R.: Learning multi-channel power allocation against smart jammer in cognitive radio networks. In: International Conference on Military Communications and Information Systems (ICMCIS), Brussels, Belgium, pp. 1–7 (2016)
8. Yang, D., Xue, G., Zhang, J., Richa, A., Fang, X.: Coping with a smart jammer in wireless networks: a Stackelberg game approach. IEEE Trans. Wirel. Commun. **12**, 4038–4047 (2013)
9. Jeung, J., Jeong, S., Lim, J.: Adaptive rapid channel-hopping scheme mitigating smart jammer attacks in secure WLAN. In: Military Communications Conference (MILCOM), pp. 1231–1236 (2011)
10. Lu, D., Wu, R., Li, P., Su, Z.: GPS smart jammer suppressin algorithm based on spatial APES. In: International Symposium on Intelligent Signal Processing and Communication Systems, pp. 88–91 (2007)
11. Xiao, L., Liu, J., Li, Q., Mandayam, N.B., Poor, H.V.: User-centric view of jamming games in cognitive radio networks. IEEE Trans. Inf. Forensics Secur. **10**, 2578–2590 (2015)
12. Garnaev, A., Trappe, W.: The eavesdropping and jamming dilemma in multichannel communications. In: IEEE International Conference on Communications (ICC), Budapest, Hungary, pp. 2160–2164 (2013)
13. Aziz, F.M., Shamma, J.S., Stuber, G.L.: Resilience of LTE networks against smart jamming attacks. In: IEEE Global Communications Conference (GLOBECOM), pp. 734–739 (2014)
14. Garnaev, A., Trappe, W.: Bandwidth scanning when facing interference attacks aimed at reducing spectrum opportunities. IEEE Trans. Inf. Forensics Secur. **12**, 1916–1930 (2017)
15. D'Oro, S., Galluccio, L., Morabito, G., Palazzo, S., Chen, L., Martignon, F.: Defeating jamming with the power of silence: a game-theoretic analysis. IEEE Trans. Wirel. Commun. **14**, 2337–2352 (2015)
16. Namvar, N., Saad, W., Bahadori, N., Kelley, B.: Jamming in the internet of things: a game-theoretic perspective. In: IEEE Global Communications Conference (GLOBECOM), Washington, DC, pp. 1–6 (2016)

17. Cumanan, K., Ding, Z., Xu, M., Poor, H.V.: Secure multicast communications with private jammers. In: 17th IEEE International Workshop on Signal Processing Advances in Wireless Communications (SPAWC), Edinburgh, UK (2016)
18. Thaler, R.H.: Misbehaving: The Making of Behavioral Economics. Allen Lane (2015)
19. de Lamare, R.C.: Massive MIMO systems: signal processing challenges and future trends. URSI Radio Sci. Bull. **2013**(347), 8–20 (2013)
20. Zhao, Y., Haggman, S.-G.: Intercarrier interference self-cancellation scheme for OFDM mobile communication systems. IEEE Trans. Commun. **49**, 1185–1191 (2001)
21. Tang, T., Heath Jr., R.W.: Space-time interference cancellation in MIMO-OFDM systems. IEEE Trans. Veh. Technol. **54**, 1802–1816 (2005)
22. Garnaev, A., Trappe, W.: To eavesdrop or jam, that is the question. In: Mellouk, A., Sherif, M.H., Li, J., Bellavista, P. (eds.) ADHOCNETS 2013. LNICSSITE, vol. 129, pp. 146–161. Springer, Cham (2014). https://doi.org/10.1007/978-3-319-04105-6_10
23. Garnaev, A., Trappe, W., Petropulu, A.: Equilibrium strategies for an OFDM network that might be under a jamming attack. In: 51st Annual Conference on Information Systems and Sciences (CISS), Baltimore, MD, pp. 1–6 (2017)
24. Altman, E., Avrachenkov, K., Garnaev, A.: Closed form solutions for water-filling problem in optimization and game frameworks. Telecommun. Syst. J. **47**, 153–164 (2011)
25. Garnaev, A., Trappe, W.: An OFDM-based dual radar/communication system facing uncertain jamming power. In: IEEE Conference on Communications and Network Security (CNS), Las Vegas, NV, pp. 1–9 (2017)

Quantifying the Information Leak in IEEE 802.11 Network Discovery

Otto Waltari[✉] and Jussi Kangasharju

Department of Computer Science, University of Helsinki, Helsinki, Finland
otto.waltari@helsinki.fi

Abstract. Wi-Fi is often the easiest and most affordable way to get a device connected. When a device connects to any Wi-Fi network its identifier (SSID) is stored in the device. These SSIDs are sometimes intentionally exposed to the outside world during periodic network discovery routines. In this paper we quantify the information leak that is present in the current network discovery protocol. Our collected data shows how common it is for a device to leak information and what can be derived from the names of networks a user has connected to in the past. We introduce a way to measure the uniqueness of an entity, which is based on the set of leaked SSID names. We apply previously proposed methods of MAC address randomization reversal on our data and evaluate entity uniqueness. We show how unique SSID names backfire against attempts to obfuscate user devices. Finally we evaluate an existing alternative network discovery scheme that does not leak information.

1 Introduction

One of the most essential properties of smart phones and other mobile devices is the ability to stay connected to the outside world. Cellular data can provide connectivity in most areas where people spend their time. However, in many countries cellular data can be quite expensive, which often motivates users to utilize free Wi-Fi where ever it is provided by some local entity, e.g. shopping mall, airport, cafe or hotel. This is especially true when travelling and data roaming has an extra cost. Terms for using this kind of a public or free Wi-Fi is often displayed to the user upon connection, and it is up to the user whether he trusts the Wi-Fi provider.

What the user often does not know is that the name of each connected network is stored on the device in a *preferred networks list* (PNL). Due to design features in the IEEE 802.11 wireless standard [1] these network names are sometimes exposed to the outside world during so-called *active network discoveries*. Privacy preserving ways of network discovery have been proposed [4,6], but our collected data set for this paper shows that still 30–40% of collected probe requests contain SSID names. Other studies [2,3,13] also show that probing is still widely used. Another concern in wireless networking is traceability of users. Since Wi-Fi is a wireless medium eavesdropping is trivial with any portable networked device. It can even be done without the subject device never knowing that

© IFIP International Federation for Information Processing 2018
Published by Springer Nature Switzerland AG 2018. All Rights Reserved
K. R. Chowdhury et al. (Eds.): WWIC 2018, LNCS 10866, pp. 207–218, 2018.
https://doi.org/10.1007/978-3-030-02931-9_17

frames it transmitted were recorded by a third party. This was exploited by Pang et al. [9] over a decade ago. A popular countermeasure against tracking is MAC address randomization [5,11], which has already made its way to recent mobile operating systems (Android 6.0 and iOS 8). However, several studies [7,8,12] have shown that MAC address randomization can be reversed.

In this paper we present a method to quantify the potentially private information that is leaking through exposed SSID names. We show that the network SSID names themselves have an impact on how unique a client device may become. We present a classification of SSID names based on how unique they are, and then introduce a measure to quantify the uniqueness of an entity based on its PNL. We show the uniqueness distribution of entities in a data set we collected. We apply de-randomization methods on our data set that reverses the effects of MAC address randomization and quantify the information value again and compare it to the results from the raw data. We also show how SSID leakage can be stopped with passive network discovery and measure the performance impact it has compared to active network discovery.

The rest of this paper is structured as follows. In Sect. 2 we explain the reasons why SSID names are exposed to the outside. Section 3 explains how we collected our data set, how we reverse the effects of MAC address randomization, and classify different types of SSID names. We also introduce a metric called *uniqueness*, which indicates how unique an entity is based in its PNL. In Sect. 4 we discuss our findings. In Sect. 5 we evaluate an alternative way of network discovery and evaluate it. In Sect. 6 we discuss related work, and finally conclude the paper in Sect. 7.

2   Background

The IEEE 802.11 wireless standard [1] specifies a network discovery protocol and a set of management frames designed for the purpose. A user device, or *station* (STA), that is looking for networks to connect to is periodically broadcasting probe request frames. A network access point (AP) may respond to the client with a probe response. If the user device decides to connect to an AP that responded the devices proceed to an authentication and association phase.

Probe requests can be either broadcast or directed. A broadcast probe has the broadcast address (ff:ff:ff:ff:ff:ff) defined as the *destination address* (DA), which also means that it can be received by anyone. Similarly, a directed probe has its destination set to the broadcast address, but in contrast to broadcast probes it has a *service set identifier* (SSID) configured in a designated header field. Addressing probe requests based on the access point MAC address would not work since one SSID can be offered by several access points. When a STA successfully associates with a surrounding network its name, i.e. its *service set identifier* (SSID), is stored on the device in a *preferred networks list* (PNL). This is a mechanism to keep track of networks that the device has connected to in the past. IEEE 802.11 specifies that one *extended service set* (ESS) may consist of more than two APs. Distinct APs in one ESS share the same SSID so that a client can authenticate with any one of them.

In most cases APs transmit periodic beacon frames in order to advertise their own SSID. However, it is not necessary for an AP to transmit beacon frames. One may also wait quietly for incoming probe requests that carry a network SSID that matches their own. This scenario would imply that the transmitter of that probe request has knowledge of that network from before. These kinds of WLAN networks are commonly known as hidden networks. They were designed to be more safe and secure, but studies [10] have shown that the absence of beacons from an access point did not increase safety against attackers, and was merely a false impression of security.

Despite the fact that STAs can find out about surrounding networks by listening to beacons sent by APs, and that hidden APs are a bad idea and should not be configured to be that way, modern mobile devices still transmit probes that contain SSID names of previously associated networks. Occasionally some devices expose large portions, or even all entries from their PNL. This is never explicitly told to the user and on most devices it happens automatically in the background as long as Wi-Fi is enabled on the device.

Not only does SSID names and locations reveal sensitive information, but a leaked PNL can also ruin the attempt of MAC address randomization. If a sufficiently unique PNL is received from two seemingly different devices, we can with high confidence map them back to the same user. Not necessarily the same device, since some mobile operating systems can sync their PNL over the cloud to multiple devices owned by the same user. Despite that, the user behind the PNL is still the same.

3   Methodology

In this section we present the data set used for our findings later presented in this paper. We also explain reverse randomization that we apply on our data set, and classify different types of SSIDs present in our data.

3.1   Collecting the Data Set

The data set used in this paper consists of six distinct capture files collected at different events and locations. For collecting the data we used a setup similar to the one described in our previous work [13]. For the sake of portability we only monitored channels 1, 6 and 11. These are the non-overlapping 2.4 GHz Wi-Fi channels that are recommended to be used when establishing new access points. Hardware we used for collecting the data was a Raspberry Pi 2 with three Wi-Fi adapters dedicated for the channels to be monitored. Data was stored locally on the device and it was powered from a USB power brick for wireless operation.

According to the findings in our previous paper [13] we do not have to monitor all available channels to increase our chance to capture a probe from a client device. Since devices scan for networks by transmitting bursts of probes in a sweeping fashion through all available channels, we can safely assume that allocating 100% reception time for three evenly spaced and non-overlapping channels will capture the ongoing network discovery.

Table 1. Data set described in numbers

#	Data set	Probe count	Directed probes	Unique MACs	Total entities	Leaked PNLs	MAC address randomizers
1	EuroSys 2017	101.1 k	42.2 k (41.8%)	3558	2077	55.1%	608 (29.3%)
2	Pop concert	129.4 k	42.7 k (33.0%)	5225	2280	28.8%	543 (23.8%)
3	Workers day	96.9 k	33.3 k (34.4%)	10363	5541	25.3%	1376 (24.8%)
4	Movie	108.6 k	31.1 k (28.7%)	5869	2540	29.9%	678 (26.7%)
5	Shopping mall	98.4 k	32.4 k (33.0%)	7787	5567	30.8%	1030 (18.5%)
6	University campus	205.5 k	88.5 k (43.0%)	6824	2606	39.1%	652 (25.0%)

Table 1 has a listing of the data sets along with some essential statistics of the data. Set #1 was collected during EuroSys 2017 conference in Serbia. Set #2 was collected during a pop concert in Helsinki, with a predominantly teenage audience. Set #3 is collected during workers day evening celebration in a large outdoor park area in downtown Helsinki. Set #4 was collected in a movie theater during the title *Alien: Covenant.* Set #5 was collected while walking around at one of the busiest shopping malls in Helsinki. Set #6 was collected during two seminars at the Department of Computer Science at Helsinki University. All of the data sets are roughly the same size, except set #6 collected at our university campus. It is twice as large likely because there were more active Wi-Fi users (staff, researchers, students) present within range than in the other data sets.

3.2 Reverse Randomization

A recent feature on mobile devices is to use fake MAC addresses when performing network discovery [5,11], i.e. *MAC address randomization.* Purpose of this convention is to prevent tracking based on a device's static MAC address. This is achieved by intentionally changing the local MAC address and making the client device, i.e. entity look like several different entities. This would make it harder for an external party to keep track of the entity since its MAC address keeps on constantly changing. While a MAC address would be the obvious choice for a primary identification handle for tracking, randomization of the address has not been able to obfuscate entities completely. Studies have shown that MAC address randomization can be reversed [7,12] and that it is not that effective.

For this paper we implemented de-randomization methods described by Vanhoef et al. [12] and Martin et al. [7]. These methods are; *(i)* sequence control (SC) continuity, *(ii)* information element (IE) fingerprinting, *(iii)* locally/globally administered OUIs, and *(iv)* PNL matching. We applied these methods to de-randomize our data set and compared characteristics of the set before and after. Table 1 shows how much the data set was reduced and how many devices present in the set use MAC address randomization.

3.3 SSID Classification

The SSID of a network is decided by the party responsible for the network. In companies and other organizations there may be a policy that defines naming conventions, but for personal purposes there are no rules or guidelines for naming. The only restriction is that it may not be longer than 32 characters. While the SSID is only an identifier for a *service set* (BSS/ESS), the choice of its textual content can reveal more than just the presence of that particular network. Based on our data set we divide SSIDs into five categories.

Globally scattered SSIDs are often used by fast food restaurants, coffee shops and other similar type big brand companies that have several locations around the world. A free Wi-Fi provided by such entities often has the name of the franchise, but does not indicate a particular site or location. From the business point of view it makes sense, since once a user connects to their network at one location, his device remembers the network in the next location and the service is available instantly. Such SSIDs are for example "Starbucks" and "McDonald's". The information value in these kinds of SSIDs is relatively low since they cannot be pinned to a location. However, they count as elements in the PNL vector.

Public location SSIDs are often present at sites like airports, hotels or shopping malls. These kinds of SSID names can be mapped back to a place somewhere. The name can be a subtle hint, or even explicitly tell what the location is. Services like Wigle[1] can assist in giving a location for the network in case it is not explicit. An examples of such an SSID would be "Helsinki Airport Free Wi-Fi". If an SSID like this is exposed from a user via his PNL, it does not reveal too much sensitive information about the user since travelling and using available Wi-Fi is quite normal.

Private location SSID is one that has been set up by a household for private use. These are often *obvious choices*, such as "Home Wi-Fi" for a home network, which has a relatively low information value. Another common practice is to include a name in the SSID, e.g. "Smith family Wi-Fi", in which case the information value is higher since it has a descriptor making it more unique. These are not unique on a global scale, but can be used to mark out user involvement with certain non-public locations.

A **unique SSID** is such that there likely is not another network by the same name. Our collected data shows that imagination plays a major role in ending up with a unique SSID. Another common way to unknowingly end up with a unique SSID is to leave it as it is by default on several ISP provided access points. The convention in this case is that the SSID has a suffix that matches with the three right-most octets of its own MAC address. This half of a MAC address is by design supposed to be unique, which gives high chances that SSIDs like "Telenet-12-3A-BC" are globally unique.

Portable access point SSIDs are by nature mobile and no guarantees can be made about their location. The typical most common instance of such network

---

[1] https://wigle.net/.

names are "AndroidAP" and "Alice's iPhone". These are the default hot-spot names when sharing a cellular data connection over Wi-Fi to other devices. No conclusions can be drawn about the location of such SSIDs. However, generic ad-hoc hot-spot SSIDs do count as elements in a user's PNL vector.

3.4   Entity Uniqueness

In order to quantify how unique entities extracted from our data set are we introduce a metric called *uniqueness*. The uniqueness value of an entity indicates how likely there is not another entity that has PNL entries, i.e. known SSIDs in common. Uniqueness values are normalized to be between 0 and 1. A high uniqueness value means that the entity stands more out of the crowd and is less likely to have common PNL entries with other entities. A low uniqueness value indicates that the entity blends more into the crowd. For entities that do not transmit a single SSID uniqueness is defined to be 0.

Let entity e have a PNL with k distinct SSID names (1) and rank of n be the number of entities that have network n in their PNL (2):

$$PNL_e = \{n_1, n_2, ..., n_k\} \tag{1}$$
$$rank_{n_i} = |n_i| \tag{2}$$

First we calculate a significance value S for each SSID in e's PNL:

$$S_i = min\left\{\frac{|n_i|^{1+\frac{1}{k}}}{T}, 1\right\},$$

where T is the total number of distinct SSIDs in the dataset. The lower the significance value is, the more it contributes to the uniqueness of an entity. Figure 1 shows the distribution of all SSID significance values with a PNL length of 1. The figure also shows the average of every S_i in each data set, which is the same as the expected value for any given SSID. If the significance value is equal to or higher than T it is not considered to be contributing to the uniqueness of the entity. This is common in the case where an entity has a PNL length of 1, and that single SSID is a popular one. A popular SSID has a high rank by nature, and k equals 1, which yields a high significance value. On the contrary, a single unique SSID yields a small significance value regardless of the PNL length.

We calculate the uniqueness value for a given entity e with the following formula:

$$uniqueness_e = 1 - \left(S_1 \cdot S_2 \cdot ... \cdot S_k\right).$$

In Sect. 4 we use uniqueness as a metric to compare how much more unique entities become after we remove the effect of MAC address randomization from our data set.

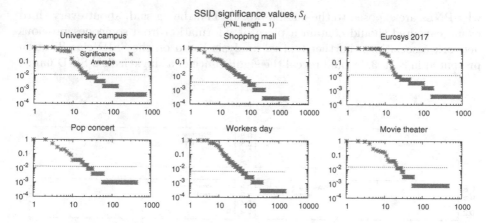

Fig. 1. Distribution of SSIDs significance values with an assumed PNL length of one. Y-axis represents significance values of distinct SSID names presented along the X-axis. Dashed line shows the average of all values. The lower the value, the more it contributes to the uniqueness of an entity.

4   Findings

For the results presented in this paper we used our data set described in Sect. 3.1. We analyzed each part of the data set separately in order to maintain spatial context in each set. Our primary measure for quantifying the information leak in 802.11 network discovery is *uniqueness* introduced in Sect. 3.4. In order to measure the uniqueness of an entity, we calculate the significance value for each SSID in that entity's PNL. Figure 1 shows the significance values of all SSIDs in the data sets. From the plots we can observe that the vast majority of dots have a small value. This means that most SSIDs have been heard from only a few different devices. The dots with higher values and closer to the top represent SSIDs that were heard from many devices. Considering the log-log scale, these are only about one percent of all SSIDs.

The CDFs in Fig. 2 illustrate the uniqueness distribution of entities before and after de-randomizing the data set. The solid line is a cumulative distribution function plot of uniqueness values from the raw data. Next to it, the dashed line represents the same data, but after it has been de-randomized. After de-randomizing the number of entities in that data set reduces. This is because several MAC addresses can be mapped back to one single entity. Table 1 shows how many devices presented in the data employ MAC address randomization. The amount is based on entities in the de-randomized set that are linked to two or more distinct MAC addresses. Based on our results, roughly one fourth of devices use MAC address randomization.

From Table 1 we can also see that roughly 30–40% of all collected probes are directed probes, which means that they carry an SSID in the frame header. This number is about 10% points lower than what Barbera et al. [2] presented in their measurement results back in 2013. Directed probes are the reason how and why PNLs are exposed to the outside world. That being said, about every third frame captured should contain a piece of information from someones previous network associations. Further textual analysis based on the SSID classification presented in Sect. 3.3 would reveal the significance of a single leaked SSID name.

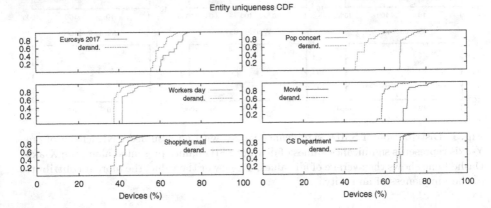

Fig. 2. Distribution of all entities' uniqueness values. Y-axis represents uniqueness values. Solid line represents the raw data set, and dashed line the same set with effects of MAC address randomization removed.

5   Fixing the Leak

Active network discovery in 802.11 works through a protocol where the client device sends out probe requests in hope for nearby access points to receive them. These probe requests can be either broadcast or directed. A broadcast probe is not addressed to any access point in particular, but may – as the name strongly indicates – be received by any access point withing range. A directed probe on the other hand is addressed to a particular *service set* (ESS/BSS). Due to the design of service sets, discovery of networks should be done based on the *service set identifier* (SSID). As the client does not initially know any access point providing access to the service set, it prepares the frame with a broadcast *destination address* (DA) and specifies the SSID in a designated field inside the probe frame header. Because the frame has a broadcast link layer destination, it is by design receivable by anyone. Since management frames, including probe requests, are unencrypted anyone can read the content. This is how PNLs leak to the external parties.

Passive network discovery is an alternative way of finding surrounding wireless networks. In this case it is required that the access point advertises itself by transmitting beacons regularly. Beacons are broadcast so that any potential client can receive the beacons. The beaconing interval can in many cases be user configured, but our measurement shows that most access points send beacons

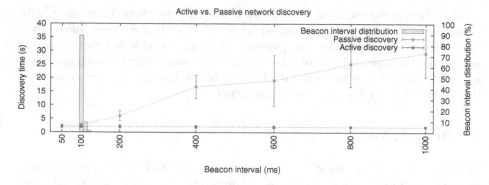

Fig. 3. Comparison of discovery times (left side Y-axis) with both active and passive network discovery. Beacon interval distribution (right side Y-axis) represents a sample of roughly 600 access points.

with a 100 to 120 ms interval, which on a wide range of access points seems to be the default setting. Once a client receives a beacon from an access point it is willing to associate with, it already knows the MAC address of the AP since it was the set as the *source address* (SA) in the beacon header. Passive network discovery by design never broadcasts SSIDs from clients, and thus is safe from potential privacy violating information leakage.

A downside with passive network discovery is that it is not as fast as active scanning. Since access points can be configured on any channel, clients have to listen to all potential channels for a predetermined time and wait for beacons. If a client does not wait long enough it could miss a beacon. Another drawback of passive network discovery is that it does not work with hidden access points. However, hiding a network does not add any security or privacy, and is thus considered to be a bad practice, or even a IEEE 802.11 protocol violation [10].

For this paper we measured association times with both an active a passive configuration. We used two laptops, where one was configured as an access point and the other one as a connecting client. Both hosts ran Debian Linux and used `wpa_supplicant`[2] and `hostapd`[3] on the AP side, which are the most widely used IEEE 802.11 software backend components. Passive scanning is a built in feature on recent versions of `wpa_supplicant`, and thus does not require anything more than a simple configuration parameter.

We measured the association times with both active and passive network discovery, and also with different beaconing intervals configured, namely 50, 100, 200, 400, 600, 800, and 1000 ms. Figure 3 shows the difference between association times between active and passive network discovery. The figure also shows the distribution of beacon interval times recorded around our university campus area and a nearby shopping mall and residential area. The capture file contains beacons from over 600 different access points.

---

[2] https://w1.fi/wpa_supplicant/.

[3] https://w1.fi/hostapd/.

Our measurements show that passive network discovery takes only 0.6 s longer in 98% of the cases compared to active scanning. Figure 3 shows that the difference between active and passive scanning is neglible at beacon interval values that the vast majority of access points are using. Since network discovery is an infrequent procedure and may happen in the background, we argue that this penalty has no impact on user experience.

6   Related Work

Probing characteristics have been studied since potential tracking and privacy concerns emerged withing the wireless community. Barbera et al. [2] did large scale measurements in public locations about probing routines in mobile devices and looked for social-network properties in the data.

Freudiger et al. [3] studied how much probes modern cellphones transmit. Their work shows that the rate at which probes are transmitted highly depends on the brand and model of the device. They conclude that a frightening amount of frames with potentially sensitive information can be collected efficiently with different antenna and wireless interface configurations. In our recent work [13] we explained and evaluated an multi channel scanning device that has full temporal coverage each channel.

Since probing makes it possible to track users, MAC address randomization has been proposed as a solution to preserve privacy. Gruteser et al. [5] proposed the use of *disposable interface identifiers*, i.e. random MAC addresses to obfuscate entities. Singelée et al. [11] proposes a more cryptographic approach in random identifiers for WPAN networks, but can be applied in the same manner to IEEE 802.11 networks aswell.

Randomization has been adopted by major operating systems (Android v. 6.0, iOS v. 8, Windows v. 10 and Linux kernel v. 3.18), and its implementation differs slightly between the platforms. A study by Vanhoef et al. [12] analyzes different implementations of MAC address randomization. Their major contribution is about reversing the effect of randomization through fingerprinting different parts of frames. Work by Martin et al. [7] claims 100% success ratio in reversing randomization by looking at low level control frame handling. They exploit an existing design flaw in current wireless chipsets and present a breakdown of MAC address randomization techniques different platforms use. Matte et al. [8] presents an alternative approach to reverse randomization by looking at the timing between transmitted frames. Their approach claims a 75% success ratio by only looking at the timing of received frames.

Privacy issues with the current IEEE 802.11 network discovery protocol has been addressed earlier. Lindqvist et al. [6] proposed a privacy preserving access point discovery protocol already back in 2009. Their solution builds on top of the existing discovery protocol. It is a key exchange protocol where the nonce-based keys are piggybacked inside probe request and response frames. The protocol requires support from both parties, and to our knowledge has not been deployed outside their lab.

7   Conclusion

The network discovery protocol specified by the IEEE 802.11 standard has by design a feature that can potentially leak sensitive information. Directed probe requests carry names of SSIDs that the device has previously been connected to. Despite the fact that they are directed, they are transmitted with a broadcast destination so that any access point can receive them. A privacy threat emerges when an eavesdropper successfully collects the whole *preferred networks list* (PNL). In this paper we presented a way to quantify the information leak that is present in the current network discovery protocol. We introduced a metric called *uniqueness* in Sect. 3.4. It is calculated based on the PNL leaked from a mobile user. We collected a data set, consisting is six separate subsets, which shows that roughly 30–40% of collected probes carry an SSID name. Also around 30% of seen entities broadcasted their PNL in the air. We calculated the uniqueness value for all entities found in our data set. Detailed information of the data set could be seen in Table 1.

MAC address randomization is a technique intended to reduce the traceability of devices. A device employing it uses disposable MAC addresses as the sender address in probe request frames. Several studies have shown that it is not as effective as expected and due to e.g. design flaws the effect of randomization can be reversed in various ways. In this paper we implemented our own version of MAC address de-randomization based on techniques presented in by others [7,12]. We de-randomized our data set and calculated the uniqueness values for the data set again, and compared the uniqueness distribution to our earlier results.

In order to prevent the information leak through PNLs, broadcast probe requests with SSIDs should not be transmitted. Passive network discovery works without actively sending probes. It works by listening to beacons sent periodically by access points. Passive network discovery is slower than active, but our evaluation in Sect. 5 indicates that in the majority of cases the penalty is not significant.

References

1. Wireless LAN Medium Access Control (MAC) and Physical Layer (PHY) Specifications. IEEE Std 802.11-2012 (Revision of IEEE Std 802.11-2007), pp. 1–2793, March 2012
2. Barbera, M.V., Epasto, A., Mei, A., Perta, V.C., Stefa, J.: Signals from the crowd: uncovering social relationships through smartphone probes. In: Proceedings of the 2013 Conference on Internet Measurement Conference, IMC 2013, pp. 265–276. ACM, New York (2013). https://doi.org/10.1145/2504730.2504742
3. Freudiger, J.: How talkative is your mobile device?: an experimental study of Wi-Fi probe requests. In: Proceedings of the 8th ACM Conference on Security & Privacy in Wireless and Mobile Networks, WiSec 2015, pp. 8:1–8:6. ACM, New York (2015). https://doi.org/10.1145/2766498.2766517

4. Greenstein, B., McCoy, D., Pang, J., Kohno, T., Seshan, S., Wetherall, D.: Improving wireless privacy with an identifier-free link layer protocol. In: Proceedings of the 6th International Conference on Mobile Systems, Applications, and Services, MobiSys 2008, pp. 40–53. ACM, New York (2008). https://doi.org/10.1145/1378600.1378607
5. Gruteser, M., Grunwald, D.: Enhancing location privacy in wireless LAN through disposable interface identifiers: a quantitative analysis. In: Proceedings of the 1st ACM International Workshop on Wireless Mobile Applications and Services on WLAN Hotspots, WMASH 2003, pp. 46–55. ACM, New York (2003). https://doi.org/10.1145/941326.941334
6. Lindqvist, J., et al.: Privacy-preserving 802.11 access-point discovery. In: Proceedings of the Second ACM Conference on Wireless Network Security, WiSec 2009, pp. 123–130. ACM, New York (2009). https://doi.org/10.1145/1514274.1514293
7. Martin, J., et al.: A study of MAC address randomization in mobile devices and when it fails. arXiv preprint arXiv:1703.02874 (2017)
8. Matte, C., Cunche, M., Rousseau, F., Vanhoef, M.: Defeating MAC address randomization through timing attacks. In: Proceedings of the 9th ACM Conference on Security & #38; Privacy in Wireless and Mobile Networks, WiSec 2016, pp. 15–20. ACM, New York (2016). https://doi.org/10.1145/2939918.2939930
9. Pang, J., Greenstein, B., Gummadi, R., Seshan, S., Wetherall, D.: 802.11 user fingerprinting. In: Proceedings of the 13th Annual ACM International Conference on Mobile Computing and Networking, MobiCom 2007, pp. 99–110, ACM, New York (2007). https://doi.org/10.1145/1287853.1287866
10. Riley, S.: Myth vs. reality: wireless SSIDs, October 2007
11. Singelée, D., Preneel, B.: Location privacy in wireless personal area networks. In: Proceedings of the 5th ACM Workshop on Wireless Security, WiSe 2006, pp. 11–18. ACM, New York (2006). https://doi.org/10.1145/1161289.1161292
12. Vanhoef, M., Matte, C., Cunche, M., Cardoso, L.S., Piessens, F.: Why MAC address randomization is not enough: an analysis of Wi-Fi network discovery mechanisms. In: Proceedings of the 11th ACM on Asia Conference on Computer and Communications Security, ASIA CCS 2016, pp. 413–424. ACM, New York (2016). https://doi.org/10.1145/2897845.2897883
13. Waltari, O., Kangasharju, J.: The wireless shark: identifying WiFi devices based on probe fingerprints. In: Proceedings of the First Workshop on Mobile Data, MobiData 2016, pp. 1–6. ACM, New York (2016). https://doi.org/10.1145/2935755.2935757

Pairing-Based Cryptography on the Internet of Things: A Feasibility Study

Ioanna Karantaidou$^{(\boxtimes)}$, Spyros T. Halkidis, Sophia Petridou (ID),
Lefteris Mamatas (ID), and George Stephanides

Department of Applied Informatics, University of Macedonia, Thessaloniki, Greece
{dai16090,halkidis,spetrido,emamatas}@uom.edu.gr, steph@uom.gr

Abstract. Pairing-based cryptography (PBC) has recently received much attention, since the mathematical building block of pairings paved the ground for devising efficient cryptographic protocols exploiting an old inspiration, i.e., to produce the public key of an entity based on its *identity*. The so-called Identity-Based Cryptography (IBC) simplifies key management procedures, since it does not require certificate-based infrastructures. Moreover, it is an elliptic curve cryptosystem which entails that it offers the same security levels as other public key systems with much smaller key lengths. The above characteristics make it an attractive solution for resource-constrained environments such as the Internet of Things (IoT), where strong confidentiality and signature schemes are necessary. In this article, we conducted feasibility tests of pairing-based cryptography for middle-class IoT devices, such as the Raspberry Pi 3 platform.

Keywords: Pairing-based cryptography · Identity-based encryption
Short signatures · Internet of things

1 Introduction

The Internet of Things (IoT) has overwhelmed the cyber-physical world with billions of interconnected, fixed or mobile, devices ranging form wearables to smartphones [1]. Providing access anytime, anywhere, anyhow, the IoT has the potential to enable innovative application in many domains such as home or building automation, automotive, transportation surveillance and health-care. However, along with its scale, the IoT augments the security concerns due to the ubiquitous nature of the IP-things which are sending private data to back-end systems, e.g., edge or core cloud, and servers [2].

Let us consider a smart health-care system where patients' wearables can either communicate directly with a hospital's IoT infrastructure or send collected data to intermediate devices, e.g., a Raspberry Pi, which gathers and forwards them to the cloud. In such a scenario, either the links, i.e., Internet connections,

K. R. Chowdhury et al. (Eds.): WWIC 2018, LNCS 10866, pp. 219–230, 2018.
https://doi.org/10.1007/978-3-030-02931-9_18

or the nodes, i.e., collaborating devices, can be untrusted. Thus, strong cryptography is required to provide efficient confidentiality and authentication solutions. At the same time, the resource-constrained nature of the IoT environment, both in terms of low rate communication links and hardware-limited devices, strives for lightweight cryptographic protocols.

Recently, pairing-based cryptography (PBC) has received much attention [3], since pairings are revealed to be the mathematical tool which makes possible the Shamir's inspiration of certificate-less Public Key Cryptography (PKC) [4]. In 1984, Shamir proposed to authenticate an entity using some form of its *identity*, e.g., the email address, instead of its certificate. The main advantage of Identity-Based Cryptography (IBC) is that enables message encryption without the need of previously distributed keys. Such a facility is attractive in IoT use-cases where keys' pre-distribution is impractical or raises security concerns. For example, when the same key is shared among all "things", the impairment of a single device exposes the security of the whole network; or when a dedicated key is established for each couple of "things", the solution is not scalable. Moreover, the IBC provides the feature of including date information to the *identity* which entails revocation support without the use of certificate revocation lists (CRLs) [3].

Two fundamental protocols, which addressed in 2001 the issue of devising efficient IBC schemes, are the Boneh and Franklin's identity-based encryption (IBE) protocol [5] and the Boneh, Lynn and Shacham's (BLS) short signature scheme [6]. IBC is public key cryptography in the sense that roughly a public key is used for encryption and a private key for decryption. However, instead of producing the public key from the private, IBC defines that public keys are issued upon pre-existing identifiers. This entails no need of Certification Authorities (CAs). Instead, a Private Key Generator (PKG) authenticates the receiver, generates his private key and provides public system parameters to the sender.

Motivated by the general advantage of IBC, i.e., it simplifies key management procedures of certificate-based public key infrastructures, in this paper, we evaluate the feasibility of the aforementioned pairing-based protocols on middleclass IoT devices, such as the Raspberry-Pi 3 platform, through experimentation. More precisely, we present the basic Boneh and Franklin's IBE scheme, namely *BasicIdent* and we implement its *FullIdent* version, which is Chosen-Ciphertext Secure, using the Relic-Toolkit library [7]. In addition we evaluate the performance of BLS short signature scheme in contrast with the Elliptic Curve Digital Signature Algorithm (ECDSA) [8]. Thus, our work focuses on encryption and decryption for IBE schemes, and on signing and verifying for signatures schemes. Feasibility is expressed in terms of protocols' execution time, memory usage and energy consumption.

Our contribution can be summarized as follows:

1. we conducted real experiments to measure the resource requirements of fundamental pairing-based crytposystems in terms of CPU time, memory and energy;
2. we implement the *FullIdent* IBE scheme inside the Relic-Toolkit library;

3. we compare the performance of *BasicIdent* and *FullIdent* IBE schemes, as well as of BLS and ECDSA signature schemes for different security levels;
4. we tested the feasibility of pairing-based algorithms for middle-class IoT devices, such as the Raspberry-Pi 3 platform.

The rest of the paper is organized as follows. A motivating use-case scenario along with pairings preliminaries are presented in Sect. 2. Section 3 reveals the algorithms and computational overhead of the Boneh-Franklin's protocols and the BLS signature scheme, while Sect. 4 provides a discussion over the experimental results. Section 5 is a brief overview of related studies. We conclude the article along with some future work insights in Sect. 6.

2 Pairing-Based Cryptography

2.1 Pairings on the IoT

To demonstrate the features and advantages of PBC in real-world IoT environments, we consider a smart health-care scenario, illustrated in Fig. 1. A patient, Peter, uses his smartphone to send some medical results to doctor David, who is on-call on the hospital Hippocrates during Friday. With traditional public key cryptography, Peter needs to know David's public key. How can Peter be sure that holds the valid David's key, and not some other key substituted by a malicious attacker? So far, certificates are the classical solution to authenticate David's key. In PBC, the string $ID = David||Hippocrates||Friday$ could be a form of doctor's *identity* for his public key. Thus, without the need of previously distributed keys, Peter can encrypt his private *Message* using the ID and public parameters announced by the PKG, which is implemented in a base station of the hospital's infrastructure.

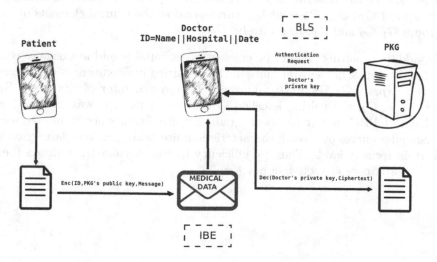

Fig. 1. An abstract view of pairing-based cryptography

Once David received the *Ciphertext* in his smartphone, he should be firstly authenticated and then proceed to data decryption. His ID can be exploited both by the signature scheme and the decryption function, since it constitutes part of his private key. The interesting feature is that the same doctor cannot access the data from his home or two days later, since his public key can be issued on-the-fly encoding information associated with his status. BLS instead of being able to authenticate a user upon his *identity*, it produces short signatures, i.e., 100s of bits in length. This is very attractive in low rates communications, since it entails shorter transmission time and fewer energy consumption in transmitters. Moreover, it is important when multiple authentication points exist. To clarify the details behind the IBE and BLS schemes used in this scenario, we provide a brief introduction to pairings.

2.2 Preliminaries on Pairings

Pairings are mathematical tools, widely used to implement the Shamir's idea for IBE and signature schemes that replace the public key of an entity with basic information about it, e.g., an *identity* string [4]. In Cryptography, a pairing, also called a (nondegenerate or admissible) bilinear pairing, is a bilinear map $e : \mathbb{G}_1 \times \mathbb{G}_2 \to \mathbb{G}_T$ where $\mathbb{G}_1, \mathbb{G}_2$ are additive groups and $\mathbb{G}_T$ is a multiplicative group, all of prime order p. We use groups in which the discrete logarithm problem is believed to be adequately hard.

A pairing satisfies the following conditions:

1. **bilinearity:** i.e., $\forall P \in \mathbb{G}_1, Q \in \mathbb{G}_2$ and $a, b \in \mathbb{Z}_p$, it holds that $e(aP, bQ) = e(P, Q)^{ab}$. $aP = P + P + \cdots + P$ (a times) and it corresponds to the scalar multiplication in the additive group.
2. **non-degeneracy:** i.e., $\forall P \neq \mathcal{O}_{\mathbb{G}_1}$ and $Q \neq \mathcal{O}_{\mathbb{G}_2}$, $e(P, Q) \neq 1_{G_T}$, which expresses the fact that the map does not send all pairs to the neutral (identity) element of $\mathbb{G}_T$. $\mathcal{O}_{\mathbb{G}_1}, \mathcal{O}_{\mathbb{G}_2}$ and 1_{G_T} correspond to the neutral elements of the groups $\mathbb{G}_1, \mathbb{G}_2$ and $\mathbb{G}_T$, respectively.

In addition, pairings should be efficiently computable and are usually constructed on elliptic curves over finite fields. A pairing environment is considered as a tuple $(p, \mathbb{G}_1, \mathbb{G}_2, \mathbb{G}_T, P_1, P_2, e)$, where P_i is a generator of the group $\mathbb{G}_i$. When $\mathbb{G}_1 = \mathbb{G}_2$, the pairing is called symmetric. This type was well-used at the dawn of PBC, but it has been gradually dismissed, since it mostly uses supersingular curves over small characteristic finite fields, i.e., very large groups for certain security levels. Thus, for efficiency reasons asymmetric pairings (i.e., $\mathbb{G}_1 \neq \mathbb{G}_2$) are more attractive in practice [9].

3   Confidentiality and Authentication Using Pairings

3.1   Identity-Based Encryption

An IBE scheme is a group of four algorithms:

- **Setup:** Run by the PKG. According to a security parameter, computes a master key that is kept secret and a system's public key P_{pub}, published as a parameter. Outputs the system parameters.
- **Extract:** Run by the PKG, takes as input the master key and an entity's identity $ID \in \{0,1\}^*$, outputs the entity's private key d_{ID}. Private keys are generated using the master key. It is the PKG's role to generate and distribute them to the communicating entities.
- **Encrypt:** Takes as input the system's public key P_{pub}, an identity ID and a message M and outputs the ciphertext C.
- **Decrypt:** Takes as input the system's public key P_{pub}, the entity's private key d_{ID} and a ciphertext C and outputs the message M or a message of failure.

3.1.1   Boneh-Franklin IBE Schemes

BasicIdent and CCA Security. The basic IBE scheme, named *BasicIdent* proposed by Boneh and Franklin in [5] is secure against eavesdropping, however it is susceptible to Adaptive Chosen Chiphertext Attacks (CCA). In a CCA, an adversary may make adaptively queries and obtain decryptions of ciphertexts different than the target ciphertext. The attack is successful when the adversary manages to obtain some information about the plaintext that corresponds to the target ciphertext.

A ciphertext C produced by the *BasicIdent* protocol has the following form: $C = (C_1, C_2) = (C_1, M \oplus H)$, where M is the message and H is the output of a hash function, both in binary format. As we can see, the ciphertext is malleable. The adversary can flip one specific bit of C_2, make a query with $(C_1, C_2') = (C_1, M' \oplus H)$ and obtain the decryption of M'. By flipping again the same bit, the message M is recovered.

FullIdent. This scheme, also proposed by Boneh and Franklin in [5], uses the Fujisaki-Okamoto transformation [10] which makes any cryptographic scheme CCA-secure. Two more cryptographic hash functions are added, the structure of the encrypted message is altered and one check at the end of the decryption process determines if the decrypted message is accepted or not. The original scheme contains symmetric pairings. In a more recent approach, the scheme is slightly adjusted to make use of asymmetric pairings [11].

The *FullIdent* is the following scheme:

- **Setup:** The PKG chooses a random $s \in \mathbb{Z}_p^*$ and keeps it as a master key. Then computes $P_{pub} = sP_1$ with P_1 being a generator for $\mathbb{G}_1$. The system parameters $(p, \mathbb{G}_1, \mathbb{G}_2, \mathbb{G}_T, P_1, P_2, e)$, P_{pub} are published. The following cryptographic hash functions are defined: $H_1 : \{0,1\}^* \to \mathbb{G}_2^*$, $H_2 : \mathbb{G}_T \to \{0,1\}^l$, $H_3 : \{0,1\}^l \times \{0,1\}^l \to \mathbb{Z}_p{}^*$ and $H_4 : \{0,1\}^l \to \{0,1\}^l$.

- **Extract:** For an identity ID, $Q_{ID} = H_1(ID) \in \mathbb{G}_2^*$ is computed and $d_{ID} = sQ_{ID} \in \mathbb{G}_2^*$ is the recipient's private key.
- **Encrypt and Decrypt:** The encryption and decryption algorithms are given by Algorithms 1 and 2, respectively.

Algorithm 1. The FULLIDENT encryption algorithm

Input: Message M with length l, system key P_{pub}, identity ID.
Output: Ciphertext $C = (U, V, W)$.
1: Compute $Q_{ID} = H_1(ID)$
2: Choose a random string σ with length l
3: Set $r = H_3(\sigma, M)$
4: $C = (rP_1, \sigma \oplus H_2(g_{ID}^r), M \oplus H_4(\sigma))$, where P_1 is a generator of $\mathbb{G}_1$ and $g_{ID} = e(P_{pub}, Q_{ID}) \in \mathbb{G}_T$.

Algorithm 2. The FULLIDENT decryption algorithm

Input: Ciphertext $C = (U, V, W)$, entity's private key d_{ID}.
Output: Message M or Failure message.
1: Compute $\sigma = V \oplus H_2(e(U, d_{ID}))$
2: Compute $M = W \oplus H_4(\sigma)$
3: Set $r = H_3(\sigma, M)$
4: Check that $U = rP_1$. If not, the ciphertext is rejected. Alternatively, the algorithm outputs the message M.

Based on the properties of pairings, the protocol is correct since:

$$e(U, d_{ID}) = e(rP_1, sQ_{ID}) = e(P_1, Q_{ID})^{sr}$$
$$= e(sP_1, Q_{ID})^r = e(P_{pub}, Q_{ID})^r = g_{ID}^r$$

The performance of the scheme depends on the cost of pairing calculations. One pairing is calculated by the sender in step 4 of Algorithm 1 and one by the recipient in step 1 of Algorithm 2. The exponentiation in step 4 of the encryption algorithm also demands notable calculation. This entails that the encryption is more time demanding compared to the decryption, and the experimental results derived confirm it.

3.2 BLS Short Signature Scheme

The BLS signature scheme produces short length signatures and it makes use of pairings only during the verification process. More precisely, this signature scheme is a group of four algorithms:

- **Setup:** The system parameters $(p, \mathbb{G}_1, \mathbb{G}_2, \mathbb{G}_T, P_1, P_2, e)$ and one cryptographic hash function $H : \{0,1\}^* \rightarrow \mathbb{G}_1$ are defined and published.
- **Key Generation:** Run by the signer. A random $x \in \mathbb{Z}_p^*$ is picked as the private key. The public key pk is computed as $pk = xP_2 \in \mathbb{G}_2$ and published.

- **Signing:** Takes as input a message M and the private key x and produces a signature $\sigma \in \mathbb{G}_1$ as $\sigma = xH(M)$.
- **Verification:** Takes as input a message M, a public key pk and a signature σ. Checks the equality $e(\sigma, P_2) = e(H(M), pk)$. If it holds, it returns a succesful verification message.

In the next section we compare the performance of *BasicIdent* and *FullIdent* IBE schemes, and we evaluate BLS in contrast to the ECDSA signature scheme. We tested the feasibility of pairing-based algorithms in terms of CPU time, memory and energy requirements for different security levels.

4 Experimental Results

We conducted our experiments on the Raspberry Pi 3 platform which has a 4 core ARM-Cortex, 1.2 GHz processor, 1 GB Memory and Raspbian GNU/Linux 8 OS. We use the elliptic curves $BN12$ and $BLS12$ from the Barreto-Naehrig and Barreto-Lynn-Scott family, respectively [12]. The curves are defined over a finite field $\mathbb{F}_q$ and are of the form $E/\mathbb{F}_q : y^2 = x^3 + b$ with $b \in \mathbb{F}_q$, embedding degree $k = 12$ and a sextic twist for faster computations. We provide results for the security levels 78, 112 and 160-bits which are defined in line with the q length. Pairing-based protocols use the efficient Optimal Ate pairing [3].

Feasibility in our study is expressed in terms of protocols' execution time, memory usage and energy consumption. The statistical evaluation of our results indicates a small standard deviation in case of IBE schemes. Therefore, the corresponding graphs depict mean values. In case of signature schemes, the standard deviation is non-negligible and, thus, both mean value and standard deviation are calculated over 1000 samples.

Figure 2 compares the encryption and decryption algorithms of the *BasicIdent* and *FullIdent* protocols' implementation in Relic-Toolkit library.

- **Execution Time:** In both protocols, encryption is more demanding than decryption, due to the overhead of the exponentiation g_{ID}^r in step 4 of Algorithm 1. The hash function H_1 that maps a value to a curve's element also consumes considerable time. It is interesting that the *FullIdent* protocol is chosen ciphertext secure with almost non time-overhead. Using hash functions and XOR operations it secures the *BasicIdent* efficiently. A slight deterioration in decryption is owed to the scalar multiplication rP_1 and an equality check in the additive group $\mathbb{G}_1$. The parameter that has serious impact on time is the security level. Moving from 112 to 160 bits adds around $550\,ms$ in the encryption process and almost $250\,ms$ in the decryption process. This is because pairing computations and scalar multiplications become time consuming in large groups of elliptic curve elements.
- **Energy Consumption:** Energy consumption is proportional to the execution time, since $E = P \times T$, where P is the power consumption and T is the algorithm's execution time. To obtain this measurement we put a USB detector between the power supply and the Raspberry Pi, and a constant

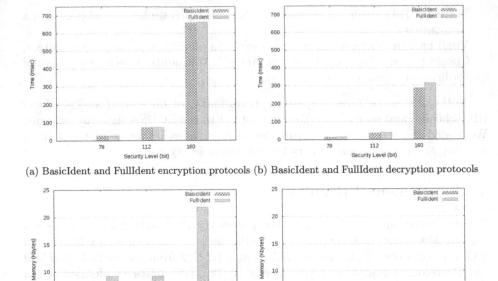

(a) BasicIdent and FullIdent encryption protocols (b) BasicIdent and FullIdent decryption protocols

(c) BasicIdent and FullIdent encryption protocols (d) BasicIdent and FullIdent decryption protocols

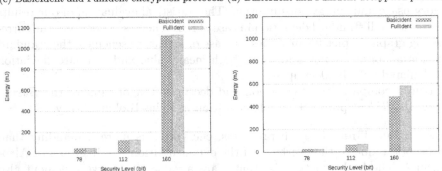

(e) BasicIdent and FullIdent encryption protocols (f) BasicIdent and FullIdent decryption protocols

Fig. 2. Execution time, memory usage and energy consumption of pairing-based encryption and decryption on the Raspberry Pi 3 platform

$P = 1702\,mW$ was observed due to the protocols' execution. During encryption, lower security levels demand less than $200\,mJ$, while 160 bit security level increases the energy demands at $1100\,mJ$ for both *BasicIdent* and *FullIdent* protocols. Decryption is more efficient, since it requires less than $100\,mJ$ in low security levels and around $500 - 600\,mJ$ for 160 bit security. These levels of energy consumption indicate that the execution of protocols is feasible in our platform.

- **Memory:** The main part of the memory being used is reserved for the integration of the Relic-Toolkit library in Contiki. Thus we measured the memory overhead caused by the protocols themselves. We observe that, during the encryption, the *FullIdent* protocol is more memory-demanding compared to the *BasicIdent* especially in higher security levels. Both protocols decrease their requirements in decryption below $5\,KB$. It can be noted that the memory used in decryption seems quite indifferent of the security level.

Figure 3 compares the signing and verification algorithms of the BLS and ECDSA protocols' implementation in Relic-Toolkit library. Both protocols use elliptic curves, but only BLS is pairing-based.

- **Execution Time:** BLS and ECDSA exhibit similar performance in signature production. This is also confirmed from Table 1, where mean values and standard deviations have been recorded (due to space limitations similar statistics for verification process are omitted). Signing includes hash functions' computations and scalar multiplications in both protocols. BLS verification is slower due to the calculation of two pairings. Keeping in mind that this process is typically executed in base stations, BLS is a good candidate given the advantage of short signatures which have impact on time and energy transmission.
- **Energy Consumption:** Both protocols demand lower than $20\,mJ$ during signing for low security levels. This raises to $95\,mJ$ for the BLS protocol and to $80\,mJ$ for the ECDSA when the security level ups to 160 bit. Verification by the BLS is more demanding than ECDSA in every security level, with a noticable difference at high security.
- **Memory:** The BLS protocol seems to be memory efficient, since it requires around $3.5\,KB$ and $1.5\,KB$ during signing and verification process, respectively, irrelevantly to the security level.

Table 1. Mean CPU time and standard deviation for signature schemes (msec)

Security level	Mean BLS	Std. Dev. BLS	Mean ECDSA	Std. Dev. ECDSA
78	3.189	0.047	3.036	0.233
112	10.349	0.742	8.0217	0.341
160	69.252	4.429	54.681	4.322

To summarize, all protocols evaluated through experimentation are shown to be feasible in middle-class IoT devices, such as the Raspberry Pi 3. Moreover, pairing-based protocols have features that make them attractive for such devices, e.g., short signatures.

5 Related Work

There is a large body of work on security and privacy issues for the IoT environment; we refer to [2] for a survey. Broadly, the Advanced Encryption Standard

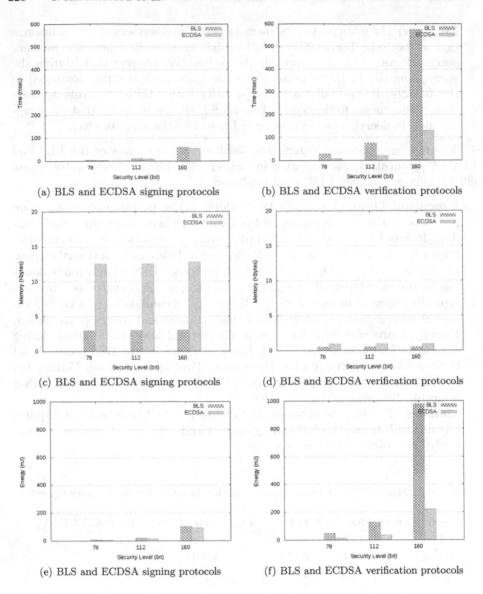

Fig. 3. Execution time, memory usage and energy consumption of pairings and not-pairings signing and verification on the Raspberry Pi 3 platform

(AES) is used in association with public-key cryptosystems to provide confidentiality, while elliptic curves' signing schemes are dominating, since an 160-bit ECC key is roughly equivalent to an 1024-bit RSA key. A step forward, our work is motivated by a recent report of the National Institute of Standards and Technology (NIST) about PBC [3]. Two seminal cryptographic schemes that use pairings on elliptic curves are introduced in 2001; i.e., the Boneh and Franklin's

IBE protocol [5] and the BLS short signature scheme [6]. Our work elaborates on the *BasicIdent* and *FullIdent* IBE protocols, and the BLS scheme in an effort to experimentally evaluate them on middle-class IoT devices. To the best of our knowledge, this is the first feasibility test of the aforementioned fundamental protocols on the Raspberry Pi 3 platform.

In [13], Szczechowiak et al. explore the application of PBC on Wireless Sensor Networks (WSNs) and their results show that pairings can be implemented in real motes, although at a high computational cost. In a more theoretical approach [14], Mandal et al. discuss decisions regarding pairings, arithmetic field, curves and key-size which influence the feasibility of PBC on WSN. A pairing-based protocol for Home Area Networks was proposed in [15], while Oliveira et al. introduced the TinyPBC, a WSN authentication scheme based on pairings [16]. Private mutual authentication and private service discovery in mobile IoT are addressed in [17] and two new protocols are introduced. This work as well as the study of Attribute-Based Encryption (ABE) for access control in IoT [18] use pairings as cryptographic primitives and Raspberry platform, among others, as IoT platform for protocols' evaluation.

6   Conclusions and Future Work

In this paper we evaluated the feasibility of fundamental PBC schemes and concluded that they can be adopted by the IoT resource-constrained devices. We implemented and evaluated the *FullIdent* IBE scheme in contrast to the *BasicIdent*. Results show that the overhead of using the extended CCA-secure is negligible. In addition, we compared the BLS short signature scheme with the well-known ECDSA. The BLS algorithm seems to be approximately equivalent to ECDSA in the signing process, while it is more time and energy consuming in the verification process.

Our future work plans include the feasibility study of pairing-based cryptography on low-class IoT platforms, e.g., Zolertia RE-Mote 2 devices, which are resource-constrained. Challenges derived by devices' communication and messages' exchange worth further research. Finally, we plan to evaluate more pairing-based protocols, which according to the bibliography are more efficient because they require a single pairing evaluation during decryption instead of one for encryption and a second for decryption.

References

1. Atzori, L., Iera, A., Morabito, G.: The Internet of things: a survey. Comput. Netw. **54**(15), 2787–2805 (2010)
2. Sicari, S., Rizzardi, A., Grieco, L.A., Coen-Porisoni, A.: Security, privacy and trust in the Internet of things: the road ahead. Comput. Netw. **76**, 146–164 (2015)
3. Moody, D., Peralta, R., Perlner, R., Regenscheid, A., Roginsky, A., Chen, L.: Report on pairing-based cryptography. J. Res. Natl. Inst. Stand. Technol. **120**, 11–27 (2015)

4. Shamir, A.: Identity-based cryptosystems and signature schemes. In: Blakley, G.R., Chaum, D. (eds.) CRYPTO 1984. LNCS, vol. 196, pp. 47–53. Springer, Heidelberg (1985). https://doi.org/10.1007/3-540-39568-7_5

5. Boneh, D., Franklin, M.: Identity-based encryption from the weil pairing. In: Kilian, J. (ed.) CRYPTO 2001. LNCS, vol. 2139, pp. 213–229. Springer, Heidelberg (2001). https://doi.org/10.1007/3-540-44647-8_13

6. Boneh, D., Lynn, B., Shacham, H.: Short signatures from the weil pairing. In: Boyd, C. (ed.) ASIACRYPT 2001. LNCS, vol. 2248, pp. 514–532. Springer, Heidelberg (2001). https://doi.org/10.1007/3-540-45682-1_30

7. Aranha, D.F., Gouvêa, C.P.L.: RELIC is an Efficient Library for Cryptography (2013)

8. Johnson, D., Menezes, A., Vanstone, S.: The elliptic curve digital signature algorithm (ECDSA). Int. J. Inf. Secur. 1(1), 36–63 (2001)

9. Galbraith, S.D., Kenneth, K.G., Smart, N.P.: Pairings for cryptographers. Discret. Appl. Math. 156(6), 3113–3121 (2008)

10. Fujisaki, E., Okamoto, T.: Secure integration of asymmetric and symmetric encryption schemes. In: Wiener, M. (ed.) CRYPTO 1999. LNCS, vol. 1666, pp. 537–554. Springer, Heidelberg (1999). https://doi.org/10.1007/3-540-48405-1_34

11. Galindo, D.: Boneh-Franklin identity based encryption revisited. In: Caires, L., Italiano, G.F., Monteiro, L., Palamidessi, C., Yung, M. (eds.) ICALP 2005. LNCS, vol. 3580, pp. 791–802. Springer, Heidelberg (2005). https://doi.org/10.1007/11523468_64

12. Barreto, P.S.L.M., Costello, C., Misoczki, R., Naehrig, M., Pereira, G.C.C.F., Zanon, G.: Subgroup security in pairing-based cryptography. In: Lauter, K., Rodríguez-Henríquez, F. (eds.) LATINCRYPT 2015. LNCS, vol. 9230, pp. 245–265. Springer, Cham (2015). https://doi.org/10.1007/978-3-319-22174-8_14

13. Szczechowiak, P., Kargl, A., Scott, A., Collier, M.: On the application of pairing based cryptography to wireless sensor networks. In: Proceedings of the 2nd ACM Conference on Wireless network security, pp. 1–12 (2009)

14. Mandal, M., Sharma, G., Bala, S., Verma, A.K.: Feasibility of public key cryptography in wireless sensor networks. J. Theor. Phys. Cryptogr. 7, 20–24 (2014)

15. Jacobsen, R.H., Mikkelsen, S.A., Rasmussen, N.H.: Towards the use of pairing-based cryptography for resource-constrained home area networks. In: Proceedings of the 2015 Euromicro Conference on Digital System Design. IEEE, Portugal (2015)

16. Oliveira, L.B., Scott, M., López, J., Dahab, R.: TinyPBC: pairings for authenticated identity-based non-interactive key distribution in sensor networks. Comput. Commun. 34(3), 485–493 (2011)

17. Wu, D.J., Taly, A., Shankar, A., Boneh, D.: Privacy, discovery, and authentication for the Internet of things. In: Askoxylakis, I., Ioannidis, S., Katsikas, S., Meadows, C. (eds.) ESORICS 2016. LNCS, vol. 9879, pp. 301–319. Springer, Cham (2016). https://doi.org/10.1007/978-3-319-45741-3_16

18. Ambrosin, M., et al.: On the feasibility of attribute based encryption on Internet of things devices. IEEE Micro 36(6), 25–35 (2016)

Aerial Networks

QoS-Based Mobility System for Autonomous Unmanned Aerial Vehicles Wireless Networks

Angelo Trotta[✉] and Luca Sciullo

Department of Computer Science and Engineering, University of Bologna,
Bologna, Italy
{angelo.trotta5,luca.sciullo}@unibo.it

Abstract. In the era of the Unmanned Aerial Vehicles (UAVs) several
kinds of applications were born to make use of these autonomous vehicles, from surveillance to emergency management, from entertainment
to package delivery. All these systems are based on the autonomous
capability of the unmanned vehicles. The common factor of such systems is the use of an ad-hoc wireless network that enables the communication among the vehicles. However, guaranteeing an effective level of
Quality-of-Service in the UAVs wireless network is hard to reach because
of the unpredictable nature of such a system. Multiple solutions have
emerged to address this problem, like enhanced communication protocols or mobility control systems that exploit the autonomous mobility of
such vehicles. Nevertheless, none of those solutions have real affect on
the end-to-end QoS performance. This paper aims to address the issue of
guaranteeing the wireless network connectivity while providing Quality-
of-Service at network layer, i.e., the proposed system will dynamically
adapt its topology in order to increase the end-to-end network performance by using nature-inspired algorithm.

Keywords: Mobility system · UAV · Wireless network · QoS
Coverage · Nature-inspired

1 Introduction

In recent days we observe the proliferation of Unmanned Aerial Vehicles (UAVs)
due to the miniaturization and cost reduction of this kind of devices. Many applications have been proposed that make use of autonomous UAVs: from video
surveillance to target recognition, from static area coverage to goods delivering, from public safety systems to disaster recovery management. In most cases,
UAVs are deployed in swarms: a fleet of autonomous UAVs that self-organize
themselves in order to accomplish the target task. In such systems, the main
challenge is the creation of a wireless communication network that enables the
cooperation among the UAVs. In literature these kind of network are called Flying Ad-Hoc Networks (FANETs) [9] and they differ from the legacy Mobile Ad-
Hoc Networks (MANETs) because of the flying nature of the devices involved.

© IFIP International Federation for Information Processing 2018
Published by Springer Nature Switzerland AG 2018. All Rights Reserved
K. R. Chowdhury et al. (Eds.): WWIC 2018, LNCS 10866, pp. 233–245, 2018.
https://doi.org/10.1007/978-3-030-02931-9_19

The challenge of using a fleet of UAVs, instead of a single one, is that vehicles need to coordinate themselves through a network that can be difficult to maintain. A key issue in most of the mentioned applications is the self-organizing capability of the flying vehicles in order to meet the Quality of Service (QoS) requirements of the user applications [5].

One of the most prominent application for self-organizing UAVs networks is the search and rescue during emergency operations [15]. In this case a fleet of UAVs is in charge of searching for survivors in the aftermath of a natural/man-made disaster and then to provide wireless connectivity to the rescue team in order to cooperate during the rescue operations. During these emergency operations, a temporary wireless communication network is created by the swarm of UAVs. The main goal of such network is to maintain the network connectivity among the whole network while guaranteeing the QoS requested by the rescue operations, e.g. end-to-end data rate to support audio/video streaming. Guaranteeing end-to-end communication QoS in a multi-hop wireless network is, in fact, still an issue for self-organizing FANETs.

Solutions for this kind of problem can use two different approaches: (i) at communication level by designing specific protocols that are able to deal with the fast movement of a UAVs network, and (ii) at mobility control level by designing a mobility control system that is able to exploit the autonomous controlled mobility of UAVs for improving the network performance. While the former approach can only adapt its parameter to the dynamics of the network, the latter approach is able to directly change the topology of the system, one of the most impact factor for the performance of a wireless communication network.

This paper focuses on the definition of a *communication aware mobility control system* that is able to both guaranteeing the QoS at the physical layer, i.e. guaranteeing the network connectivity among the whole network, and to enhance the QoS at higher communication layers in order to meet the end-to-end QoS. For these issues, we rely on the well known nature-inspired algorithm of the virtual spring forces that will enable the scenario exploration while maintaining the mesh connectivity. We first describe the algorithm that is capable of guaranteeing the network connectivity and then we improve this method to enhance the performance for the end-to-end communications.

The rest of the paper is structured as follows. In Sect. 2 we review the related literature in emergency communications and in the field of communication aware mobility systems. In Sect. 3 we introduce the system model and we describe the system we use for guaranteeing the QoS at both physical layer and higher layer. In Sect. 4, we analyze the proposed system through extensive simulations. Finally, in Sect. 5, we draw the conclusions.

2   Related Works

The use of UAVs have gained the attention of the public safety systems due to self-capability and the fast deployment especially for emergency and dangerous scenarios [10]. These vehicles, in fact, can drastically reduce the human risk by avoiding the direct participation of human operators. Due to the 3-dimensional nature of their movement and the possibility of line-of-sight link connections inside the aerial network, the UAVs wireless communication networks has become a hot research topic for temporary and emergency communication networks [15].

However, given the complexity of the UAVs movement and the high velocity that these vehicles can reach, different issues must be addressed in order to further exploit the capability of these kind of networks [9]. One key issue of a UAVs wireless network is to maintain and guarantee the connectivity of the network, i.e., trying to keep all the UAVs connected. In order to achieve this goal, there exist two main possibilities: using a *mobility-aware communication protocol* or a *communication-aware mobility control system*. The aim of the first strategy is to use network protocols that are able to foresee/react to the nodes movement, and so to a possible change of the network topology. Instead, the second strategy aims to control the motion of the nodes in order to preserve the network constraints.

In the first case, to cope with the frequent variability of the network topology, several solutions consider the possibility to redefine the routing tables by including directly inside the routing algorithms some kind of mobility-aware information. For instance, authors of [13] present P-OLSR, an enhanced version of the OLSR routing protocol [2], where the link-state index also takes into account the nodes position and their speed. Another approach, proposed in [17], considers long term link-stability indexes, since nodes disseminate their link stability and load indexes through the network. In the context of reactive routing protocols, the idea is to exploit Route Request (*RREQ*) message in the route creation operations, in order to avoid routes that are considered less stable [1].

In the second case, the UAVs mobility control system deals with the communication constraints. Typically, in these research works, the network communication ability of UAV is modeled with a fixed radius disk area. Communication between two nodes exists if and only if the two vehicles involved are respectively in the communication radius of each others. Several solutions have been deployed to guarantee the communication between nodes by guiding their movements, like for instance [16], where vehicles act as repelling and attractive forces, i.e., keeping a minimum safe-distance to avoid collision, and not going beyond a maximum distance to avoid disconnections. Of course, this strategy can be made more accurate if the communication ability is modeled keeping into account also some communication metrics, like the link budget [15], or the Signal-to-Noise-and-Interference-Ratio (SNIR) [4], or the bit-error-ratio, instead of considering only fixed and constant values for the vehicles inter-distances.

Another important aspect in the design of UAV networks is the possibility to guarantee service differentiation with Quality of Service (QoS), i.e., that particular set of features that lets the system manage multiple kinds of communication flows while enabling the deployment of reliable services. Also in this case, in order to implement the QoS, multiple solutions have been deployed through the modification or the adaptation of the communication protocols involved. For instance, a specific network transport layer introduced by [14] is used by a robust routing protocol to provide a minimum amount of data to each node.

Dealing with high mobility in an unmanned vehicles network, an efficient routing architecture is required in order to face the frequent topology change of the network. For this reason, geographical routing can be considered a good solution, since it can define route paths basing on the positions of the destination nodes. Hence, there is no need for the network to maintain all the route information. Of course, it requires a good accuracy and reliability of the positions information, whose knowledge and management cannot be considered a trivial problem [8]. One of the most common scenario where QoS is required in a UAVs network is the video streaming application, like in the case of monitoring or surveillance. Despite the huge number of works in the video streaming use case, only few works focus in the video streaming aspects in an autonomous unmanned vehicles network, especially concerning also the Quality of Experience (QoE) of the video. Some adaptive video streaming techniques have been designed basing on the transmission quality estimation [7]. This is computed taking into account the amount and the delay of the acknowledgments received for the video frames transmitted. Instead, in [12] a different approach based on the routing level is presented. In particular, the authors designed a cross-layer protocol that enhances the video transmission flows by using a geographical routing protocol combined with a path quality estimator. This lets the protocol foresee the quality deterioration and react by creating a new path before the link expires and so avoiding a video stop during the streaming.

In this paper we extend the work done in [15] by introducing a new method to improve the emergency wireless communication links and, hence, giving the rescue team a reliable and more effective communications network during the emergency operations.

3   System Model

In this Section we introduce the system model and the terminology we use throughout the paper. Let $U = \{u_1, u_2, \ldots, u_{N_{UAV}}\}$ be the set of the available UAVs. Each UAV $u_i \in U$ has, at each time instant, a specific position $p_i = \langle x_i, y_i \rangle$ defined in Euclidean space. We assume a limited scenario of dimension $S_{maxX} \times S_{maxY}$. During an emergency, all the UAVs $u_i \in U$ are deployed into the scenario by the public safety organizations. Let PS be the static wireless point managed by the public safety team. The UAVs are then released in the emergency scenario starting from the station PS. All the UAVs have the capability of adjusting their position and moving autonomously in the scenario. Without loss of generality, we assume a connected communication network among the UAVs during the deployment operations. We assume that each UAV is equipped with a GPS sensor and an on-board camera that is able to generate a video streaming of the emergency scenario. The generated video streaming is then sent toward the public safety station PS through the UAVs multi-hop wireless network. The UAVs organize themselves in a multi-hop mesh network where an UAV $u_j \in Neigh(u_i)$ if there is a 1-hop direct connection between UAV u_i and UAV u_j.

The objective of this paper is to formulate a distributed mobility model that is able to maintain the connectivity of the UAVs mesh network during the whole network lifetime and provide a QoS on the end-to-end network performance.

3.1 Distributed Mobility Model

In this Section we describe the distributed mobility model used by each UAV for the autonomous movements. At each time instant, on each UAV u_i, $n_i = |Neigh(u_i)|$ multiple forces act on it, i.e. $\overrightarrow{F}_{i,1}$, $\overrightarrow{F}_{i,2}$, ..., $\overrightarrow{F}_{i,n_i}$, where the sum of these forces defines the next position that the UAV u_i will try to reach. More formally, the total force $\overrightarrow{F}_i$ that is acting on the UAV u_i is given by the sum of all the acting forces:

$$\overrightarrow{F}_i = \sum_{u_j \in Neigh(u_i)} \overrightarrow{F}_{i \leftarrow j} \tag{1}$$

We modeled the acting forces $\overrightarrow{F}_{i \leftarrow j}$ as *virtual spring forces*, i.e. forces that act as springs. We use the well know Hooke's law as force definition:

$$\overrightarrow{F} = -k \cdot \overrightarrow{x} \tag{2}$$

where $\overrightarrow{x}$ is the displacement of the *virtual* spring from its relaxed position l_0. The constant k defines the *stiffness* of the spring, i.e. the responsiveness at the spring displacement. We keep the value of k as a constant system parameter; we plan to further investigate such parameter as future work. We modeled the relaxed position l_0 with two different methods:

- *Algo_{low}*: $l_0 = l_{0,low}$. Here, $l_{0,low}$ is a system variable that is in charge of guaranteeing the network connectivity among the UAVs network. In *Algo_{low}* we let l_0 be equal for all the forces $\overrightarrow{F}_{i \leftarrow j} \doteq \overrightarrow{F}^{low}_{i \leftarrow j}$, $\forall u_i, u_j \in U$ (described in Sect. 3.2).
- *Algo_{high}*: here l_0 is no more constant among all the forces $\overrightarrow{F}_{i \leftarrow j} \doteq \overrightarrow{F}^{high}_{i \leftarrow j}$, but it is a function of $l_{0,low}$ and of the communication network conditions. In this case the spring relaxed position will modify each communication link in order to meet the higher levels QoS (described in Sect. 3.3).

3.2 Physical Layer Quality of Service

We introduced the spring forces to enable the UAVs network to maximize the coverage of the scenario while maintaining the UAVs communication network connected. In this Section we describe in more details the *Algo_{low}* where the relaxed position of each virtual spring force is: $l_0 = l_{0,low}$.

We derived this technique from [3, 15], where the virtual spring force acting on the UAVs u_i and generated from the UAV u_j, located respectively in positions p_i and p_j, is defines as follow:

$$\overrightarrow{F}_{i \leftarrow j}^{low} = -k \cdot \Delta l_{i \leftarrow j}(l_{0,low}) \cdot \frac{\overrightarrow{(p_j - p_i)}}{|(p_j - p_i)|} \tag{3}$$

where k is the stiffness characterizing the spring forces and $\Delta l_{i \leftarrow j}(l_0)$ is the spring displacement between the actual length of the spring, $l_{i \leftarrow j}$, and the relaxed, or natural, length of the spring l_0, that is defined by $l_{0,low}$ in $Algo_{low}$.

For the definition of the $\overrightarrow{F}_{i \leftarrow j}^{low}$ spring force length we used the *link budget* (LB) index that UAV u_i receive from the UAV u_j. The LB index, or fading margin [11], captures the physical layer QoS because it defines the reliability of the communication link and indicates whether it is going to break or not. Here, $l_0 = l_{0,low}$ is the user defined parameter that indicates the requested QoS at physical layer and $l_{i \leftarrow j}$ defines the actual value of the LB index. The $l_{i \leftarrow j}$ index is evaluated on UAV u_i after receiving a message from UAV u_j and is calculated as follow:

$$l_{i \leftarrow j} = P_{i \leftarrow j}^{rx} - R_i^{thr} \tag{4}$$

Here, $P_{i \leftarrow j}^{rx}$ is the power received by UAV u_i from a message sent by UAV u_j, while R_i^{thr} is the radio receiver threshold that indicated the minimum amount of energy that a receiver device needs in order to be able to properly receive a message. Without loss of generality, we assume homogeneous characteristic of the radio receiver, i.e. $\forall u_i \in U$, $R_i^{thr} = R^{thr}$. Finally, the spring displacement $\Delta l_{i \leftarrow j}(l_0)$ is calculated as follow:

$$\Delta l_{i \leftarrow j}(l_0) = \begin{cases} 1 - \sqrt[\alpha]{\frac{l_0}{l_{i \leftarrow j}}} & \text{if } l_{i \leftarrow j} < l_0 \\ \sqrt[\alpha]{\frac{l_{i \leftarrow j}}{l_0}} - 1 & \text{if } l_{i \leftarrow j} > l_0 \\ 0 & \text{otherwise} \end{cases} \tag{5}$$

where α is the propagation decay exponent that describes the propagation characteristic of the environment. Figure 1 shows the $\Delta l_{i \leftarrow j}(l_0)$ value for different environment characteristics.

We can notice from Eqs. 3 and 5 that the force $\overrightarrow{F}_{i \leftarrow j}^{low}$ is repulsive against the UAV u_j when the received message is too strong ($l_{i \leftarrow j} > l_0$) and is attractive if the calculated LB index is too low ($l_{i \leftarrow j} < l_0$).

In order to execute the $Algo_{low}$ method, each UAV $u_i \in U$, every t_{beacon} seconds, broadcasts a $BEACON_{low}$ message to inform the neighborhood of its position. The beacon message sent by the UAV u_i is formed as follow:

$$BEACON_{low} = \langle ID_i, p_i \rangle \tag{6}$$

where ID_i is the identifier of the UAV u_i.

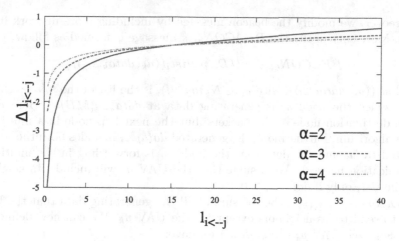

Fig. 1. The displacement $\Delta l_{i \leftarrow j}$ for different values of α as a function of $l_{i \leftarrow j}$. Here, l_0 is set to $15\,\text{dBm}$.

3.3 Higher Layer Quality of Service

The forces defined in $Algo_{low}$ and introduced in the previous Sect. 3.2 are able to guarantee only a low level of QoS, i.e. they are able to maintain the UAV network connected and to keep a user-defined LB value on each communication link. However, these forces are not able to guarantee any application layer QoS, like throughput, packet delivery ratio (PDR), end-to-end delay, etc. For this reason, in this paper, we propose a model that is able to exploit the autonomous vehicle mobility to improve the aforementioned QoS indexes.

We saw in previous Sect. 3.2 that in $Algo_{low}$, the value of the reference link budget used as natural spring length l_0 is constant and defined by the system variable $l_{0,low}$. This method, however, manages all the communication links in the same way, without taking in consideration of the network condition of each particular link. In this Section we describe the $Algo_{high}$ that is capable of exploit the difference between each communication link improving the network performance. The calculus of the spring forces is similar to the Eq. 3:

$$\overrightarrow{F}_{i \leftarrow j}^{high} = -k \cdot \Delta l_{i \leftarrow j}(l_{0,high}^{i \leftarrow j}) \cdot \frac{\overrightarrow{(p_j - p_i)}}{|\overrightarrow{(p_j - p_i)}|} \qquad (7)$$

with the only difference in the definition of the spring relaxed position that is no more the constant $l_{0,low}$, but the value $l_{0,high}^{i \leftarrow j}$ that is different for each link $i \leftarrow j$. Before defining the $l_{0,high}^{i \leftarrow j}$ value, we need to describe the network variables used in this context. In Eq. 4 we saw how an UAV u_i is able to easily calculate the link budget $l_{i \leftarrow j}$ of the link $i \leftarrow j$. We can also assume that the UAV u_i is able to estimate the packet error rate (PER) $per_{i \leftarrow j}$ on the link $i \leftarrow j$ [6]. While the link budget is useful for the connectivity issue since it indicates if a specific link is going to break, the PER index gives more information about the link state specifying the error probability on the link.

Moreover, we modify the beacon message by including more network information. More specifically the $BEACON_{high}$ message is formed as follow:

$$BEACON_{high} = \langle ID_i, p_i, list_i(\langle u_k, data_{k \leftarrow i}\rangle)\rangle \tag{8}$$

where $list_i(\langle u_k, data_{k \leftarrow i}\rangle)$, with $u_k \in Neigh(u_i)$, is the list of the u_i's neighbors toward which the node u_i is generating data at $data_{k \leftarrow i}[MB/s]$. Here u_k is not the destination node of the packets, but the next-hop node in a multi-hop routing algorithm. Furthermore, the generated $data_{k \leftarrow i}$ includes both the packet generated by u_i and the data that the node u_i is forwarding in the multi-hop communication network. We assume that the UAV u_i will include its neighbor u_k in the $list_i$ only if $data_{k \leftarrow i} > 0$.

Let $data_{Neigh(u_i)\backslash\{k\} \leftarrow i}$ be the sum of all the generating data that the UAV u_i has to send to its neighbors except for the UAV u_k. We can now define the $l_{0,high}^{i \leftarrow j}$. For each UAV $u_j \in Neigh(u_i)$ we have:

$$l_{0,high}^{i \leftarrow j} = \begin{cases} inc_{LB}^{i \leftarrow j} & \text{if } data_{i \leftarrow j} > 0 \text{ OR } data_{j \leftarrow i} > 0 \\ dec_{LB}^{i \leftarrow j} & \text{if } data_{Neigh(u_j)\backslash\{i\} \leftarrow j} > 0 \text{ AND } data_{Neigh(u_i)\backslash\{j\} \leftarrow i} > 0 \\ l_{0,low} & \text{otherwise} \end{cases} \tag{9}$$

Essentially, the $Algo_{high}$ will increase the reference link budget if u_i is transmitting data towards u_j, or vice versa, while it will decrease the reference link budget if u_i and u_j is transmitting data towards any other UAV. If both u_i and u_j are not transmitting the $Algo_{high}$ will behave like $Algo_{low}$. The functions $inc_{LB}^{i \leftarrow j}$ and $dec_{LB}^{i \leftarrow j}$ are defined as follows:

$$inc_{LB}^{i \leftarrow j} = \left((l_{0,high}^{max} - l_{0,low}) \cdot \left(1 - \frac{1}{e^{data_{i \leftrightarrow j} \cdot per_{i \leftarrow j}}}\right)\right) + l_{0,low} \tag{10}$$

$$dec_{LB}^{i \leftarrow j} = \left((l_{0,high} - l_{0,low}^{min}) \cdot \frac{1}{e^{data_{i \leftrightarrow j} \cdot per_{i \leftarrow j}}}\right) + l_{0,high}^{min} \tag{11}$$

where $l_{0,low}^{min}$ and $l_{0,high}^{max}$ are user defined variable, such that $l_{0,low}^{min} \leq l_{0,low} \leq l_{0,high}^{max}$. Furthermore, we need to define $data_{i \leftrightarrow j} = max(data_{i \leftarrow j}, data_{j \leftarrow i})$ and $data_{i \leftrightarrow j} = max(data_{Neigh(u_j)\backslash\{i\} \leftarrow j}, data_{Neigh(u_i)\backslash\{j\} \leftarrow i})$. In Fig. 2(a) and (b) we draw the $inc_{LB}^{i \leftarrow j}$ and $dec_{LB}^{i \leftarrow j}$ functions, respectively. In Fig. 2(a) we see that the value increases asymptotically till the value of $l_{0,high}^{max}$. We notice also the effect of the $per_{i \leftarrow j}$ index on the resulting reference link budget: the less the $per_{i \leftarrow j}$ is, the faster the reference link budget increase. In this way a poor quality link will be recovered faster due to an higher reference link budget. On the other side, if the link has already a good quality, there is no need for increasing the reference link budget. In Fig. 2(b) is shown the $dec_{LB}^{i \leftarrow j}$ function. In this case the UAVs u_i and u_j have data to transmit, but no data packet for each other and hence we need to reduce the interference among them. In order to do this, we reduce the reference link budget that will distance the two UAVs. Also in this case, if the link quality index is poor (high $per_{i \leftarrow j}$), we move the UAVs farther away to reduce the interference.

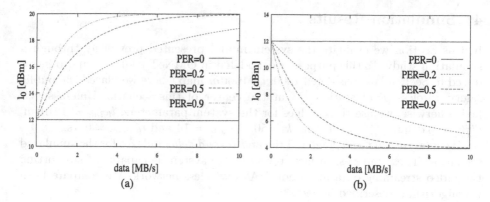

(a)   (b)

Fig. 2. Example of $inc_{LB}^{i\leftarrow j}$ (a) and $dec_{LB}^{i\leftarrow j}$ (b) with $l_{0,low} = 12\,\mathrm{dBm}$, $l_{0,low}^{min} = 4\,\mathrm{dBm}$ and $l_{0,high}^{max} = 20\,\mathrm{dBm}$ for different value of $per_{i\leftarrow j}$.

In Fig. 3 we show a possible scenario with $N_{UAV} = 8$. In this example scenario we have that the UAV u_1 and u_4 are generating the streaming video for the PS station. The data flow generated by u_1 is passed through u_2 and u_3, while the data flow generated by u_4 is passed through u_5. Here we can appreciate how the $Algo_{high}$ works: since there is a flow along the path $u_1 \rightarrow u_2 \rightarrow u_3 \rightarrow PS$, the communication link belonging to this path becomes shorter due to the increment of the reference link budget (see Eq. 9). The same happen to the path $u_4 \rightarrow u_5 \rightarrow PS$. On the other side, the links between these two data flow paths ($u_1 \leftrightarrow u_4$, $u_2 \leftrightarrow u_4$, $u_2 \leftrightarrow u_5$, $u_3 \leftrightarrow u_5$), become longer to reduce the interference among the them. The UAVs u_6, u_7, u_8 are not affected by these data flows and their links length remain constant.

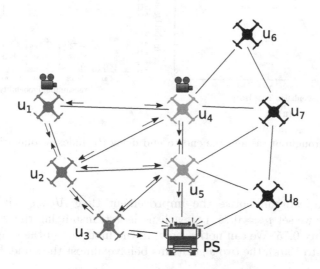

Fig. 3. Example of $Algo_{high}$ in action. In this scenario UAVs u_1 and u_4 are streaming the video toward the station PS.

4   Simulation Results

In this Section we evaluate the system model presented previously through a simulation study. To this purpose, we modeled in OMNeT++ the scenario introduced in Sect. 3. We considered $1000m \times 1000m$ map where we placed the public safety wireless point station PS at the center of this scenario. Unless specified otherwise, we use these values for the system parameters: $l_{0,low} = 12\,\text{dBm}$, $l_{0,low}^{min} = 4\,\text{dBm}$, $l_{0,low}^{max} = 20\,\text{dBm}$, $k = 50$, $N_{UAV} = 14$ and $t_{beacon} = 0.5\,\text{s}$.

We analyze the *throughput* and the *end-to-end delay* indexes for the simulated scenarios. These indexes, in fact, reveal if the system is capable of supporting the video streaming on a multi-hop UAVs wireless network. We compare both the algorithms described in Sect. 3:

- $Algo_{low}$ where the natural spring length of the forces l_0 is constant and set to $l_{0,low}$;
- $Algo_{high}$ where the natural spring length of the forces l_0 is parametric to the wireless link characteristic between each pair of UAVs u_i, u_j.

At the beginning of each simulation test, we release the set U of UAVs close to the station PS, assuring an initial connectivity of the wireless mesh. During the initialization phase of 60 s, we let the UAVs move without generating any video stream. In this way, the UAVs will cover the emergency scenario forming the wireless covering mesh. After this initialization phase, each UAV, with probability p_S, will generate a video streaming flow of $400\,\text{kB/s}$ toward the station PS.

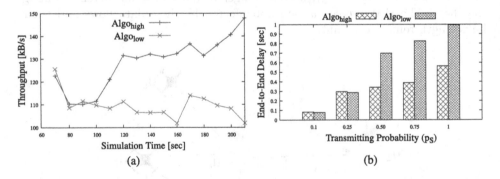

(a)   (b)

Fig. 4. The throughput (a) and the end-to-end delay (b) indexes comparing $Algo_{high}$ and $Algo_{low}$.

In Fig. 4(a) we can notice the improvement that $Algo_{high}$ has over the $Algo_{low}$. Here we set $p_S = 0.75$, i.e. each node is transmitting the video stream with probability 0.75. We can notice how, in the first part of the graph (simulation time 70 s to 100 s), the two algorithms behave almost the same. However, as soon as the UAVs using the $Algo_{high}$ activate the adaptive value of l_0, the performance of the system improve meaningfully. On the other side, the throughput index for the $Algo_{low}$ method, remains almost stable during the time. Figure 4(b) shows the average end-to-end delay index of the network varying the transmitting probability p_S of the UAVs. We can notice that at low traffic load, the difference between the two algorithms is neglectable. However, when more UAVs start the video streaming, the $Algo_{low}$ is no more able to support the streaming. On the other side, we have that the $Algo_{high}$ that is capable of halving the end-to-end delay, giving hence more support for real-time video streaming. In Fig. 5(a) and (b) we show the network performance changing the number of deployed UAVs. As we can see, the $Algo_{high}$ outperforms always $Algo_{low}$ in both the throughput and the end-to-end delay indexes. In Fig. 5(a) we have that the throughput decrease while increasing N_{UAV} because of the multiple generation of streaming data and hence the number of packet collisions in the wireless channel. In Fig. 5(b) we notice that in $Algo_{high}$ the end-to-end delay remains approximately half of the $Algo_{low}$.

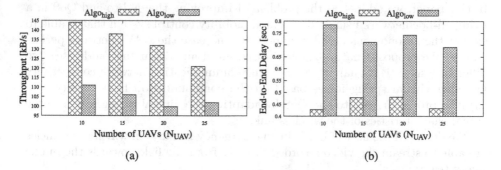

Fig. 5. The throughput (Fig. 4(a)) and the end-to-end delay (Fig. 4(b)) indexes comparing $Algo_{high}$ and $Algo_{low}$ varying the number of UAVs.

We want to point out that the proposed mobility algorithm $Alogo_{high}$ is agnostic on the routing protocol that is being used, because the only thing that the algorithm needs to know is the next-hop node in the multi-hop wireless network. In the previous settings we used $AODV$ as routing protocol. In Fig. 6 we changed the routing algorithm with the $GPSR$ protocol. As we can see from the figure, also in this case there is a significant improvement in both the throughput and the end-to-end delay performance indexes.

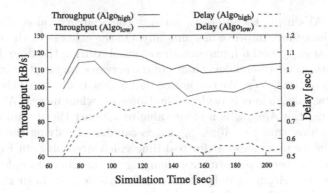

Fig. 6. The throughput and the end-to-end delay indexes comparing $Algo_{high}$ and $Algo_{low}$ using GPSR as routing protocol.

5   Conclusions

In this paper, we addressed the problem of improving the end-to-end QoS in a flying ad-hoc network using a distributed mobility control system that is able to exploit the autonomous mobility in order to increase the UAVs network performance. We proposed nature-inspired distributed algorithm that addresses two different issues: (i) it guarantees the flying communication network connectivity by using virtual spring forces based on the communication links quality, and (ii) it improves the end-to-end QoS by adapting the virtual spring forces to the actual characteristics of the wireless link.

We deployed the fleet of UAVs in an emergency scenario in which the vehicles are able to stream the video recorded directly from the field towards the public safety team.

We showed through extensive simulation the QoS improvement that the network gains by using the proposed method. The results pointed out that maintaining the network connectivity is not enough to support the rescue operation during an emergency scenario. The communication network, in fact, needs of additional improvement to be capable of supporting the emergency operations, especially for real-time data streams. Our work goes exactly in this direction by exploiting the self-organizing capability of the UAVs network.

References

1. Biomo, J.-D.M.M., Kunz, T., St-Hilaire, M.: Routing in unmanned aerial ad hoc networks: introducing a route reliability criterion. In: 2014 7th IFIP Wireless and Mobile Networking Conference (WMNC), pp. 1–7. IEEE (2014)
2. Clausen, T., Jacquet, P.: Optimized link state routing protocol (OLSR). Technical report (2003)
3. Derr, K., Manic, M.: Extended virtual spring mesh (EVSM): the distributed self-organizing mobile ad hoc network for area exploration. IEEE Trans. Ind. Electron. **58**(12), 5424–5437 (2011)

4. Dixon, C., Frew, E.W.: Optimizing cascaded chains of unmanned aircraft acting as communication relays. IEEE J. Sel. Areas Commun. **30**(5), 883–898 (2012)
5. Gupta, L., Jain, R., Vaszkun, G.: Survey of important issues in UAV communication networks. IEEE Commun. Surv. Tutor. **18**(2), 1123–1152 (2016)
6. Han, B., Lee, S.: Efficient packet error rate estimation in wireless networks. In: 2007 3rd International Conference on Testbeds and Research Infrastructure for the Development of Networks and Communities, pp. 1–9, May 2007
7. Kacianka, S., Hellwagner, H.: Adaptive video streaming for UAV networks. In Proceedings of the 7th ACM International Workshop on Mobile Video, pp. 25–30. ACM (2015)
8. Kuiper, E., Nadjm-Tehrani, S.: Geographical routing with location service in intermittently connected manets. IEEE Trans. Veh. Technol. **60**(2), 592–604 (2011)
9. Bekmezci, İ., Sahingoz, O.K., Temel, Ş.: Flying ad-hoc networks (FANETs): a survey. Ad Hoc Netw. **11**(3), 1254–1270 (2013)
10. Okereafor, D.T., Diala, U., Onuekwusi, N., Uzoechi, L.O., Chukwudebe, G.: Improving security and emergency response through the use of unmanned vehicles. In: 2013 IEEE International Conference on Emerging Sustainable Technologies for Power ICT in a Developing Society (NIGERCON), pp. 263–269, November 2013
11. Rappaport, T.: Wireless Communications: Principles and Practice, 2nd edn. Prentice Hall PTR, Upper Saddle River (2001)
12. Rosario, D., Zhao, Z., Braun, T., Cerqueira, E., Santos, A., Alyafawi, I.: Opportunistic routing for multi-flow video dissemination over flying ad-hoc networks. In: IEEE 15th International Symposium on a World of Wireless, Mobile and Multimedia Networks (WoWMoM), pp. 1–6. IEEE (2014)
13. Rosati, S., Krużelecki, K., Heitz, G., Floreano, D., Rimoldi, B.: Dynamic routing for flying ad hoc networks. IEEE Trans. Veh. Technol. **65**(3), 1690–1700 (2016)
14. Stephan, J., Fink, J., Charrow, B., Ribeiro, A., Kumar, V.: Robust routing and multi-confirmation transmission protocol for connectivity management of mobile robotic teams. In: IEEE/RSJ International Conference on Intelligent Robots and Systems (IROS 2014), pp. 3753–3760. IEEE (2014)
15. Trotta, A., Felice, M.D., Bedogni, L., Bononi, L., Panzieri, F.: Connectivity recovery in post-disaster scenarios through cognitive radio swarms. Comput. Netw. **91**, 68–89 (2015)
16. Yanmaz, E.: Connectivity versus area coverage in unmanned aerial vehicle networks. In: 2012 IEEE International Conference on Communications (ICC), pp. 719–723. IEEE (2012)
17. Zheng, Y., Wang, Y., Li, Z., Dong, L., Jiang, Y., Zhang, H.: A mobility and load aware OLSR routing protocol for UAV mobile ad-hoc networks (2014)

Implementing a System Architecture for Data and Multimedia Transmission in a Multi-UAV System

Borey Uk, David Konam, Clément Passot, Milan Erdelj[(✉)], and Enrico Natalizio

Sorbonne Universités, Université de Technologie de Compiègne, UMR CNRS 7253 Heudiasyc, Compiègne, France
{borey.uk,david.konam,clement.passot}@etu.utc.fr,
{milan.erdelj,enrico.natalizio}@hds.utc.fr

Abstract. The development of Unmanned Aerial Vehicles (UAV) along with the ubiquity of Internet of Things (IoT) enables the creation of systems that can provide real-time multimedia and data streaming. However, the high mobility of the UAVs introduces new constraints, like unstable network communications and security pitfalls. In this work, the experience of implementing a system architecture for data and multimedia transmission using a multi-UAV system is presented. The system aims at creating a bridge between UAVs and other types of devices, such as smartphones and sensors, while coping with the multiple fallbacks in an unstable communication environment.

1 Introduction

The development of UAVs and their applications in different domains opens new possibilities in natural disaster management [1,2]. In UAV-assisted disaster management applications, UAVs not only report the affected area but also establishes and maintains a communication network between multiple types of actors, like smartphones or web clients.

This work describes the communication architecture for a system of systems composed of UAV, smartphones, and sensors to transmit telemetry and data streaming, which we proposed in the framework of the project IMATISSE (Inundation Monitoring and Alarm Technology In a System of SystEms). The main contributions of this work are the following:

1. We review the state of the art of the technologies for multimedia streaming in dynamic networks;
2. We identify a set of technologies that can be used within a framework composed of different kinds of mobile communication devices;
3. We propose a whole novel communication architecture for disaster management that includes UAVs, smartphones and sensors.

© IFIP International Federation for Information Processing 2018
Published by Springer Nature Switzerland AG 2018. All Rights Reserved
K. R. Chowdhury et al. (Eds.): WWIC 2018, LNCS 10866, pp. 246–257, 2018.
https://doi.org/10.1007/978-3-030-02931-9_20

In the rest of the paper, multimedia streaming approaches are reviewed in Sect. 2, we present the data transmission architecture in Sect. 3 and its implementation in Sect. 4. Conclusions are drawn in Sect. 5.

2 Background on Multimedia Streaming

This section, first, surveys the existing protocols for video streaming. It ranges from protocols designed for Video on Demand to real-time low latency protocols. Then, it presents the encoding/decoding algorithms that play an important role in providing low latency and high quality multimedia transmission.

2.1 Network Protocols

Streaming Protocols - RTSP/RTMP. Back in the 90s, videos served over HTTP needed to be fully downloaded before they can be played. The creation of *progressive download* - video can be played as soon as a fragment of video is downloaded - helped a bit with giving a sense of streaming. However, functionality was still limited. As an example, there was no look-ahead seeking control.

The RTSP (Real Time Streaming Protocol) stack was designed in the 90s as an answer to these issues, and is composed of the following protocols:

- RTP (real time transport protocol): transport layer, built on top of UDP;
- RTCP (real time control protocol): session layer, quality control;
- RTSP (real time streaming protocol): presentation layer, "network remote control".

This suite of protocols was the basis for the RTMP (Real Time Messaging Protocol), the leading protocol for multimedia streaming at the time. The main concept of RTSP and RTMP is to create a stateful connection between the server and the client. Thus, the protocol offers multimedia functionality to the client, like fast-forwarding or rewinding. Moreover, as the protocol suite has control over the transport, session and presentation layer, it performed better than HTTP at the time. Transfer rates were faster and bandwidth was saved, in comparison to HTTP Progressive Downloading. Latency was also fairly low, averaging delay in seconds. However, RTMP and, by extension, RTSP, had heavy restrictions regarding the client and server. Indeed, as RTMP is based on another protocol, it required the use of a special player and server, and the stateful connection implied increased network usage. This need of an additional infrastructure and lack of compatibility with HTTP was a burden for the clients and the servers. As Adobe Flash (the main technology mandatory for RTMP) is being phased out and is now unsupported by a rising numbers of device and software, the need for a replacement started to grow.

HTTP Streaming - HLS and DASH. As described in [12], there was a need for a user-convenient video streaming protocol, which can be used without using any other software than a web browser. One of the first "new generation" HTTP-based streaming technology alternative to RTMP was HLS (HTTP Live Streaming), a protocol developed by Apple. It used the "Progressive Download" design, by breaking the stream into small files, letting the user play each file at a time. It also adapted the bit-rate according to the internet connection: more than *Progressive Download*, HLS was *Adaptative Streaming*. As HLS was proprietary and designed by Apple, it was not widely supported by other devices or browsers.

DASH (Dynamic Adaptive Streaming over HTTP) is now the open-source standard protocol for HTTP Video Streaming. The main concept is the same than HLS, but differs in the sense that it is codec agnostic, open-source, and clearly defined by a international standard [4]. DASH is now a standard technology and is used by Netflix or YouTube, as described in [4].

In [5], the usage of DASH for low-latency communications is described. DASH was not designed as a low-latency solution, in fact it rather targets multimedia usages like video serving on YouTube. DASH has, on average, more latency than RTMP solutions, as described in [13], mainly due to the segmentation and downloading process. However, by tweaking the segment size and other parameters, the authors of [5] achieve a best-case 240ms lag on a local network. It is important to note here that DASH relies on HTTP/1.1, which has a lot of overhead for real-time communications.

HTTP/2, Websockets and WebRTC. HTTP/2 is the successor of HTTP/1.1, defined by the IETF (Internet Engineering Task Force) in 2015. Since the 90s, Internet and its content has changed: from text and images, Internet is now mainly composed of multimedia content, like video and audio. HTTP/2 aims at removing the protocol overhead of HTTP/1.1 while reducing latency, lowering the number of connections and enabling data streaming [14]. Furthermore, HTTP/2 introduces *server push*, which means that a server can push data to the client. HTTP/2 seems to be the ideal transport protocol for DASH, which is currently implemented over HTTP/1.1. Indeed, the implementation of DASH over HTTP/2 is still a work in progress.[1] While we are waiting for HTTP/2 to become mainstream, there are other ways to have real-time communication in a web browser, like WebRTC or WebSockets.

WebRTC is a browser-based real-time protocol API for web browsers. It is still in a draft state but the main web browsers support it.[2] WebRTC provides peer-to-peer communication between two browsers and at a transport layer, it can transfer any type of data (sound, video, binary data, etc). However, WebRTC does not include signaling, therefore a user would still need a signaling server to

---

[1] A draft is available here https://www.iso.org/obp/ui/#iso:std:iso-iec:23009:-6:dis:
    ed-1:v1:en.
[2] Support for iOS browsers was added with iOS 11, while Google Chrome, Mozilla
    Firefox and (partially) Microsoft Edge supports WebRTC.

coordinate data exchange between two browsers.[3] Furthermore, WebRTC also requires the use of "STUN" and "TURN" servers: the "STUN" server exposes a public IP for each of the peers whereas the "TURN" server is a cloud fallback server which is used if a peer-to-peer communication cannot be used. As a consequence, WebRTC can be quite complex to deploy and use. Still, an implementation of DASH over WebRTC is described in [11]. In this paper, authors achieve a latency of 170ms, which is lower than described in [5].

The WebSocket protocol was standardized in 2011 by the IETF. Like WebRTC, it enables full-duplex communication between a web browser and a server. Even if the WebSocket protocol differs from the HTTP protocol, they are compatible. WebSocket is not inherently designed for multimedia communication, and may be less performing than WebRTC for video transmission. Nevertheless, WebSocket is supported by all the browsers, and is simpler to use than WebRTC. A solution for low-latency video streaming would be to use WebSockets to transfer raw video data and use the browser to decode it, which is the solution proposed in this paper.

2.2   Encoding and Decoding

Each multimedia container format supports different video, audio formats and compression types. There are numerous video file formats, each with different features and benefits.

Encoding with FFmpeg. FFmpeg is a multimedia framework, able to decode, encode, transcode, multiplex and stream multimedia flows. It supports the most obscure ancient formats up to the cutting edge. It is also highly portable – FFmpeg compiles, runs under a wide variety of build environments, machine architectures, and configurations.

Decoding with JSMpeg. JSMpeg is a video player written in JavaScript, that consists of MPEG-TS demuxer, MPEG1 video and MP2 audio decoders, WebGL and Canvas2D renderers and WebAudio sound output. JSMpeg can load static videos via Ajax and allows low latency streaming via web sockets. It can work in any modern browser (Chrome, Firefox, Safari, Edge). JSMpeg can connect to a web socket server that sends out binary MPEG-TS data. When streaming, JSMpeg tries keeping latency as low as possible - it immediately decodes everything it has, ignoring video and audio timestamps altogether.

We need to keep in mind that MPEG1 is not as efficient as modern codecs. MPEG1 needs quite a bit of bandwidth for HD video (for example, 720p video quality begins to look acceptable at 2 Mbits/s throughput). Also, the higher the bitrate, the more work JavaScript has to do to decode it.

---

[3] http://io13webrtc.appspot.com/.

2.3 Image Processing

In the context of natural disaster management, in addition to receive the video stream in real time, it could be useful to notify the users of a web application with information related to the detection of human beings hit by the disaster or the detection of the source of the disaster (fire for instance). For this reason, in the following subsections we will review some solution for image processing.

WebAssembly. WebAssembly (or wasm) is a portable and load-time-efficient format suitable for compilation to the web. It is currently being designed as an open standard by a W3C Community. It is efficient and fast because the wasm stack machine is designed to be encoded in a size-binary format. WebAssembly executes at native speed by taking advantage of common hardware capabilities available on a wide range of platforms.

OpenCV. OpenCV (Open Source Computer Vision) is a library of programming functions mainly aimed at real-time computer vision for all the operation related to image processing. The library is composed of around 3000 algorithms, which include a set of both classic and cutting edge computer vision and machine learning algorithms. These algorithms can be used to detect and recognize faces, identify objects, classify human actions in videos, track camera movements, track moving objects, extract 3D models of objects. The architecture proposed in this paper relies on this technology due to its richness in the algorithms it offers.

3 Data Architecture

We will now focus on the data side of the solution we want to build. Other than video streaming, our system has to manage telemetry data and commands message, so we have to decompose our system into functional blocks.

3.1 Functional Architecture

In the target system, 4 segments can be identified: UAVs, UAV server, web server, and clients (smartphones and web browsers), as in Fig. 1.

The *UAVs* are gathered by fleets, where each fleet of UAV sends telemetry data, while each UAV sends its video. All the data sent by the UAVs is received by the *UAV server*, which is connected to the UAVs through a local wireless network. In return, the UAVs receive Mavlink commands from the UAV server. The UAV server centralizes all the data sent by the UAVs. Additionally, it also exposes each videostream for the *web clients* and also receives the command messages sent by the web server. The **Web server** is the main element of the architecture: it stores telemetry and stream processing data into a database, and also provides an API to the web clients. The core of the web server is a program written in Golang which is responsible for launching the different modules in several threads. The web server comprises the following modules:

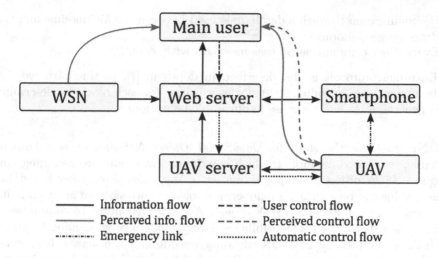

Fig. 1. Proposed architecture

- API: Responsible for exposing a RESTful API to the clients. Enables two-way communication between the clients and the UAVs. On one hand, the web application can query the database through the API module to retrieve data such as the last telemetry of a UAV or retrieve a snapshot of the video stream. On the other hand, clients can also send commands to the UAV fleet.
- Processing modules: This set of modules are responsible for processing data coming from the UAV fleet. Each type of data is assigned to a specific sub-module:
  - `Streaming`: Manages the websocket stream video servers. Synchronizes the different video inputs (UAV streams) with the outputs (video players which are requesting a given stream).
  - `Screenshot`: Manages the reception of the snapshot resulting from the video stream and its analysis by OpenCV (use of face-detection algorithm). It also allows the recording of streaming information into the database (addresses where UAVs publish their streams, and the addresses where the web client can retrieve them).
  - `Telemetry`: Process telemetry data received and stores them in a database.

3.2 Dataflow and Encoding

As described in [7], there are three ways of communicating between software blocks, using a database, services, or messages. In our architecture, we make use of these three ways:

- Communication through a service is used between the API module and the clients;

- Communication through a database is used between the API module and the Processing submodules;
- Every other communication uses messages with *ZeroMQ*.

Encoding protocols is also described in depth in [7]. In this part, we will explain which data encoding technologies we chose for each block, by describing their general usage and their use in our implementation.

JSON. *JSON* is the short for *JavaScript Object Notation*. It is a human-readable, text-based file format, which is independent of any programming language. A *JSON* object is composed of a set of key/value pairs: a key is a string while a value can be a string, a number, a boolean expression, an array containing a value or even another *JSON* object. As *JSON* is simple to comprehend, it boasts a wide range of compatibilities. Every modern programming language has a library implementing JSON encoding/decoding, which makes this format effortless to use. However, even if *JSON* is lighter than *XML*, it is still heavier than other binary formats, like *FlatBuffers*.

Protocol Buffers. *Protocol Buffers.* - or *protobuf* - is a binary encoding technology. Protocol Buffers functions with *protocol buffer message types*, which are language-agnostic files defining the messages that the user want to serialize. These *protocol buffer message types* are then used with a specific compiler, *protoc*, which generates an encoding/decoding library for the majority of modern languages - C++, Java, Go, Javascript, etc.

Protocol Buffers was designed by Google, and is tightly coupled with *gRPC*, a RPC-based framework also developed by Google and based on HTTP/2. However, Protocol Buffers is also usable without gRPC as a serialization framework. Indeed, a message encoded with Protocol Buffer is generally lighter than the equivalent in JSON, thus faster to transfer over the network. The use of generated encoder/decoder functions also ensures speed, compared to JSON. Nevertheless, using a binary protocol like Protocol Buffers also have some drawbacks: each party wanting to communicate with this type of encoding technology has to be compatible with it. We also need to generate files for each language that we want to use, and so we have to ensure that Protocol Buffers is compatible with the target programming language. These issues are common to every binary serializing technology. However, Protocol Buffers also have room for improvement: the decoding step can be avoided to lead to a greater speed. That is the goal of the successor of Protocol Buffers: FlatBuffers.

FlatBuffers. It is an efficient cross platform serialization library and it was originally created at Google for performance critical applications. What makes FlatBuffers special is that it represents hierarchical data in a flat binary buffer, in such a way that it can still be accessed directly without parsing and unpacking, while also still supporting data structure evolution. FlatBuffers require only small amounts of generated code, and just a single small header as the minimum dependency, which is very easy to integrate. According to benchmarks, it is lighter than JSON.

3.3 Storing Data

MongoDB. MongoDB is an open-source document-oriented database program. It supports sharding, which permits horizontal scaling by dividing a collection of documents across a cluster of nodes, thus making reads faster. In addition, Mongo offers replication in two modes: master-slave and replica sets. Mongo is schema-less, that means it will store any document you decide to put into it. There is no upfront document definition requirement. Ultimately, documents are grouped into collections, which are equal as tables in a relational database. Collections can be defined on the fly as well. Documents are stored in a binary JSON format, called BSON, and encapsulate data represented as name-value pairs. JSON documents in Mongo do not force particular data types on attribute values. That is, there is no need to define the format of a particular attribute. Working with MongoDB is not without challenges. For starting, Mongo requires a lot of memory, preferring to put as much data as possible into working memory in order to have fast access. Besides, data is not immediately written to disk after an insert and a background process eventually writes unsaved data to disk. This makes writing extremely fast, but corresponding reads can occasionally be inconsistent. As a result, running Mongo in a non-replicated environment courts the possibility of data loss. Furthermore, Mongo does not support the notion of transactions, which is a touchstone of the database world. As with traditional databases, indexing in Mongo must be thought through carefully. Improperly indexed collections will result in degraded read performance. Moreover, while the freedom to define documents at will provides a high degree of agility, it has repercussions when it comes to data maintenance over the long term. Random documents in a collection present search challenges.

InfluxDB. InfluxDB is a time series, metrics, and analytics database. Time series databases are designed to tackle the problem of storing data resulting from successive measurements made on a period of time. This data consists of items such as system metrics. The longer a system operates, the greater the amount of data accumulated. InfluxDB provides a solution for efficiently storing this data. Indeed, the InfluxDB data model has key-value pairs as labels, which are called tags. In addition, InfluxDB has a second level of labels called fields, which are more limited in use. InfluxDB supports timestamps with up to nanosecond resolution. InfluxDB uses a variant of a log-structured merge tree for storage with a write ahead log, sharded by time. This is much more suitable to event logging. Influx accepts queries via an SQL-like query language. It already supports filtering using where clauses, in addition to aggregates using group by, merge and join. InfluxDB also includes a feature called continuous queries, which allows users to "precompute expensive queries into another time series in real-time". Language bindings already exist for Javascript, Ruby, Python and

Node.js. However, according the purpose, we may find that interacting directly with the HTTP API was already simple enough. Coupled with Grafana which is a visualization tool, InfluxDB allows data visualization by producing graphs and charts.

ElasticSearch. Elasticsearch is a distributed search engine based on Apache Lucene. It has become one of the most popular search engines, and is commonly used for log analytics, full-text search, and operational intelligence cases. When coupled with Kibana, a visualization tool, Elasticsearch can be used to provide real time analytics using large volumes of log data. Elasticsearch offers REST API, a simple HTTP interface, and uses schema-free JSON documents making it easy to index, search, and query data. *Elasticsearch* uses an index to achieve fast search responses.

4 System Implementation

The technologies chosen for the proof of concept system are the following:

- Database: ElasticSearch
- Data visualisation: Kibana
- Data format: Flatbuffers
- Communication library: ZeroMQ
- Programming languages: NodeJS and Golang
- Image processing library: OpenCV
- Video reading library: JSMPEG.

4.1 Multimedia Transmission

The system implements a multimedia server in Node.js that offers an access point available to UAVs allowing them to send their video streams, and an access point to allow web clients to retrieve the stream. With this method using the publisher/subscriber pattern, the server automatically manages the different UAVs in a completely independent and transparent way (Fig. 2).

4.2 Architecture Adaptation and Fault Tolerance

The autonomy of UAVs in the system facilitates two aspects of fault tolerance:

- Error confinement with the isolation of the suspected faulty agent so as to preserve the system reliability;
- System readjustment – agents have adaptability capacities that will ensure in case of loss of some agents, the continuation of services.

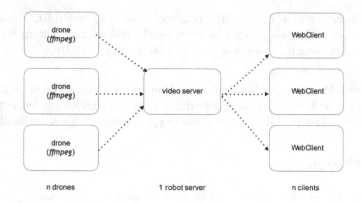

Fig. 2. Multimedia transmission architecture.

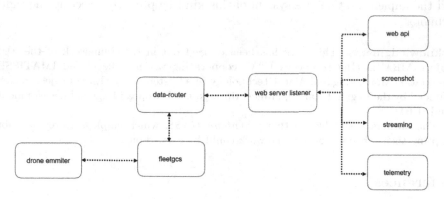

Fig. 3. Multi-agent system approach.

Our architecture includes different units that can be called agents with the multi-agent system approach. Indeed, these units are independent and operate autonomously, the whole communicating via ZeroMQ. We can notice that the architecture has been sufficiently decomposed so that the units have well identified services. For example, the UAV emitter only takes care of sending information and video streams while the screenshot unit deals only with snapshot and image processing (Fig. 3).

4.3   Security

The purpose of this part is to enumerate quickly the security vulnerabilities that have been considered in our architecture and that motivated some of our technologies choices. As described before, the data-streaming architecture relies on two encoding technologies: *Mavlink* and *FlatBuffers*.

Mavlink. Security-wise, the *Mavlink* protocol offers a 12-round RC5-based message encryption. Such encryption is considered efficient for text up to 2^{44}-bit length. Mavlink security issues are tackled extensively in [9,10].

FlatBuffers. Messages are binary-encoded but not encrypted by default. Thus, we need to encrypt messages with a symmetric key, which we can encrypt itself with an asymmetric key. RSA encryption is recommended for its reliability.

5   Conclusion

This paper presents an overview of technologies useful for building a system architecture for data and video streaming with UAVs. It also details the design and the implementation of a system of this kind by properly selecting the right technology.

Acknowledgments. This work has been carried out in the framework of the FUI project AIRMES (Heterogeneous UAVs cooperating within a fleet) and IMATISSE (Inundation Monitoring and Alarm Technology in a System of SystEms) project, which is funded by the Region Picardie, France, through the European Regional Development Fund (ERDF).

The authors would like to thank *Syntony GNSS*, which employs Borey Uk, for adapting their schedule so that this work could be carried out.

References

1. Erdelj, M., Natalizio, E., Chowdhury, K.R., Akyildiz, I.F.: Help from the sky: leveraging UAVs for disaster management. IEEE Pervasive Comput. **16**(1), 24–32 (2017)
2. Erdelj, M., Król, M., Natalizio, E.: Wireless sensor networks and multi-UAV systems for natural disaster management. Comput. Netw. **124**, 72–86 (2017)
3. Bajer, M.: Building an IoT data hub with Elasticsearch, Logstash and Kibana. In: 2017 5th International Conference on Future Internet of Things and Cloud Workshops (FiCloudW) (2017)
4. Krishnappa, D.K., Bhat, D., Zink, M.: DASHing YouTube: an analysis of using DASH in YouTube video service. In: 38th Annual IEEE Conference on Local Computer Networks, Sydney, NSW, pp. 407–415 (2013)
5. Bouzakaria, N., Concolato, C., Le Feuvre, J.: Overhead and performance of low latency live streaming using MPEG-DASH. In: The 5th International Conference on Information, Intelligence, Systems and Applications, Chania, IISA 2014, , pp. 92–97 (2014)
6. Anton, D., Kurillo, G., Yang, A.Y., Bajcsy, R.: Augmented telemedicine platform for real-time remote medical consultation. In: Amsaleg, L., Guðmundsson, G.Þ., Gurrin, C., Jónsson, B.Þ., Satoh, S. (eds.) MMM 2017. LNCS, vol. 10132, pp. 77–89. Springer, Cham (2017). https://doi.org/10.1007/978-3-319-51811-4_7
7. Kleppmann, M.: Designing Data-Intensive Applications. O'Reilly Books, Sebastopol (2017)

8. Ravindran, R., Chakraborti, A., Amin, S.O., Azgin, A., Wang, G.: 5G-ICN: delivering ICN services over 5G using network slicing. IEEE Commun. Mag. **55**(5), 101–107 (2017)
9. Domin, K., Marin, E., Symeonidis, I.: Security analysis of the UAV communication protocol: fuzzing the MAVLink protocol. In: Proceedings of the 37th Symposium on Information Theory in the Benelux. Werkgemeenschap voor Informatie-en Communicatietheorie, January 2016
10. Butcher, A.N., et al.: Securing the MAVLink Communication Protocol for Unmanned Aircraft Systems (2014)
11. Zhao, S., Li, Z., Medhi, D.: Low delay MPEG DASH streaming over the WebRTC data channel, pp. 1–6 (2016). https://doi.org/10.1109/ICMEW.2016.7574765
12. Li, B., Wang, Z., Liu, J., Zhu, W.: Two decades of internet video streaming: a retrospective view. ACM Trans. Multimed. Comput. Commun. Appl. **9**(1s), Article 33 (2013)
13. Lohmar, T., Einarsson, T., Frojdh, P., Gabin, F., Kampmann, M.: Dynamic adaptive HTTP streaming of live content. In: IEEE International Symposium on a World of Wireless, Mobile and Multimedia Networks (WoWMoM) (2011)
14. Borysov, A.: Enabling Googley microservices with HTTP/2 and gRPC. JavaDay Kyiv (2016)
15. Pohl, D., Nickels, S., Nalla, R., Grau, O.: High quality, low latency in-home streaming of multimedia applications for mobile devices, In: 2014 Federated Conference on Computer Science and Information Systems, Warsaw, pp. 687–694 (2014)

Wireless Nanosensor Network with Flying Gateway

Rustam Pirmagomedov[1]([⊠]), Mikhail Blinnikov[2], Ruslan Kirichek[2],
and Andrey Koucheryavy[2]

[1] Peoples' Friendship University of Russia,
Moscow 117198, Russian Federation
prya.spb@gmail.com
[2] St. Petersburg State University of Telecommunication,
St. Petersburg 193232, Russian Federation
michael.blinnikov@gmail.com, kirichek@sut.ru,
akouch@mail.ru

Abstract. The use of unmanned aerial vehicles (UAVs) with a nano communication networks can significantly expand the network's capabilities. In addition, UAVs can automate the process of data collection and reduce its cost. This article expands the application that uses UAV to collect data from passive nanosensor devices. The article considers the specifics of the THz frequency range for the energy supply of nanodevices, as well as for communication with them. The paper presents a mathematical model of these processes and simulation results.

Keywords: Nanonetworks · Nanosensors · UAV

1 Introduction

At this point, developments in wireless sensor networks have achieved significant results. These networks consist of numerous miniature nodes, equipped with a transceiver, microprocessor, power unit, and sensor. This article considers one of the types of wireless sensor networks – passive wireless sensor networks. In this case, sensor units do not have an onboard power supply. The energy harvested from electromagnetic waves provides sufficient power for the functioning of the passive sensor unit and the signal transmission to the gateway (reader).

Passive sensor units do not require any maintenance, have a long service life, and low cost. That is why they continue to gain popularity in many industries including medicine, production processes monitoring, smart cities, etc. The development of nanotechnologies has served as an impetus for the improvement of sensor unit technologies, with many efforts being devoted to the development of devices for nanocommunication networks. Several of these devices use the unique properties of graphene to transmit data in the THz frequency range, with some elements having been patented [1]. The devices have microscopic dimensions; an example is the passive acoustic graphene nanosensor [2, 3], the elements of which are placed on a graphene board with geometric dimensions of 200×200 µm.

K. R. Chowdhury et al. (Eds.): WWIC 2018, LNCS 10866, pp. 258–268, 2018.
https://doi.org/10.1007/978-3-030-02931-9_21

Many problems and questions are associated with methods of data collection from passive sensor units since they do not possess a permanent communication channel with other network elements. To communicate, these devices should be provided with energy levels sufficient to both perform the measurement by integrated sensor and transference of the measured values to the network gateway. In many cases, this is done manually with the help of employees who bring readers to the sensor devices. An alternative is the use of automated means, such as UAVs.

In this article, we will consider communication aspects of data collection from the passive nanosensor devices located in a specific area, by means of UAVs, using a THz frequency range for wireless communication.

The article is organized in the following way: Sect. 2 describes the application, its operating principle, structure, and aims. Section 3 considers the mathematical model of data collection in the THz frequency range. Section 4 presents results of a simulation using the developed model. In conclusion, the results of the work are analyzed, with ideas for future research being considered.

2   Application Description

To begin with, we can assume that there is a field (or a particular surface), which needs to be monitored. In this application, sensor devices are being used for monitoring purposes. These devices can measure physical parameters. To seed sensor devices on the field, the UAV (Fig. 1) deposits them randomly. When we are ready to take measurements from sensors, we will also use the same UAV. It is already oriented to fly over the field, utilizing the existing sensors in a predetermined route using GPS (Fig. 2) and then communicates with the sensors.

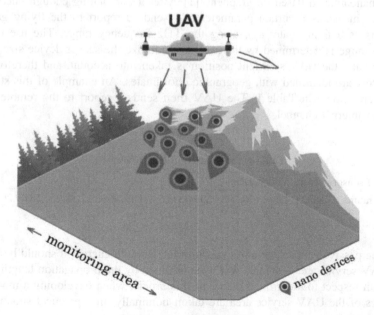

Fig. 1. Sensors installation

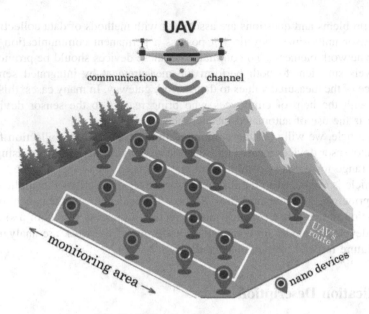

Fig. 2. Collecting data from sensors

Flying over the territory where passive nanosensor units are randomly located, the UAV emits electromagnetic (EM) waves of the THz range, the energy of these waves accumulates in the sensor devices by converting the SPP waves into electricity (NOTE: the electrical characteristics of nanosensor devices are not considered in this article). The reason of using of THz range is small size of the sensor devices, in particular plasmon nanoantenna based on graphene [1] After accumulating enough energy, the nanosensor measures a certain parameter and sends a report to the flying gateway (UAV acts as a flying gateway), using the THz frequency range. The use of THz frequency range is determined by the need to minimize the sensor device size. When collecting data, the UAV's current position is taken into account, and therefore data from sensors are identified with geographic coordinates. An example of this structure and data are shown in Table 1. The UAV then sends a report to the remote server through an Internet channel.

Table 1. Structure and data example

Type of sensor	Sensor model	Data	Location	Time	Date
Temperature	XFD3112	34.211	59.903176, 30.491099	12:32:03	22.09.2017

For the passive nanosensor unit to accumulate enough energy, it should be located in the UAV service area – an area that is determined by the propagation length of EM waves with respect to the ground plane. In this article, when developing a model, the boundaries of the UAV service area are taken nominally; in a practical situation, the boundaries can depend on parameters like the THz transmitter capacity, the opening angle and the antenna gain parameter, as well as the UAV's altitude, and flight speed among others.

The system is adaptable and can be useful for many spheres of industry. For instance, better control of the soil conditions in agriculture, monitoring environmental pollution and remediation, or control of constructed linear objects (pipelines, dams, dikes). The information obtained will allow a more exact determination of potential accidents or breakdowns, predicting them and fixing before they worsen.

3 Modeling

To determine the total delay time t_{tot} between the entry of the passive nanosensor unit into the flying gateway service area and the receipt of a sensor report, it is necessary to take into account the time t_{ch}, during which the nanosensor accumulates enough energy, as well as the delay in data transmission t_{sg}:

$$t_{tot} = t_{ch} + t_{sg} \tag{1}$$

The time for data transmission t_{sg} is an integral index that directly depends on the size of the packet being transferred, data transmission technology, time for processing and encapsulation; it is assumed as $t_{sg} = 10$ ms. The time spent for accumulating the energy by nanosensor can be characterized by the formula (2)

$$t_{ch} = \frac{E_{tot}}{P_{rx} r_c} \tag{2}$$

where E_{tot} – total energy demands required for transmission of the one sensor report; P_{rx} – amount of energy, being receiving by passive nanosensor per second. It is necessary to take into account the conversion coefficient of electromagnetic energy into electric energy $r_c = 0.5$.

In order to calculate electric energy expended by the passive nanosensor unit for transmission of one sensor report to the flying gateway, it's necessary to take into account energy expended on maintaining the nanosensor in working order (until it measures the required parameter), for processing the information received, and the encapsulation of data and sending the packet to the UAV (3) [4].

$$E_{tot} = E_s + E_p + E_{packet-tx} \tag{3}$$

where E_s – energy demands of nanosensor device for measuring the indicator value; E_p – energy demands for data processing; $E_{packet-tx}$ – energy demands for sending the data packet to the flying gateway.

During modeling, the values for energy consumption of nanosensors values of the Ultra-Low-Power Smart Visual Sensor [5] were used, as its energy consumption is quite low. Thus, $E_s = 1.06$ µJ and $E_p = 0.73$ µJ.

In order to calculate energy expended for sending one data packet there is offered [6] an Eq. (4) depending on its volume

$$E_{packet-tx} = N_{bits} W E_{pulse-tx} \qquad (4)$$

where N_{bits} – the number of bits contained in the transmitted packet; W – the code weight, i.e., the probability of transmitting the pulse ("1") instead of keeping the mute mode ("0"), $E_{pulse-tx}$ – the energy expended for transmission of one pulse.

Using the THz range has a number of features that affect the power of received signal (5)

$$P_{rx} = \frac{P_{tx} G(f)}{A(f)} + N_T(f) + N_{mol}(f) \qquad (5)$$

where P_{tx} – power of the transmitted signal; $G(f)$ – antenna gain parameter; $A(f)$ – total attenuation ratio; $N_T(f)$ – thermal noise; $N_{mol}(f)$ – molecular-based absorption noise.

The thermal noise of graphene antennas has yet to be fully explored, but it is suggested to be negligibly small due to the inherent features of this material [7].

For the calculation of the attenuation ratio, it is necessary to take into account not only the attenuation of the signal during propagation in the A_{fspl} space but also the molecular-based absorption A_{mol} [8–10]. Thus, the total attenuation ratio can be characterized by the formula (6):

$$A(f) = A_{fspl}(f) A_{mol}(f) \qquad (6)$$

Free space losses consider attenuation because of wave propagation in the environment [8]. Signal attenuation during propagation in space can be defined as follows:

$$A_{fspl}(f) = \left(\frac{4\pi f d}{c}\right)^2 \qquad (7)$$

where d – distance from the transmitter to receiver; f – transmission frequency; c – light velocity.

A feature of using the THz range for wireless communication is the presence of molecular-based absorption, caused by the vibrations and rotation of molecules. Molecular-based absorption of the EM energy is an effect that occurs when the signal is transmitted at frequencies close to, or equal to, the resonance frequencies of molecules, which absorb part of the signal energy and produce noise $N_{mol}(f)$ at the same frequencies due to the internal kinetic energy of the molecules [4].

$$A_{mol}(f) = e^{k(f)d} \qquad (8)$$

where k – the average absorption coefficient.

The molecular-based absorption coefficient determines the ability of a molecule to absorb energy and is determined by its physical properties (molecular communications, spatial orientation, etc.) [7]. According to [8], the losses of the molecular-based absorption are calculated depending on the transmission frequency, the distance between the receiving and transmitting antenna, and the environmental conditions where the signal propagates. In this article the molecular-based absorption coefficient was determined by means of the HITRAN database [11, 12] for ambient conditions corresponding to the "USA model, mean latitude, summer", H = 0 (mixture correlations: H_2O = 1.860000%, CO_2 = 0.033000%, O_3 = 0.000003%, N_2O = 0.000032%, CO = 0.000015%, CH_4 = 0.000170, O_2 = 20.900001%, N_2 = 77.206000%) at a temperature of 296 K and a pressure of 1 atm.

Thus, according to (5–8), we have

$$P_{rx} = \frac{P_{tx}G(f)c^2}{(4\pi fd)^2 e^{k(f)d}} + N_{mol}(f) \qquad (9)$$

As a result of research [7, 8] it was determined that in some frequency ranges the absorption is excessively large and can cause a significantly reduced communication distance. However, there are transparency windows, where the absorption is much less than in other parts of the spectrum. It is worth noting that k does not depend on the transmission distance, but only on the ambient conditions and the frequency of the transmitted signal.

In accordance with [7] when the transmittance coefficient values are lower than 94.5% (equivalent to the absorption coefficient values of the environment higher than 5.5%), the molecular-based absorption noise N_{mol} becomes equal to the maximum value of −203.89 dB/Hz ($\approx 10^{-20}$ W/Hz), which corresponds to the Johnson-Nyquist thermal noise level.

Since there is no need to use high transmission speeds for sensor reports, and therefore no current need to use a broadband channel, a bandwidth of 100 kHz per one nanodevice is used in the model. This article considers the frequency range of 0.1–0.15 THz. Consequently, taking into account that the environment transmission coefficient in the transparency windows is always above 95.5% at small and medium distances, and the molecular-based noise per 1 Hz of the used frequency band is about $\approx 10^{-20}$ W, we obtain N_{mol} = 1 fW, which allows considering the molecular-based noise value as negligibly small.

As mentioned above, the model considers the frequencies of the first transparency window f_1 = 0.1 THz and f_2 = 0.15 THz. It's also assumed that during the entire flight the distance between the passive nanosensor device and the flying gateway varies from the minimum distance d_{min} = 40 cm to the maximum distance d_{max} = 50 cm, and therefore, calculations are made for these two distances, and the interference capacity of the flying gateway $P_{tx} * G$ = 10 mW. The results of the calculations performed, as well as the values of the primary parameters, are presented in Table 2.

According to [13], the number of "1" and "0" bits in the packet is approximately the same, and therefore, W = 0.5. The energy of one pulse is equal to $E_{pulse-tx}$ = 1 pJ for transmission to a distance of 10 mm [14]. In this article, the distance from the passive nanosensor to the flying gateway d directly depends on the UAV's flight altitude h, and therefore taking h = 40 cm and the radius of the UAV's service area R = 30 cm. Consequently $E_{pulse-tx, min}$ = 1.6 nJ and $E_{pulse-tx, max}$ = 2.5 nJ. Thus, taking into account that the total packet volume containing the sensor report is taken to be $V_s = 16$ bytes, $N_{bit} = 128$ bits, [15] it became possible to calculate the energy of one packet $E_{packet\text{-}tx,\ min} = 0.21$ μJ and $E_{packet\text{-}tx,\ max} = 0.32$ μJ. Therefore, in accordance with (3), the total energy demands for transmission of one sensor report is about $E_{tot,\ min} \approx 2$ μJ and $E_{tot,\ max} \approx 2.11$ μJ.

Table 2. Variables, constants and their units of measure

Name	Identification	Value
THz-reader capacity	$P_{tx} * G$	10 mW
Transmission frequency (1st case)	f_1	0.1 THz
Transmission frequency (2nd case)	f_2	0.15 THz
Frequency band width	Δf	100 kHz
Minimum distance between the passive nanosensor and the flying gateway	d_{min}	0.4 m
Maximum distance between the passive nanosensor and the flying gateway	d_{max}	0.5 m
Absorption factor (0.1 THz)	k_1	2.58×10^{-5} m^{-1}
Absorption factor (0.15 THz)	k_2	1.01×10^{-4} m^{-1}
Energy demands of the passive nanosensor for transmitting one sensor report (40 cm)	$E_{tot,\ min}$	2 μJ
Energy demands of the passive nanosensor for transmitting one sensor report (50 cm)	$E_{tot,\ max}$	2.11 μJ
Capacity at the input of the passive nanosensor (0.4 м, 0.1 THz)	$P_{rx1,\ min}$	3.57 nW
Capacity at the input of the passive nanosensor (0.4 м, 0.15 THz)	$P_{rx2,\ min}$	1.59 nW
Capacity at the input of the passive nanosensor (0.5 м, 0.1 THz)	$P_{rx1,\ max}$	2.28 nW
Capacity at the input of the passive nanosensor (0.5 м, 0.15 ТГц)	$P_{rx2,\ max}$	1.01 nW
Time of charging the passive nanosensor (0.4 m, 0.1 THz)	$t_{ch1,\ min}$	0.011 s
Time of charging the passive nanosensor (0.4 m, 0.15 THz)	$t_{ch2,\ min}$	0.025 s
Time of charging the passive nanosensor (0.5 m, 0.1 THz)	$t_{ch1,\ max}$	0.019 s
Time of charging the passive nanosensor (0.5 m, 0.15 THz)	$t_{ch2,\ max}$	0.041 s
Time of data transmission from the passive nanosensor to the flying gateway	t_{sg}	0.010 s

4   Simulation Results

The simulation model was designed using Python software, the positioning data of the passive nanosensor is unknown and set randomly, and the UAV moves linearly at a constant speed v and a service area radius R.

The number of packets received by a flying gateway directly depends on the time of the passive nanosensor presence in the UAV's service area, t_{ex} (10):

$$t_{ex} = \frac{D}{v} \tag{10}$$

where D $(D \leq 2R)$ – data exchange range.

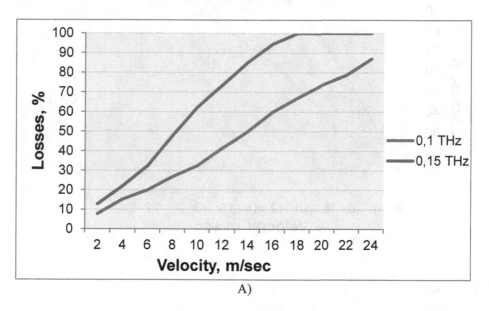

A)

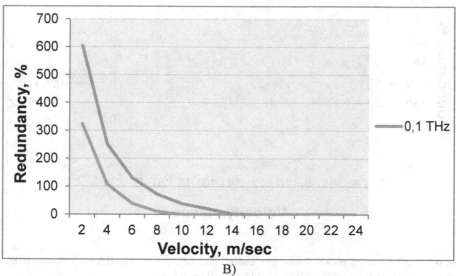

B)

Fig. 3. Dependence of packet losses (A) and redundancy (B) on the UAV's velocity at the transmission frequencies of 0,1 THz and 0,15 THz (D = 0,4 m)

What is more, if the condition $t_{ex} \geq (t_{ch} + t_{sg})$ is not fulfilled packet loss occurs. However, if $t_{ex} \geq n(t_{ch} + t_{sg})$, one nanodevice transmits 'n' copies of packets, the energy accumulation and report transmission cycle succeeds several times. This can result in data redundancy.

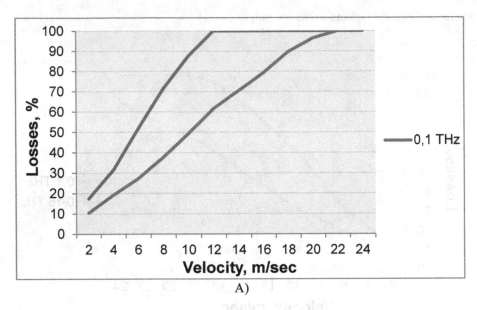

A)

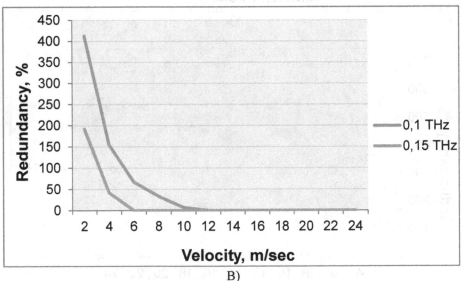

B)

Fig. 4. Dependence of packet losses (A) and redundancy (B) on the UAV's velocity at the transmission frequencies of 0,1 THz and 0,15 THz (D = 0,5 m)

For determining the distance D, the circle line picking method is used [16]

$$D = 2R(\frac{\pi}{2}F(s))$$

(11)

$$F(s) = \frac{2}{\pi}\arcsin\left(\frac{s}{2}\right) + C$$

(12)

where $F(s)$ – probability density function within a circle; s – the distance between two points on the circle of the UAV's service area; C – constant.

In the capacity of the simulation results the dependency diagrams of losses and redundancy of the transmitted packets on the UAV's velocity for two frequencies (Figs. 3 and 4):

From the simulation results it can be seen that when operating at a frequency of 0.1 THz and low UAV flight speeds (2–4 m/s), the considered data collection system has a loss of no more than 20%, which can likely be compensated by the redundancy in the number of nanosensor devices. In order to reduce losses, it is possible to have the UAV "hovering" in the air over the sensor field area. However, it should be taken into account that the UAV has a limited battery capacity and therefore a limited operating time.

Regarding the redundancy in the number of sensor reports transmitting to the flying gateway, creating high traffic in the "flying gateway – user" channel, it is possible to use an algorithm that considers data accumulation and its transmission as one large packet [17]. Such an algorithm uses the Internet connection more efficiently since it reduces the amount of transmitted signaling information (packet headers).

5   Conclusion

Integration of wireless sensor networks and UAVs can reduce the cost and simplify the data collection process through automation. The usage of nanotechnologies will expand the scope of application of such networks for those industries where the size of the sensor devices is the primary consideration.

This article analyzed the use case of data collection from passive nanosensor devices using a flying gateway, which the UAV is an example of, and uses the THz frequency range for both energy harvesting and data transmission. The article takes into account the characteristics of signal transmission in the THz frequency range, calculates the energy expended by the sensor device, and also presents the numerical results of the simulation. The application of graphene-based components will reduce energy consumption. Since device charging will take less time, the delay time in the collection and transmission of sensor reports will also decrease, which will further reduce the resulting packet losses. At the same time, the model presented in this article does not take into account the possible influence of the weather and the presence of additional obstacles between a UAV and the sensors; these factors will be taken into account in future works. Moreover, for future research it's expected that technological enhancements will bolster the UAV's characteristics (battery capacity and energy consumption), application prototyping and practical testing.

Acknowledgment. The publication has been prepared with the support of the "RUDN University Program 5-100".

References

1. Akyildiz, I.F., Jornet, J.M.: Graphene-based plasmonic nano-antenna for terahertz band communication. U.S. Patent No. 9,643,841, 9 May 2017
2. Aznakayeva, D.E., Yakovenko, I.A., Aznakayev, E.G.: Passive acoustic graphene nanosensor modeling. In: Radar Methods and Systems Workshop (RMSW). IEEE (2016)
3. Aznakayeva, D.E., Yakovenko, I.A., Aznakayev, E.G.: Numerical calculation of passive acoustic graphene nanosensor parameters. In: Radar Methods and Systems Workshop (RMSW). IEEE (2016)
4. Blinnikov, M., Pirmagomedov, R.: Wireless identifying system based on nano-tags. In: Proceedings of 18th International Conference on Advanced Communication Technology (ICACT) 2018. — Phoenix Park, Korea – in publishing
5. Rusci, M., Rossi, D., Lecca, M., Gottardi, M., Farella, E., Benini, L.: An event-driven ultra-low-power smart visual sensor. IEEE Sens. J. **16**(13), 5344–5353 (2016)
6. Jornet, J.M., Akyildiz, I.F.: Joint energy harvesting and communication analysis for perpetual wireless nanosensor networks in the terahertz band. IEEE Trans. Nanotechnol. **11** (3), 570–580 (2012)
7. Boronin, P., et al.: Capacity and throughput analysis of nanoscale machine communication through transparency windows in the terahertz band. Nano Commun. Netw. **5**(3), C72–C82 (2014)
8. Jornet, J., Akyildiz, I.: Channel modeling and capacity analysis for electromagnetic wireless nanonetworks in the terahertz band. IEEE Trans. Wirel. Commun. **10**(10), 3211–3221 (2011)
9. Kokkoniemi, J., Lehtomäki, J., Umebayashi, K., Juntti, M.: Frequency and time domain channel models for nanonetworks in terahertz band. IEEE Trans. Antennas Propag. **63**(2), 678–691 (2015)
10. Tsujimura, K., Umebayashi, K., Kokkoniemi, J., Lethomäki, J.: A study on channel model for THz band. In: 2016 International Symposium on Antennas and Propagation (ISAP) (2016)
11. Rothman, L.S.: The HITRAN molecular spectroscopic database and HAWKS (HITRAN atmospheric workstation): 1996 edition. J. Quant. Spectrosc. Radiat. Transfer **60**(5), 665–710 (1998)
12. http://hitran.iao.ru/
13. Jornet, J.M., Akyildiz, I.F.: Low-weight channel coding for interference mitigation in electromagnetic nanonetworks in the terahertz band. In: Proceedings of IEEE International Conference on Communication, pp. 1–6 (2011)
14. Jornet, J.M., Akyildiz, I.F.: Information capacity of pulse-based wireless nanosensor networks. In: Proceedings of 8th Annual IEEE Communications Society Conference on Sensor, Mesh and Ad Hoc Communications and Networks, pp. 80–88 (2011)
15. Pirmagomedov, R., Hudoev, I., Shangina, D.: Simulation of medical sensor nanonetwork applications traffic. In: Vishnevskiy, Vladimir M., Samouylov, Konstantin E., Kozyrev, Dmitry V. (eds.) DCCN 2016. CCIS, vol. 678, pp. 430–441. Springer, Cham (2016). https://doi.org/10.1007/978-3-319-51917-3_38
16. Weisstein, EW.: Circle line picking. From MathWorld–A Wolfram Web Resource (2004)
17. Pirmagomedov, R., Blinnikov, M., Glushakov, R., Muthanna, A., Kirichek, R., Koucheryavy, A.: Dynamic data packaging protocol for real-time medical applications of nanonetworks. In: Galinina, O., Andreev, S., Balandin, S., Koucheryavy, Y. (eds.) NEW2AN/ruSMART/NsCC - 2017. LNCS, vol. 10531, pp. 196–205. Springer, Cham (2017). https://doi.org/10.1007/978-3-319-67380-6_18

3D Folded Loop UAV Antenna Design

Alexander Pyattaev[1], Dmitri Solomitckii[2], and Aleksandr Ometov[2(✉)]

[1] Peoples' Friendship University of Russia (RUDN University), Moscow, Russia
[2] Tampere University of Technology, Tampere, Finland
`aleksandr.ometov@tut.fi`

Abstract. Utilization of Unmanned Aerial Vehicles (UAVs), also known as "drones", has a great potential for many emerging applications, such as delivering the connectivity on-demand, providing services for public safety, or recovering after damage to the communication infrastructure. Notably, nearly any application of drones requires a stable link to the ground control center, yet this functionality is commonly added at the last moment in the design, necessitating compact antenna designs. In this work, we propose a novel electrically small antenna element based on the 3D folded loop topology, which could be easily located inside the UAV airframe, yet still delivering good isolation from the drones own noise sources. The complete manufacturing technique along with corresponding simulations/measurements are presented. Measurements and evaluations show that the proposed antenna design is an option to achieve genuinely isotropic radiation in a small size without sacrificing efficiency.

1 Introduction

Unmanned Aerial Vehicles (UAVs) are viral today in a variety of applications, ranging from civilian entertainment all the way to the military use [1–4]. In all of those cases, it is critical for the UAV to keep the telemetry/control link with its operator at all time (in case the flight is not fully autonomous), as to ensure that the UAV remains in controlled flight [5].

In addition, for certain applications of drones reliable communication is the whole point of operation (even if the drone itself is automated). For instance, an area may be left without any connectivity due to the natural disaster [6]. To address this, a cell relay [7] or a stand-alone base station (BS) [8] may be considered. However, this is always very costly to do [9], and thus the use of UAVs [10] as relays may be attractive.

The primary challenge of any ground-to-air comms could be formalized as that most of the antennas utilized today are not isotropic, and thus their gain may vary depending on the orientation of the UAV relative to the operator [11]. Preferably, a UAV should be equipped with an isotropic antenna, as to ensure predictable levels of radio signal irrespective of the orientation. In addition, the number of antennas used should be minimal to save weight.

© IFIP International Federation for Information Processing 2018
Published by Springer Nature Switzerland AG 2018. All Rights Reserved
K. R. Chowdhury et al. (Eds.): WWIC 2018, LNCS 10866, pp. 269–281, 2018.
https://doi.org/10.1007/978-3-030-02931-9_22

Of course, merely placing an isotropic antenna onto the UAV does not solve the problem, since the body of the aircraft is not entirely transparent to radio signals, and thus will block the signal depending on the position of the antenna. Due to small sizes of the typical UAV's compared to larger aviation, the design requirements for the antenna become very strict [12], as it also has to fit inside the UAV body for best aerodynamic performance.

The primary goal of this work was to design an antenna system for a fixed-wing UAV that would ensure uniform illumination around the airplane, while at the same time minimally interfering with the other aspects of UAV design. The results, however, are equally applicable to quadrotors and ground vehicles.

The remainder of the manuscript is as follows. First, we explain the key constraints in more details in Sect. 2. Section 3 provides the design process, discussion and simulation results. Then, we continue to the actual manufacturing process description and measurement results in Sect. 4. The last section concludes the manuscript.

2   Antenna Requirements

As stated before, the goal of this work is to develop an antenna system for a UAV. We aimed at the airplane structure built with a conventional aerodynamic scheme in mind (single straight wing with classic tail assembly), keeping in mind that similar structure should be applicable to rotorcraft as well. The schematic drawing of the airframe is given in the Fig. 1.

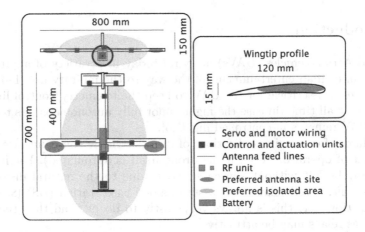

Fig. 1. Selected UAV schematics.

The key requirements chosen for the developed system are summarized as follows:

- Isotropic radiation pattern in the far-field around the airplane;
- At least −20 dB isolation from the electrics inside the airplane body;

- Mounting inside the airfoils of the airplane (no parts of antenna sticking outside of the plane);
- Small size and weight (wire antenna preferred to horns and patches);
- Single operating frequency around 2.5 GHz;
- At least 95% radiation efficiency (for maximal coverage).

The requirements listed before are based on the previous experience making UAV's for entertainment purposes, and problems observed with RF interferences as a result thereof. Further, we referred to the commercial examples of UAV antenna design [13].

As discussed above, the isotropic radiation pattern is key to the sustained, reliable control of the airplane. The isolation requirement stems from the fact that most of the avionic controls are brushed electric motors, which are known for massive commutation noise levels. Similarly, control units employ Pulse-width modulation (PWM) techniques to change the power supplied to the primary motors, which, in turn, use MOSFET switches, all of them creating high-frequency noise harmonics.

Further, large lengths of wires and metallic structural components such as landing gear in the airplane could interfere with the operation of the antennas if not taken care of properly, while carbon fiber elements are excellent RF absorbers at certain frequencies. Therefore, it is highly preferred to isolate the airplane from the antenna altogether, as to simplify its design. As a direct consequence of these requirements, we may easily identify the locations best suited for the antenna placement. Those are located in the wing tips and are highlighted in gray in Fig. 1. The wingtips are far away from most motors, and are usually composed of plastic (and are thus transparent to the radio waves of the selected frequency). Furthermore, they are mostly empty inside since they have very low structural load. In what follows, we will use the wingtip geometry (see Fig. 1) as our guideline for the size limits on the antenna elements. Mainly, we are limited by the wingtip height being about 15 mm for most consumer-grade UAVs.

One should note that in commercial airplanes it is commonly preferred to position the antenna outside of the fuselage since the body is made of aluminum and is not RF-transparent. Further, the relatively small antenna elements do not cause significant drag compared to the plane itself. In small gliders and UAV's, however, even thin wire antennas cause significant aerodynamic drag and thus should be positioned inside the body of the airplane.

Based on the proposed use-case, the antenna system should provide uniform coverage in a horizontal plane (3 dB fluctuations are OK), and near-uniform coverage in a vertical plane (5 dB fluctuations are OK). Next, based on the geometry of our example aircraft, the antenna elements must be located in areas $120 \times 15 \times 200$ mm in size symmetrically on the tips of the airplane wings. The spacing between antennas is approximately 800 mm.

From the efficiency and cost point of view, the Standing wave ratio (SWR) for the antenna must not exceed -20 dB; antenna should be matched to 50 Ohm for coupling with standard radios.

3   Antenna Design – 3D Folded Loop

The simplest wire antenna - a dipole - does not provide the desired performance due to its high vertical size (much more than allowed 15 mm), inappropriate coverage pattern and potentially high coupling to the airplane electrics. However, two dipoles separated by $\lambda/4$ can produce a cardioid pattern, and its null can be used to negate the coupling with airplane electrics, thus addressing most of the requirements. The only questions then become (a) how to make the dipoles fit into the wing's 15 mm height without losing efficiency, and (b) how to address the lack of coverage strictly downwards, which could be important for some applications.

The most natural alternative to a conventional dipole is the loop antenna. Unlike comparable dipole, it better conforms with the shape of the wing. Controversially, the diameter of the loop ends up being so large $(c/2500\,\mathrm{MHz}/pi \approx 38\,\mathrm{mm})$, that the two loops needed to produce a cardioid pattern $(c/2500\,\mathrm{MHz}/4 \approx 30\,\mathrm{mm})$ overlap with each other. Of course, there is a possibility to bend the loop antenna into a more "rectangular" shape without changing its radiation pattern too much, but unfortunately, this results in mutual coupling between loops, and the desired array pattern is not achieved.

Faced with the problem of making a loop antenna even smaller, one has two paths that can be followed: (i) To place the loop on dielectric substrate as to reduce its size (sacrificing efficiency); (ii) To fold the loop even further to make it electrically small.

Since the dielectric substrate option inevitably causes loss of efficiency, we have taken the challenge to follow the second path, and design an array element that would be small enough to fit into a wing and stay isolated from the other element, yet at the same time be efficient as a full-size antenna. The antenna we have used is commonly known as 3D folded loop (3DFL) structure.

In practical engineering, 3DFLs are sometimes used by amateur radio enthusiasts to make small-size, long-wavelength antenna due to the simplicity of manufacturing and modeling with NEC-like tools [14]. Academically, however, the 3DFL theory is very poorly developed in the literature (the only example is found in work [15]), and thus does not find wide commercial use. However, it is straightforward to explain the fundamental principles behind 3DFL antennas.

3DFL antenna is a 3D hybrid structure combining loop and meander antenna principles, and consists of at least three components:

- The first radiating loop, which is smaller than the full wavelength and would normally radiate at a very high frequency. This loop is fed in the middle and matched to 50 Ohm feed line;
- The connecting structure, which acts as transmission line and delays the wave, thus effectively enlarging the antenna;
- The second radiating loop, which complements the first one and balances the entire structure. The second loop may be oriented almost arbitrarily with respect to the first one, but best characteristics are usually achieved when it is coplanar to the first one.

Overall, the full wire length of the 3DFL antenna is almost equal to the resonant wavelength, and electrically it acts as a resonant, free-space antenna. Externally, however, it ends up being smaller than its dipole or loop counterparts.

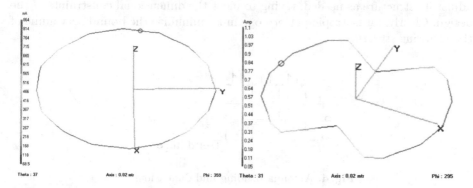

Fig. 2. Conventional (left) and bent (right) loop antenna current distributions.

The design starts with a conventional, resonant loop antenna. It is clear that there are two active zones based on the current intensity distribution, as shown in Fig. 2, and two regions which barely have any current flow at all. Those can be folded and bent in any way desired with minimal effects on the current distribution, antenna pattern or efficiency. The amount of bending that can be done with minimal impact is quite generous, and the optimal amount is a subject of separate research.

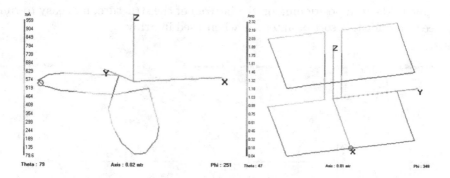

Fig. 3. 3DFL transition: bending off-plane (left) and completed 3DFL (right).

The logical next step is to bend the antenna off its plane, transitioning from flat into the 3D structure, as it is shown in Fig. 4. This allows to further work towards a truly 3D structure, as can be seen in Fig. 3. As before, the pattern and operating frequency are almost unaffected by those manipulations as long as the antenna perimeter (i.e., the full length of all wires) remains constant, and bending occurs at the points with minimal current density. As there is no clear way to analytically model 3DFL structures, through the bending process, one must constantly check the resonant frequency of the resulting antenna, and adjust its structure as needed, trying to meet the dimensional constraints of the design. Clearly, for isotropic pattern one must minimize the bounding volume of the resulting structure.

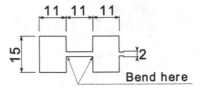

Fig. 4. Antenna bending and dimensions.

Note, that 3D bending design can produce a structure which is essentially a cube, and thus has the maximal surface area with minimal volume, which is the desired effect. In fact, the completed 3DFL antenna has almost three times smaller side than equivalent planar structure, occupying just $11 \times 11 \times 15\,\mathrm{mm}$ volume (see Fig. 4), compared to planar loop's 38 mm diameter. As a result, resonant 3DFL structure has nearly isotropic pattern (since it is so small), and can be packed much tighter to other element, including desired $\lambda/4$ spacing needed to produce cardioid pattern.

On the other hand, just like full-size loop structures, they have reasonably good resonant characteristics and are very robust to near-field obstructions. Further, due to the feed positioning on the bottom of the structure, it is easy to run the feed lines for this sort of antennas when used in array.

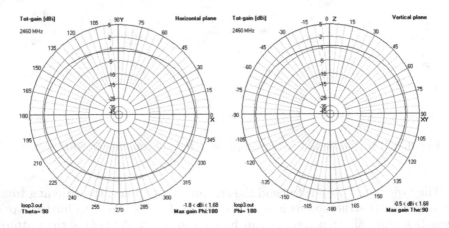

Fig. 5. Radiation pattern for 3DFL: horizontal (left) and vertical (right) patterns.

The resulting 3DFL structure, even though it is resonant, does have several curious properties. First and most important one is that it is essentially a perfect isotropic radiator. As can be seen from Fig. 5, the pattern is indeed uniform in every direction within 1 dB(!) tolerance. There are no hidden nulls/cavities in this pattern, and it is only natural that this antenna radiates in such a way. Since its radiating parts are so much shorter than λ, in fact as short as $\lambda/8$, it is as an electrically small antenna and thus has near isotropic pattern. On the other hand, just like a full-size resonant antenna, it has near about 99% theoretical radiation efficiency, since no dielectric was used to reduce its size.

On its own, the 3DFL antenna is not well-matched to 50 Ohms and requires external lumped component matching network. However, the typical component values are minimal (5 pF capacitors and 5 nHenry inductors) and present no significant engineering issue. With the lumped component matching network in place, 3DFL antenna shows outstanding performance at operating frequency, as shown in Fig. 6.

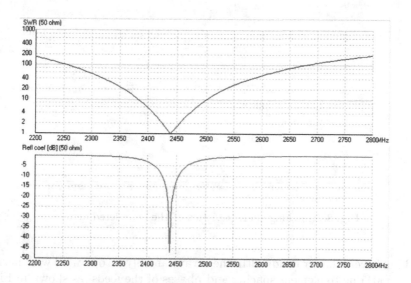

Fig. 6. Radiation pattern for 3DFL structure.

Array matching of 3DFL antennas is a somewhat tedious process, as they couple to each other and there is a need to perform matching after the array is constructed. In addition, at this stage one needs to balance the impedances and ensure correct power distribution between elements (otherwise one element tends to radiate more energy, harming the array performance). However, resulting system shows good performance within our test airplane (see Fig. 7 for crucial performance data).

Electrically, the resulting antenna array is a narrowband (about 1% fractional bandwidth), resonant structure with high efficiency. Even though the matching

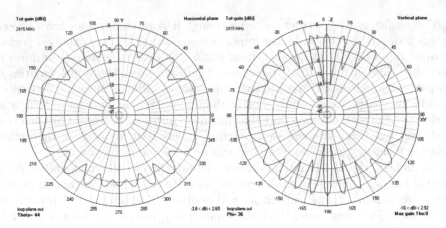

Fig. 7. Simulations of the finalized antenna array: horizontal (left); vertical (right).

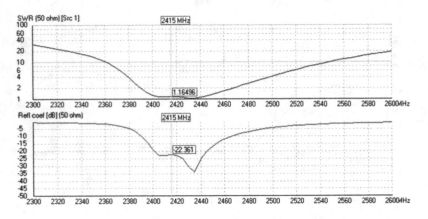

Fig. 8. Matching characteristics of the completed array.

would hold over a larger bandwidth, the array can only be operated with narrow-band signals due to element spacing and phases of the feeds, as shown in Fig. 8.

Another interesting observation may be found in Fig. 9. Here, when operating under incorrect frequency, the antenna pattern of individual sub-arrays turns into quasi-omnidirectional, with a spectacular set of grating lobes. Therefore, even though antenna elements do radiate fine under different frequencies, their use within arrays must be targeted at one specific frequency. However, two individual elements may be used if motor noise isolation is not required to provide isotropic coverage.

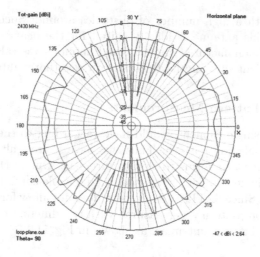

Fig. 9. Off-frequency array operation (+35 MHz).

4 Measurements and Resulting Antenna Element Specification

4.1 Post-manufacturing

Since the development of the entire array structure with equipment avaialbe proved to be a complex task, we have decided to evaluate a single antenna element as to prove the feasibility of the design. Single elements of this antenna require matching after manufacture and can be tuned in the wide range of frequencies. In this example, we have tuned a testing antenna to operate at 2.5 GHz (see Fig. 10).

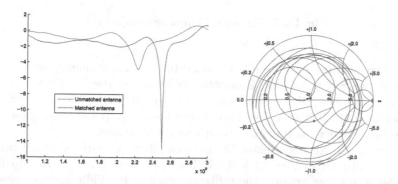

Fig. 10. Measured characteristics of the manufactured antenna before/after matching.

The practical antenna appears to be insensitive to interfering metal objects at distances above 3 cm. Thus, it is a very robust antenna for applications requiring small footprint with a high number of obstacles around. Such tight near field also means that this antenna is ideally suited for the near-field measurement applications. The manufactured and matched antenna was taken to SATIMO[1] StarLab measurement site, and its field pattern was thoroughly measured.

4.2 Radiation Pattern Measurements

In the far field, a single element should have (according to the simulations) an almost perfectly isotropic pattern. Thus, we have thoroughly tested that the manufactured element conforms to this requirement. One of the main concerns was the effect of the feed point, where the coaxial cable could interfere with the antenna radiation. Since SATIMO equipment does not allow for full 360° vertical sweep, the radiation pattern was measured with two different orientations of the antenna, and two different antennas, as shown in Fig. 11.

Fig. 11. Radiation field measurement setups.

The two antennas have been both tuned to the same frequency, and oriented such that the feed point loop is oriented vertically in the XZ plane (with the feed coming from negative Z direction) or horizontally in the XY plane (with the feed coming from positive Y direction). Since their patterns are omnidirectional, the precise alignment of the orientation was not necessary.

To better numerically see how the pattern differs for various mount orientations, one can refer to Figs. 12 and 13. The scale used here is −15 : 15 dB, to more clearly see how uniform the radiation pattern is. While making measurements of such antennas, one must take care to always use the right scaling on all axes, as most software tends to over-emphasize the irregularities in the pattern.

---

[1] Microwave Vision Group: StarLab: http://www.mvg-world.com/en/products/ field_product_family/antenna-measurement-2/starlab.

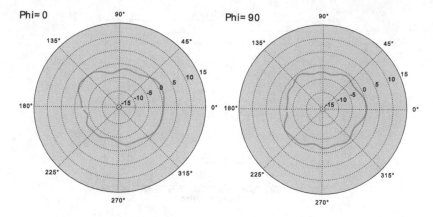

Fig. 12. Measured radiation pattern, vertical slices

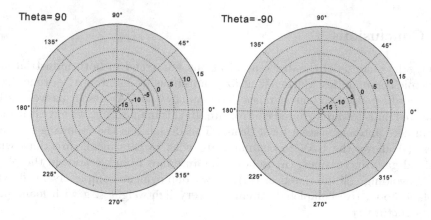

Fig. 13. Measured radiation pattern, horizontal slices

The antenna element radiation pattern is nearly isotropic. The isotropic property holds in both orientations (A and B) and with changing the measured antenna element. The minimal observed gain has been −2.5 dB, the maximal observed gain was +2.0 dB. We believe that the final element design well meets its design specifications, despite limitations of manufacturing facilities.

Finally, the efficiency of the antenna is, as expected, very good at the operating frequency, which can be seen from Fig. 14. Numerically, the efficiency is about 90% for all produced antenna elements.

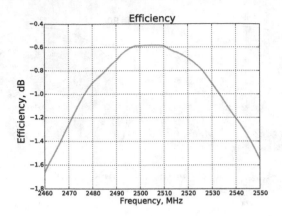

Fig. 14. Radiation efficiency

5   Conclusions

Today, the analysis of the drone applications is a trend in both industrial and academic communities. Currently utilized antennas to maintain the drone flight may be affected by the interference delivered by the UAV itself, as well as by undesired nulls towards ground control site. In this manuscript, we have designed a complete antenna system for a drone. The design has the following key features: (i) allows the UAV to communicate with targets in all directions with minimal gain fluctuations; (ii) isolates the antennas from electrics in the plane itself, avoiding self-interference; (iii) allows deployment completely inside the airplane body; (iv) completed antenna is very lightweight (2 g with foam support structure).

The antenna system uses a novel type of element, 3D folded loop, which is a state of the art antenna structure, only recently becoming popular. The manufacturing technique was also developed to produce the 3DFL antennas in the lab environment with minimal equipment available. Singular elements have been successfully produced and tested, confirming their unique properties (minimal size of $\lambda/10$ with 90% measured radiation efficiency, isotropic pattern). This manuscript delivers a complete set of instructions to produce the 3DFL antenna along with its properties.

Measurements and evaluations show that 3DFL is a relatively easy way to achieve truly isotropic radiation in a small size without sacrificing efficiency. We believe that 3DFL-based antennas will often be used for UAVs and other size-weight-critical systems. However, we would not recommend producing such structures without appropriate equipment, such as metalization 3D printers.

Acknowledgment. The publication has been prepared with the support of the "RUDN University Program 5-100".

References

1. Bor-Yaliniz, I., Szyszkowicz, S.S., Yanikomeroglu, H.: Environment-aware drone-base-station placements in modern metropolitans. In: IEEE Wireless Communications Letters (2017)
2. Orsino, A., et al.: Effects of heterogeneous mobility on D2D-and drone-assisted mission-critical MTC in 5G. IEEE Commun. Mag. **55**(2), 79–87 (2017)
3. Paramonov, A., Nurilloev, I., Koucheryavy, A.: Provision of connectivity for (Heterogeneous) self-organizing network using UAVs. In: Galinina, O., Andreev, S., Balandin, S., Koucheryavy, Y. (eds.) NEW2AN/ruSMART/NsCC -2017. LNCS, vol. 10531, pp. 569–576. Springer, Cham (2017). https://doi.org/10.1007/978-3-319-67380-6_53
4. Mäkitalo, N., Ometov, A., Kannisto, J., Andreev, S., Koucheryavy, Y., Mikkonen, T.: Safe and secure execution at the network edge: a framework for coordinating cloud, fog, and edge. IEEE Softw. **35**, 30–37 (2018)
5. Secinti, G., Darian, P.B., Canberk, B., Chowdhury, K.R.: SDNs in the sky: robust end-to-end connectivity for aerial vehicular networks. IEEE Commun. Mag. **56**(1), 16–21 (2018)
6. Ometov, A., Sopin, E., Gudkova, I., Andreev, S., Gaidamaka, Y.V., Koucheryavy, Y.: Modeling unreliable operation of mmWave-based data sessions in mission-critical PPDR services. IEEE Access **5**, 20536–20544 (2017)
7. Müller, W., et al.: Secure and interoperable communication infrastructures for PPDR organisations. In: SPIE Defense+ Security, International Society for Optics and Photonics (2016)
8. Deruyck, M., Wyckmans, J., Martens, L., Joseph, W.: Emergency ad-hoc networks by using drone mounted base stations for a disaster scenario. In: Proceedings of 12th International Conference on Wireless and Mobile Computing, Networking and Communications (WiMob), pp. 1–7. IEEE (2016)
9. ICS Industries PTY LTD: Cell on Wheels: Engineered for All Environments (2017). http://www.icsindustries.com.au/downloads/brochures?download=37: cell-on-wheels,
10. Solomitckii, D., Gapeyenko, M., Semkin, V., Andreev, S., Koucheryavy, Y.: Technologies for efficient amateur drone detection in 5G millimeter-wave cellular infrastructure. IEEE Commun. Mag. **56**(1), 43–50 (2018)
11. Fabra, F., Calafate, C.T., Cano, J.C., Manzoni, P.: On the impact of inter-UAV communications interference in the 2.4 GHz band. In: Proceedings of 13th International Wireless Communications and Mobile Computing Conference (IWCMC), pp. 945–950. IEEE (2017)
12. Moses, A., Rutherford, M.J., Valavanis, K.P.: Radar-based detection and identification for miniature air vehicles. In: Proceedings of IEEE International Conference on Control Applications (CCA), pp. 933–940. IEEE (2011)
13. Cobham Antenna Systems: Cobham Antenna Systems. Unmanned Systems Antennas Airborne Platforms, UAVs, Ground Vehicles, Robots. Technical report (2010)
14. Cuthbert, D.: The 3-D folded loop antenna. Technical report (2003)
15. Chiu, C.W., Chang, C.H., Chi, Y.J.: A compact folded loop antenna for LTE/GSM band mobile phone applications. In: Proceedings of International Conference on Electromagnetics in Advanced Applications (ICEAA), pp. 382–385. IEEE (2010)

Vehicular and Content Delivery Networks

D2D Data Offloading in Vehicular Networks with Delivery Time Selection

Loreto Pescosolido[✉], Marco Conti, and Andrea Passarella

Institute for Informatics and Telematics (IIT),
Italian National Research Council (CNR), Pisa, Italy
{loreto.pescosolido,marco.conti,andrea.passarella}@iit.cnr.it

Abstract. Within the framework of a Device-to-Device (D2D) data offloading system for cellular networks, we propose a Content Delivery Management System (CDMS) in which the instant for transmitting a content to a requesting node, through a D2D communication, is selected to minimize the energy consumption required for transmission. The proposed system is particularly fit to highly dynamic scenarios, such as vehicular networks, where the network topology changes at a rate which is comparable with the order of magnitude of the delay tolerance. Through extensive system level simulations, we compare the energy consumed by the devices to perform D2D data offloading using the proposed scheme with the energy consumed when using a benchmark scheme (proposed in previous works) without optimal transmission instant selection. The results show that, in specific scenarios, compared to the benchmark system in which the transmission instant is not optimized, the proposed system allows a reduction of the energy consumed for D2D communications above 90%.

Keywords: D2D data offloading · Power control
Delay-tolerant applications · Radio resource management

1 Introduction

Device-to-Device (D2D) data offloading in cellular networks [1] is a powerful means to decrease congestion at the base stations, reduce the energy consumption of the overall system, and increase spectral efficiency. The idea is that, whenever a content is requested by a node, if the content is available at any of its neighbors, it must be obtained from it, rather than from the network infrastructure. We indicate the nodes that can potentially hand the desired content to a requesting node as *potential content providers*. The set of potential content providers, for a given content request, depends on scenario parameters, like the node density and the content popularity, and on the specific protocol design. For delay-tolerant applications, an interesting protocol design option is that, in case a node issuing a content request has no potential content provider in its

© IFIP International Federation for Information Processing 2018
Published by Springer Nature Switzerland AG 2018. All Rights Reserved
K. R. Chowdhury et al. (Eds.): WWIC 2018, LNCS 10866, pp. 285–297, 2018.
https://doi.org/10.1007/978-3-030-02931-9_23

neighborhood at the time of request, it waits for a predefined interval, called *content timeout*, within which it is still possible to obtain the content from a new neighbor, encountered in the meantime [2,3]. Only at the expiration of the content timeout, if the content has not yet been obtained, it is transmitted by the infrastructure nodes through an Infrastructure-to-Device (I2D) transmission. This approach is particularly effective in highly dynamic scenarios, such as vehicular networks, where the network topology changes at a fast rate. The use of a content timeout allows to increase the population of potential content providers beyond the set of the requesting node's neighbors at the time of request, extending such population to the nodes that will become its neighbors in the future. In this way, the system obtains an increase of the offloading efficiency, defined as the percentage of contents delivered by using D2D communications between peer nodes (vehicles), rather than using I2D transmissions from the infrastructure nodes, bringing along the aforementioned system-level benefits.

In our prior works [4,5], we have shown that the considered type of D2D data offloading protocols for delay-tolerant applications, are very effective in reducing the overall energy consumption at system level. More in general, this is true for most D2D data offloading protocols, especially when power control is in use. However, there is still significant room for improving the performance of D2D transmissions, by taking *full* advantage of the delay tolerance of requests.

Consider two nodes, and let us define them as neighbors if and only if their distance is less than or equal to a (nominal) maximum transmission range d_{max}. In previous works that follow the above described approach, *in the case at the time of a content request there are no potential content providers within a range d_{max} from the requesting node* (i.e., no neighbor has the requested content in its cache), as soon as the requesting node encounters a potential content provider, the content is transmitted. In this case, it is clear that the transmission takes place at the maximum transmission range of the devices. Therefore, in a system with distance-based power control, all the requests that are not fulfilled at the time of request, inherently require the use of the maximum D2D transmit power. Furthermore, *in the opposite case, in which at the time of request there is already a potential content provider, say at distance $d < d_{max}$*, the content delivery requires a transmit power that is higher than what would be required if the delivery was postponed to a later instant, at which the involved (or any other) content provider would be closer than d to the requesting node.

Motivated by this observation, in this work we propose the following approach. When a new request arrives, a controller, running, e.g., at the eNodeB (eNB), exploits knowledge of nodes positions and predicted movements in the near future (in the following content timeout window), to estimate which potential content providers will be in radio range of the requesting node within the content timeout. The content transmission is scheduled with the potential content provider that is predicted to be at the minimum distance from the requesting node, at the point in time when this will happen. In this way, provided that a distance-dependent transmit power control is in use, the smallest possible transmit power will be required. We will show that using this approach the energy consumption of the considered protocol for delay-tolerant application can be dramatically reduced.

The paper is organized as follows. We position our work with respect to the recent research trends in this area in Sect. 2. In Sect. 3 we describe our system set-up and a possible MAC (adapted from an existing solution) for an in-band implementation of the proposed D2D Data offloading scheme. In Sect. 4 we present the proposed Content Delivery Management System (CDMS). In Sect. 5 we evaluate the performance of the proposed system through the analysis of system-level simulations results, in terms of the average energy consumption per content delivery required to satisfy a given system-wise traffic demand. Finally, Sect. 6 concludes the paper summarizing our contribution.

2   Related Work

The use of D2D communications to offload traffic from infrastructure nodes has been investigated for years by the researchers of different communities. Works like [6,7] aim at investigating scaling laws and network throughput from a fundamental limits perspective. Works like [8,9] (amongst many others), aim at devising radio resource allocation strategies, and/or other physical layer parameters, like coding rates and transmit power levels, assuming that D2D and/or I2D links to be accomodated are given as an input to the problem. More specific protocol-oriented works have been appearing in the last years as well. The interested reader may want to check, e.g., [1] for an extensive survey. In these works, the objective is to determine and schedule I2D and D2D offloading communications as a function of the request patterns (as opposed to the above mentioned works, in which the link to schedule are an input to the problem). In [2], the peculiarity of D2D data offloading for delay-tolerant applications was first addressed. In [3], a CDMS for contents originated from delay-tolerant applications, suited to a vehicular network scenario, was proposed. In [10], in a scenario in which content delivery mostly relies on D2D-offloading, a strategy for I2D re-injection of contents in the network is proposed to mitigate the effect of temporal content starving in a certain areas. In [11], in the framework of a content dissemination problem (i.e., when contents need to reach all the nodes, without having been explicitly requested), the authors propose a mixed I2D-multicast and D2D-relaying reinforcement-learning-based strategy, which determines which users should receive the contents through a direct I2D transmission or through D2D relaying from a neighboring device. The above mentioned works, although providing interesting insights from the perspective of offloading efficiency maximization, devote less attention to performance metrics which are closer to physical quantities, like energy consumption and spectrum efficiency. Our work is motivated by the need to take into account such metrics in the system design, and optimize it to maximize them. With the focus on energy consumption minimization, we have been working on a CDMS inspired by [3], and evaluated analytically its performance in [5]. The work in [5] investigates the effect of content popularity and vehicles speed on the D2D transmit power by proposing and validating an analytical model for computing the offloading efficiency and the energy consumption, and then selecting the best value for the maximum D2D transmission range. The CDMS considered in [5] does not optimize the D2D transmission time, letting the nodes transmit a requested content as soon as they encounter a node requesting it. In this work, differently from the above mentioned ones, we leverage the degree of freedom entailed by delay tolerance by deferring the D2D transmission instant to the time it will require the lowest power, thus achieving impressive performance gains in terms of energy consumption. Finally, we deem it appropriate to take into account accurate channel models, since using relatively simplistic models may result in an inaccurate estimation of the performance gain of a particular design [4]. Furthermore, we consider it necessary, when dealing with the type of performance metrics discussed above, to integrate in the performance evaluation an actual radio resource management technique. Among the many available, we found it useful to implement the solution proposed in [9].

3   System Model

3.1   Network Topology, Node Mobility, and Content Requests

We consider a Region of Interest (ROI) consisting of a bidirectional street chunk which vehicle enter, traverse, and exit from both ends, as shown in Fig. 1.

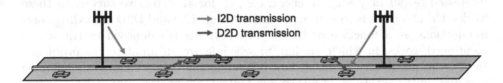

Fig. 1. Sketch of the considered scenario.

Vehicles enter the street according to a given stationary temporal arrival process, with an average arrival rate of λ_t vehicles per second ($\lambda_t/2$ vehicles per second on each end). Each vehicle n traverses the ROI at an average speed v_n, selected as a random variable with probability density function $p_V(v)$. Particularly, we select $p_V(v)$ as a uniform random variable in a limited speed range $[v_{min}, v_{max}]$. Each vehicle has onboard a mobile device, which can be either a human hand-held device or part of the vehicle equipment. Along the street, a set of eNBs is regularly placed. At each instant, each device (vehicle) is under the coverage of an eNB. Each device issues content requests according to a given stationary content request process with an average content request rate of λ_Z requests per second, by sending requests messages to the eNB it is associated to at the time of request. The specific content being requested is drawn according to a content popularity distribution $p_Z(z)$. Similarly to [2,3], we assume that the content requests can be fulfilled with some delay tolerance, i.e., they must be served at most within a content timeout τ_c. A request may be fulfilled either by a potential content provider, through a D2D communication, or by an eNB. In this work we assume that, within the content timeout, the first option (delivery through D2D) is always privileged, and I2D content deliveries are performed only at the end of the content timeout, if it has expired before any potential content provider has been found. The rationale of this is that, in this way, we maximize the advantage of D2D transmissions in *offloading* traffic from the cellular infrastructure, which is one of the primary goals of any offloading system. A final important notion to introduce is that of the *sharing timeout*, τ_s. This is defined as the time each device keeps a received content in its cache, available for other nodes that it encounters, and after which, to avoid an indefinite increase of the cache occupation, it removes.

The above assumptions are quite general. It is clear that, for the purpose of performance evaluation, specific models need to be assumed for all the involved random processes. For the sake of readability, we leave the description of the specific assumptions used for our performance evaluation to Sect. 5.

3.2 MAC and Physical Layer Implementation

The purpose of this work, besides the presentation of the proposed CDMS, is also the evaluation of its performance with realistic medium access control and radio resource management strategies, also including physical layer aspects such as multipath frequency selective fading of the radio channels. We focus on in-band D2D offloading, in which D2D communications and I2D ones share the same spectrum. We have considered a LTE-like multi-carrier system in which the radio resources are organized as a time-frequency grid of Physical Resource Blocks (PRBs) of fixed bandwidth and duration. We have selected a very flexible Radio Resource Reuse (RRR) scheme, which allows concurrent D2D and I2D communications. Particularly, we have implemented, with some modifications, the resource-sharing oriented scheme recently proposed in [9]. However, we adapted the algorithms in [9] to use different transmit power levels across concurrent links, and included multiple eNBs and spatial frequency reuse for I2D communications (besides D2D ones) in the design. Additionally, it is worth mentioning that the solution proposed in [9] is evaluated under a flat fading channel assumption, whereas our implementation includes frequency selective channels. Further details on the considered channel model are provided in Sect. 5.

Time is organized in control intervals. In each control interval, a set of ID2 and D2D links have to be scheduled for transmission. The set of I2D and D2D links to schedule in each control interval is determined by the CDMS according to the procedure described in Sect. 4. Radio Resource allocation is performed by a RRR agent residing at the eNBs. We assume that the position of each device is known to the RRR agent, and hence, it can compute the distance between any node pair.

First, the RRR agent, taking in input the distance d between transmitter and receiver of each link to be scheduled, computes the transmit power of each link. This is done by inverting an expression for the nominal per-subcarrier capacity

C, of the kind $C = \log_2(1 + P_c g(d)/\sigma_c^2)$, with respect to the per-subcarrier transmit power P_c. In the above expression, σ_c^2 is the thermal noise power on each subcarrier[1] and $g(d)$ is a *nominal* (deterministic) path loss expression[2], which is selected by the system according to the deployment scenario (urban, dense-urban, rural, micro-cell, macro-cell, I2D, D2D, etc.). The so obtained value of P_c is increased by a suitable link margin M, which is required to compensate the presence of random fluctuations and frequency selectivity, and of the interference that may come from concurrently transmitting links. Note that both these effects are taken into account in the implementation we used in our performance evaluation.

Second, the set of links is partitioned[3] into RRR sets in order to satisfy a set of cross-interference mitigation constraints. The constraints are computed using an estimation of the interference across links obtained by computing the nominal channel gain g between any link transmitter and any link receiver among the set of links to be scheduled. A suitable amount of PRBs is assigned to each RRR set. This amount is a function of the number and size of the contents that have to be transmitted by each link in the RRR set. D2D links in the same RRR set can use the same radio resources, since their belonging to the same set stands for the fact that their cross-interference is sufficiently low not to compromise the communications. I2D links originating from the same eNB are assigned radio resources in an exclusive way, selected as a portion of the pool of PRBs assigned to the RRR set they have been included in. In its portion of PRBs, however, each I2D link is subject to the interference coming from the D2D links included in the same RRR set. Finally, I2D links originating from different eNBs, that are included in the same RRR set, can be assigned the same portion of PRBs within the pool of PRBs assigned to that RRR set. If the RRR set partitioning and consequent PRBs allocation to each RRR set, due to the cross-interference constraints and to the limited number of PRBs in a control interval, prevent to accomodate the transmission of all the data required by any of the links, the data to be transmitted are pruned until reaching a feasible amount. The pruned transmissions will be rescheduled in the next control interval. Pruning is performed giving a higher scheduling priority to content deliveries related to requests whose content timeout is closer to expire. Therefore, I2D communications have a higher priority then D2D ones, since they are by design related to content requests whose timeout has already expired. If, due to pruning, the content timeout of any content request expires, the corresponding delivery is redirected to be performed by an eNB.

---

[1] σ_c^2 is computed as the thermal noise power spectral density $N_0 = -174\,\text{dBm/Hz}$, plus a 10 dB receiver noise figure, times the subcarrier bandwidth.

[2] The function $g(d)$ is one of the components of our channel model, the other component being random frequency selective fluctuations added on top of $g(d)$, see Sect. 5. In this work, we assume that $g(d)$ is computed according to Eqs. 5-4, 5-5, and 5-6 in [12]. Interestingly, the considered channel model distinguishes between I2D and D2D channels, using different path loss functions in the two cases. This is one of the main reasons to opt for this model.

[3] The RRR set partitioning algorithm is similar to [9, Algorithm 1].

A more detailed description of the considered RRR scheme and physical layer model is outside the scope of this work, and will be provided in a future work.

4 Content Delivery Management System with Optimized Delivery Time

In this work, we assume that the proposed protocol is executed under the supervision of an entity that we call CDMS. This is a distributed software agent under the control of the network operator. Most of its functions, explained in the following of this section, are executed at the eNBs. Whenever a content request is generated by a user, it reaches the CDMS, which is responsible for handling it from the time it is issued by a device until its fulfillment, deciding how and when the content request will be satisfied, either through D2D or through I2D communications. The basic functions of such a CDMS have been described in detail in our previous work [5] (see also [13]). The main contribution of this paper, thus, consists in a novel algorithm used by the CDMS to estimate the optimal transmission instant for D2D communications.

The CDMS acts on a distributed database containing the up-to-date list of each node's position and an estimation of their trajectories for the next τ_c seconds. Each device may obtain a running estimation of its speed and trajectory in the next seconds, either through the use of GPS or, if it is part of the vehicle electronic equipment, directly from the speedometer, and send it periodically to the eNBs. Alternatively, the devices can send the GPS information only to the eNB, leaving the burden of trajectory estimation to the CDMS. In general, different combinations are possible, whose details are outside the scope of this work. In this way, essentially, the CDMS has a picture of how the network topology will evolve in the next seconds[4]. Each device k has an internal content cache $\mathcal{C}_k$ populated with previously downloaded contents. We assume that, at any time, the CDMS also has an index of the contents in each node's cache, and the instants at which each content will be removed from the node's cache due to the expiration of the associated sharing timeout. Each eNB keeps the above described information for all the nodes in its coverage and all the nodes in the adjacent eNBs cells. This is obtained by a periodic exchange of information among eNBs performed through high speed fiber connections, or dedicated radio channels, forming a mesh-type backhaul network. A high level abstraction of the CDMS architecture is depicted in Fig. 2.

On a coarse timescale, with respect to a given content request, the requesting node and the proposed CDMS act as follows. Upon receiving a request of content z from a node j, the eNB performs the following operations:

1. It compares the estimated trajectory of the requesting node j, for the next τ_c seconds, with those of all the nodes that have content z in their caches. In

---

[4] In this work, we assume a perfect prediction of the vehicles' trajectory for an amount of time equal to the content timeout, leaving the evaluation of the robustness of the system with respect to trajectory prediction errors to a future work.

practice, the set of potential content providers is limited by a maximum speed parameter v_{max}, the content timeout τ_c, and the maximum D2D transmission range d_{max}. These parameters are system parameters known to the CDMS and which determine the set of nodes that the requesting node j is supposed to encounter before the content timeout for the request of content z expires.

2. It truncates the estimated trajectory of each potential content provider with the instant its *sharing* timeout for content z will expire, if such instant comes before the expiration of the considered request *content* timeout, obtaining what we call "filtered" trajectories.

3. On the basis of the filtered trajectories of all the potential content providers, it computes which potential content provider, say device k, will reach the shortest distance from device j, the value of such distance, say $d_{(j,k)}^{(z)}$, and the instant $t_{(j,k)}^{(z)}$ at which the two nodes are going to find themselves that close to each other.

4. It schedules the transmission of content z from the potential provider k to the requesting node j at the time instant $t_{(j,k)}^{(z)}$.

5. During the content timeout, the CDMS, with respect to the considered content request, keeps track of any device other than j and k which (i) is not included in the initial set of potential content providers and (ii) is supposed to encounter node j within the content timeout. If any such node receives the same content z during the content timeout, the closest distance it will reach from node j is computed, and if it is found to be shorter than $d_{(j,k)}^{(z)}$, the content delivery is rescheduled to be performed by the newly found potential provider, say k', at the time it will supposedly be at the newly found shortest distance.

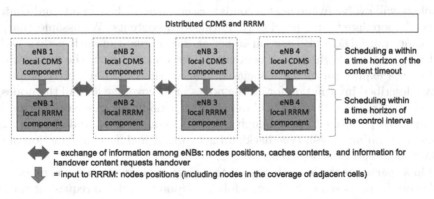

Fig. 2. High level abstraction of the distributed CDMS.

The requesting node, upon issuing a request, just waits for the content to be delivered to it. At the end of the content timeout, if it has not yet received the content, it will anyway receive it from the network infrastructure through an I2D transmission.

On a finer time scale, the operations described above are executed, in practice, in discrete-time, according to control intervals of duration typically much lower than the content timeout. For instance, the content timeout can be in the order of one minute, and the control interval duration is in the order of 1 s. The scheduled content delivery instants $t_{(j,k)}^{(z)}$ are hence computed in terms of number of control intervals, and mapped to the future control intervals, contributing, at the prescribed time, to the input to the RRR and allocation scheme described in Sect. 3.2.

5   Performance Evaluation

To evaluate the performance of our system, we used a custom simulator written in Matlab[5]. Our simulator implements a state of the art frequency selective channel model selected from [12,14], which includes random Lognormal shadowing and Rician small scale multipath fading[6].

We considered a two-lane street chunk of length 1.8 Km and width 20 m. The two lanes correspond to opposite marching directions. Four eNBs are placed at the horizontal coordinates of 0, 600, 1200, and 1800 m, respectively, at the center of the street (see Fig. 1), with height 10 m. The distance between the center of the two lanes is 10 meters. This is also the closest distance a vehicle can get to any vehicle marching in the opposite direction. We modeled the vehicles arrival as a temporal Poisson Point Process (PPP). In all the simulations whose results are presented in the following, the vehicle arrival rate was kept fixed at $\lambda_t = 1/3$ vehicles per second. Similarly, we used a PPP for modeling the request arrival process of each node, and kept the content request rate per device fixed at $\lambda_Z = 1/6$ requests per second (10 content requests per minute). The content requests processes of different devices were set to be statistically independent. The selected content popularity distribution was a Zipf distribution with parameter $\alpha = 1.1$, i.e., $p_Z(z) \sim \frac{1}{\zeta(\alpha)} z^{-\alpha}$, truncated to a library size of 10^4 contents. The sharing timeout was also fixed and equal to $\tau_s = 600$ s. The content size was fixed and equal to a payload of 500 KBytes, which we assumed to

---

[5] The reason to use a custom simulator, as opposed to classic network simulators like ns-3 or OMNET++, is to obtain a fine grain control on the physical layer aspects, retaining an acceptable level of scalability, using a state of the art channel model.

[6] We implemented the Geometry-based Stochastic Channel Model (GSCM) described in [12,14], up to the detail of generating the spatially correlated large scale parameters (LSPs): delay spread, shadow fading standard deviation, and Rician K-factor mean and variance, according to the procedure described in [12]. These parameters are then used to generate the random component of the set of spatially correlated frequency selective channels between any two points in a square grid with spatial step-size of 5 m, representing the region of interest. The frequency response experienced by each transmission is obtained by adding the so generated random component on top of the deterministic path loss component $g(d)$ described in Sect. 3.2, taking the random component between the grid points closest to the transmitter and receiver, respectively.

be encoded in a packet of 625 KBytes using a FEC coding rate equal to 0.8. The MAC parameters we used (see Subsect. 3.2) are as follows: each control interval lasts one second, and is divided in time slots of duration 1 ms. Each PRB lasts for 1 time slot and has width 200 KHz. In each PRB bandwidth, there are 12 subcarriers, the overall system bandwidth is 10 MHz, and in each control interval, a maximum of 50000 PRBs could be scheduled to concurrent I2D and D2D transmissions (possibly spatially reusing the same PRBs across non-interfering links).

The following set of results shows the performance obtained by letting a system parameter vary while keeping the rest of the parameters fixed. We focus on three parameters: the speed range $[v_{min}, v_{max}]$ in which each vehicle's speed falls, the content timeout τ_c, and the maximum D2D transmission distance. For each value of the varying system parameter, we run 10 independent i.i.d simulations, each lasting 1 h, reinitializing the random number generator seed with the same state at the beginning of each batch of 10 simulations. Each simulation is initialized with a random number of vehicles, positions, speeds, and cache content of each node according to the results in our previous work [5], in which we computed the steady state average number of vehicles and cache content distribution. In each simulation, we used a different independent realization of the whole set of random component of the channels between any two points in the grid, and between any eNB and any point in the grid. The next figures show the average value of the offloading efficiency and of the energy, E_{D2D}, consumed by D2D transmissions, measured in dB Re 1mJ[7]. Each value is displayed along with the related 95% confidence interval. Dark bars refer to a benchmark scheme, in which offloading is performed as soon as there is a potential content provider within range. Light bars refer to the proposed scheme.

Figure 3 shows the system performance with different selections of the speed range (measured in m/s). The increase in offloading efficiency with increasing vehicles speed, although a higher speed entails a lower vehicles' density (if the vehicle arrival rate is the same), is due to the fact, with higher speeds, the rate at which vehicles encounter each other increases, and hence the number of potential content providers met during the content timeout increases. From the energy consumption point of view, it can be seen that the proposed system allows for a more than 10 dB reduction of the energy consumed by the devices, on average, to deliver contents to their neighbors. This reduction is considerable, since it represents a more than 90% energy saving, and is consistent across the different selected values of the speed range.

Figure 4 shows the behavior of the two systems with different values of the maximum range d_{max} within which potential content providers, for each content request, are searched by the CDMS. The offloading efficiency increases accordingly to the increase of d_{max}, but the energy consumption increases as well. This happens because the additional D2D offloading opportunities obtained by widening the potential content providers search space, come at the price of a higher

---

[7] $E_{D2D}[\text{dB Re 1mJ}] = 10 \log_{10}(E_{D2D}[\text{mJ}])$, e.g, a value of 10 dB Re 1mJ means that $E_{D2D}[\text{mJ}] = 10$ mJ. A value of -10 dB Re 1mJ, means that $E_{D2D}[\text{mJ}] = 0.1$ mJ.

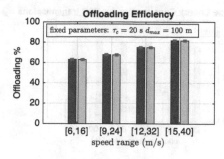

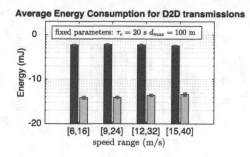

Fig. 3. Offloading efficiency and energy consumption with varying speed range. Benchmark offloading scheme (dark bars) and proposed scheme (light bars).

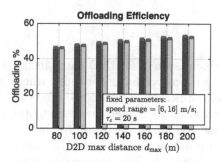

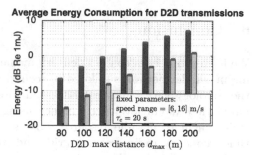

Fig. 4. Offloading efficiency and energy consumption with varying maximum D2D transmission distance d_{max}. Benchmark offloading scheme (dark bars) and proposed scheme (light bars).

required transmit power (for those additional opportunities), since the related involved transmission range is inevitably higher. Keep in mind that, due to the finite content timeout, the requesting node cannot wait indefinitely for those additional, farthest, potential content providers, to come close to it. The relative gain of the proposed D2D offloading transmission instant selection scheme, however, is consistently in the order of magnitude of 10 dB, with worst case 7 dB, which represents an 80% energy saving.

Finally, Fig. 5 displays the performance trend with respect to an increase of the content timeout. As expected, for both the benchmark and the proposed system, the offloading efficiency increases, since possibility of encountering potential content providers, within a larger time window, obviously increases. What is even more interesting, however, is the increase of the relative gain, in terms of energy consumption, of the proposed system with respect to the benchmark, with larger content timeouts. This happens because, with larger a time window, the probability that a potential content provider comes *very* close to the requesting device increases, thus entailing a lower transmit power during the content transmission. With a content timeout of 120 s, the energy saving for D2D offloading transmissions achieves 97%.

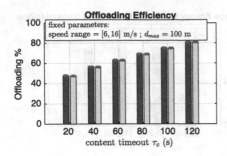 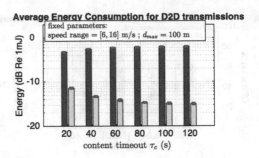

Fig. 5. Offloading efficiency and energy consumption with varying content timeout. Benchmark offloading scheme (dark bars) and proposed scheme (light bars).

6   Conclusion

We have proposed a content delivery management system for D2D data offloading in cellular networks tailored to scenarios, such as vehicular networks, where the topology varies at a fast rate, and to delay-tolerant applications. We evaluated the system level performance using an accurate system level simulator which includes a radio resource reuse scheme for allocating resources over a time-frequency radio resource grid, and incorporates a quite detailed channel model including small scale frequency selective fading. The proposed system, in which the D2D transmission instant is selected to minimize the transmission range, allows energy savings of around 90% in most of the considered settings, peaking at 97% for a delay tolerance of 2 min. The proposed system exploits the availability of nodes mobility predictions at the CDMS. As a future research direction, we plan to investigate the effect of trajectory prediction mismatches.

Acknowledgement. This work was partially funded by the EC under the H2020 REPLICATE (691735), SoBigData (654024) and AUTOWARE (723909) projects.

References

1. Rebecchi, F., et al.: Data offloading techniques in cellular networks: a survey. IEEE Commun. Surv. Tutor. **17**(2), 580–603 (2015)
2. Whitbeck, J., Lopez, Y., Leguay, J., Conan, V., de Amorim, M.D.: Push-and-track: saving infrastructure bandwidth through opportunistic forwarding. Pervasive Mob. Comput. **8**(5), 682–697 (2012)
3. Bruno, R., Masaracchia, A., Passarella, A.: Offloading through opportunistic networks with dynamic content requests. In: Proceedings of the IEEE MASS 2014, October 2014
4. Pescosolido, L., Conti, M., Passarella, A.: Performance evaluation of an energy efficient traffic offloading protocol for vehicular networks. In: Proceedings of the 1st International Balkan Conference on Communications and Networking (BalkanCom 2017), Tirana, AL, 30 May–2 June 2017 (2017)

5. Pescosolido, L., Conti, M., Passarella, A.: Performance analysis of a device-to-device offloading scheme for vehicular networks. In: Proceedings of the IEEE WoW-MoM 2018, Chania, Greece, 12–15 June 2018 (2018)
6. Ji, M., Caire, G., Molisch, A.F.: Wireless device-to-device caching networks: basic principles and system performance. IEEE J. Sel. Areas Commun. 34(1), 176–189 (2016)
7. Ji, M., Caire, G., Molisch, A.F.: Fundamental limits of caching in wireless D2D networks. IEEE Trans. Inf. Theory 62(2), 849–869 (2016)
8. Lin, X., Andrews, J.G., Ghosh, A.: Spectrum sharing for device-to-device communication in cellular networks. IEEE Trans. Wirel. Commun. 13(12), 6727–6740 (2014)
9. Yang, Y., Liu, T., Ma, X., Jiang, H., Liu, J.: FRESH: push the limit of D2D communication underlaying cellular networks. IEEE Tran. Mob. Comput. 16(6), 1630–1643 (2017)
10. Rebecchi, F., de Amorim, M.D., Conan, V.: Circumventing plateaux in cellular data offloading using adaptive content reinjection. Comput. Netw. 106, 49–63 (2016)
11. Rebecchi, F., Valerio, L., Bruno, R., Conan, V., De Amorim, M.D., Passarella, A.: A joint multicast/D2D learning-based approach to LTE traffic offloading. Comput. Commun. 72, 26–37 (2015)
12. ICT METIS Project Deliverable 1.4: METIS Channel Models. Technical Report (2015)
13. Pescosolido, L., Conti, M., Passarella, A.: Performance analysis of a device-to-device offloading scheme in a vehicular network environment (2018). https://arxiv.org/pdf/1801.09082
14. 3GPP: Study on 3D channel model for LTE (Release 12). 3rd Generation Partnership Project; Technical Specification Group Radio Access Network, T.R. 36.873, V12.4.0, March 2017

Adaptive V2V Routing with RSUs and Gateway Support to Enhance Network Performance in VANET

Jims Marchang[1]([✉]), Benjamin Sanders[2], and Dany Joy[3]

[1] Department of Computing, Sheffield Hallam University, Sheffield, UK
jims.marchang@shu.ac.uk
[2] Department of Computing, University of Winchester, Winchester, UK
Ben.Sanders@winchester.ac.uk
[3] Department of Computing, University of Plymouth, Plymouth, UK
dany.joy@plymouth.ac.uk

Abstract. In a VANET communication, link stability can neither be guaranteed nor make the established route link permanent due to the dynamic nature of the network. In V2V communication without the involvement of any infrastructural units like RSU access points or gateway, the probability of successful link establishment decreases when vehicle's speed varies, red traffic light increases, cross-road increases and finally when the density of the running vehicles is sparse. To ensure route establishment and control route request broadcast in a sparse VANET with cross-road layout, RSUs are used in this paper for route discovery within one gateway zone when a next hop vehicle to relay the route request packet is unavailable. RSUs are static but the vehicles are dynamic in nature, so relying completely on RSU for forwarding data is not recommended because chances of link failure, link re-establishment, and handoff overhead will be high. So, in this paper, RSUs and Gateways are evoked for route discovery and data forwarding only when necessary. Moreover, a local route repair is attempted in this paper when the path length is high to reduce or avoid loss of buffered packets along the route and to maintain a more stable link with the help of RSUs.

Keywords: VANET · RSU · Gateway · Ad Hoc Networks · Local link repair

1 Introduction

In building and integrating a smart traffic management system and incorporate each vehicle to become a part of the Internet of Things (IoT) entity, Vehicle Ad Hoc Network (VANET) is a vital component. In a dynamic multi-hop wireless network environment where vehicles can stop, speed up, slow down, take different turns and may collide, the density of the vehicles along any road or highways can vary depending on the time, situation, surrounding events and environmental factors like rain, snow, cyclone, accident etc. In such environment, setting up a stable end-to-end link is a challenge because the state of the network may change dynamically over time. So, a topology based reactive routing protocol like AODV [1] suits well in such dynamic

© IFIP International Federation for Information Processing 2018
Published by Springer Nature Switzerland AG 2018. All Rights Reserved
K. R. Chowdhury et al. (Eds.): WWIC 2018, LNCS 10866, pp. 298–310, 2018.
https://doi.org/10.1007/978-3-030-02931-9_24

network settings [2]. However, route undiscoverable situation in V2V is not uncommon especially when vehicle density is too low, and the destination is too far away because the probability of missing next hop link increases because of the dynamic nature of the vehicles in VANET and the physical structure of roads and highways (straight, cross-road, curve etc.). Since the hop count of a path is inversely proportional to the end-to-end throughput [3] in a Multi-hop Ad-Hoc network, the route with the least possible hop should be considered. In a V2V communication, to collect local information of the passing vehicles and to distribute information, Road Side Units (RSU) is installed and their mobility is restricted in general.

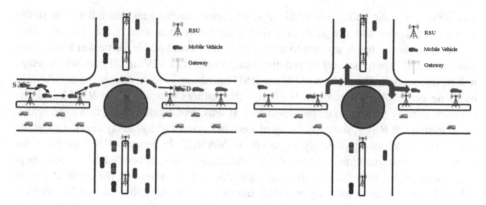

Fig. 1. V2V communication in a high dense VANET.

Fig. 2. V2V communication in a low dense VANET.

Some may argue that without RSU, information collection and distribution from and to the vehicles can be executed directly using internet; however, in a bandwidth hungry world with limited wireless network resources, RSUs and Gateways play a crucial role in collecting and disseminating information from and to the vehicles by targeting only the region of interest. RSUs can help in ensuring safety and security by monitoring speed limits and vehicles activity, provide traffic condition information, report accident or road blockade etc. all in real time with least possible delays and without interrupting internet bandwidth. In fact, RSUs offload the internet bandwidth and make the V2V communication viable by optimizing the utilization of limited wireless bandwidth. Activities of road or highway can be relayed to the gateway through RSUs to propagate and distribute information via Wide Area Network (WAN) or internet to enhance connectivity with the rest of the region or globally if necessary.

In a multi-hop VANET communication as shown in Fig. 1, if the vehicle density is high and the distribution is uniform then a communication link is stable. However, if vehicle distribution density is low and if one of the potential relay vehicles accelerate or slows down or take a turn in the ring road as shown in Fig. 2, the link stability between the source and destination decreases. In order to ensure a more stable link, this paper proposed a routing mechanism which uses the support of RSUs in absence of next hop relay vehicle and conducts a local link repair if the link is broken closer to the destination to reduce route discovery overhead and overall data loss. However, the limitation of the model is the use of RSUs for routing in absence of vehicle to relay.

The remainder of the paper is organized as follows. Related work is presented in Sect. 2 and assumptions are listed in Sect. 3. In Sect. 4, an adaptive routing is proposed. It is followed by simulation results and discussion in Sect. 5; and finally, conclusion and future directions are highlighted in Sect. 6.

2 Relevant Background Study

The RSUs are static and available always, so various authors take an advantage of the presence of RSUs and use in discovering path between a source and a destination. However, it should be clear when to use and when to avoid RSUs for packet forwarding otherwise RSUs purpose will be redefined and the V2I or I2V or I2I bandwidth usage will be overloaded. The authors of [4] use RSU backbone to route packets to in VANETs by using geographic forwarding. However, the authors depend on the RSU backbone network to relay packets to distant locations. It was investigated in [5] that even with a small number of RSUs, the probability of network connectivity, delay and the message penetration time are significantly improved in VANET. In general, RSU are place for information dissemination, so it is vital to understand the number of RSU requirement and placement for better connectivity as analyzed in [6]. Moreover, the connectivity of VANET is not determined only by RSU, but rather there are other factors like vehicle density, distribution, traffic lights, vehicles speed and communication range in governing the connectivity in VANET [7]. The authors of [8] investigate the Network dwell time (Time Before Handover and Exit Time) by considering the overlapping RSUs transmission ranges, to help in predicting the handover time and make a successful proactive handover to maintain a better connectivity. In order to increase network performance, a hybrid (vehicle-to-vehicle and vehicle-to-RSU) communications scheme is designed in [9] where two nodes can communicate only when they have consensus about a common idle channel and next hop node has the minimum message delivery time. However, in an ever-changing dynamic network due to high mobility maintaining accuracy about minimum message delivery time to relay within its neighborhood will be a challenge. The path from source to destination is made by using road id's and Gateway nodes assist in locating the destination and forward packets from one segment of a road to other [10]. In order to ensure limited delay, bound packet forwarding, RSUs are used by placing minimal number of RSUs in the system at the right spots [11]. Many authors used RSUs to forward packets, however in this paper RSUs will be invoked if and only if the next hop vehicle is not within its transmission range and conduct local route repair if necessary to reduce packet loss when link is broken.

3 Assumptions

In implementing and testing to validate the proposed routing mechanism, using network simulator NS2, there are some assumptions considered about the test environment. As described by the authors of [12], this work also follows a simple wireless communication model with a perfect radio propagation channel as used in academic practice with the following assumptions:

  i. The surface of communication is flat.
 ii. A radio's transmission area is circular.
iii. If node A can hear node B, then node B can also hear node A (symmetry) when nodes don't move and use same transmission power.
 iv. If node A can hear node B at all, node A can hear node B perfectly.
  v. Signal strength is a function of distance.

Other assumptions include, vehicles travel with the same average speed at all time and the RSUs are functional at all time and a local gateway is installed in every ring-road as shown in Fig. 3.

4 Proposed Adaptive Routing

The proposed routing protocol is called an adaptive V2V routing with RSUs and Gateway support (AV2VR) where the RSUs are invoked for routing only when one or more vehicles connecting the source and destination are missing or if the link is broken due to acceleration or slow down or due to changing direction in cross road. It is a reactive routing protocol like AODV. The proposed mechanism is to ensure connectivity in a sparse V2V network either in highways or in city traffic as shown in Fig. 5. In order to maintain efficient network traffic management, information distribution, and storage, a local gateway can be assigned for each zone or for multiple zones depending on the area size and traffic condition of a highway or city traffic as shown in Fig. 3. In this paper, the study covers the aspect when a next hop vehicle in V2V communication between source and destination is mission; it also covers the aspect when a link is broken around the destination so that a local link repair could be conducted. However, the study does not cover the aspect when the destination is not within the same zone as the source. Nodes are considered to be within the same zone when they all lie within a same local gateway as shown in Fig. 5.

In a V2V communication, RSUs are generally used to disseminate or collect information from or to the vehicles; however, in this proposed routing mechanism RSUs are used to define additional responsibilities as highlighted below:

- Firstly, it records the identity of all the vehicles passing within its vicinity along with its speed, so that RSU can keep track of the destination and either stop rebroadcasting of route request (R_{req}) or forward as deemed necessary to reduce route discovery overheard. If the destination is not recorded in RSU then the R_{req} is forwarded only to the RSUs or local Gateway by using a unique ID tag of RSUs or Gateway to increase the chances of discovering the destination as shown in the flowchart of Fig. 4. A route reply (R_{reply}) is initiated only when a destination is discoverable within a zone via V2V or via RSUs or mixture of V2V and RSUs. Moreover, in this study, if the Gateway could not locate the destination within the surrounding RSUs of a ring-road, the R_{req} is not forwarded to other gateways of other zones.

- Secondly, RSUs are invoked and involved in route discovery when next hop vehicle to forward the route request are unavailable or link is broken due to missing of possible relay vehicle because of acceleration or slow down or changing movement direction or halt due to accident.

Another contribution of this paper is that when link failure occurs due to broken link or vehicle acceleration or slow down or changing direction, link repair is initiated from a point where link failure occurs and local link repair is performed *if and only if* $R \geq 5$ and $F \geq 3$ in this study, where R is the path length of the route and F is the number of hops up to the point of failure from the source and $R = F + \Delta$, where Δ is the number of hops from the point of failure to the destination. It means that link repair is conducted only for high path length and when a link failure point is closer to the destination compared to the source's hop count. The reason is that if the link failure occurs closer to source, it's better to re-initiate the route discovery since number of buffered packets along the route will be less compared to a high hop path length where buffered packets along the route is high and if new route is established from the source then all the old buffered packets along the earlier route will be lost and local repair can also avoid a fresh generation of heavy flooding route request initiating from the source.

In a real V2V network scenario, unavailability of next hop vehicle is highly likely because it is not realistic to always assume that there will be a continuous presence of vehicles along a highway or any city road. Thus, during a route discovery RSU are involved in forwarding the route request packets *if and only if* a next hop possible relay vehicle is missing. Thus, the approach is a hybrid of V2V, V2I, I2V, and I2I for effective route establishment in a very dynamic and a sparse VANET. In the process, the IDs of the vehicles, RSUs, and local Gateways are given different tags to associate, represent and uniquely identify their own category during route discovery and route reply process. The local Gateway keep track of all the RSUs associated within a zone.

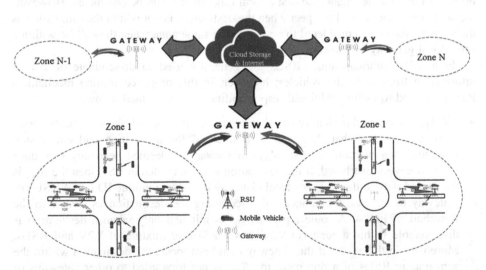

Fig. 3. An Architecture of VANET with infrastructural RSU and communication backbone setup.

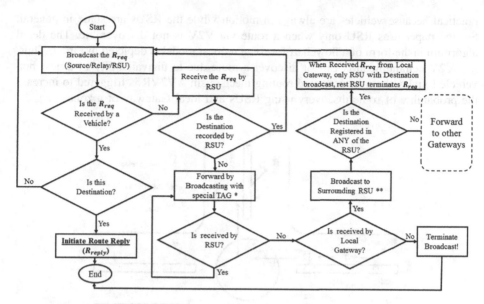

Fig. 4. Flow chart of route request in presence of V2V, V2I, I2I, and I2V.

In an event of missing next hop vehicle in V2V communication, during the route request initiation, the route request packets are not forwarded throughout the network in this study, rather the relay or forwarding of the route request packets are restricted by the record in RSUs or local Gateway. If the RSU does not hold the record of a destination, then the route request is forwarded via the neighboring RSUs or the local Gateway. When the RSUs could not locate the destination and the local Gateway of a zone could not get respond from surrounding RSUs of the ring-road then the forwarding of route request is terminated to reduce unnecessary flooding of route request broadcast activity. When one of the RSUs respond to the local Gateway about the destinations, the rest of the other RSUs in the ring-road terminates the route request broadcast. If the search of destination is to be expanded beyond the zone, then the route request is forwarded to gateways of other zones (this aspect is however not covered in this study as mentioned earlier). The route reply steps are like that of a reactive AODV routing protocol, however, the destination initiate route reply through V2V link if the route exists, otherwise, a route with a combination of V2V and RSUs (V2I, I2V, and I2I) are considered as shown in Fig. 5.

Thus, RSUs, local Gateway and the next hop vehicles are used in discovering route and if a route is discovered through V2V then the route discovered via RSUs are ignored, because when a route is established via moving vehicles, the chances of link stability is higher compared to route discovered via RSUs which are static in nature. However, when vehicles don't move in same direction or have a broken link due to acceleration or slow down then RSU can help in providing a better connectivity especially when vehicle density is sparse, and which is the motivation of this paper. So, the RSUs are considered only when a next hop vehicle is missing or not available to forward or relay packets. Relying completely on RSU for packet forwarding is not practical because vehicles are always in motion while the RSUs are static in general. So, the paper uses RSU only when a route via V2V is not discoverable. The detail algorithm in the form of a flowchart for route request model is depicted in Fig. 4. Thus, if a V2V communication cannot discover a route due to unavailability of a next hop vehicle to relay then the proposed routing mechanism AV2VR is triggered to increase the probability of route discovery using RSUs and local Gateway of a zone.

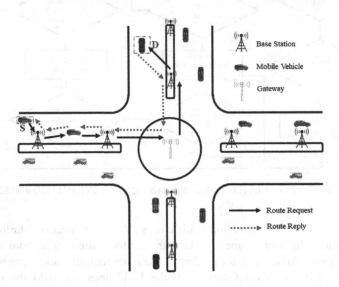

Fig. 5. Link support via RSU in a sparse VANET communication.

In order to avoid frequent re-routing or re-discover of route due to vehicle's speed, direction, density and limited transmission range of the vehicles, the transmission range of the RSUs can be made much higher to maintain longer link stability and provide better scope of handoff since RSUs are stationary in nature. However, in this paper, the transmission power of all the vehicles and RSUs are made equal to 250 m.

5 Network Settings, Results, and Discussion

To analyze the performance of the proposed routing protocol a network topology of Fig. 5 is considered, where vehicles are sparsely spaced and tested with an average speed of 20 m/s and 40 m/s. The simulation is conducted using NS2 with CBR traffic and each round of simulation is conducted for 100 s each. The distance between the moving vehicles and the consecutive RSUs are 200 m apart. The distance between the local Gateway and RSUs of a ring-road of a given zone is also considered as 200 m. The path length between the source and the destination is separated by at least six hops and the data packet size is a constant 1000 bytes. Moreover, after the selected destination is traveled for 1 km, it turns left in a roundabout and proceeds with the same initial speed while the source and rest of the vehicles continue traveling on the same straight road. For a RSU with a transmission range of 250 m, a vehicle with a speed of 20 m/s will take 25 s to cover from one end to the other i.e. 500 m [*Time = Distance/Speed*]. Since the transmission range is fixed, the duration of link stability will also depend on the speed of vehicle, quickness of seamless handoff and duration of local link repair. The proposed AV2VR is compared with a local link repair AODV based routing protocol [13]. The network parameters used in the simulation is listed in detail in Table 1.

Table 1. Network simulation setup parameters.

Parameter	Value/protocol used
Grid size	10,000 m^2
Routing protocol	LL repair AODV/AV2VR
MAC	IEEE 802.11b
Queue type	DropTail
Queue size	100
Bandwidth	11 Mb/s
SIFS	10 μs
DIFS	50 μs
Length of slot	20 μs
Default power (Pt)	24.49 dBm
Default *RXThresh*	−64.37 dBm
Default *CSThresh*	−78.07 dBm
CPThresh	10.0
Max_{Retry}	7
Simulation time	100 s
Traffic type	CBR
Frame size	1000 bytes
Speed	20 m/s and 40 m/s

As shown in Fig. 6, the end-to-end network performance increases as the offered load increases, however, the network gets saturated above 750 kb/s offered load. The saturation point will be different depending on the path length of the route since the throughput is inversely proportional to the hop. The local link repair AODV yield comparatively low throughput because once the link is broken and if the link repair cannot be completed the source may continue to send packet up to the point where the link is broken with a hope of repairing the broken link. However, in a sparse network environment where there is no next hop vehicle to forward or relay then the packets will never get delivered to the destination. Unlike LL Repair AODV, the proposed AV2VR uses the nearest RSUs in absence of the next hop vehicle to forward and relay packets when link is broken by establishing a route via the available RSUs to deliver the packets to the destination vehicle. When the offered load is 1000 kb/s, the end-to-end throughput is approximately 1.6 times the performance of LL Repair AODV. Even if the vehicles are moving and destination is moving on different direction as shown in network topology of Fig. 5, the overall network performance is increased despite the increased in the path length because of forwarding the packets via RSUs in absence of next hop relay vehicle in V2V communication.

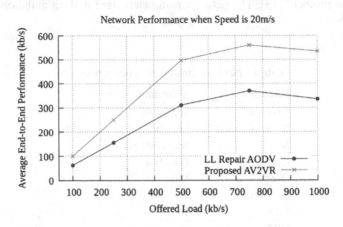

Fig. 6. Network performance when the average speed of the vehicles is normal i.e. 20 m/s.

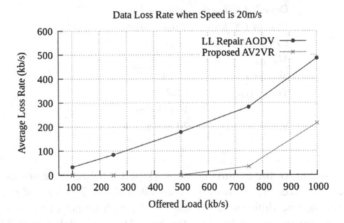

Fig. 7. Average loss rate along the route when the average speed of the vehicles is normal i.e. 20 m/s.

In a distributed data communication of wireless networks, loss of data is mainly due to buffer overflow, data collision, exceeding the data retransmission limit and total link failure leading to loss of buffered packets. The loss rate is depicted in Fig. 7 when the average speed of the vehicles is 20 m/s. Here in this study, the loss is focused on the buffer overflow and loss due to link failure. In LL repair AODV based routing the loss is evident from low offered load of 100 kb/s to a high network offered load of

1000 kb/s as shown in Fig. 7. When the offered load is high i.e. 1000 kb/s, the loss is as high as nearly 50% of the offered load. In this network setup, with a speed of 20 m/s, the destination vehicle turns to left direction of a ring road at the 50th second i.e. after traveling 1 km from its initial position. It means that shortly after the half of the simulation time, the destination vehicle breaks the link. Once the link is broken by the destination vehicle because of moving in different direction and due to sparse vehicle density, it becomes impossible to re-establish a route in LL repair AODV. So, packets keep forwarded from the source vehicle hoping to eventually repair the broken link, but it never happened, rather the buffer gets overflowed and packets get dropped eventually, leading high loss rate as the offered load increases. Unlike LL repair AODV protocol, in the proposed mechanism AV2VR, when a link is broken, it conducts a local link repair by using the nearest RSU to relay the packets and eventually forward to the destination. When the offered load is up to 500 kb/s there is hardly any loss of packets because the rate of forwarding was faster than the packet buffering rate. When the offered load is high i.e. 1000 kb/s, the loss due to buffer overflow is only approximately 20% in the proposed AV2VR routing mechanism, but the loss in LL repair AODV is as high as approximately 50% because LL repair AODV could not conduct local link repair because of lack of next hop relay vehicle in a sparse vehicle density. Thus, the approach of using nearby RSU to route packets in absence of next hop relay vehicle is proven to be effective.

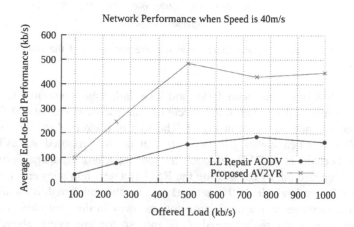

Fig. 8. Network performance when the average speed of the vehicles is high i.e. 40 m/s.

As shown in Fig. 8, when the speed of the vehicles is increased to high speed i.e. 40 m/s which is 144 km/h, the end-to-end throughput drops heavily in LL repair AODV and performs under 200 kb/s irrespectively of the offered load. This is mainly because the link breakage point reaches faster as the speed increases. In this network setting, the destination vehicle reaches the crossroad at the 25th second before taking a turn and move in different direction and breaks the link and due to the absence of potential relay neighborhood vehicle, the local link repair could not be conducted in LL repair AODV. Due to early link breakage and inability to recover the link state, the end-to-end performance sinks as the speed of the vehicle increases. However, in the proposed AV2VR routing mechanism, in absence of next hop relay vehicle in a sparse vehicle density, a neighbor RSU is discovered to relay packets to the destination. Thus, a high end-to-end throughput is achieved without much loss. As the offered load increases beyond 500 kb/s the throughput saturates between 400 kb/s to 500 kb/s for AV2VR. The performance of AV2VR routing provides much higher throughput compared to LL repair AODV and achieve a throughput of 3 times more with any given load.

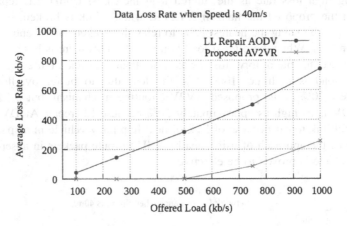

Fig. 9. Average loss rate along the route when the average speed of the vehicles is high i.e. 40 m/s.

When the link breakage occurs faster and local link repair could not be conducted due to lack of relay vehicle then it is expected to have a lesser end-to-end throughput and a higher loss rate as shown in Fig. 9. The loss of packets along the route in LL repair AODV is much higher compared to that of the proposed AV2VR routing mechanism, because in AV2VR protocol, as soon as a link breakage occurs, a link repair steps is carried out by considering the RSU as a next hop relay entity in absence of a next hop forward vehicle. In this network setting, the path length is initially at least 6 hops and it increases as the destination moves away in different direction, and the vehicles are moving at a higher speed of 40 m/s, so the loss rate is above 742 kb/s when the offered load is 1000 kb/s in case of LL repair AODV, while with the proposed AV2VR, loss rate is only 256 kb/s. In case of AV2VR routing, there is no buffer overflow loss until the offered load crosses 500 kb/s and when the offered load is 750 kb/s, the loss rate stands only at 87 kb/s while LL repair AODV loss rate stands above 500 kb/s. It is also observed that the loss rate of the proposed AV2VR routing mechanism is low irrespective of the speed of the vehicles because of successful link repair which is conducted with the help of the RSUs in absence of the next hop relay vehicle unlike LL repair AODV which could not conduct local link repair in absence of the relay vehicle. When a local link repair could not be conducted and a new route is established then all the earlier buffered packets along the older routes are dropped, so local link repair is a must when path length has high hop, which is the reason why a local link repair is conducted in AV2VR if the route path length $R \geq 5$.

6 Conclusion and Future Direction

The proposed AV2VR routing mechanism which uses the support of RSUs in absence of next hop relay vehicles in a sparse VANET ensures a much higher end-to-end throughput with less packet loss rate irrespective of the offered load or the speed of the vehicles. It is also observed that if a local link repair could not be performed as seen in LL repair AODV, sources should be informed about the indiscoverable or unrecoverable link state otherwise the loss rate increases, and end-to-end throughput decreases because source forward packets with a hope that link can be recovered locally, but it never happens in absence of relay neighborhood.

This work is an initial study to reduce the broadcast route request and increase the link stability in absence of next hop relay vehicle with the help of RSUs and conduct local link recovery if link failure occurs. Future work will cover discovery of an unrecorded destination within a zone and conduct a well-informed smart routing with least possible route discovery overhead. The future work will also cover the optimization of path length, RSU installation and explore its corresponding theoretical analysis aspect. The extended work will cover an estimation of energy consumption and cover the detail analysis with different data traffic model, different data rates, different network density and build an average requirement of RSUs based on transmission ranges and established a relationship between RSUs requirement and vehicle density. In future, when a local route repair fails then the buffered packets will be redirected to reduce or avoid any possible loss and inform the source to reduce the overall loss of packets and reduce unnecessary network contention leading to unprofitable network congestion.

References

1. Perkins, C., Belding-Royer, E., Das, S.: Ad hoc on-demand distance vector (AODV) routing (no. RFC 3561) (2003)
2. Abdelgadir, M., Saeed, R.A., Babiker, A.: Mobility routing model for vehicular ad-hoc networks (VANETs), smart city scenarios. Veh. Commun. 9, 154–161 (2017)
3. Marchang, J., Ghita, B., Lancaster, D.: Hop-based dynamic fair scheduler for wireless ad-hoc networks. In: 2013 IEEE International Conference on Advanced Networks and Telecommunications Systems (ANTS), pp. 1–6. IEEE (2013)
4. Mershad, K., Artail, H., Gerla, M.: ROAMER: roadside units as message routers in VANETs. Ad Hoc Netw. 10(3), 479–496 (2012)
5. Sou, S.I., Tonguz, O.K.: Enhancing VANET connectivity through roadside units on highways. IEEE Trans. Veh. Technol. 60(8), 3586–3602 (2011)
6. Cavalcante, E.S., Aquino, A.L., Pappa, G.L., Loureiro, A.A.: Roadside unit deployment for information dissemination in a VANET: an evolutionary approach. In: Proceedings of the 14th Annual Conference Companion on Genetic and Evolutionary Computation, pp. 27–34. ACM (2012)

7. Kafsi, M., Papadimitratos, P., Dousse, O., Alpcan, T., Hubaux, J.P.: VANET connectivity analysis. arXiv preprint: arXiv:0912.5527 (2009)
8. Ghosh, A., Paranthaman, V.V., Mapp, G., Gemikonakli, O.: Exploring efficient seamless handover in VANET systems using network dwell time. EURASIP J. Wirel. Commun. Netw. **2014**(1), 227 (2014)
9. Ghafoor, H., Koo, I.: Infrastructure-aided hybrid routing in CR-VANETs using a Bayesian model. In: Wireless Networks, pp. 1–19 (2017)
10. Amjad, Z., Song, W.C., Ahn, K.J.: Two-level hierarchical routing based on road connectivity in VANETs. In: 2016 International Conference on Industrial Engineering, Management Science and Application (ICIMSA), pp. 1–5. IEEE (2016)
11. Li, P., Huang, C., Liu, Q.: Delay bounded roadside unit placement in vehicular ad hoc networks. Int. J. Distrib. Sens. Netw. **11**(4), 937673 (2015)
12. Kotz, D., Newport, C., Gray, R.S., Liu, J., Yuan, Y., Elliott, C.: Experimental evaluation of wireless simulation assumptions. In: Proceedings of the 7th ACM International Symposium on Modeling, Analysis and Simulation of Wireless and Mobile Systems, pp. 78–82 (2004)
13. Jain, J., Gupta, R., Bandhopadhyay, T.K.: On demand local link repair algorithm for AODV protocol. Int. J. Comput. Appl. (0975–8887), 20–25 (2011)

DFCV: A Novel Approach for Message Dissemination in Connected Vehicles Using Dynamic Fog

Anirudh Paranjothi[1(✉)], Mohammad S. Khan[2],
and Mohammed Atiquzzaman[1]

[1] School of Computer Science, University of Oklahoma, Norman, OK, USA
{anirudh.paranjothi,atiq}@ou.edu
[2] Department of Computing, East Tennessee State University,
Johnson City, TN, USA
khanms@etsu.edu

Abstract. Vehicular Ad-hoc Network (VANET) has emerged as a promising solution for enhancing road safety. Routing of messages in VANET is challenging due to packet delays arising from high mobility of vehicles, frequently changing topology, and high density of vehicles, leading to frequent route breakages and packet losses. Previous researchers have used either mobility in vehicular fog computing or cloud computing to solve the routing issue, but they suffer from large packet delays and frequent packet losses. We propose Dynamic Fog for Connected Vehicles (DFCV), a fog computing based scheme which dynamically creates, increments and destroys fog nodes depending on the communication needs. The novelty of DFCV lies in providing lower delays and guaranteed message delivery at high vehicular densities. Simulations were conducted using hybrid simulation consisting of ns-2, SUMO, and Cloudsim. Results show that DFCV ensures efficient resource utilization, lower packet delays and losses at high vehicle densities.

Keywords: Fog computing · Cloud computing · VANET · Connected vehicles

1 Introduction

Intelligent Transport Systems (ITS) recently developed applications to enhance vehicle safety based on vehicle-to-vehicle (V2V) and vehicle-to-infrastructure communication (V2I). V2V and V2I communication in Vehicular Ad-hoc Network (VANET) depend on Dedicated Short Range Communication (DSRC) [1] which consists of a set of protocols for transmitting messages between vehicles and between vehicles and the roadside infrastructure in a connected vehicular environment. As a result, VANET emerged as the most promising wireless network for a variety of applications from road safety to entertainment.

In a connected vehicular environment, information transmitted among the vehicles in terms of messages. However, many challenges still exist due to the difficulties in deployment and management of resources [2]. In specific, the current techniques for V2V and V2I communications do not provide guaranteed message delivery resulting in

© IFIP International Federation for Information Processing 2018
Published by Springer Nature Switzerland AG 2018. All Rights Reserved
K. R. Chowdhury et al. (Eds.): WWIC 2018, LNCS 10866, pp. 311–322, 2018.
https://doi.org/10.1007/978-3-030-02931-9_25

messages being dropped before reaching the destination. It is due to an instability of DSRC, arising from the frequency band used by DSRC, as the number of vehicles increases. Furthermore, the current techniques for message dissemination have limitations such as the efficient utilization of resources, delay constraints due to high mobility and unreliable connectivity, and Quality of Service (QoS) [3].

Previous authors used either mobility in vehicular fog computing or cloud computing techniques to solve the instability, resource utilization and QoS problems mentioned above. Wang et al. [4] and Grewe et al. [5] illustrated the possibility of mobility based fog computing for broadcasting information in a vehicular environment. However, the authors did not address various scenarios, including fog-split and fog-merge, in a connected vehicular environment. Moreover, the proposed approach for broadcasting messages [4, 5] has limitations, such as high delay and frequent loss of connectivity. Agarwal et al. [6] discussed techniques to transmit the information between the clouds but creates instability in the cloud if the load increases. In addition, the approach is not suitable for the highly dynamic vehicular environment.

To address the shortcomings, we introduce a fog-based layered architecture, called Dynamic Fog for Connected Vehicles (DFCV) for the dissemination of messages. It consists of two emerging paradigms: (1) fog computing (also known as edge computing), and (2) cloud computing. In contrast to previous methods, DFCV incorporates all possible scenarios for disseminating the messages, including split and merge, in a connected vehicular environment. The *difference* between DFCV and the previous approach [4–6] is the techniques used in deployment and management of resources including broadcasting messages. Previous methods used either cloud computing or mobility in vehicular fog computing to solve the problems, whereas, DFCV uses a three-layered architecture consisting of fog computing and cloud computing techniques, thereby ensuring efficient resource utilization, rapid transmission of messages, decreases in delay and better QoS.

Our *objective* is to lower the delay and to provide guaranteed message delivery at high vehicle densities in a connected vehicular environment. To the best of our knowledge, we are the first to implement the dynamic fog for the dissemination of messages in a connected vehicle environment. The messages are broadcasted to intended recipients using single-hop or multi-hop. Once the message is successfully transmitted, DFCV dismantles the fog. We considered three previously used schemes for comparing with DFCV: (1) Named Data Networking (NDN) with mobility [4], (2) Fog-NDN with mobility [4], and (3) PEer-to-Peer protocol for Allocated REsource (PrEPARE) protocols [7].

The simulations are performed using network simulator (ns-2), Simulation of Urban Mobility (SUMO) and Cloud Simulators (cloudsim). Our *results* lead to an exciting conclusion that the DFCV provides guaranteed message delivery and reduce latency and performs up to 35% better than the current techniques at high vehicle densities and simulation times. The *contributions* of the paper are: (1) developing a framework to broadcast the messages in a connected vehicular environment with guaranteed message delivery, less delay and improved QoS and (2) comparative analysis of the schemes based on the mobility in fog computing.

The rest of this paper is organized as follows: We first discuss related work in Sect. 2. The proposed system model and the various scenarios involved in it are illustrated in Sect. 3. Based on the proposed approach, we analyze the performance of our algorithm in Sect. 4. Performance evaluation of our system is discussed in Sect. 5. We validate our analysis through extensive simulation in Sect. 6, before concluding the paper in Sect. 7.

2 Related Work

This section is divided into two main subsections: (1) mobility in vehicular fog computing, and (2) cloud computing.

2.1 Mobility in Vehicular Fog Computing

In vehicular fog computing, nodes are equipped with enhanced storage space, communication and computational capabilities at the edge of the internet, usually Road Side Unit (RSU) or base station [8]. Roman et al. [9] illustrated the possibility of fog computing based mobility support, in other words, Mobile Edge Computing (MEC) regarding bringing the resources close to the vehicles in a connected vehicle environment. Furthermore, the authors mentioned about advantages of mobility support in fog including location awareness, availability, low latency, etc. Sun et al. [10] proposed a hierarchical fog computing architecture associated with Virtual Machines (VM) to handle the data generated from terminals such as vehicles, smartphones, etc. at the mobile-edge. Chaudhary et al. [11] explained resource allocation management in fog computing for different application requirements along with the mobility nature of fog users. However, the existing approaches [8–11] has the following limitations: (1) high overhead due to frequent loss of connections and packets and (2) high delay.

2.2 Cloud Computing

Botta et al. [12] discussed the integration of cloud computing and the internet of things. Also, they illustrated the service available in the cloud regarding both proprietary and open platforms along with future directions. Paranjothi et al. [13] discussed the performance and outcomes of the mobile cloud in allocation and management resources along with the integration of mobile cloud computing and internet of things. Agarwal et al. [6] proposed a system to perform automatic data placement across geographically distributed data centers. Moreover, the authors discussed various services given by the cloud to its users. The shortcomings of existing approaches [6, 12, 13] are: (1) high maintenance cost, and (2) delay associated with accessing and allocating resources in the cloud.

3 Proposed Architecture of DFCV

In this section, we discuss the system model and the scenarios involved in evaluating DFCV.

3.1 System Model

Our proposed fog-based layered architecture, called DFCV, is shown in Fig. 1. DFCV consists of three layers: (1) Terminal layer, (2) Fog layer, and (3) Cloud layer.

Terminal Layer. This layer closest to the physical environment and end user. It consists of various devices like smartphones, vehicles, sensors, etc. As the motive of our approach is to broadcast the messages in a connected vehicular environment, only vehicles are represented in the terminal layer. Moreover, they are responsible for sensing the surrounding environment and transmitting the data to the fog layer for processing and storage.

Fog Layer. Fog layer is located at the edge of a network. It consists of fog nodes, which includes access points, gateways, RSUs, base station, etc. In DFCV, RSUs and base stations play a major role in disseminating the messages. Fog layer can be static at a fixed location or mobile on moving carriers such as in the vehicular environment. Also, they are responsible for processing the information received from the terminal device and temporarily store it or broadcast over the network.

Cloud Layer. The main function of the cloud computing in DFCV is to keep track of the resources allocated to each fog node and to manage interaction and interconnection among workloads on a fog layer, popularly known as fog orchestration.

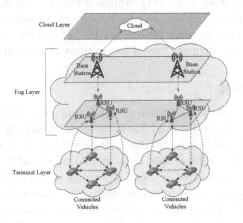

Fig. 1. Three layers of our proposed DFCV architecture for dissemination of messages.

DFCV. In our approach, the vehicle senses surrounding environment and when it encounters a situation like potholes, road accident, icy road, brake failure, etc. it sends the information to the fog layer or acquires the properties of resources such as RSU and base station from fog layer to broadcast it. As we broadcast the messages in a highly dynamic connected vehicular environment, we coined our approach as DFCV. Our approach supports one to one, one to many and many to many communications.

3.2   Scenarios Involved in Evaluating DFCV

Case 1: Split. Fog split will occur in two scenarios: (1) either the capacity of the DFCV is greater than the threshold capacity (Sect. 5.2), or (2) the distance between the vehicle increases from the view of the sender, also known as first observer. One possible situation explained in Fig. 2. At time interval (*t1*), the vehicles V3 and V4 connected to RSU 1 and vehicles V1 and V2 connected to RSU 2 respectively. Assume the vehicle V3 need to transmit messages to vehicles V2 and V1. First, messages from V3 transmitted to RSU 1, and then, it relayed to the base station. From the base station, the messages disseminated to the vehicles in it. The cloud monitors the resources used in this activity and keeps track of resources allocated to fog layer.

Consider the same scenario at a time interval (*t2*), since the vehicles are continuously moving in a forward direction and due to frequent topology changes, vehicles V3 and V4 connected to RSU 2 and vehicles V2 and V1 connected to RSU 3 respectively. Here the RSUs are connected to different base stations, and thus, the fog layer splits vertically into two different layers fog layer 1 and fog layer 2. The messages from V3 transmitted to the target base station where the intended recipients (V2, V1) are located using a handshaking technique.

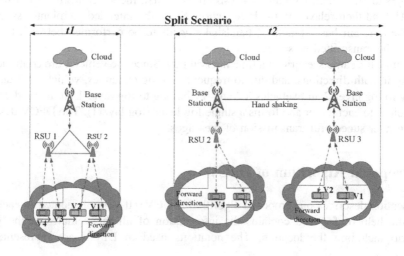

Fig. 2. The split scenario of our proposed architecture DFCV for splitting the fog into multiple fogs.

Case 2: Merge. Fog merge will occur in two scenarios: (1) either the capacity of the DFCV is lesser than the threshold capacity, or (2) the distance between the vehicles is lesser than the minimum distance. At time interval (*t1*), consider the vehicles move in both directions. The vehicles V3 and V4 connected to RSU 2 and vehicles V1 and V2 connected to RSU 1 respectively. Since vehicles V3, V4, and V2, V1 located in a region of different base stations, it gets connected to two different fog layers; fog layer

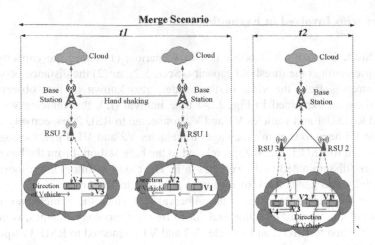

Fig. 3. The Merge scenario of our proposed architecture DFCV for merging multiple fogs into a single fog.

1 and fog layer 2 as represented in Fig. 3. Assume the vehicle V1 need to transmit messages to the vehicles V3 and V4 respectively. First, messages from V1 transmitted to RSU 1and then relayed to the base station. Since the intended recipients associated with the different base stations, a handshake needs to be performed between them to receive the transmitted message.

Assume the same scenario at a time interval (*t2*). Since the vehicles are continuously moving in both directions, and due to frequent topology changes, vehicles V3 and V4 belong to fog layer 2 and vehicles V2 and V1 belong to fog layer 1 are merged as they come close to each other and forms a single fog layer (fog layer1). The DFCV destroys the fog after successful transmission of messages.

4   Proposed Algorithm of DFCV

This section describes our proposed algorithm (DFCV). It is implemented in each cell with the help of fog and contains the information of all the vehicles in the given scenario including the location. The notations used in DFCV are represented in Table 1.

DFCV aims to transmit the messages to the neighboring vehicles using fog computing technique. It mainly concentrates on merge and split scenarios as discussed in Sect. 3.2. The split is a primitive operation performed by DFCV using *split()* function. The steps are as follows: First, the distance between the vehicles is calculated using the *distance()* function. It is calculated based on the distance from the sender, and then, the capacity of the DFCV is determined using *th_cap()* function based on the equation formulated in Sect. 5.2. The split accomplished when the distance exceeds the minimum distance (d_{min}) or the capacity of the DFCV (f_c) surpass the threshold capacity. Here, a single fog will split into two parts. After the split, messages are relayed to the base station with the help of the RSU and send() function is used to send the input message to the vehicles in a corresponding base station (bs_i).

Algorithm: DFCV (input_msg, veh$_{rec}$)

---

for all (veh$_{send}$ ∈ bs$_i$)
    for all (v ∈ c)
        calculate distance()
        calculate th_cap()
      if (distance > d$_{min}$ || f$_c$ > th_cap)
        split (v ∈ c)
        split fog_layer
        fog_layer← v
        bs$_i$ ← send (input_msg)
        veh$_{rec}$← bs$_i$
    else
        merge (v ∈ c)
        merge fog_layer
        fog_layer ← v
        bs$_i$ ← send (input_msg)
        veh$_{rec}$← bs$_i$
  print message transmitted to an intended recipient(s)
      end if
  end for
  end for

Table 1. Notations used in DFCV algorithm.

Variables	Purpose
veh_{send}	Set of the vehicle(s) that need to transmit messages
veh_{rec}	Intended recipient(s)
$input\_msg$	Input message from veh$_{send}$ to Veh$_{rec}$
d_{min}	The minimum distance between the vehicles
f_c	DFCV capacity
bs_i	Base station associated with veh$_{send}$
$v ∈ c$	Set of vehicles belongs to the communication range of base station

Merge is another primitive operation performed by DFCV using *merge()* function based on the following constraints: the distance is lesser than the minimum distance (d_{min}), or the capacity of the DFCV (f_c) is lesser than the threshold capacity (Sect. 3.2). It combines two or more fog layers under the same base station (bs_i) into a single fog layer. Then, the messages are broadcasted to the neighboring vehicle using *send()* function.

5 Performance Evaluation

The performance of DFCV is evaluated using two different analyses: (1) analysis of DFCV and (2) capacity of DFCV. Each analysis is formulated and explained briefly in the following subsections.

5.1 Analysis of DFCV

In this analysis, we calculated the probability of failure. Failure of the system can occur due to loss of connectivity or a resource, insufficient capacity of fog, and excessive delays, etc. The probability of system failure ($P_{sysfail}$) is calculated by:

$$P_{sysfail} = \sum_{i=0}^{n_{v,tmax}} \binom{n_{v,tmax}}{i} d_f^i (1 - d_f)^{n_{v,tmax}-i} \tag{1}$$

Where n_v, is the number of vehicles in the fog, $tmax$ is the maximum time taken by the vehicles to get connected, and d_f is the probability of success in the fog. Like Quality of Service (QoS), the probability of system failure contributes to the performance of the system. A minimum number of failures leads to the maximum performance of the fog.

5.2 Capacity of DFCV

In this analysis, the capacity of DFCV (f_c) calculated, and compared with the threshold capacity of the fog (th_{cap}). The threshold capacity is calculated based on the resources allocated to the fog node. If the DFCV capacity (f_c) is less than the threshold capacity (th_{cap}), the communication link established between the vehicles located in that region. Otherwise, a new fog created. The capacity of DFCV is given by:

$$f_c = \frac{n_v}{t_v} \tag{2}$$

$$\begin{cases} f_c \le th_{cap}, & \text{establish a communication link between vehicles} \\ f_c > th_{cap}, & \text{split the fog} \end{cases}$$

Where f_c is the DFCV capacity, n_v is the number of vehicles connected to the fog; t_v is the total vehicles located in the region, th_{cap} is the threshold capacity of the fog.

6 Simulation Results

The simulation results to evaluate DFCV are divided into two subsections: (1) simulation setup, explains the various parameters considered for the simulation of DFCV, (2) simulation results, depicts the outcome of our experiments performed using various simulators.

6.1   Simulation Setup

Simulation of DFCV algorithm (Sect. 4) is accomplished based on the architecture and scenarios discussed in Sect. 3. The analyses of DFCV illustrated in Sect. 5 are used in simulation to measure the stability of the system (Sect. 5.1) and to specify when the fog split should occur (Sect. 5.2) in a given scenario. To simulate the trace of vehicles movements, we used open source traffic simulator SUMO. The output of the SUMO simulator (i.e., the trace of vehicles) given as input to the ns-2 simulator. NS-2 is a discrete event simulator, consisting of many modules to perform the simulation. Following modules are considered for simulation: (1) node deployment model for dynamic placement of nodes, (2) node mobility model for dynamic network topologies, (3) wireless signal propagation model for transmitting radio waves between the vehicles, and (4) packet loss model to identify the number of packets dropped in transmission. Finally, the cloudsim simulator is used to deploy a cloud to monitor the resources allocated to the fog. The simulations are performed based on the parameters, represented in Table 2.

Table 2. Parameters used in simulation of DFCV.

Parameters	Value
Road length [m]	1000
Number of vehicles [#]	40–240
Number of lanes [#]	4
Vehicle speed [mph]	30–65
Transmission range [m]	300
Message size [bytes]	256
Simulator used	ns-2, SUMO, cloudsim
Data rate [bps]	2 M
Technique used	Multi-hop, Fog, Cloud
Protocol	IEEE802.11p

6.2   Simulation Results

We performed simulation in two parts, (1) urban scenario and (2) highway scenario. The urban scenario shows the results of the simulation in an urban environment where splitting or merging takes place less frequently, and the highway scenario shows the results of a simulation performed during the fog split in a highway environment (Fig. 2). As mentioned in Sect. 3.2, fog split takes place when the distance between the vehicle increases or the capacity of DFCV increases in a region.

Urban Scenario. Simulation of DFCV in an urban scenario is performed based on the metrics such as (1) end-to-end delay, (2) probability of message delivery, and (3) collision ratio. During the simulation, DFCV is analyzed based on the equation formulated in Sect. 5.1 to ensure the stability of the system.

End-to-end Delay. The DFCV is aware of the location of the intended recipients; hence, it reduces the time taken for an initial setup across a network from source to destination and disseminate the messages much quicker than existing approaches such as fog-NDN with mobility, NDN with mobility and PrEPARE protocols. Thus, the end-to-end delay of the DFCV is relatively low, represented in Fig. 4a. The end-to-end delay is calculated against the number of vehicles, and it increases as the number of users increases in the system due to a large number of messages need to be delivered within a specific time interval.

Probability of Message Delivery. In our approach, we considered the probability of message delivery with respect to the number of vehicles. For each user, the probability of message delivery is distributed in the range of (0–1), as represented in Fig. 4b. From the figure, we can observe that the probability of message delivery decreases marginally as the number of users increases due to the increase in load on the fog. Moreover, DFCV outperforms existing approaches at high vehicle densities.

Collision Ratio. To observe the number of packets colliding before reaching the destination, we performed this experiment at a time interval (t) and observed that the collision ratio of our approach is lower at high vehicle densities, and it increases slightly as the number of users increases in the system, as shown in Fig. 5a. It is due to the additional packets generated being more likely to encounter another packet and resulting in a collision.

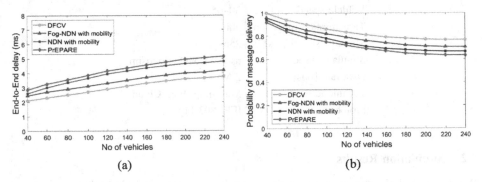

(a)   (b)

Fig. 4. Simulation results of DFCV: (a) comparison of end-to-end delay in an urban scenario, (b) comparison of the probability of message delivery in an urban scenario.

Highway Scenario. Simulation of DFCV in a highway scenario (split condition) is performed based on the metrics discussed in an urban scenario. As the vehicles are moving at high speed, handover occurs frequently, leading to the fog split situation, as represented in Fig. 2. We displayed two possible areas of the split during the simulation in Fig. 5b. It is calculated based on the equation formulated in Sect. 5.2. If the split occurs in the yellow region (split 1), the probability of message delivery and end-to-end delay of DFCV is not affected due to the fewer number of vehicles. Whereas, if the split occurs in the blue region (split 2), as the number of vehicles is higher, the end-to-end delay increases when compared to the split 1. However, the performance of

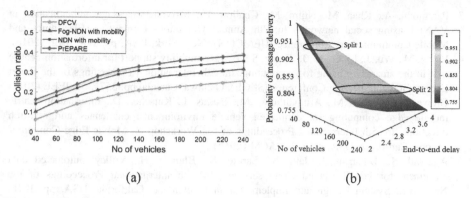

Fig. 5. Simulation results of DFCV: (a) comparison of collision ratio in an urban scenario, (b) split condition in a highway scenario

DFCV does not deteriorate due to fog split. Furthermore, DFCV yields better performance when compared to existing approaches such as fog-NDN with mobility, NDN with mobility and PrEPARE protocols.

7 Conclusion

We studied Connected Vehicle challenges, such as poor resource utilization, increase in delays and frequent vehicle disconnection notably in dense vehicle regions. To address these problems in a connected vehicle environment, we used two emerging paradigms, fog computing, and cloud computing. In this paper, we proposed a novel approach, called DFCV, which ensures less delay and guaranteed message delivery to nearby vehicles. DFCV also supports one to one, one to many, and many to many communications between vehicles. We have analyzed the probability of message delivery, end-to-end delay and the collision ratio by modeling buffers at vehicles and performed simulation using ns-2, SUMO, and cloudsim simulators. The results showed that DFCV is robust, efficient and provides the best performance at all vehicle densities for a number of current schemes available in the literature.

Acknowledgements. This work is supported by a grant (RDC # 18-023sm) awarded to the second author from East Tennessee State University.

References

1. Outay, F., Kammoun, F., Kaisser, F., Atiquzzaman, M.: Towards safer roads through cooperative hazard awareness and avoidance in connected vehicles. In: 31st International Conference on Advanced Information Networking and Applications Workshops (WAINA), Taipei, China, pp. 208–215. IEEE (2011)
2. Hasan, A., Hossain, M., Atiquzzaman, M.: Security threats in vehicular ad hoc networks. In: 5th International Conference on Advances in Computing, Communications, and Informatics (ICACCI), Jaipur, India, pp. 404–411. IEEE (2016)

3. Paranjothi, A., Khan, M., Nijim, M., Challoo, R.: MAvanet: message authentication in VANET using social networks. In: 7th Annual Ubiquitous Computing, Electronics and Mobile Communication Conference (UEMCON), New York, USA, pp. 1–8. IEEE (2016)
4. Wang, M., Wu, J., Li, G., Li, J., Wang, S.: Toward mobility support for information-centric IoV in the smart city using fog computing. In: 5th International Proceedings of the Smart Energy Grid Engineering Conference (SEGE), Oshawa, Canada, pp. 357–361. IEEE (2017)
5. Grewe, D., Wagner, M., Arumaithurai, M., Psaras, I., Kutscher, D.: Information-centric mobile edge computing for connected vehicle environments: challenges and research directions. In: 5th International Proceedings of the Workshop on Mobile Edge Communications, California, USA, pp 7–12. ACM (2017)
6. Agarwal, S., Dunagan, J., Jain, N., Saroiu, S., Bhogan. H.: Volley: automated data placement for geo-distributed cloud services. In: 7th International Proceedings of the Networked System Design and Implementation Conference, California, USA, pp. 1–16. USENIX (2010)
7. Meneguette, R., Boukerche, A.: Peer-to-peer protocol for allocated resources in vehicular cloud based on V2V communication. In: 15th International Proceedings of the Wireless Communications and Networking Conference, California, USA, pp 1–6. IEEE (2017)
8. Ni, J., Zhang, A., Lin, X., Shen, X.: Security, privacy, and fairness in Fog-based vehicular crowdsensing. IEEE Commun. Mag. 55(6), 146–152 (2017)
9. Roman, R., Lopez, J., Mambo, M.: Mobile edge computing, Fog et al.: a survey and analysis of security threats and challenges. Future Gen. Comput. Syst. 78(2), 680–698 (2018)
10. Sun, X., Ansari, N.: EdgeIoT: mobile edge computing for the Internet of Things. IEEE Commun. Mag. 54(12), 22–29 (2016)
11. Chaudhary, R., Kumar, N., Zeadally, S.: Network service chaining in Fog and Cloud computing for the 5G environment: data management and security challenges. IEEE Commun. Mag. 55(11), 114–122 (2017)
12. Botta, A., De Donato, W., Persico, V., Pescapé, A.: Integration of cloud computing and Internet of Things: a survey. Future Gen. Comput. Syst. 56(1), 684–700 (2016)
13. Paranjothi, A., Khan, M., Nijim, M.: Survey on three components of mobile cloud computing: offloading, distribution and privacy. J. Comput. Commun. 5(1), 1–31 (2017)

Parametric-Decomposition Based Request Routing in Content Delivery Networks

Tuğçe Bilen[1(✉)], Dinçer Salih Kurnaz[2], Serkan Sevim[2], and Berk Canberk[1]

[1] Department of Computer Engineering, Faculty of Computer and Informatics,
Istanbul Technical University, Ayazaga, 34469 Istanbul, Turkey
{bilent,canberk}@itu.edu.tr
[2] Medianova, Mecidiyeköy, 34387 Istanbul, Turkey
{dincersalih.kurnaz,serkan.sevim}@medianova.com

Abstract. Content Delivery Networks (CDNs) enable the rapid web service access by meeting the client requests using the optimal surrogate server located at their nearby. However, the optimal surrogate server can suddenly be overloaded by the spiky characteristics of the high-bandwidth client requests. This accumulates both the drop rates and response times of the client requests. To solve these problems and balance the load on surrogate servers, we propose a Parametric-Decomposition based request routing at the surrogate servers in CDNs. With the Parametric Decomposition method, we combine the high-bandwidth client requests on origin server with our proposed Superposition and Queuing procedures. Then, we split these requests into more than one surrogate server through proposed Splitting and Adjustment procedures. We model the origin and surrogate servers based on G/G/1 queuing system to determine the load status. In case of high congestion on the origin server, we split client requests to the different surrogate servers instead of selecting one. The split sizes of whole content are adjusted by defining a novel splitter index parameter based on the queuing load and waiting time of surrogate servers. The results reveal that the proposed strategy reduces the load on surrogate servers by 42% compared to the conventional approaches. Moreover, the latency and request drops are decreased by 44% and 57% compared to the conventional approaches, respectively.

Keywords: Content Delivery Networks · Load balancing
Request routing · Queuing theory

1 Introduction

With the rise of next generation cloud networking, the usage of CDNs enables higher throughput, accessibility, and bandwidth with smaller mean response time in internet core infrastructure [1]. Here, the high number of client requests to access web services may increase the congestion and bottleneck problems [2]. With the evolution of the CDNs, surrogate servers solve this congestion problem

© IFIP International Federation for Information Processing 2018
Published by Springer Nature Switzerland AG 2018. All Rights Reserved
K. R. Chowdhury et al. (Eds.): WWIC 2018, LNCS 10866, pp. 323–335, 2018.
https://doi.org/10.1007/978-3-030-02931-9_26

through content replication. In this way, client requests are intelligently routed to get original content from the nearest server.

Request routing is one of the most crucial functionality of CDNs. The main aim of the request routing is to direct the client requests to the nearest surrogate server. In this way, clients can reach the requested content with smaller response time and higher throughput. On the other hand, the nearest surrogate server may not be the best server in every situation. Accordingly, the load status, response, and waiting times of the surrogate servers must be taken into consideration during the routing procedure to select the optimal server.

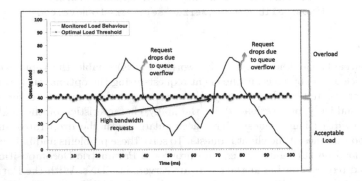

Fig. 1. Surrogate server overload caused by high-bandwidth requests

In some cases, clients can transfer many requests for high-bandwidth content. If these requests are routed to a specific server, the queuing load on that server is increased dramatically as shown in Fig. 1. This overload also increases the waiting times of the client requests in the queue. At this point, drop rate and response time of the clients begin to suddenly increase. These drops observed during the transfers make the web latency 5-times slower [3]. This situation causes a reduction in the client experience. For example, every 100ms increase in latency will reduce the profits by 1% for Amazon [4]. Therefore, the selection of optimal server without considering the request size decreases the performance of the CDN.

Thus, through this paper, we aim to investigate the effects of a high bandwidth client requests on the CDN request routing procedure. Also, we come up with a complete novel method called as Parametric-Decomposition to overcome this problem. The parametric-decomposition enable us to incorporate the high-bandwidth client requests on origin server and split again into more than one surrogate servers in a more autonomous way.

1.1   Related Work

As mentioned above, request routing distributes the client requests to the optimal surrogate servers to achieve load balancing. There are different request routing mechanisms in the literature as dynamic or static. Dynamic algorithms collect information from the network and servers to use in the routing decision. On the other hand, static algorithms cannot use any data gathering mechanism. As summarized in [5], the Random algorithm distributes the requests to the surrogate servers with uniform probability as a static approach. In the Round Robin, different surrogate servers are selected during each routing. Thus, the same number of the client request is transferred to each surrogate server statically. The Least-Loaded algorithm transfer the client requests to the least loaded server [6]. Similarly, the work in [7] executes the routing according to the available bandwidth and round-trip latency of the surrogate servers. Two Random Choices algorithm route the request to the least loaded server among the two choices [8]. The [9] proposes a network cost aware request routing to assign the user requests by reducing the server charging volume. In [10], the client requests are routed to other CDNs when the request for a video in a particular CDN could not be found. Also, the proximity and load on the servers are considered during these procedures. Similarly, [11] executes the CDN interconnection request routing with the help of Application-Layer Traffic Optimization. The article [12] solves the request mapping and routing problems at the same time with the distributed algorithm based on Gauss-Seidel to optimize the performance and cost. However, the routing of high-bandwidth client requests is not considered in none of these works.

Contributions. In this paper, we propose a Parametric-Decomposition based request routing in CDNs. With the Parametric-Decomposition, the incoming client requests to the origin server can be combined and split again into the different surrogate servers. We aim to route the high-bandwidth client requests to more than one server with this strategy. In this way, we can reduce the load on a specific surrogate server causing from high-bandwidth requests. Also, we can reduce the latency and drop rates of the clients. The main contributions of the paper can be summarized as follows:

- We model the origin and surrogate servers according to the G/G/1 queuing system.
- In the modeling of the origin server, we define two procedures as Superposition and Queuing to determine the load status. We use load information of origin server in the content split decision.
- In the modeling of surrogate servers, we also define two procedures called as Splitting and Adjustment. The Splitting enables the queue load and waiting time parameters to the Adjustment procedure.
- In Adjustment procedure, the split content sizes are adjusted by a novel proposed splitter index parameter based on the queue load and waiting time of surrogate servers.

The rest of the paper is organized as follows: the proposed content delivery network architecture is given in Sect. 2. In Sect. 3, the request routing model is detailed. The performance of the proposed approach is evaluated in Sect. 4. Lastly, we conclude the paper in Sect. 5.

2   Content Delivery Network Architecture

In this paper, we use the partial-site approach as a basis for our CDN request routing method. In this approach, client requests are transferred to the origin server to return the main content. Then, the requests are sent to the optimal surrogate server to take the high-bandwidth contents as shown in Fig. 2a.

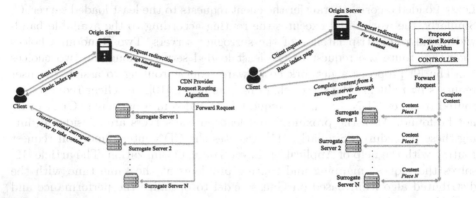

(a) Partial Site Request Routing Approach   (b) Proposed Request Routing Approach

Fig. 2. CDN Request Routing Architectures for Traditional and Proposed Approaches

At this point, instead of selecting only one server, we split the client requests to different surrogate servers which are in the geographical proximity of the client as shown in Fig. 2b. For this aim, in this paper, we consider a CDN network architecture consisting of controller, clients, origin and surrogate servers as shown in Fig. 2b. The origin server contains the original data and distributes it to each of the surrogate servers accordingly. In this paper, we particularly use the cooperative push-based approach for content outsourcing which is based on the pre-fetching of content to surrogates [1]. The controller can communicate with the client, origin and surrogate servers to manage the proposed request routing approach as explained in the following section.

3   Request Routing Model

The proposed request routing approach is managed by the controller. For this purpose, the controller consists of the *Congestion Determination, Content Distribution, and Content Combination Modules* as shown in Fig. 3. The details of these modules are explained in following subsections.

3.1   Congestion Determination Module

In this module, first, the controller evaluates congestion level of the origin server to apply the proposed request routing approach. If the client sends a request

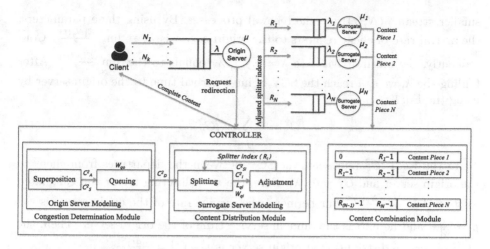

Fig. 3. Proposed system framework

for high-bandwidth content and the congestion level of the origin server rises above the optimal threshold, then we use our proposed request routing model. For this purpose, this module takes the client requests arriving at origin server as input. Respectively, it gives the congestion status information of the origin server. The congestion determination module also includes the *Origin Server Modeling* submodule with *Superposition* and *Queuing* procedures as explained in the following part.

Origin Server Modeling. In this paper, we use an approximation based on the two-parameter characterization of the arrival processes [13]. For the origin server two-parameter characterization, the first parameter λ is the mean arrival rate of the client requests to the origin server and it is equal to the $1/E[A]$. Here, A shows arrival time of the client requests to the origin server. The second parameter C_A^2 is the Squared Coefficient of Variation (SCV) of inter-arrival times. These two parameters λ and C_A^2 are related to the first and second moment of interarrival times. Correspondingly, we can observe the arrival characteristics of the client requests by using these parameters. For this purpose, we decompose the origin server modeling into two procedures as *Superposition* and *Queuing* as shown in Fig. 3.

Superposition: The client requests cannot reach to the origin server in a specific distribution. These requests come as random arrivals with high variability. Also, the total arrival stream of client requests to the origin server is the superposition of all requests transferred by the client. Therefore, we model the origin server according to the *G/G/1* queuing model. Appropriately, $N_j(t)$ is the number of transferred requests from the client to origin server by time t. The combined arrival process to origin server is equal to the $N(t) = \sum_{j=1}^{k} N_j(t)$, ($k$ is the maximum request number of client). At this point, the total $(N(t))$ and each of the smaller streams $(N_j(t))$ are the renewal processes. By using these parameters, the arrival rate of client requests to the origin server is $\lambda_j \equiv \lim_{t \to \infty} \frac{E[N_j(t)]}{t}$. Consequently, the mean arrival rate $\lambda = \sum_{j=1}^{k} \lambda_j$ equals to the $\lim_{t \to \infty} \frac{E[N(t)]}{t}$. After finding the λ, we can reach the SCV of inter-arrival time to the origin server by using the Eq. 1.

$$C_A^2 = \frac{1}{\lambda} \sum_{j=1}^{k} \lambda_j C_j^2 \tag{1}$$

In the Eq. 1, C_j^2 represents the SCV between the departures from client to the origin server and $C_j^2 = \vartheta_i / \lambda_j$. Here, the ϑ_j is limiting factor and calculated as $\vartheta_j \equiv \lim_{t \to \infty} \frac{Var[N_j(t)]}{t}$. Furthermore, the service rate of the origin server is the $\mu = \frac{1}{E[S]}$ and here, S is the random service time of the origin server. Then, the SCV of service distribution at origin server is the $C_S^2 = \frac{Var[S]}{E[S]}$.

Queuing: The client requests first arrive at the origin server, receive basic content, and then transferred to the surrogate servers through the controller for taking the high-bandwidth contents. Hence, the SCV between departures (C_D^2) from the origin server is found as given in Eq. 2.

$$C_D^2 = \rho^2 C_S^2 + (1 - \rho^2) C_A^2, \quad (\rho = \frac{\lambda}{\mu}) \tag{2}$$

According to the $G/G/1$ queuing model, the approximation of queue waiting time (W_{q_o}) for the origin server is found as given in Eq. 3.

$$W_{q_o} = E(S) \frac{\rho}{1 - \rho} \frac{C_A^2 + C_S^2}{2}, \quad (\rho = \frac{\lambda}{\mu}) \tag{3}$$

Also, by using Eq. 3, $I = \frac{W_{q_o}}{E(S)}$ is defined as the congestion index of the origin server. If the congestion index approaches to 1, then the origin server starts to be congested and this is an indicator of the heavy traffic (asymptotically exact as $\rho \uparrow 1$). Similarly, the values of C_A^2 and C_S^2 show variability level of the arrival and service distributions. The variability accumulates congestion, therefore, higher values of these parameters show congestion on the origin server. Therefore, in addition to the I, the controller uses C_A^2 and C_S^2 parameters to determine congestion status of the origin server. In the overload case, we split the client requests to different surrogate servers. At this point, the calculated C_D^2 value is transferred to content distribution module for use in the client request splitting procedure to the surrogate servers as explained in the following subsection.

3.2   Content Distribution Module

In this module, first client requests leaving from the origin server are split to the different surrogate servers in equal sizes through the controller. Then, the split content sizes are determined with the *splitter index* parameter by considering the queue load and waiting time of the surrogate servers by the aid of SCV parameters. For these purposes, the content distribution module includes the *Surrogate Server Modeling* submodule with *Splitting* and *Optimization* procedures as explained in the following part.

Surrogate Server Modeling. We also use the *G/G/1* queuing system for modeling the surrogate servers. The arrival and service times of the surrogate servers are independent and identically distributed (IID). Accordingly, the arrival and service rates of the surrogate servers are $\lambda_i = \frac{1}{E[A_i]}$ and $\mu_i = \frac{1}{E[S_i]}$. Here, A_i and S_i represent the arrival and service times of the surrogate servers, respectively.

Splitting: The client requests for high-bandwidth contents are split to different surrogate servers by the controller. The SCV between these routed arrival requests to the specific surrogate server is calculated by using the Eq. 4.

$$C_i^2 = R_i C_D^2 + (1 - R_i), \quad \forall i = 1, ..., N \tag{4}$$

In this equation, C_D^2 is obtained from the Queuing procedure as given in Eq. 2. Also, we define a R parameter called as *splitter index* based on the queue load and waiting time of surrogate servers to determine the split piece sizes of whole content in Adjustment procedure. Subsequently, to determine the splitter index (R_i), we require the queue loads and waiting times of the surrogate servers. According to the *G/G/1* queuing model, the queue waiting time approximation of the surrogate server is found as given in Eq. 5.

$$W_{q_i} = E(S_i) \frac{\rho_i}{1 - \rho_i} \frac{C_i^2 + C_{Si}^2}{2}, \quad (\rho_i = \frac{\lambda_i}{\mu_i}) \tag{5}$$

In Eq. 5, $C_{Si}^2 = \frac{Var[S_i]}{E[S_i]}$ is the SCV of the service distribution at the surrogate server. Moreover, according to the Little's theorem, the queue loads of the surrogate servers are found as given in Eq. 6.

$$L_{q_i} = \frac{\rho_i^2}{1 - \rho_i} \frac{C_i^2 + C_{Si}^2}{2}, \quad (\rho_i = \frac{\lambda_i}{\mu_i}) \tag{6}$$

Adjustment: As explained above, the high-bandwidth client request is split into different surrogate servers and R_i is the *splitter index* to determine the optimal split size of the whole content to a specific surrogate server.

Initially, we take the *splitter index* parameters of surrogate servers are equal ($R_i = \frac{1}{N}$, $i = 1, 2, .., N$) and so, the content is divided into pieces of equal sizes ($\frac{K}{N}$, K: size of whole content). Then, to determine the optimal split sizes of content, we adjust the splitter index according to the queue loads and waiting

Table 1. Key notations

Notation	Explanation
λ, μ	Arrival and service rates of origin server
λ_i, μ_i	Arrival and service rates of surrogate servers
R_i	Splitter index
C_A^2, C_S^2	SCVs of inter-arrival time and service distribution at origin server
C_D^2	SCV between departures from origin server
C_j^2	SCV between departures from client to origin server
C_i^2, C_{Si}^2	SCVs of routed arrival requests and service distribution at surrogate server

times of surrogate servers by the aid of SCV parameters. Therefore, we define the splitter index as a function of the queue load and waiting time as given in Eq. 7.

$$R_i = \frac{\frac{L_{q_i}(C_i^2, C_{Si}^2)}{\sum_{i=1}^{N} L_{q_i}(C_i^2, C_{Si}^2)} + \frac{W_{q_i}(C_i^2, C_{Si}^2)}{\sum_{i=1}^{N} W_{q_i}(C_i^2, C_{Si}^2)}}{2}, \forall i = 1, 2, .., N \qquad (7)$$

In the definition of R_i, the first parameter in sum is obtained from the *queue load based R_i adjustment*. After finding the $R_i = \frac{1}{N}$, we calculate the C_i^2 values of the corresponding surrogate servers with Eq. 4. Then, the calculated C_i^2 is used in Eq. 6 to find L_{q_i}. These procedures are executed for all surrogate servers and corresponding load values are collected to obtain a total load value. The second parameter in sum comes from the *queue waiting time based R_i adjustment*. Here, the same procedures are executed on the W_{q_i} parameter. Finally, we take the average of the load and queue waiting time-based adjustments to find the splitter index. Therefore, the splitter index (R_i) parameter of each surrogate server is found as given in Eq. 7. Finally, each splitter index (R_i) is multiplied by K to find the split size of whole content to that server. The procedures to adjust the split content size is also summarized in Algorithm 1. Also, the key notations used in all equations through the paper is given with Table 1.

3.3 Content Combination Module

As mentioned above, the controller transfers split content to different surrogate servers according to the calculated splitter index (R_i) parameters. Before transferring whole content to the client, the controller should combine split content pieces taken by these surrogate servers again. To ease the combination of content pieces, we define a sequence range in the packet header. Accordingly, the controller should add the sequence range to the header of each transferred content piece according to R_i parameters. Therefore, the controller combines content pieces according to these sequence ranges before transferring the client as given in Fig. 3.

Algorithm 1. Content Size Splitting

```
1:  L_T = 0
2:  W_T = 0
3:  for i ⟵ 1 to N do
4:      Calculate R_i = 1/N
5:  end for
6:  Queue Load Based Adjustment()
7:  for i ⟵ 1 to N do
8:      Calculate C_i^2 with Eq. 4
9:      Calculate L_{q_i} with Eq. 6
10:     Add L_{q_i} to L_T
11: end for
12: Queue Waiting Time Based Adjustment()
13: for i ⟵ 1 to N do
14:     Calculate C_i^2 with Eq. 4
15:     Calculate W_{q_i} with Eq. 5
16:     Add W_{q_i} to W_T
17: end for
18: for i ⟵ 1 to N do
19:     R_i = (L_{q_i} + W_{q_i}) / (2(L_T + W_T))
20:     Assign KR_i to surrogate server i
21: end for
```

4   Performance Evaluation

4.1   Simulation Setup and Methodology

The efficiency of the proposed approach is evaluated through simulations by comparing with Round Robin, Least-Loaded, and Two Random Choices request routing algorithms. The simulations are executed by using the ns2 network simulator. To the best of our knowledge, the current simulators do not include any tool for evaluating the different request routing mechanisms. Accordingly, we benefit from the new library added to the ns2 network simulator during the implementation of our request routing approach [14]. Also, we use network topology of the Medianova Company. Each node on this network corresponds to a surrogate server which connects to the end users and an origin server. The metrics used to evaluate performance are queue load, the latency of client, and request drops due to queue overflow.

4.2   Performance Results

Queue Load. We first evaluate the queue load behavior of a specific surrogate server according to the time. The queue length of this server in time help us to observe the load behavior and we use the Eq. 6 for this purpose. Here, requests from the client are transferred to this surrogate server in Round Robin, Least-Loaded, and Two Random Choices request routing algorithms. In our approach, we use other servers in addition to this server during the high-bandwidth client requests.

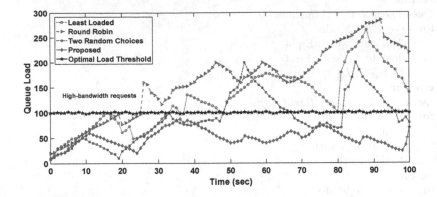

Fig. 4. Queue load behavior of a server

The Round Robin does not collect information about the network and server status due to it is a static algorithm. Although the Least-Loaded and Two Random Choices algorithms are dynamic, they do not consider the routing of high-bandwidth client requests. Accordingly, as shown in Fig. 4, the transferred two different high-bandwidth requests cause overloading of the server in these three algorithms. On the other hand, we use other servers to meet the client requests based on Algorithm 1. Accordingly, as shown in Fig. 4, we have roughly 42% less load on this specific server compared to other three algorithms.

Latency of Client. We also evaluate the latency of client until the request is met. We define this latency as the difference between the sending time of request by the client and its response time by the surrogate server. During this duration, client requests are kept in the queues of the origin and surrogate servers. Therefore, we use the waiting times of the client requests in these queues.

Accordingly, we use the Eqs. 3 and 5 for the origin and surrogate server waiting times calculations, respectively. Additionally, the load status of the surrogate servers affects the latency of the requested client. The increased number of client accumulates the requests waiting in queues of servers. Therefore, we investigate the latency according to the client number parameter. As shown in Fig. 5, in the Round Robin, Least-Loaded, and Two Random Choices algorithms, the latency of a client increases with growing request number. More specifically, client observes more latency during the high-bandwidth request transfers. In these durations, high-bandwidth requests of client and other increased requests accumulates the latency and drops. On the other hand, we do not overwhelm the

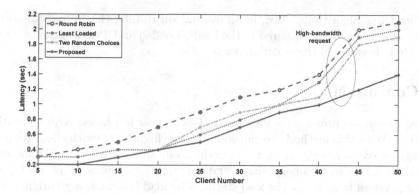

Fig. 5. Latency of a client with increased request numbers

specific server with high-bandwidth requests in a very demanding environment based on Algorithm 1. Therefore, as shown in Fig. 5, we have roughly 44% less client latency compared to other three algorithms.

Request Drops Due to Queue Overload. To show that our proposed approach does not overload the queues of servers, we investigate the dropped requests of clients by the surrogate servers. We observe the request drops again the client number parameter. As explained above, loads of surrogate server queues are accumulated with increasing client and request numbers. This load on the surrogate servers increases the request drops of clients. For this reason, as shown in Fig. 6, we observe an increase in the drops during the incoming of high-bandwidth requests for the Round Robin, Least Loaded, and Two Random Choices Algorithms. But, we do not overload a server with high-bandwidth requests in our approach. Accordingly, we do not monitor an increase in dropped client requests. Therefore, as shown in Fig. 5, we reduce the request drops roughly 57% according

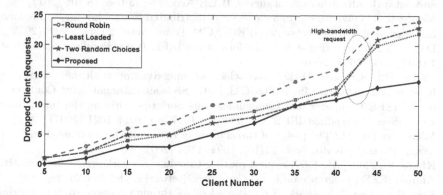

Fig. 6. Request drops due to queue overload

to other three algorithms. Also, in all evaluation results, the Round-Robin has the worst performance compared to the Least-Loaded and Two Random Choices algorithms because of the static characteristic.

5 Conclusion

In this paper, we proposed a Parametric-Decomposition based request routing in CDNs. With this method, we can combine the high-bandwidth client requests on origin server and split again to more than one surrogate server. We modeled the origin server with superposition and queuing procedures based on $G/G/1$ queuing system to estimate the load status. The load information of origin server is used for split decision of client requests. Moreover, the surrogate servers are modeled with splitting and adjustment procedures based on $G/G/1$ queuing system. The queue loads and waiting times of surrogate servers are used to calculate the splitter index. We adopt the splitter index parameter to determine the optimal content split sizes to the surrogate servers. According to the simulation results, the proposed approach reduces the load on surrogate servers by 42% compared to the conventional approaches. Also, the latency and request drops are decreased by 44% and 57% compared to the conventional approaches, respectively.

References

1. Pathan, A., Buyya, R.: A taxonomy and survey of content delivery networks. Technical report, GRIDS-TR-2007-4, February 2007
2. Bilen, T., Canberk, B., Chowdhury, K.R.: Handover management in software-defined ultra-dense 5G networks. IEEE Netw. **31**(4), 49–55 (2017)
3. Flach, T., et al.: Reducing web latency: the virtue of gentle aggression. In: Proceedings of the ACM Conference of the Special Interest Group on Data Communication (SIGCOMM 2013) (2013)
4. Jia, Q., Xie, R., Huang, T., Liu, J., Liu, Y.: The collaboration for content delivery and network infrastructures: a survey. IEEE Access **5**, 18 088–18 106 (2017)
5. Manfredi, S., Oliviero, F., Romano, S.P.: A distributed control law for load balancing in content delivery networks. IEEE/ACM Trans. Netw. **21**(1), 55–68 (2013)
6. Dahlin, M.: Interpreting stale load information. IEEE Trans. Parallel Distrib. Syst. **11**(10), 1033–1047 (2000)
7. Carter, R.L., Crovella, M.E.: Server selection using dynamic path characterization in wide-area networks. In: INFOCOM 1997, Sixteenth Annual Joint Conference of the IEEE Computer and Communications Societies. Driving the Information Revolution, Proceedings IEEE, vol. 3, April 1997, pp. 1014–1021 (1997)
8. Mitzenmacher, M.: The power of two choices in randomized load balancing. IEEE Trans. Parallel Distrib. Syst. **12**(10), 1094–1104 (2001)
9. Khare, V., Zhang, B.: CDN request routing to reduce network access cost. In: 37th Annual IEEE Conference on Local Computer Networks, October 2012
10. Kee, H.S., Lau, P.Y., Park, S.K.: Peered-CDN through request routing peering system for video-on-demand. In: 2013 13th International Symposium on Communications and Information Technologies (ISCIT), September 2013, pp. 66–71 (2013)

11. Arumaithurai, M., Seedorf, J., Paragliela, G., Pilarski, M., Niccolini, S.: Evaluation of ALTO-enhanced request routing for CDN interconnection. In: 2013 IEEE International Conference on Communications (ICC), June 2013, pp. 3519–3524 (2013)
12. Fan, Q., Yin, H., Jiao, L., Lv, Y., Huang, H., Zhang, X.: Towards optimal request mapping and response routing for content delivery networks. IEEE Trans. Serv. Comput. **PP**(99), 1 (2018)
13. Gross, D., Shortle, J.F., Thompson, J.M., Harris, C.M.: Fundamentals of Queueing Theory, 4th edn. Wiley-Interscience, New York (2008)
14. Cece, F., Formicola, V., Oliviero, F., Romano, S.P.: An extended ns-2 for validation of load balancing algorithms in content delivery networks. In: 2010 Proceedings of the 3rd International ICST Conference on Simulation Tools and Techniques, pp. 32:1–32:6 (2010)

Author Index

Printed in the United States
By Bookmasters